Walking Places in Florida

OTHER TITLES AVAILABLE FROM OUT THERE PRESS

Guides to Backcountry Travel & Adventure

Arkansas
Georgia
North Carolina
Pennsylvania
South Carolina
Virginia
West Virginia

Sea Kayaking Florida & the Georgia Sea Islands
Sea Kayaking the Carolinas

Coming Soon

Walking Places in Washington DC
Walking Places in New England

Walking Places in Florida

by Diane Marshall

out there press
asheville, north carolina
www.outtherepress.com

Walking Places in Florida

© 2000 Diane P. Marshall

Out There Press
PO Box 1173
Asheville, NC 28802
www.outtherepress.com

Maps by Simply Maps

Library of Congress Catalog Card Number: 00-100022
ISBN: 1-893695-01-8

The author and publisher have made every effort to ensure the accuracy of the information contained in this book. Nevertheless, they can not be held liable for any loss, damage, injury, or inconvenience sustained by any person using this book. Readers should keep in mind that walks in wilderness areas of county, state, and national parks have some risk. Please be careful.

Cover photographs: James Bannon (St. Augustine), Diane Marshall
Cover design: James Bannon

Manufactured in the United States

10 9 8 7 6 5 4 3 2 1

For my Mom, Dad, husband John, and the Pointer Sisters.

Different places on the face of the earth have different vital effluence, different vibration, different chemical exhalation, different polarity with different stars: call it what you like. But the spirit of place is a great reality.

—D.H. Lawrence, "The Spirit of Place"

Table of Contents

Acknowledgments

I am particularly indebted to Jim Bannon, the publisher, who suggested this project. He opened the doors to the eco-heritage tourism universe. Like James Howard Kunstler, author of The Geography of Nowhere and Home From Nowhere, I "have been unusually sensitive to the issue of place" since I was a little girl. I traveled the world with a military family and experienced in those impressionable years a strong sense of place. I didn't know then what it was that stirred my heart. This book has led me to the answer.

When I moved to the Florida Keys in my late 30s, I was dismayed by the ugly sameness of the architecture in the Keys (with the exception of Key West). I fought an urge to round up the architects who had designed the hideous structures and, in *A Clockwork Orange* fashion, pin their eyes open and force them to see repeated images of their crude creations. Fortunately, there were others who felt the same way, among them architects like Robert Garant, who over recent years has designed pastel-colored houses with broad porches, deep roof overhangs, and ornamental details, in a tropical island style befitting the Keys. The limited other parts of Florida that I had seen gave me little hope that they were any different. Researching this book showed me that I was very wrong about the rest of Florida.

As I traveled up and down the state, I met many people who share a strong sense of place, who work to preserve Florida's cultural and ecological heritage, and do their utmost to curb the further Disney-ization of the state. I am particularly indebted to the Florida Trust for Historic Preservation (FTHP), which accepted my late application to attend their annual conference in Gainesville, where I was allowed to discuss the project with preservationists, city planners, architects, museum directors, and developers.

Jodi Rubin of Orlando played an important part in this project. She introduced me to Master Site Files and explained the historic preservation process. She also suggested that I attend the (FTHP) conference and when there went out of her way to introduce me to her colleagues and assure them that I would take good care of their files. I also must personally thank the following people who allowed me access to their files, spent their days off showing me their towns and parks, and gave me insights into the complex dilemmas of eco-heritage tourism and preservation: Joan Jennawine of Ybor City, Lucretia Freed-West in Mount Dora, Diana Colburn Kyle of Pinellas County Park Department in Clearwater, Greg

Utech of Timucuan Ecological & Historic Preserve in Jacksonville, Patricia Crass of Micanopy, Alicia Addeo of Fort de Soto County Park in St Petersburg, Jane S. Kirschner and Debra Flynt-Garrett in Sarasota, Amy David and Betty Quibell in Safety Harbor, Joseph LeGath, Melody Staunton, and Vance Perkey of Philippe Park in Safety Harbor, Jeffries Bolden at J.N. "Ding" Darling National Wildlife Refuge in Sanibel, Christy Gibson of the Beaches of South Walton (Seaside), Alan Baggett of Lakeland Area Chamber of Commerce, Historic Lakeland Inc, Patricia Crass and the Micanopy Historical Society, Steve Orlando at the University of Florida, Robyn De Ridder at Cypress Gardens, Del Acosta at the City of Tampa, historical researcher Melanie V. Barr of Gainesville, the St Augustine Historical Society, Nancy Hamilton of Lee Island Coast Visitor & Convention Bureau, Kelly Earnest of Tampa/Hillsborough Convention & Visitors Association, Jeffries Bolden of J.N. "Ding" Darling National Wildlife Refuge, Anne Mullins at the City of Fort Myers, Caroline Pomeroy Ziemba at the Stuart Heritage Museum, and John Bailey, who gave me a tour of Ybor City.

Finally, I must thank my husband, who sent me packages, paid the bills, and took good care of our home and the Pointer Sisters, our two lab-German shorthair pointers, for three months while I traveled around the state.

Preface

Commenting on the placelessness of contemporary American culture, Jane Jacobs writes in *The Death and Life of Great American Cities*, "every place becomes more like every other place, all adding up to Noplace." The book in your hands is about Places. Places where people recognize the importance of Place, the importance of permanence, the importance of belonging. They recognize that their communities are not like every other place, but instead are an accumulation of the many unique people who lived there and the events that unfolded there.

Many of the Places in this book are revitalized older residential neighborhoods that disintegrated when they were abandoned for suburban communities dominated by green lawns, identical box houses with tall privacy fences, gated entries, monotonous strip malls, and huge discount stores with vast parking lots. Over the last 10 years, however, a growing number of people have tired of the long, frustrating automobile-dependent commutes to the suburbs, the lack of connectivity to a community, and suburban cookie-cutter sameness. These urban pioneers are returning to the abandoned cities and reclaiming them. Today, they take great pride in preserving the unique historical identity of their communities.

Other Places in the book, such as Seaside in the Panhandle, are new "developments." I use the word loosely, because they are only developments in that they were developed. They differ substantially from conventional developments because they were designed with a keen sense of Place. No two houses are alike. The architecture reflects Florida's climate. In the words of Andres Duany and Elizabeth Plater-Zyberk, the architects who designed many of them, these new communities returned "to first principals, laying out brand new towns according to old-fashioned fundamentals, with the locations of stores, parks, and schools precisely specified from the outset, with streets that invite walking, with stylistic harmony that avoids the extremes of either architectural anarchy or monotony."

The Places in this book are all pedestrian-friendly. As Duany and Plater-Zyberk say, they "invite walking." You will feel it as you walk through revived historic neighborhoods, where residents sit on big, wide porches and greet passersby, whether they are friends, neighbors, or strangers. You will feel it as you pass buildings that are rich in architectural character and local history. You will feel it along the slow, narrow residential streets and sidewalks lined with hundred-year-old live oaks, acacias, tamarinds, and palms.

A portion of the book is also devoted to the Natural Places of Florida. They too have suffered, as millions of acres of wilderness have been filled, drained, and converted to dust under developers' bulldozers. Gone with them are entire species of plants and animals. Our parks reveal a basic sense of Place. Where else can we see the eagles soar and the bison roam? Where else can we hear the pig frogs snort and the limpkin wail *kurr-ee-ow?* Where else can we get a sense of our natural history, of what was here before we were? Our parks must be preserved.

Almost a century before the Pilgrims clamored up Plymouth Rock, European settlers struggled to survive in the Sunshine State's never-before-seen environment. Centuries before them, sophisticated Native Americans thrived in agricultural and fishing communities that traded with other aboriginal cultures as far away as Ohio. Men and women like Henry Morrison Flagler, Thomas Edison, Henry Ford, Alan Shepard, Marjory Stoneman Douglas, Zora Neale Hurston, and Marjorie Kinnan Rawlings molded and shaped Florida long before Disney arrived to, in the words of Herbert L. Hiller in *Guide To The Small And Historic Lodgings of Florida*, "capitalize on modernity's extravagant rejection of the past by recasting tradition as nostalgia and completing the illusion that Old Florida and its legendary hospitality no longer exist." Within these pages, I strive to demonstrate that Florida is not just about the mouse with big ears. Old Florida's legendary hospitality—as well as its historic hotels, houses, and neighborhoods—does indeed exist.

Lastly, I have tried to be faithful to the theme of the book, by including—whenever possible—the restaurants, accommodations, and attractions within or on the periphery of each community that contribute to the community's sense of Place.

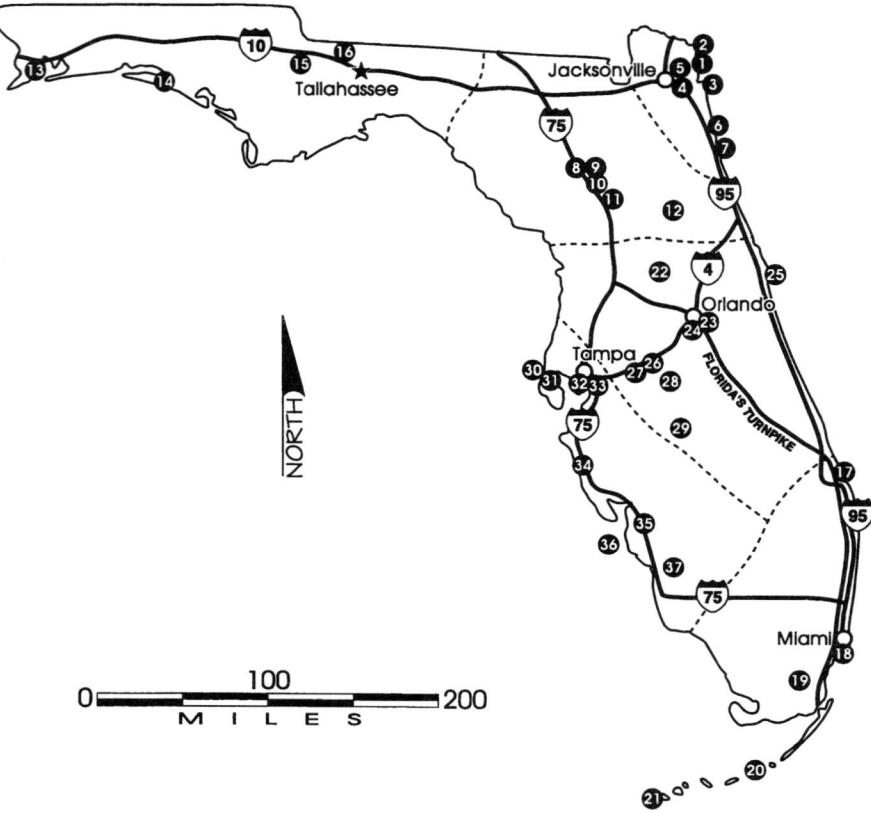

NORTHEAST
1. Downtown Fernandina
2. Fort Clinch State Park
3. Talbot Islands State Park
4. Jacksonville
5. Timucuan Ecological
   & Historic Preserve
6. St Augustine
7. Washington Oaks State Park

NORTH CENTRAL
8. University of Florida
9. Morningside Park
10. Paynes Prairie State Park
11. Micanopy
12. Ocala National Forest

NORTHWEST
13. Pensacola
14. Seaside
15. Torreya State Park
16. Quincy

SOUTHEAST
17. Stuart
18. Miami Beach
19. Everglades National Park
20. Pigeon Key
21. Key West

SOUTH CENTRAL
22. Mount Dora
23. Lake Cherokee Historic District
24. Harry P. Leu Gardens
25. Merritt Island NWR
26. Florida Southern College
27. Munn Park Historic District
28. Cypress Gardens
29. Highlands Hammock State Park

SOUTHWEST
30. Caladesi Island State Park
31. Safety Harbor
32. Hyde Park
33. Ybor City
34. Sarasota
35. Fort Myers
36. Ding Darling NWR
37. Corkscrew Swamp Sanctuary

Introduction

History

In 1976 the United States proudly boasted of its 200-year history. That same year, I sat in a restaurant built in a 14th-century wine *cave* in Dijon, France, and reflected that it seemed somewhat absurd to refer to our 200-year existence as "history." However, the real absurdity is not in thinking that 200 years is not long enough to be considered a history, but in thinking that our history begins with the 13 colonies, Declaration of Independence, and American Revolution.

Likewise, some people gauge Florida's history in terms of the mouse with the big ears. Was there really a Sunshine State before Disney arrived? Sure there was. Remember that Spanish guy who came looking for the Fountain of Youth? Well, he didn't find age-reversing waters, but he did find people. People whom historians believe first arrived in Florida about 10,000 to 9,000 BC. The largest numbers settling along the coasts as hunters and gatherers. By 3000 BC major settlements existed throughout the state. The Timucuans, the largest group, settled the northeast; the Apalachee lived in the Panhandle; the Tocobaga inhabited the area between Tallahassee and Tampa; the Calusa and Matecumbe dwelled along the southwest coast and Florida Keys, the Ais colonized the east central region, and the Jaega and Tequesta lived on the southeast coast. By 600 to 500 BC many of these cultures exhibited highly developed agricultural, artistic, and engineering skills.

Although these early Floridians left no written records, evidence of their cultures has been found in burial mounds. Archaeologists have unearthed artifacts of pottery, tools, weapons, arrowheads, bone fragments, spears, pipes, ornaments, and other signs that reveal well-defined cultures. There also are shell mounds, or middens, used as garbage heaps comprised primarily of discarded oyster and mussel shells.

When Juan Ponce de Leon arrived in Florida in 1513 in search of gold and the Fountain of Youth, he christened the land *La Florida* and claimed it all for Spain. His first encounter with Native Americans at Charlotte Harbor, on the southwest, was hostile. (Just think. Had he been more diplomatic, we might be celebrating Thanksgiving in April instead of November.) He returned in 1521 with a small army, priests, horses, and a plan to convert the natives to Catholicism. He and several men were wounded. They fled to Cuba, where de Leon died. Several other Spanish attempts to settle the wild land also failed, including a settlement at Pensacola, which was abandoned after three years in 1561.

Africans joined the early Spanish explorers, not enslaved, but free, as artisans, seamen, navigators, and adventurers. In the early 1500s Juan Garrido took part in the expeditions of Ponce de Leon in Puerto Rico and Florida as well as with Hernando Cortez in Mexico. Esteban joined Panfilo de Narvaez as he traveled through the Gulf Coast and the Southwest. In later years, the Spanish granted African slaves freedom and asylum in their territories. This would increase friction between Spain and England in the next century and be the impetus for battles fought over Florida.

Initial French attempts at colonization proved equally unsuccessful. Jean Ribault built a French fort on the St Johns River near present-day Jacksonville. The Spanish, having claimed the land, dispatched Pedro Menéndez de Avilés in 1565 to remove the French. De Avilés landed 30 miles south at present-day St Augustine to mount a defense. He succeeded in routing the French and establishing the first permanent settlement in the United States at St Augustine.

Over the next 200 years, Spain, France, and England battled over Florida. Under the First Treaty of Paris in 1763, Spain turned over Florida to England. Under the Second Treaty of Paris, the English returned Florida to Spain in 1783. By that time, the aboriginal population had dwindled due to European diseases, enslavement, and outright murder. However, Native Americans did not disappear from Florida's history. In the late 1700s, the Oconee Creeks, ancestors of today's Seminole tribesmen, migrated from Georgia to Florida.

With the number of white settlers growing, there was pressure for the government to remove the Native Americans to reservations in the West. Following the defeat of the Creeks in the Battle of Horseshoe Bend in Alabama, Andrew Jackson, who led the assault in Alabama, used the victory as an excuse to chase the Creeks into Florida and massacre entire villages, thus initiating the First Seminole War in 1817. After Jackson was elected President of the United States in 1828, Congress passed the Indian Removal Act of 1830. This precipitated the Second and Third Seminole Indian wars, which ended in 1858 when Chief Billy Bowlegs agreed to take his people west. Some Seminoles remained in Florida, retreating to the Everglades. Today, there are Seminoles and related Miccosukees living on four federal reservations northwest of Lake Okeechobee, near Hollywood, outside Tampa, and in the Everglades.

At the height of the Seminole Wars, Florida joined the Union, only to secede from it 16 years later in 1861 over the issue of slavery. Although no deciding battles were fought in Florida during the Civil War, the

Confederate army relied upon it to supply beef from its huge cattle ranches in the center of the state. When the war ended, Florida had lost 5,000 men and suffered $20 million in damage.

Migration to Florida for its sun-kissed climate, good soil, and cheap land began in the early 1800s. Cigars, citrus, and tourism became the major industries, which really took off when the railroads stitched Florida's widespread cities together with the rest of the eastern seaboard. The most important railroad baron was Henry Morrison Flagler. His Florida East Coast Railroad eased down Florida's Atlantic coast in 1885, stopping at St Augustine, Daytona, Palm Beach, Miami, and Key West. Each time, he transformed the city into a major tourist destination by building a series of posh hotels for well-to-do tourists. On the west coast, Henry Plant's Atlantic Coastline Railroad linked Richmond, Virginia with Tampa. Cities sprang up along the coasts in between.

Tourists returned north boasting of warm, sunny winter vacations. Soldiers returned to their northern homes after being stationed in Florida during the Spanish-American War. Their tales prompted thousands to migrate south, launching Florida's first major boom in 1920. Land speculators became millionaires overnight. The boom lasted until 1926, when their paper fortunes collapsed. The 1929 Depression came on the heels of the bust, and Florida didn't fully recover until World War II, when it served as a training station and embarkation point for troops. After the war, many soldiers again returned to settle in Florida, initiating another boom.

The next major upheaval came in 1959 when Fidel Castro overthrew the government in Cuba. Hundreds of thousands of Cubans came to South Florida between 1960 and 1980. The opening of Walt Disney World in 1971 fueled a huge population expansion in central Florida that lasted about 20 years as Disney grew and other theme parks opened their doors. Another shift came in South Florida with additional migrations from Cuba, the Caribbean, and Latin America that lasted well into the 1990s. They were joined by hundreds of thousands of Americans from northern states. The flow continues, with Florida's population growing at more than 800 new arrivals every day.

How to Use this Book

This guide is divided into six travel regions as illustrated on the map of Florida on page xiv. Each of the regions begins with an introduction, followed by walks in cities, towns, villages, parks, and forests.

Each walk is presented as a complete package. It begins with information to help you get started, such as historical background, visitor centers, directions, suggested readings, organized and guided walking tours, and seasonal highlights. The walks are presented as a "walking" narrative of the structures, sites, and flora and fauna observed along the way. Then follow listings and descriptions of nearby accommodations and eateries. In the historic districts and small towns, we've also included nearby museums, galleries, bookstores, and nightlife. All of the walks return to their starting points. There is no indication of difficulty because Florida's basically flat terrain—the highest point is 345 feet in the Panhandle—makes all of the walks pretty easy. Instead, the distance and approximate time for a leisurely pace are included for each walk.

Many worthy cities and natural areas were not included due to space limitations, others were not included because they did not have a tourism infrastructure within a reasonable drive.

Finally, in the cities, towns, and villages, please respect the privacy of the people living in the neighborhoods. Be friendly and say hello. If you see them outside and like their house, let them know. Most people are very proud of their preservation efforts. If a building is a semi-public structure such as a church, commercial facility, or bed & breakfast, ask permission to see inside. Feel free to enter other public buildings such as courthouses, libraries, post offices, banks, and museums.

Enjoy your walk!

Cultural Heritage Walks

The cultural heritage walks explore the districts and neighborhoods that reflect each city's history and cultural heritage. Also included are two college campuses and the New Urbanist town of Seaside, which embodies many of the characteristics that make old neighborhoods places where people want to be.

Each walk begins at a convenient point, usually a chamber of commerce, visitor center, park, attraction, or other site. In commercial and mixed-use areas, there are often restaurants and cafes where you can stop to eat or drink along the way. The maps illustrate the routes as well as tour highlights, roads, and visitor centers.

Natural Area Walks

Florida's government is committed to preserving the state's unique natural heritage—which ranges from mangrove swamps and barrier islands with beach dunes to wet and dry prairies and tropical hardwood hammocks. This book includes walks through Florida's extensive system of county, state, and national parks, preserves, refuges, sanctuaries, and rails-to-trails, as well as botanical gardens—some private, some within the park system.

The nature walks start at a visitor center or trailhead that has plenty of parking. In addition to pointing out wildlife and vegetation, we note interpretive signs, trail markers, trail crossings, roads, observation decks and towers, blinds, and bridges along the trails. Stay on the marked trails. Wandering off the trails destroys habitat and stresses the wildlife. The maps indicate the route and any significant structures.

Many of the parks require admission. At state parks the cost is generally $3–$4 per vehicle. If you plan to visit several state parks, an annual or vacation pass may be more cost effective. An individual 15-day vacation pass costs $20, plus tax. An individual annual pass costs $30; the annual family pass, good for up to 8 passengers, costs $60. Passes for national parks are also available. The annual Golden Eagle Passport costs $50; the lifetime Golden Age Passport for seniors 62 years and over costs $10. The Golden Access Passport for disabled visitors is free.

Lastly, in wilderness areas, please respect the animals and plants. Don't approach them. You're likely to get a better, longer view if you keep your distance. And always, take only pictures and leave only footprints.

Flora and Fauna

No other state can match the variety of flora and fauna found within Florida. According to the National Audubon Society's *Field Guide to Florida*, "Nearly 900 vertebrate species and at least 4,000 plants are native or naturalized in the state, and the number of naturalized species grows annually as humans introduce nonnative plants and animals."

A multi-zone climate and an abundant water supply account for its exceptional biodiversity. The state makes a nearly 450-mile stretch from the Georgia border to the Florida Keys. Along the way the climate changes from temperate to subtropical or tropical. In the northern regions the trees change colors in fall. At the southern end bananas, palms, and mangroves grow tall.

Everywhere there is water. Florida is not only surrounded by water on three sides, but it has abundant rainfall, nearly 8,000 lakes, and numerous rivers, springs, and ponds. These aquatic habitats are biologically rich, supporting myriad species of plants and animals.

Among the most common mammals found in natural areas are armadillos, white-tailed deer, raccoons, squirrels, coyotes, foxes, otters, feral pigs, bats, opossum, and nutria. Less common are bobcats and four of the country's most endangered mammals, Florida black bears, Florida panthers, Key deer, and manatees.

As the last (going south) and first (going north) large landmass along the migratory flyway, Florida is host to millions of migratory birds. Other birds spend the winter here. And with plenty to eat, many birds reside in Florida year-round.

Reptiles and snakes, six of which are poisonous, are also abundant. There are native alligators and crocodiles, and introduced caimans. Geckos, iguanas, sea and land turtles live alongside toads, treefrogs, salamanders, and sirens. (See Pests and Dangers below).

Supporting the widely varied flora and fauna are numerous habitats, including coral reefs, beaches and dunes, salt marshes, mangrove swamps, rivers and lakes, freshwater marshes and swamps, prairies, and upland wooded areas.

Practical Information

State Tourism Information
For information about visiting the Sunshine State, including a free Florida Vacation Guide that has a decent state map, contact VISIT FLORIDA, toll-free 888/7FLAUSA; 850/488-5607; 661 E Jefferson St, Suite 300, Tallahassee, FL 32301; www.flausa.com. An emergency toll-free help line is available 24 hours a day by calling 800/656-8777.

National Park Service & US Forest Service
The National Park Service provides information on its recreation areas. Contact them at The Department of the Interior, National Park Service, Office of Public Inquiries, PO Box 37127, Room 1013, Washington, DC 20013; 202/208-4747; www.nps.gov. For recreation in National Forests, contact the US Forest Service, US Department of Agriculture, Washington, DC 20250; 800/245-6340, 202/720-1127; or USDA Forest Service, Woodcrest Office Park, 325 John Knox Rd, Suite F-100, Tallahassee, FL 32303; 850/942-9300; www.fs.fed.us.

Other Outdoor Organizations

Nearly 900 miles of the continuous Florida Trail, a designated National Scenic Trail that extends the length of Florida through public and private lands, has been completed by the Florida Trail Association (FTA). Eventually, the trail will encompass an additional 400 miles. Some of the walks in the book cross or include parts of the Florida Trail. For additional information, contact FTA, PO Box 13708, Gainesville, FL 32604-1708; 800/343-1882, 352/378-8823; fta@florida-trail.org, www.florida-trail.org/~fta; or visit their offices at 5415 SW 13th St in Gainesville.

The Cross Florida Greenway State Recreation and Conservation Area is a 70,000-acre, 110-mile-long corridor that stretches through natural areas from the St Johns River to the Gulf of Mexico. It features historical sites and numerous areas to walk, hike, bike, fish, canoe, horseback ride, camp, and observe wildlife. For information, contact the Florida Department of Environmental Protection, Office of Greenways and Trails, 325 John Knox Rd, Bldg 500, Tallahassee, FL 32303; 904/488-3701.

In Florida, the Rails-To-Trails Conservancy (RTTC) maintains nine trails that were converted from abandoned rail corridors. These are generally well-marked flat, paved trails that pass through natural areas and small towns and are suitable for walking, biking, skating, and wheelchairs. Some of the walks in the book are on the rail trails. For information, contact the Office of Greenways and Trails (see above), or the RTTC, 1400 Sixteenth St NW, Suite 300, Washington, DC 20036; 202/797-5400.

When to Go

Late fall to early spring are the most comfortable periods. This is also the height of tourist season, when the state, especially South Florida, is crowded with snowbirds and vacationers. Most hotels are more expensive then, too.

Florida's climate ranges from subtropical in the south to temperate in the north. It is characterized by long, hot, humid summers that range from the 80s to the 90s throughout the state, and mild, dry winters ranging from the 50s to the 70s with occasional cold fronts that plunge temperatures into the 20s in the north and central areas, 30s and 40s in coastal and south areas, and 50s to 60s in the Keys. Rain is infrequent except in summer, when short rain showers with lightning may occur almost daily.

What to Wear

Wear comfortable shoes. Blisters that start forming a mile from the car will be mush by the time you limp back teary eyed. Aside from that advice, remember that Florida's climate dictates what you should wear. Before you say, "That's obvious," keep in mind that temperatures in the sunshine state vary greatly north to south, especially in the winter. While Miami and the Florida Keys might be enjoying a balmy 72 degrees in January, a cold front may be making Orlando, Jacksonville, Pensacola, and other northern cities feel more like winter in Maine with temperatures in the 30s or 40s. That said, dress in layers in winter. In summer, a nice breeze at Ding Darling National Wildlife Refuge, Merritt Island National Wildlife Refuge, and other coastal parks or towns might make the 88-degree, 80-percent humidity day feel comfortable, but that same heat and humidity in historic downtown Orlando or Ocala National Forest in the middle of the state would feel unbearable.

Shorts, loose clothing, sunglasses, sunscreen and mosquito repellent, and a hat are your best bets for summer. Also bring a bathing suit, especially if you're planning to walk in parks and towns along the coast or that have natural springs. Restaurants are very casual in Florida, even nice shorts with a collared shirt for men and a matching blouse for women would be acceptable in fine restaurants during the day.
In summer it's prudent to bring an umbrella and/or foldable poncho. Sudden afternoon thunderstorms might get you a little wet.

What to Bring

Good maps of Florida and the cities you plan to visit are indispensable. You can get them free from the state tourism office (see above), local visitor centers (see each walk), some chambers of commerce (see each walk), and AAA (if you're a member).

I also found a pedometer useful for measuring the distance, keeping time (mine even has a clock), counting calories, and number of steps. They are available through sporting goods stores and catalogs for $15 to $25.

Binoculars come in handy on the wildlife walks. Cameras, too. Be sure to use a film that's appropriate for Florida's bright, sunny days.

Water is essential on any walk, especially in summer. Drink frequently and before you are thirsty to avoid dehydration.

Did I already say bring sunscreen and mosquito repellent, especially in summer?

Pests and Dangers

Natural
Alligators and Snakes
Alligator mississippiensis, the American alligator, hatches from mid-August through September. During the months after that, watch for them and listen for their high-pitched grunting cry. Do not approach a baby alligator. Mama is usually close by and will hiss and possibly charge if she feels her babies are threatened.

Florida has six species of poisonous snakes: three rattlesnakes and the copperhead, cottonmouth water moccasin, and coral snake. They generally avoid people and are most likely to be encountered when sitting or stepping in areas around logs, debris, and piled leaves.

Insects
Ticks and chiggers are the most common problematic crawling insects. Lyme disease is rare in Florida, but it's possible to contract other tick-borne flu-like illnesses. Mosquitoes and yellow, deer, and horse flies are the most common annoying flying insects. All four are most prevalent from May to August. You can protect yourself from them by applying insect repellent.

Scorpions and two poisonous spiders—brown recluse and black widows—deliver painful but not lethal stings or bites. They're most commonly found in wood piles, under logs, and in structures that are seldom used.

Fire ants can deliver severe, painful bites that can cause secondary infection and allergic reactions. Avoid standing on mounds found in fields and open woods.

Hurricanes
Hurricane season runs from June through November. Florida's vulnerability increases in September and October, when the hurricane activity shifts to the western Caribbean. Tourists are the first to be evacuated during a hurricane, so tune in to local weather at least once a week during the season.

Lightning
Florida has the highest number of deaths by lightning in the country. If a thunderstorm approaches while walking outdoors, immediately seek

shelter anywhere but under trees. They are especially vulnerable to lightning strikes.

Poisonous Plants

Florida's diverse plant life includes numerous poisonous or injurious plants, the largest number of which are found in South Florida. Be cautious before touching or picking up any flower, twig, or leaf until you've identified the plant. Better still, avoid touching them. Among the most common plants that are poisonous or injurious just by touching are poisonwood (*Metopium toxiferum*), poison sumac (*Toxicodendron vernix*), poison ivy (*Toxicodendron radicans*), poison oak (*Toxicodendron toxicarium*), tread softly (*Cnidoscolus stimulosus*), and manchineel (*Hippomane mancinella*).

Manmade Dangers
Hunters

Hunting may be allowed in some of the natural areas, especially parts of the national forests and preserves. Although hunting isn't allowed anywhere near any of the trails, it would be prudent to ask rangers about hunting regulations in these areas.

Crime

In the four months and several hundred miles I walked alone in cities and natural areas to research this book, there was never a time when I felt unsafe. That said, in natural areas I always let someone on the park staff know when I walked and when I expected to return and I carried my cellular phone in my backpack.

Transportation

Florida is dotted with airports served by major and regional airlines, including Air Canada (800/776-3000), America West (800/235-9292), American (800/433-7300), Canadian Airways (800/426-7000), Continental (800/523-3273), Delta (800/221-1212), Northwest (800/225-2525), Southwest (800/435-9792), TWA (800/221-2000), United (800/241-6522), and US Airways (800/428-4322).

Amtrak (800/872-7245) and Greyhound (800/231-2222) have extensive networks throughout the state.

All of the major rental car companies are represented, including Alamo (800/327-9633), Avis (800/331-1212; in Canada 800/879-2847), Budget (800/527-0700), Dollar (800/800-4000), Enterprise (800 /736-8222), Hertz (800/654-3131; in Canada 800/263-0600), National (800/227-7368), and Thrifty (800/367-2277). Florida rates start around $36 a day, $150 a week, but can vary greatly by city, season, holiday, and demand.

Architecture

Up until the last 50 years, Florida's distinctive architecture was a response to its environment. Before the advent of air conditioning, the sultry climate prompted the earliest nonnative Floridians, known as Crackers, to surround their houses with wide, shady porches, high, pitched roofs, and big windows through which cooling breezes could blow. They avoided the wet soil by raising the structures off the ground on wooden or brick piers and they used readily available building materials found in the abundant pine, cypress, and hardwood hammocks around them. And always, the buildings were simple and utilitarian. Many of these weathered buildings still stand, particularly along country roads.

Later arrivals, particularly those in the cities and along the coasts who had access to other building materials and who were influenced by northerners and Europeans, incorporated more sophisticated styles. But they retained many aspects of classic Cracker vernacular design, especially the practical elements.

Fires, hurricanes, and storm surge inspired the need for stronger technologies like concrete and steel. Along with wood, these materials were incorporated into the new architectural darlings—Mediterranean Revival-, Tudor Revival-, Prairie-, Craftsman-, and Bungalow-style buildings—that shot up during the land boom of the 1920s. Even these styles were adapted to Florida's hot, humid climate, utilizing high ceilings, porches, shaded courtyards, and cupolas.

On the heels of those styles came the International, Art Moderne, and Art Deco movements. They were especially popular in South Florida. With the exception of adjustable louvered-glass windows that let in breezes, concrete eyebrows that shaded the windows, and the occasional balcony that substituted for porches, they had little in common with the vernacular style. But then, this was the beginning of the age of air-conditioned living.

Starting in the mid-1940s, most Florida architects seemed to design with no notice of the bright sunshine, humidity, or hurricanes, storms, and their accompanying winds. Instead, they focused on the financial rewards to be made during the post-WWII real estate boom. They threw up cheap, unimaginative tract houses as fast as a hammer could pound in the nails. While fast-buck builders still drive the local industry, there is a major move underway to reform Florida's unappealing post-WWII architectural landscape. In pockets around the state, a few architects are again designing buildings that hearken back to the vernacular principles that respond to the environment rather than fight it.

Recommended Reading

Listed below are a few of the books that I used to research *Walking Places in Florida*. I've also noted a few in the First Steps section of some of the walks. Those are not repeated here.

Fiction
• *A Land Remembered* by Patrick D. Smith
• *Cross Creek* by Marjorie Kinnan Rawlings
• *Florida Stories: Tales From the Tropics* edited by John and Kirsten Miller
• *Nine Florida Stories* by Marjory Stoneman Douglas
• *Palmetto Leaves* by Harriet Beecher Stowe
• *The Yearling* by Marjorie Kinnan Rawlings
• *Their Eyes Were Watching God* by Zora Neale Hurston
• *To Have and Have Not* by Ernest Hemingway

Non-Fiction
• *Beyond the Theme Parks* by Benjamin D. Brotemarkle
• *Black Florida* by Kevin M. McCarthy
• *Changing Places* by Richard Moe and Carter Wilkie
• *Classic Cracker: Florida's Wood-Frame Vernacular Architecture* by Ronald W. Haase.
• *Florida Country Inns* by Robert Tolf
• *Florida's Past: People and Events That Shaped the State (vol. 1,2,3)* by Gene M. Burnett
• *Florida's Vanishing Architecture* by Beth Dunlop
• *Florida: A Guide to the Southernmost State* by the Federal Writers' Project
• *Guide to the Small and Historic Lodgings of Florida* by Herbert L. Hiller

- *In Praise of Wild Florida* by Archie Carr
- *National Audubon Society Field Guide to Florida*
- *The Book Lover's Guide to Florida* edited by Kevin M. McCarthy
- *The Everglades: River of Grass* by Marjory Stoneman Douglas
- *The Florida Reader: Visions of Paradise from 1530 to Present* edited by Maurice O'Sullivan and Jack C. Lane
- *The Geography of Nowhere* by James H. Kunstler
- *Travels of William Bartram* edited by Mark Van Doren

Lodgings and Restaurants

Evaluating hotels and restaurants, like evaluating anything, is subjective, open to varying opinions. Our goal was not to rate the establishments. Rather it was—whenever possible—to select accommodations and eateries that contribute to the life and vibrancy of the city or historic district in which they are located. Even with the walks in natural areas, we tried to find places that were not run-of-the-mill, places that had lots of character and that you wouldn't find at home. We looked for lodgings and restaurants that had history, that were in historic or otherwise significant buildings, that reflect the regional cuisine and style, and that were operated by someone special. In areas where the selections are limited, we chose facilities that are clean, comfortable, and welcoming.

Price/Standards for Lodgings
The prices are based on a standard double room. Within the text, two prices are shown, representing rates during the high/low seasons.
$ under $50
$$ $50–$100
$$$ $101–$150
$$$$ over $150

Price/Standards for Restaurants
Prices are based on dinner for one person, including, appetizer, main course, and dessert. They do not include drinks, tax, or tip.
$ under $15
$$ $15–$20
$$$ $20–$30
$$$$ over $30

Miscellaneous

We have made every effort to be accurate. However, time brings changes. Historic buildings are torn down or altered, streets are closed off, park trails are closed due to weather or wildlife needs, telephone numbers are changed, and businesses are shut down. Areas codes are especially subject to change these days. If you have trouble reaching a number, first call the operator and verify the area code.

Please Write

We'd like to know whether you enjoyed the walks in this book. Was a walk a waste of time? Did the description of the restaurants and lodgings we recommended meet your expectations? We welcome your feedback, positive and negative, so that we can create better books. If you have a favorite walk or you discovered a walk, restaurant, or hotel that we haven't included and you would like to share, please let us know. We'll check it out. Also, please send corrections, errors, and omissions. We'll include them in the next book. You can reach us by email at: jim @outtherepress.com. Or write to us at Out There Press, PO Box 1173, Asheville, NC 28802.

Northeast Florida

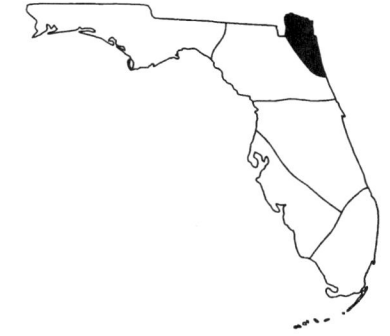

"People have to work in the cities, they can't live in the woods anymore. But they ought to have a place in the woods they can go to."—Willie Browne, turn-of-the-century owner who willed his land to the Timucuan Ecological and Historic Preserve

Introduction

Long before the Pilgrims landed at Plymouth Rock, life in Northeast Florida was unfolding like a soap opera. Native Americans had cultivated crops and traded with other groups in the southeastern United States for 12,000 years. Then Juan Ponce de León anchored near St Augustine in April 1513, waded ashore, and announced to the Timucuan Indians—who didn't understand a word he was saying—that he was renaming their land *La Florida* and taking it for Spain. He left, returned eight years later with 200 people and animals and tried to establish a settlement. The Timucuans ran him off.

The French followed in 1562 with Jean Ribault exploring Amelia Island. Two years later his colleague, René Goulaine de Laudonnière, a Protestant Huguenot, established Fort Caroline at the mouth of the St Johns River, near Jacksonville. The Spanish dispatched Pedro Menéndez de Avilés across the Atlantic to remove the French. He massacred all of the French except for the women, children, artisans, and men who professed a belief in Catholicism.

Menéndez renamed the fort San Mateo, manned it with Spanish soldiers, and went south a few miles to establish St Augustine, the first permanent European settlement in the United States. The French retaliated by murdering the Spanish soldiers at the fort.

Great Britain entered the drama, sending Sir Francis Drake to loot and burn St Augustine in 1586. And so it went for almost 250 years: Europeans fighting over St Augustine—and the rest of Florida—until Spain ceded Florida to the United States in 1821. In the interim, the Native Americans were enslaved, converted, killed, infected with European diseases, and eventually annihilated.

The Civil War years proved only a little less dramatic, as Florida joined the Confederacy, Union troops occupied Jacksonville and Amelia Island, and the Confederacy won a battle at Olustee, 40 miles southwest of Jacksonville.

After the war, Jacksonville became a major port, Henry Flagler opened the first railroad bridge across the St Johns River, steamboats brought visitors from the north, and tourist hotels sprang up in coastal cities from Amelia Island to St Augustine. With these four components, the Northeast flourished beginning in the 1870s and harbingered modern-day Florida.

Northeast Florida had much to offer early visitors. Beaches, dunes, barrier islands, rivers, freshwater and saltwater marshes, tidal estuaries, coastal flatwoods, and hardwood hammocks provided alluring glimpses of natural beauty and opportunities for year-round outdoor recreation.

Though millions more people now inhabit Northeast Florida and the effects on wildlife and natural habitat are disheartening, numerous parks and vast green spaces cover the region, reflecting the way Florida appeared in more primitive times.

Downtown Fernandina Beach

Today's Fernandina Beach is a lively, tourist-oriented resort town with a 30-block historic district, turn-of-the-century B&Bs, and numerous beachfront vacation rental houses and mom-and-pop motels.

The town owes its existence to its strategic location on the north end of Amelia Island, Florida's northernmost barrier island. Native Americans recognized this and lived on the 13.5-mile by 2-mile island for centuries. Jean Ribault, the first European to arrive, planted the flag for France in 1562. Spain already claimed everything south of Georgia, and they quickly ran the French out. It remained in the hands of the Spanish, who named the town after Queen Isabella's consort, until the arrival of the English, who named the island after George II's daughter. These countries plus five others raised the flag on the island, making it the only US city to have flown eight flags.

In the early 1800s the port, again under Spanish control, became the smuggler's port of entry for enslaved Africans after it became illegal to import them into the US. That ended when Spain ceded Florida to the US in 1821. Florida became a state in 1845.

The entire town moved south a half-mile to a less marshy area so a railroad could be built to the mainland in 1853. Spearheaded by Senator David Yulee, who had petitioned for Florida's acceptance into the Union, the railroad carried freight from ocean-going ships across the state to the Gulf of Mexico.

Following the Civil War, many northern soldiers returned to the sunny island, starting Fernandina Beach's first tourist boom. Major tourist hotels flourished as wealthy northerners came down on steamships directly from New York. The bust came when Henry Flagler built his luxurious hotel in St Augustine and the shipping industry moved 32 miles southwest to Jacksonville. Fires in 1876 and 1883 destroyed the first few blocks from the waterfront east.

Today, with two large, posh resorts south of town and careful preservation of its historic downtown, Fernandina Beach again enjoys a reputation as a resort destination.

Now, as earlier, Centre Street remains the most important thoroughfare. Though overly touristy—it's lined with mostly tasteful shops, bars, and eateries—the street retains much of its historic flavor, especially from the second floor up.

Information

Amelia Island Chamber of Commerce, 102 Centre St, PO Box 472, Fernandina Beach, FL 32034; 800/2AMELIA, 904/261-3248; aifbychamber@net-magic.net; www.ameliaisland.org. The **Amelia Island Museum of History**, 233 S 3rd St, Fernandina Beach, FL 32034; 904/261-7378.

Getting there

Take I-95 to exit 129 (Hwy A1A) east to S 8th St, then left onto Centre St. There are plenty of directional signs to the Historic District. Jacksonville International Airport is about 20 minutes south at exit 127 (Airport Rd). The closest train and bus depots are in Jacksonville: Amtrak's (800/USA RAIL, 904/766-5110) station is at 3570 Clifford Lane. Greyhound (800/231-2222, 904/356-9976) has a station downtown at 10 N Pearl St.

First steps

For area maps and information, contact the **Amelia Island Chamber of Commerce**. Centre Street becomes Atlantic Street east of 7th Street. Books of interest include *The Golden Age of Amelia Island* by Suzanne Davis Hardee and *The Best of Amelia Now* by Helen Gordon Litrico. The Amelia Island Museum of History publishes several books on the island's history, including *Churches of The Golden Age of Amelia Island* and *The Golden Age of Amelia Island*, both by Suzanne Davis Hardee.

Seasonal highlights

During the low season, October through February, chamber of commerce members offer Amelia Island Midweek Retreat, for midweek savings of up to 33 percent on accommodations and other discounts.

Tours

The **Amelia Island Museum of History** gives museum tours daily at 11 am and 2 pm and historic district tours on Thursday and Friday or by request at 3 pm, departing from the Chamber of Commerce. Tours are only by request June to August.

Historic downtown Fernandina Beach. *This two-mile route covers the 30-block Historic District. It can be walked in 90 minutes, but allow three hours if you plan to go inside any of the churches, inns, historic eateries, or other buildings.*

Start at the Chamber of Commerce. At the west end of town, on the corner of Centre and Front streets, is the gabled, rectangular brick **Railroad Depot** dating from the cross-state railroad days in the mid 1800s. It's now the chamber of commerce. Across the street the **Duryee Building** (101

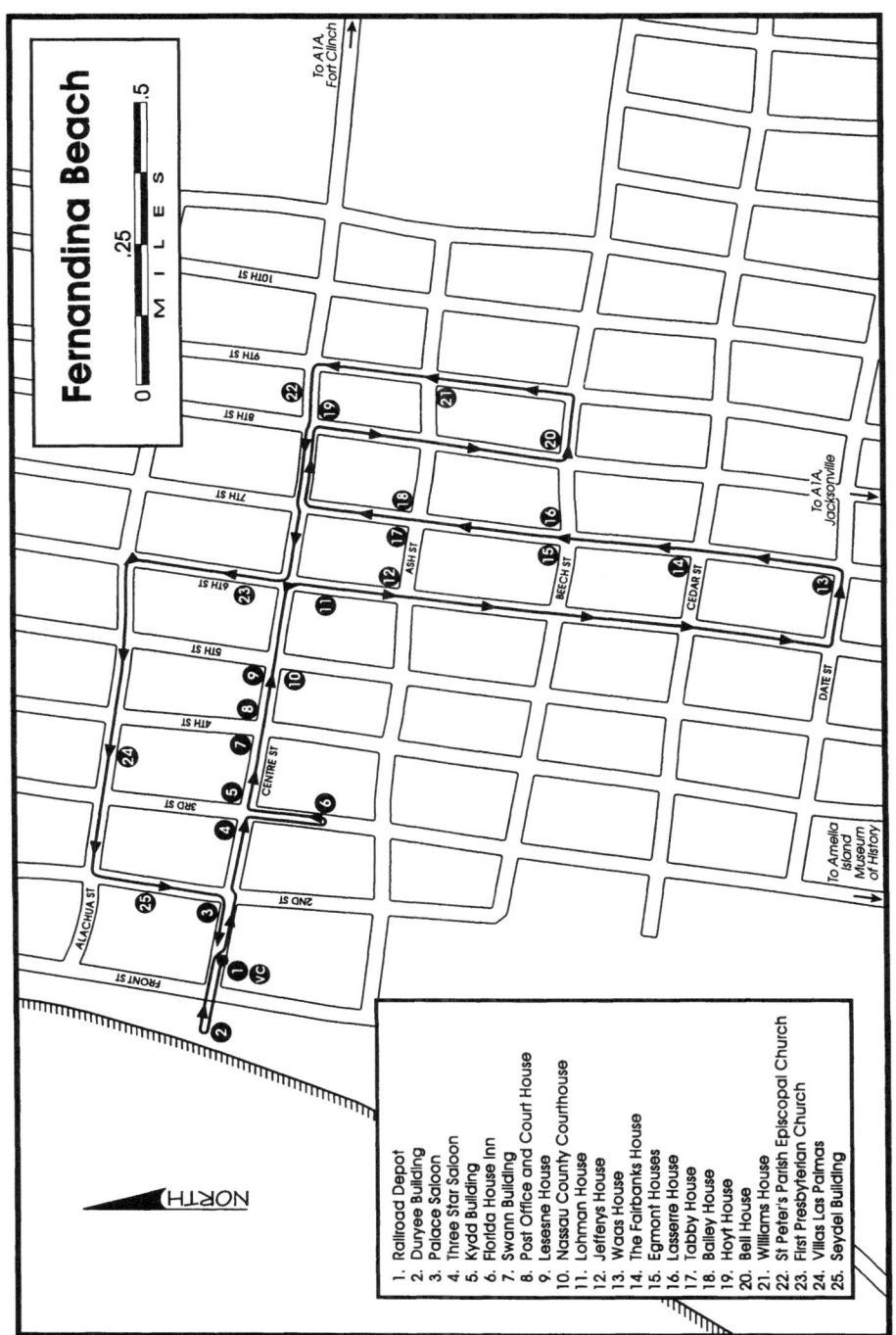

Fernandina Beach

MILES

0   .25   .5

NORTH

1. Railroad Depot
2. Dunyee Building
3. Palace Saloon
4. Three Star Saloon
5. Kydd Building
6. Florida House Inn
7. Swann Building
8. Post Office and Court House
9. Lesesne House
10. Nassau County Courthouse
11. Lohman House
12. Jefferys House
13. Waas House
14. The Fairbanks House
15. Egmont Houses
16. Lasserre House
17. Tabby House
18. Bailey House
19. Hoyt House
20. Bell House
21. Williams House
22. St Peter's Parish Episcopal Church
23. First Presbyterian Church
24. Villas Las Palmas
25. Seydel Building

Centre) once served as the offices of the namesake Union· officer who returned after the war and sold feed. It's now a restaurant. *Continue east on Centre St.*

Note the **Palace Saloon** (113 Centre St) a few doors down, which has operated continuously since it opened in 1903, except during Prohibition, when it served ice cream. Stop to see the intact interior, which features hand-carved details. Three stars decorate the face of the brick **Three Star Saloon**, built in 1877. The **Kydd Building** (corner Centre and 3rd), was the first brick building on the street. It once housed J&T Kydd's Dry Goods. *Detour south half way down 3rd St to* the **Florida House Inn** (22 S 3rd), which hosted such notables as Mary Pickford, Ulysses S. Grant, and freedom fighter Jose Marti. The railroad opened it in 1859 as an upscale tourist hotel. The colorful, striking building is still a restaurant and inn. *Return to Centre St.* On the northwest corner is the **Swann Building**, whose metal façade connects it to the building next door. It has a decorative cornice and stepped side roofline. Across 4th St is the Mediterranean Revival **Post Office and Court House** (401 Centre) built in 1910. The cast-iron lamp posts were the first standardized types approved for Federal buildings. Inside is a feast of marble, original wood counters, railings, and molding. Next door is the **Lesesne House**, built in 1860 for Dr. John Lesesne, who left during the Civil War and didn't return.

Across the street, the 1891 **Nassau County Courthouse** (416 Centre) has a red brick Victorian Revival design with cast-iron columns and a central tower and clock that still keeps time. It has beautiful ornamentation. *Continue east on Centre, turn right onto 6th St.* The **Lohman House** (19 S 6th) and the **Jeffreys House** (NE corner 6th and Ash) both show ornately detailed balustrades, wood spindles, and brackets. The Lohman House was originally located on Centre St. *Continue south on 6th St, turn left onto Date St, then left again onto 7th St.*

When it was originally built in 1856, the **Waas House** (corner of Date and 7th) was much smaller, simpler, and faced Date St. In 1901, its new owner, Dr. W.T. Waas, changed its orientation and design to its present Queen Anne style. On the corner of the next block sits **The Fairbanks House** (227 7th), known as Fairbanks' Folly, an excellent example of Italianate architecture. It was designed by architect Robert S. Schuyler for Confederate army Major George Fairbanks, an historian, citrus grower, and editor of the *Florida Mirror*.

In the next block, the four houses at numbers 131, 127, 123, and 119 are called the **Egmont Houses** because they were built on the site of and with the wood from the elegant 19th-century Egmont Hotel. They all feature gabled roofs. Across the street, the **Lasserre House** (130 S 7th) is one of nine houses built by the Bell brothers, identical twins who were river pilots from North Carolina. All of their houses feature elaborate detailing.

Schuyler was also the architect for the **Tabby House** (27 S 7th), the town's only house made of tabby construction, using a poured concrete aggregate of oyster shell. The 2.5-story house has a 2-story verandah with carved posts, balustrades, and brackets. Cross the street to admire one of the town's prettiest houses, the Queen Anne **Bailey House** (28 S 7th). Now a B&B, it features stained-glass windows, multiple fireplaces, and beautiful architectural detailing. *Go to Centre St and turn right, then right again onto 8th St.*

In 1905 Fred Hoyt, a merchant and bank owner, had **Hoyt House** (corner of 8th St and Atlantic Ave) built, modeled after the Rockefeller Cottage on Jekyll Island. It has bay window rooms, seven fireplaces, and pine floors. **Bell House** (801 Beech) is another fine example of Victorian "gingerbread" built by the Bell brothers. Today, it's the Beech Street Grill. *Turn left onto Beech St, then left again onto 9th St.*

The lovely **Williams House** (103 S 9th), another B&B, was built in 1856, and later purchased by Marcellus Williams and his wife, a descendant of the King of Spain. They hired Schuyler to add the elaborate gingerbread detailing. *Turn left onto Centre St.*

On the right is Schuyler's masterpiece, **St Peter's Parish Episcopal Church** (corner of Centre and 8th). The concrete Gothic Revival structure was built in 1884, then rebuilt after a fire in 1893. Go inside to look at the open-timbered roof and stained-glass windows, especially the Yellow Fever window, which memorializes two doctors who died while treating patients. *Continue west on Centre St, then turn right onto 6th St.*

The 1860 **First Presbyterian Church** (19 N 6th) is the town's oldest house of worship. It was built on land possibly donated by Senator David Yulee. During the Civil War, Union forces occupied it. *Turn left onto Alachua St.*

Lumber baron Nathaniel Borden impressed his new bride with the huge **Villas Las Palmas** (315 Alachua) built in 1910 with plenty of room for entertaining. Among its many features are a wide front porch, cedar shingles, clay roof tiles, and semi-circular parapet wall at the dormers. *Walk two blocks, then turn left onto 2nd St.*

The **Seydel Building** (31 N 2nd) was constructed as a store in 1877. It now houses a restaurant. *Return to Centre St and turn right to return to the Railroad Depot.*

Lodging
Weekend, festival, and winter guests fill the B&Bs, which, besides the resorts, provide the finest accommodations. Small motels along the Atlantic Ocean are a popular low-price option. The two exclusive resorts are at the very high end. Chain hotels are almost non-existent. Visitors staying a week or longer can choose among scores of beachfront rental homes. Rates are higher in summer.

Visitors can totally immerse themselves into the town's history by staying in one of the historic B&Bs on the tour or nearby. The **Addison House** ($$–$$$, 904/277-1604), constructed in 1876, has sunny rooms with private porches and four-poster beds. Guests can dine indoors or on the verandah at 614 Ash St. One of the most beautiful houses on the tour is the **Bailey House** ($$–$$$, 904/261-5390), a charming 1895 Queen Anne furnished with antiques at 28 S 7th St. The sprawling antebellum **Williams House** ($$$–$$$$, 904/277-2328) features fireplaces and large rooms at 103 S 9th St. If your dream runs more toward an Italianate villa, the 1885 **Fairbanks House** ($$$–$$$$, 904/277-0500) at 227 S 7th St will fulfill them with 12 antique-filled rooms, suites, and cottages. There's even a pool.

The island is well known for two first-class resorts, **The Ritz-Carlton Amelia Island** ($$$–$$$$, 800/241-3333, 904/277-1100) at 4750 Amelia Island Pkwy, and **Amelia Island Plantation** ($$$–$$$$, 800/874-6878 or 904/261-6161) at 3000 First Coast Hwy.

The two-story **Hampton Inn** ($$, 904/321-1111) at 2549 Sadler Rd, and the **Inn at Fernandina Beach** ($$, 904/277-2300) next door at 2707 Sadler Rd, have standard rooms, pools, and complimentary breakfast and are two miles from the historic district and one block from the beach.

Options for mom-and-pop style beachfront—or near beachfront—motels that offer simple, but clean rooms and efficiencies include **Amelia Motel** ($–$$, 904/261-5735) at 1997 S Fletcher Ave; **Surf Restaurant, Motel & Lounge** ($–$$, 904/261-5711), which has live entertainment on weekends in the lounge at 3199 S Fletcher Ave.

Arts & culture
The owner collects fine arts and crafts from regional artists to exhibit at the **Art & Antiques Centre** at 702 Centre St. More than 50 Nassau County artists belong to the cooperative **Island Art Association** at 205 Centre St, which presents monthly exhibits. **Waterwheel Art Gallery**'s two locations showcase original oils, watercolors, bronze sculptures by local artist at 5047 First Coast Hwy and at 316-A Centre St.

Amelia Community Theatre (904/261-6749) has performances September through May at 209 Cedar St. Likewise, the **Fernandina Little Theatre** (904/321-1595, 904/277-2202) stages productions of from February through May at 1014 Beech St.

The **Amelia Island Museum of History** is located in the former jail that was active from 1878 to 1975 at 233 S 3rd St. Its best features include enlarged photos of the town during the 19th century. Docents give tours ($3) daily at 11 am and 2 pm. They also lead tours of the historic district (see Tours).

The **Book Loft** at 214 Centre St and **Books Plus** across the street at 215 Centre St have a large section of local interest works.

Food & drink

Fernandina Beach is a haven of good eating in historic settings. The choices range from cheery Irish pubs and intimate French bistros to elegant steak houses and waterfront seafood cafes. Prices run moderate to high.

With wood planking and nautical accents, the **Crab Trap** ($–$$, 904/261-4749) at 31 N 2nd St in the historic Seydel Building, looks like a longshoreman's bar. Located a block off Centre Street and the river, it's a good choice before or after the tour. Service is super, as is the mostly seafood menu of oysters any way you like; Alaskan, Dungeness, king and blue crab; plus crab, fish, and beef burgers. The *Wine Spectator* and *Jacksonville Magazine* both laud **The Beech Street Grill** ($$–$$$, 904/277-3662) an intimate eatery at 801 Beech St, in the Bell House that prepares innovative veal, beef, pork loin, venison, lamb, and seafood dishes. **Joe's 2nd Street Bistro** ($$–$$$, 904/321-2558) occupies a restored turn-of-the-century house at 14 S 2nd St, where the menu features seafood, duck, lamb, and steaks.

Outside of the historic district your best bets are the very healthy and innovative **River Place** ($–$$; 904/277-2336), which also has a deli and takeout service on the west side of the Shave Bridge and Hwy A1A; the award-winning oceanfront **Grill** ($$–$$$, 904/277-1028) at The Ritz-Carlton at 4750 Amelia Island Pkwy; a not-to-be-missed Sunday brunch (as well as other great meals) at the **Amelia Inn** ($$–$$$, 904/321-5050) at the Amelia Island Plantation at 3000 First Coast Hwy; and the seafood and live entertainment at **The Surf** ($–$$, 904/261-5711) at 3199 S Fletcher St (A1A).

Nightlife

Rustic, laid-back **O'Kane's Irish Pub & Eatery** at 318 Centre St is a popular spot with the locals for food, fun, and live entertainment Wed to Sun. Just down the block is **The Palace Saloon**, Florida's oldest saloon operating in the same location at 117 Centre St. The popular **Brass Rail Saloon** schedules live bands Friday and Saturday nights at 12 N Second St. Away from the downtown area there's disco at

Sliders at 1998 S Fletcher Ave; live bands booked several nights a week at **Sandy Bottoms** at 2910 Atlantic Ave; and nightly entertainment ranging from piano tunes to a vocalist to dance bands at the **Ritz-Carlton's** Lobby Lounge at 4750 Amelia Island Pkwy.

Events
The annual Isle of **Eight Flags Shrimp Festival** (800/2AMELIA) attracts some 300,000 visitors the first weekend in May. The annual **December Holiday Tour of Historic Treasures** (800/2AMELIA) showcases 10 B&Bs and historic churches all decorated for the season. **Fort Clinch** (904/277-7274), located a few miles north of the historic district, holds Civil War period re-enactments, garrison weekends, holiday encampments and candlelight viewings the first weekend of each month. (See Fort Clinch Walking Tour.)

Fort Clinch State Park

Fort Clinch, a well-preserved double-wall fortification built of brick and stone, occupies 1,121 acres on the north end of Amelia Island, Florida's northernmost barrier island. It overlooks Georgia across the Cumberland Sound and the St Mary's River. The Atlantic Ocean laps its eastern shore, the Intracoastal Waterway and Amelia River front its western shore.

The US began building the fort to guard the mouth of the St Mary's River and defend Fernandina's deep-water port in 1847, naming it after Duncan Lamont Clinch, a general in the Second Seminole War. It was never completed. The Confederate militia took it over at the beginning of the Civil War, but withdrew when Union forces returned in 1862. Construction resumed until 1867, when it was deactivated. Troops returned for brief periods during the Spanish-American War and World War II. After Florida purchased it in 1935, the Civilian Conservation Corps developed it into a state park.

Visitors may explore almost every nook and cranny, including the museum that has interpretive displays and artifacts. On most days, park rangers are dressed up as Union soldiers re-enacting daily life and providing historical information.

The natural park is quite a showplace too. Giant live oaks draped with Spanish moss form a sun-dappled tunnel along the main three-mile road. There is a natural beach along the Atlantic Ocean, campgrounds, restrooms, picnic and fishing areas, and three trails, two about a quarter mile and one about six miles. The trails are for hikers and bikers, so the best time to visit is during the week. There is also less traffic then. Alligators, squirrels, armadillos, and birds are the most common animals along the trails.

Information

Fort Clinch State Park, 2601 Atlantic Ave, Fernandina Beach, FL 32034; 904/277-7274. Department of Environmental Protection, Division of Recreation and Parks, 3900 Commonwealth Blvd, Tallahassee, FL 32399; 850/488-9872. Amelia Island Chamber of Commerce, 102 Centre St, PO Box 472, Fernandina Beach, FL 32034; 800/2AMELIA or 904/261-3248; aifbychamber@net-magic.net; www.ameliaisland.org.

Getting there

Take I-95 to exit 129 (Hwy A1A) east to S 8th St, turn right onto Centre St, which becomes Atlantic Ave east of 8th St. Jacksonville International Airport is about 20 minutes south at exit 127 (Airport Rd). The closest train and bus depots are in Jacksonville.

First steps

For park information, contact **Fort Clinch State Park**, which is open daily from 8 am to sunset, or the **Department of Environmental Protection**. The **Amelia Island Chamber of Commerce** provides area maps and information. Admission is $3.25 per car with up to 8 people; $1 for pedestrians and bicyclists. There's an additional $1 charge to tour the fort and museum

Tours

Rangers lead candlelight tours ($2, plus park admission) of the fort the first weekend of the month.

Seasonal highlights

Painted buntings and other migratory birds are common late spring to early fall.

Natural Fort Clinch. *This 3.5-mile walk covers a half-mile tour of the fort, a half-mile walk around Willow Pond, plus 2.5 miles of trails that parallel the park's main road. It can be lengthened up to 7 miles by continuing along the trails that parallel the road to the ranger station. Trailheads along the trail allow you to cross the road and return at various points.*

Start at the fort. After touring the museum, enter the fort and walk around, viewing the bastions, blacksmith shop, living quarters, bakery, and other areas. Then climb onto the rampart for a bird's-eye view of the surrounding waters and Cumberland Island, Georgia. *Exit the fort and walk across the parking lot to the trailhead.*

The trail is single track and has very gentle changes in terrain as it passes through a coastal hammock of live oak (*Quercus virginiana*), hackberry (*Celtis laevigata*), sparkleberry (*Vaccinium arboreum*), cabbage palm (*Sabal palmetto*), and southern magnolia trees (*Magnolia grandiflora*)**. Primary shrubs and vines include crape myrtle (*Lagerstroemia indica*), coral bean (*Erythrina herbacea*), yaupon (*Ilex vomitoria*), American (*Ilex opaca*) and dahoon (*Ilex cassine*) holly. The understory is thin.

A half mile in, the trail crosses the main park road. A tenth of a mile farther is a confusing directional sign. It's meant to give bikers the option of going around or crossing a ditch. Take either side. Both meet the road a tenth of a mile farther. *Don't cross, instead walk 20 feet right and rejoin the trail on the same side.*

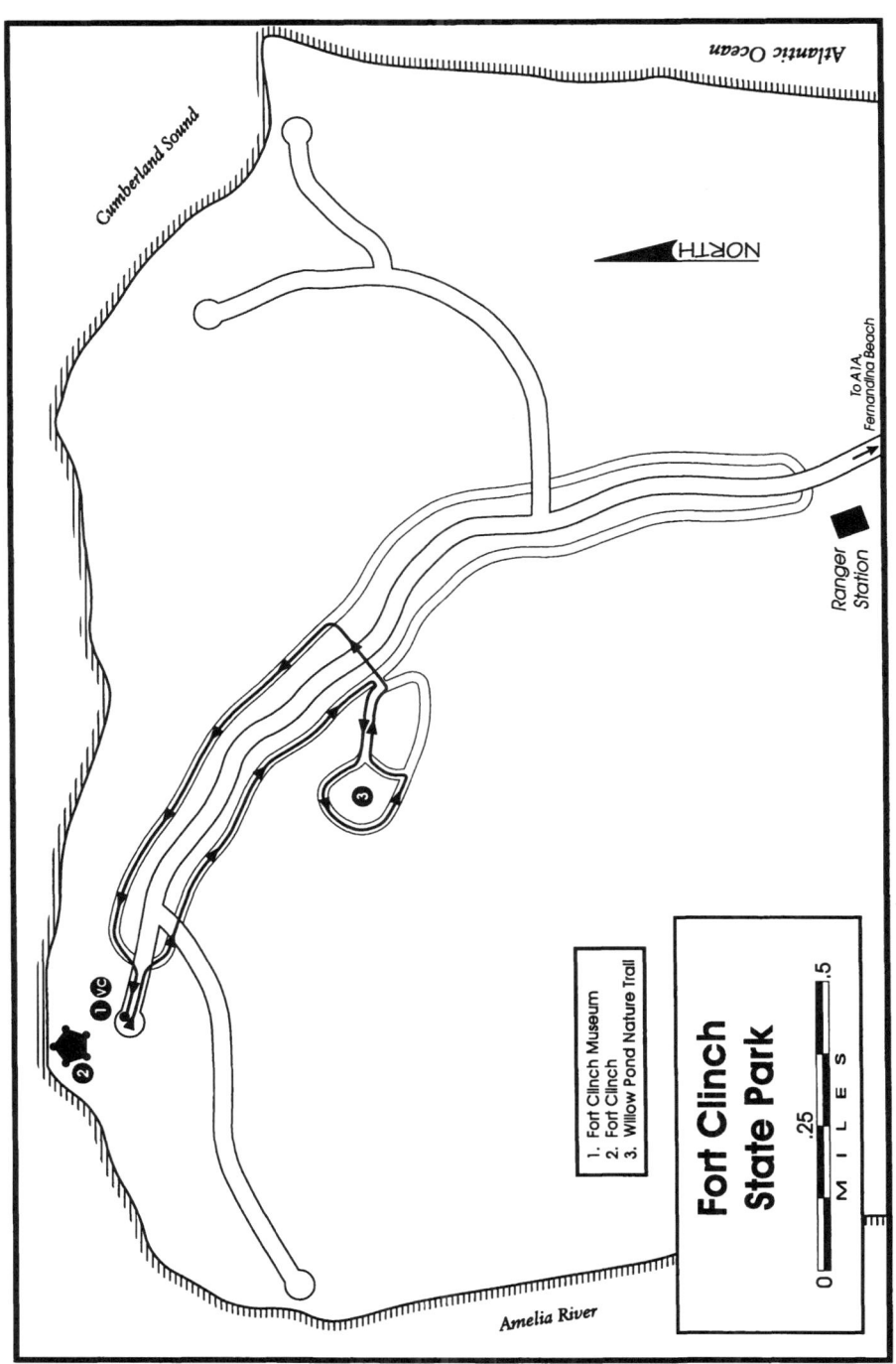

Atlantic Ocean

Cumberland Sound

NORTH

To A1A,
Fernandina Beach

Ranger
Station

1. Fort Clinch Museum
2. Fort Clinch
3. Willow Pond Nature Trail

Fort Clinch
State Park

.25

.5

0

M I L E S

Amelia River

At a little under a mile, there's a small glen of bright green saw palmettos, just before the trail meets the road and picks up 20 feet along the same side to bypass another ditch.

At a mile and a quarter, the trail emerges at the Willow Pond Nature Trail, where you can choose to walk one or two loops. Both loops start at the same place, but at the first intersection, stay to the right. Interpretive displays describe the vegetation along the trail. There's also a sign regarding alligators. If you're lucky, you'll see one.

Bird life is abundant because of the pond. You'll see dozens and hear many more. Painted buntings, American redstarts, mockingbirds, herons, crows, and warblers are among them. At the pond, cross over the short wooden bridge. The trail continues on a dike that traverses the pond. Look for alligators on either side. When not sunning themselves on the bank, they're usually partially or completely submerged under the duckweed that covers the pond. Notice where the vegetation is matted on both sides of the dike. These are alligator crossings. You can see their tracks in the mud.

Bear right at the next fork. It continues across the pond. At the next intersection there's a short overlook on the right with a clear view of the pond, a bench, and an interpretive display on freshwater plants. *Regain the trail, and continue to the Willow Pond trailhead. Then cross the road and follow the trail back to the fort on the east side of the main road.*

Lodging, food & drink
See Downtown Fernandina Beach Walking Tour.

Events
Full garrison re-enactments of the fort's Union occupation take place in May. In October, Confederate soldiers regain control.

Talbot Islands State Parks

Five barrier islands lay along Florida's northeast coast, from the St Mary's River—the dividing line between Florida and Georgia—south nine miles to the St John's River on the north edge of Jacksonville. They're collectively called the Talbot Islands after Charles Baron Talbot, who served as the Lord High Chancellor of England during the mid 1700s. Individually, they are Amelia Island, Big Talbot Island, Long Island, Little Talbot Island, and Fort George Island. Eco-cultural tourism couldn't have a better setting. The four islands, most of which form Talbot Islands State Parks, offer culture, history, unspoiled beaches, dunes, coastal hammocks, and marshlands.

Amelia Island (see page 5), the northernmost, is a mix of small towns, posh resorts, and two state parks: Fort Clinch (see page 12) and Amelia Island State Recreation Area. The latter is just south of the developed tourist and residential areas of Amelia Island. It is 200 acres of undeveloped beaches, salt marshes and coastal maritime forests. There's fishing, hiking, sunning, birdwatching, and guided horseback riding along the beach.

The southernmost, Fort George Island is lush, with moss-draped laurels and live oaks creating a shady canopy. It has one of the highest points on the Atlantic coast south of New Jersey: Mount Cornelia rises to 55 feet. The island was home to its namesake, Fort Saint Georges, built in 1736 by General James Oglethorpe, founder of the Georgia Territory. While the fort is gone and its exact location on the island is uncertain, it's easy to find the Fort George Island State Cultural Site, Rollins Bird and Plant Sanctuary, the 4.4-mile trail, and Kingsley Plantation, a restored cotton and indigo plantation now operated as an historic cultural site by the National Park Service. Bicycling and hiking are the main activities at Fort George Island State Cultural Site. A new 1.5-mile loop bicycle trail of sand, grass, and leaf litter is ideal for walking.

In between stretch Big Talbot Island and Little Talbot Island. Save for a few residences on the south end of Big Talbot Island, the two islands remain undeveloped park lands.

Anyone tiring of Florida's flat landscape need only visit Big Talbot Island. While folks from the Washington, Oregon, California coastline may snicker at their height, they won't be able to deny that the bluffs here make the island one of the most scenic spots in the state.

As you walk from the parking lot, the first thing you'll be impressed by is the large oaks with a cleared understory. As you get closer, you'll realize that you're on a bluff. Then the real drama unfolds as you take the first steps down the wooden stairs that descend from the top of the bluff to the beach below. (The steps were seriously damaged by Hurricane Floyd. At publication, the date for repair was undecided.) Ancient, weathered giant oaks that tumbled with the eroding bluff lie along the beach like felled behemoths on a battle field. Their twisted shapes form beautiful pieces of natural art. This is a place that invites lingering. Several short trails course the island's beach and hammocks.

A bridge on the north end connects Big Talbot to Amelia Island, and you can walk along the beach to the southern point when the tide is out. Along the way, you'll pass people parked on lawn chairs at the water's edge surf fishing. You can still access the beach from the north end of the island.

Little Talbot Island is one of the few remaining totally undeveloped barrier islands in Florida. The entire 2,500-acre island is a state park with about six miles of wide, hard-packed sand beaches, rolling dunes, as well as a maritime forest. The combination attracts more than 190 birds that inhabit the island along with raccoons, opossum, bobcats, and marine animals.

Parking, bath houses, a campground, dune walkovers, trails, an observation platform, campfire programs, and seasonal guided walks make the island accessible to visitors.

A fifth island, Long Island, sandwiched between Big Talbot Island and Little Talbot Island, was recently acquired by the state park system. A few facilities will be added in the future.

Information

Little Talbot Island State Park, 12157 Heckscher Dr, Jacksonville, FL 32226; 904/251-2320. Jacksonville and the Beaches Convention & Visitors Bureau, 201 E Adams St, Jacksonville, FL 32202; 800/733-2668, 904/798-9111; www.jaxcvb.com.

Getting there

Take I-95 to Jacksonville exit 124 (Heckscher Dr/Hwy 105) east. Turn north onto Hwy A1A, for 15 miles to the Little Talbot Island State Park entrance. The four other islands can be reached by driving north or south of Little Talbot on Hwy A1A. From the north, take exit 129 (Hwy A1A) east toward Amelia Island. Drive south to reach the other islands. Jacksonville International Airport is about 15 minutes north of the city at exit 127 (Airport Rd). Amtrak's (800/USA RAIL, 904/766-5110) station is at 3570 Clifford Lane. Greyhound (800/231-2222, 904/356-9976) has a station at 10 N Pearl St.

First steps

For trail maps and park information, contact **Little Talbot Island State Park**. For area maps and information, contact the **Jacksonville and the Beaches Convention & Visitors Bureau**, which also has visitor centers at the airport and downtown at Jacksonville Landing. Admission to Little Talbot Island State Park is $3.25 per car (up to 8 passengers), $1 for pedestrians and bicyclists. The honor system is used to collect the fee of $1 at Big Talbot Island State Park and Amelia Island State Recreation Area. Fort George is free.

The trailhead is before the park entrance. Don't park there. Enter the park and leave the car in one of the lots near the ranger station. It's a short walk, about 0.10 miles, to the trailhead. In the summer, the beach areas of the walk can be very hot. Bring water.

Tours

While there are few ranger-led tours of the islands, every weekend there are programs about history, plants, and animals.

Natural Little Talbot Island. *This 4-mile route covers a coastal hammock, a progression of dunes, and the beach. Allow two to three hours, depending on how long you want to spend observing the plants along the way. On sections where the trail crosses the inland dunes, walking in the sand can be slow going.*

Start at the Trailhead 0.10 miles from the Ranger Station on the main park road. The floor of the arms-width trail begins as sand beneath a blanket of small, crisp, brown live oak leaves (*Quercus virginiana*), then quickly becomes sand before passing under a canopy of pines and live oaks. The sand makes it easy to spot telltale signs of animal life. Look for wriggly lines crossing the trail, where a snake has passed. Look for bird tracks and raccoon tracks. As you leave the maritime forest and descend the first small dune, the trail is lined with magnolias (*magnolia grandiflora*), southern red cedar (*Juniperus virginiana* var. *silicicola*), and saw palmettos (*Serenoa repens*).

Gopher turtles move quickly across the trail and dive into their burrows near vegetation. Their elaborate burrows and tunnels are also used by other animals for shelter and food. If you're walking during the spring and fall migrations or in early summer, you'll see warblers flitting about from branch to branch. The terrain is very gently rolling. At 0.5 miles, there's a low bluff on the right and a small creek on the left.

Note the deeply furrowed, papery, unevenly rectangular plates that look like quilt squares on the bark on the slash pines (*Pinus elliottii*). The

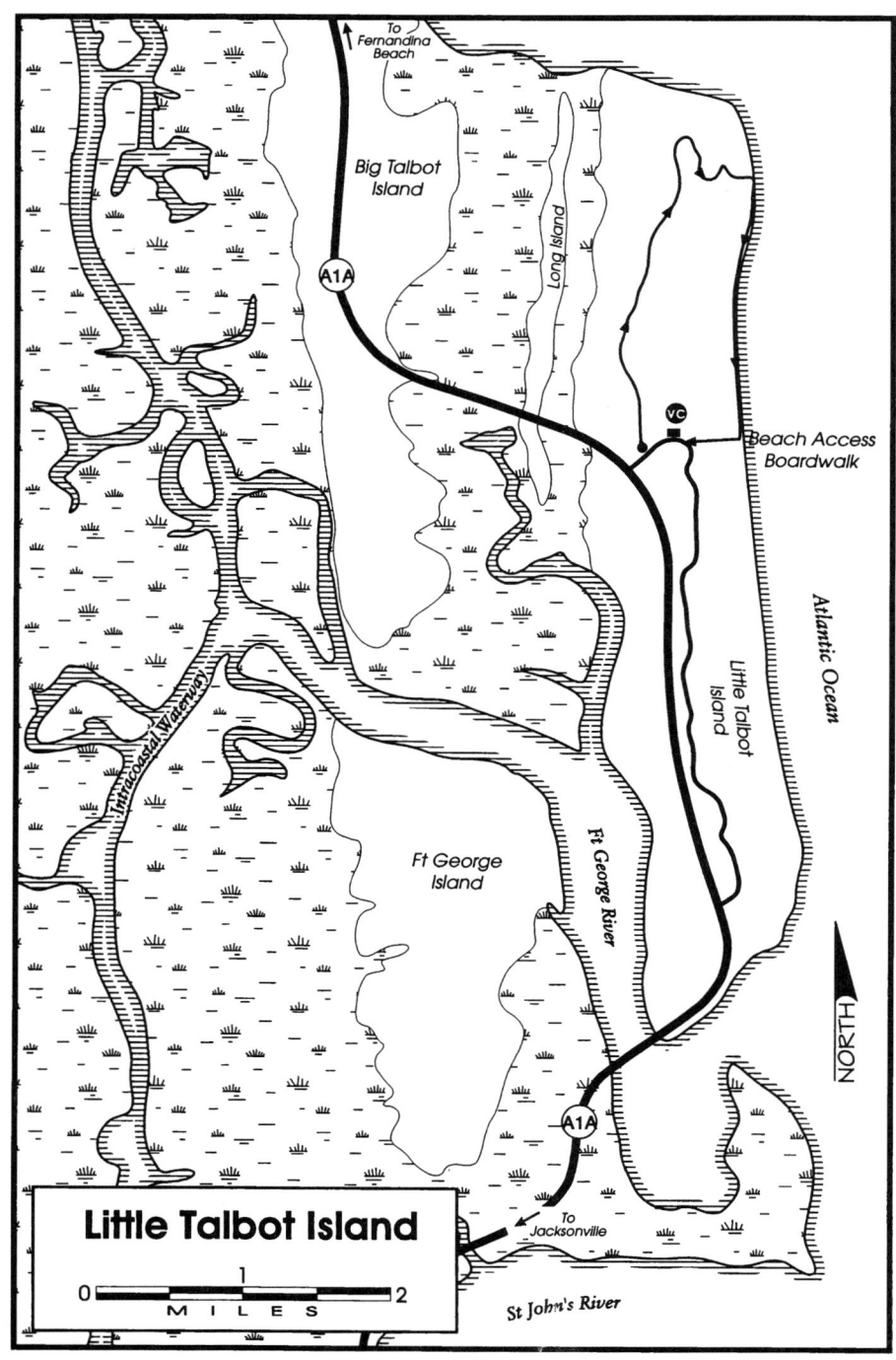

To
Fernandina
Beach

Big Talbot
Island

Long Island

A1A

VC

Beach Access
Boardwalk

Atlantic Ocean

Little Talbot
Island

Ft George River

Ft George
Island

Intracoastal Waterway

NORTH

A1A

To
Jacksonville

St John's River

Little Talbot Island

0   1   2
M I L E S

bark on its relative, the sand pine (*Pinus clausa*), is usually more gray and has narrow ridges.

At about 1 mile, the trail begins a gradual climb up the dune. The ground is wetter and ground ferns appear along the trail and resurrection ferns (*Polypodium polypodioides*) appear on the tree branches. At the interpretive display for sparkleberry (*Vaccinium arboreum*), look for the tree's green to blue-black berries.

More graceful live oaks border the trail as it continues. At 1.75 miles, a large live oak branch over the trail is covered with a huge mat of resurrection ferns. They will appear dry and shriveled if it has not rained recently, bright green and showy if it has, hence its name. Stop for a closer look at this unique plant. Understory plants to look for include the American holly (*ilex opaca*) and yaupon holly (*Ilex vomitoria*). You can tell them apart by looking at the leaves. The leaf edges of the American holly are sharp and pointed, typical of the holly seen at Christmas time. Yaupon holly's leathery leaves have round teeth. Both produce a beautiful red berry that is NOT edible by humans.

Look for a large cabbage palm (*sabal palmetto*) on the left. Its light gray trunk is latticed with old leaf bases. This is the tree that produces the heart of palm used in salads.

As you pass through a wash between dunes, the scenery changes to pines with no understory. A thick layer of pine needles carpets the ground. At 2 miles the trail opens onto a sand dune clearing with a bluff on the right. From this point, you can hear the sound of the waves. The sand gets deeper, the walking slower.

The trail veers left under pines again with cones and needles on the ground. This is quickly followed by more sand and dunes as the sound of the waves becomes louder. It's very tempting to touch the pretty, white, trumpet-shaped, five-lobed flowers that bloom from March to October at the trail's edge. Don't. It's tread softly (*Cnidoscolus stimulosus*). Although also called stinging nettle, it's a member of the spurge family. Do take a closer look at the long clusters of pretty cuplike rose-pink flowers that bloom year round on the coral vine (*Antigonon leptopus*). Watch for butterflies around this plant.

The trail continues through a series of dunes. More coral vines and woody, barbed, tangled wild blackberries (*Rubus cuneifolius*) grow along the trail's edge and hillside. The one-inch, purple-black edible berries are ripe from June to October. In spring, the white flowers attract pollinators.

Look for a single cabbage palm on the right near a saw palmetto with fan-shaped, deeply palmate leaves and prickle-edged leafstalks growing next to it. On the left is another small native tree, the wax myrtle (*Myrica cerifera*) or southern bayberry. Its small clustered flowers, which bloom from April to June, look like furry brownish green caterpillars.

As you climb the last dune, the trail curves left and opens onto the beach. *Just before you reach the beach, there's a "Hiking Trail Return" sign. Turn right.*

The beach scenery is beautiful, especially at low tide, when the beach is wide and flat. There's nothing manmade as far as you can see. Small ghost crabs scamper sideways across the hard-packed gray and tan sand as it slopes very gradually to the water. Gnarled driftwood decorates the landscape. Flocks of pelicans glide on air currents looking like an approaching squadron of B52s.

The waterside dunes above the maximum high-tide line are spotted with cabbage palms and clumps of sea oats (*Uniola paniculata*). The latter have deep roots that help anchor the sand dunes. They are protected by state law, so don't touch.

Most of the seashells are broken as they tumble to shore across a deep shelf. Be sure to walk down to the water's edge, where the sand is so hard-packed that you hardly leave a footprint. The beach trail continues for about 1.5 miles. *On the right look for a sign and boardwalk marked "Hiking Trail Return" or "Section F."* Turn right and follow the trail through the parking lot, then turn right again and walk to the road, which leads back to the ranger station.

Lodging, food & drink
See Amelia Island and Jacksonville Walking Tours.

Events
In March the park hosts the annual **Archaeology Festival** at Little Talbot Island. That's followed in November by the **Kingsley Celebration**, a joint project between the National Park and State Park, at Kingsley Plantation on Fort George Island.

Downtown Jacksonville

In area, Jacksonville is the largest city in the United States, covering 840 square miles. In population, it's a mere 15th, with around 1 million residents.

It owes its sprawling layout to two factors. In the late 1960s city and county governments merged, creating one huge municipality. And the St Johns River flows north through the city on its way to the Atlantic Ocean. With waterfront property being very desirable, neighborhoods grew up all along both banks of the river.

The result is a downtown through which almost everything must pass. Once in sharp decline, today downtown is a lively redeveloped area with a performing arts center and theater, museums, hotels, restaurants, and shops on both banks of the river. In keeping with the spirit of a user-friendly downtown, the city will unveil a new downtown trolley system in early 2000.

The river also creates prime recreational areas for hiking, canoeing, swimming, camping, briding, and wildlife watching within minutes of downtown.

The city sprang up on the banks of the St Johns River at a site Native Americans called *Wacca Pilatka*, which means place where cows cross. The English called it Cow Ford and crossed the site to link their colonies in the north with St Augustine in the late 1700s.

The town was laid out in 1822 in a 20-block section bounded by the river and Duval, Ocean, and Catherine streets, still part of the heart of downtown. It took its name from Andrew Jackson, a hero of Florida's Seminole Wars before becoming the seventh president of the United States. Wealthy northern vacationers and a shipping industry spurred rapid growth. By the time the 1854 fire devastated downtown, Jacksonville had grown to 36 blocks. It went through another boom, bust, and boom, only to be destroyed in 1901 by a fire whose smoke was reported to have been seen 500 miles north in Raleigh, North Carolina. It wiped out more than 2,500 buildings and left 8,600 people homeless.

Jacksonville owes its current wealth of diverse architecture to the many architects and builders who flocked to the city after the 1901 fire. They brought with them bold ideas and new technologies.

As elsewhere across the country, people left the downtown to live in the suburbs in the 1950s and 1960s, and the wrecking ball swung wildly on the deteriorating downtown during the 1970s. Preservation groups stepped in to advise, inventory, and promote preservation.

While this tour covers downtown Jacksonville, the bordering residential communities of Riverside, Avondale, and San Marco—which were early affluent suburbs—also have extensive historic districts worth seeing.

Information

Jacksonville and the Beaches Convention & Visitors Bureau, 201 E Adams St, Jacksonville, Florida 32202; 800/733-2668, 904/798-9111; www.jaxcvb.com. Jacksonville Historical Society, 317A Philip Randolph Blvd, Jacksonville, FL 32202; 904/665-0064, provides information about the city's early days. Starting in early 2000, Jacksonville Transportation Authority (904/630-3181), will operate a trolley that will circulate through downtown every 5 minutes during peak hours, every 10 minutes at other times on weekdays. It will connect with the Skyway, which runs between the Northbank and Southbank.

For information about Riverside, Avondale, and San Marco, contact Riverside-Avondale Preservation, Inc, 2623 Herschel St, Jacksonville, FL 32204; 904/389-2449; and the San Marco Preservation Society, 1652 Atlantic Blvd, Jacksonville, FL; 904/396-4734.

Getting there

Take I-95 to exit 117 (Union St), then turn right onto Main Street. Follow signs to Jacksonville Landing parking. Jacksonville International Airport is about 15 minutes north at exit 127 (Airport Rd). Amtrak's (800/USA RAIL, 904/766-5110) station is at 3570 Clifford Lane. Greyhound (800/231-2222, 904/356-9976) has a station at 10 N Pearl St.

First steps

For area maps and information, contact the Jacksonville and the Beaches Convention & Visitors Bureau, which also has visitor centers at the airport and downtown at Jacksonville Landing, where the tour starts. The latter is open Monday to Saturday 10 am to 8 pm and Sunday noon to 5:30 pm. For an in-depth look at Jacksonville's architecture and history, read *Jacksonville's Architectural Heritage* ($50) by Wayne W. Wood compiled for the Jacksonville Historic Preservation Commission.

Seasonal highlights

In April, Riverside-Avondale Preservation, Inc presents its annual Tour of Homes (904/389-2449) showcasing 10 homes in the two historic residential neighborhoods across the river from downtown.

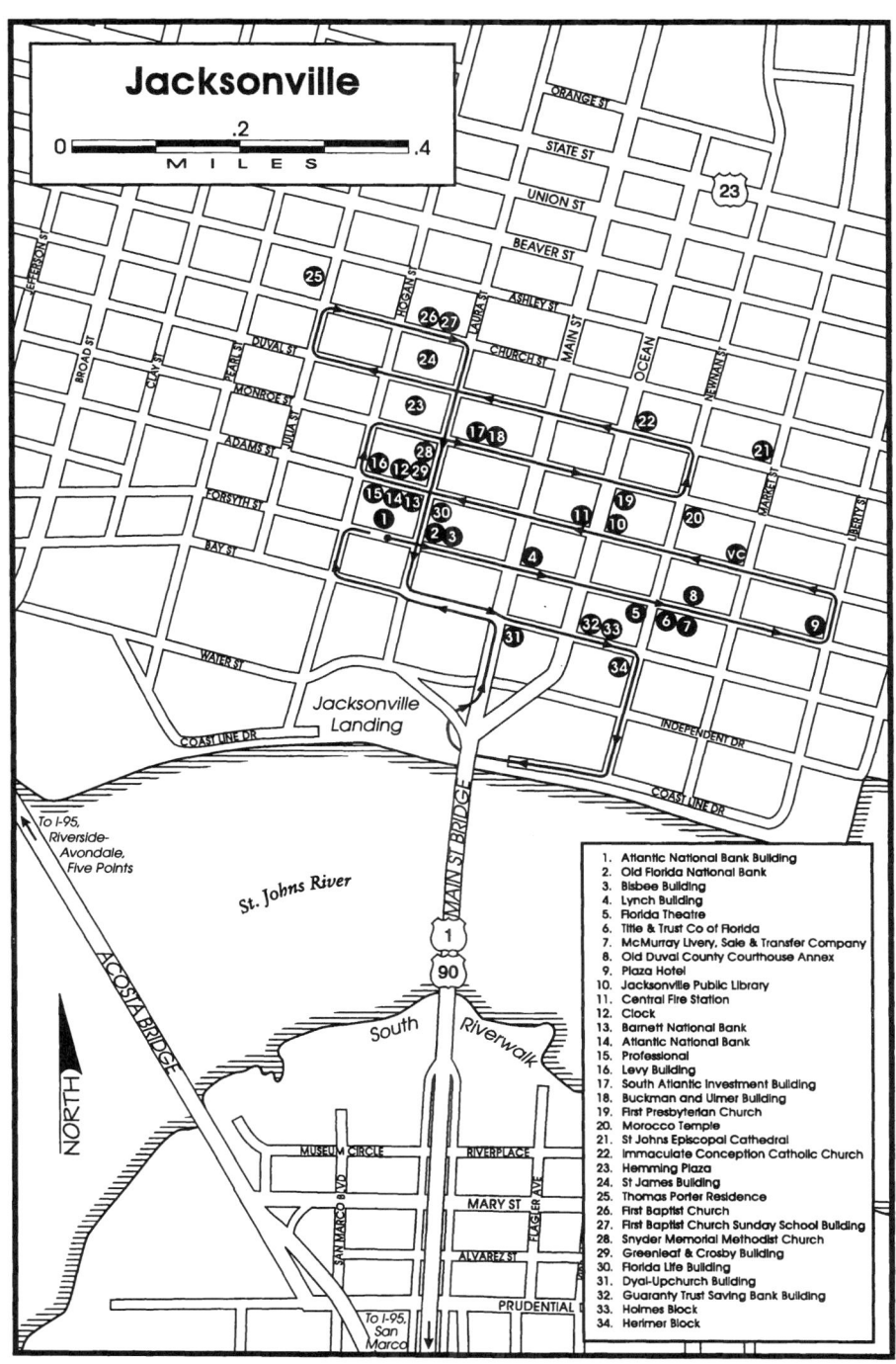

Jacksonville

0 |=======| .2 |=======| .4
M I L E S

1. Atlantic National Bank Building
2. Old Florida National Bank
3. Bisbee Building
4. Lynch Building
5. Florida Theatre
6. Title & Trust Co of Florida
7. McMurray Livery, Sale & Transfer Company
8. Old Duval County Courthouse Annex
9. Plaza Hotel
10. Jacksonville Public Library
11. Central Fire Station
12. Clock
13. Barnett National Bank
14. Atlantic National Bank
15. Professional
16. Levy Building
17. South Atlantic Investment Building
18. Buckman and Ulmer Building
19. First Presbyterian Church
20. Morocco Temple
21. St Johns Episcopal Cathedral
22. Immaculate Conception Catholic Church
23. Hemming Plaza
24. St James Building
25. Thomas Porter Residence
26. First Baptist Church
27. First Baptist Church Sunday School Building
28. Snyder Memorial Methodist Church
29. Greenleaf & Crosby Building
30. Florida Life Building
31. Dyal-Upchurch Building
32. Guaranty Trust Saving Bank Building
33. Holmes Block
34. Herimer Block

Historic downtown Jacksonville. *This 3-mile route covers the most important historic buildings downtown. Allow yourself two to three hours for a leisurely trip. There are lots of restaurants that cater to the downtown business district along the route.*

Start at the corner of Bay Street and Main Street, on the north side of Jacksonville Landing (2 Independent Dr) on the St Johns River. At the center of a small garden is an 8-ft cast-stone ornament featuring a lion's head and the monogram M. It was rescued from the McConihe building—one of the first buildings constructed after the 1901 fire—which was replaced in 1971. *Walk west on Bay St. Turn right on Hogan St, then right onto Forsyth St.*

In a race to see who could build the first "new" steel-frame style skyscraper, the 10-story **Atlantic National Bank Building** (121 W Forsyth) came in second behind the Bisbee Building (see below). It has lots of ornate detailing and columns that frame the entrance.

In the next block, two buildings were originally constructed at half their width. Built in 1902 as the Mercantile Exchange Bank (51 W Forsyth), it was sold three years later and expanded in the same Neo-Classical Revival style by the **Old Florida National Bank.** The six columns and façade are marble, hence its nickname, the Marble Bank. Now the Jacksonville National Bank, it has been completely restored to its 1916 splendor. The **Bisbee Building** (47 W Forsyth) was designed by Henry Klutho. It was the first reinforced-concrete frame high-rise office building. The concept proved so popular that it was completely rented before it was finished. So the owner had the east wall removed and a duplicate section added alongside.

On the next corner, the 17-story **Lynch Building** (11 E Forsyth) has lovely polychromatic terra cotta panels above each window. It was built in 1926 at a cost of $1 million. Two blocks down on the opposite side of the street is the 1927 **Florida Theatre** (128-134 E Forsyth). A marvel of its day, the seven-story Mediterranean Revival building featured more than a million bricks, elaborate terra cotta ornamentation, air-conditioning, central heating, and a central vacuum system. Among its performers were Sally Rand, Bob Hope, and in 1956, Elvis Presley. It's now a city-owned performing arts center, and worth a look inside at the restored wood, tile, and marble work. On the adjacent corner is the Classical Revival **Title & Trust Co of Florida** (200 E Forsyth), built in 1928. Note the entrance's columns and Doric pilasters. It was designed by Marsh & Saxelbye, one of the most sought-after architectural firms during the 1920s building boom.

Founded in 1880, the **McMurray Livery, Sale & Transfer Company** (220 E Forstyh) moved here in 1905 and operated out of this red-and-white brick building until the automobile made its services redundant. Long before that, the site was significant as the location of Jacksonville founder Isaiah D. Hart's original log cabin in 1821.

Across the street stands the **Old Duval County Courthouse Annex** (231 E Forsyth). It was built in 1914 in a Neo-Classical Revival style. Partially hidden behind trees at the corner of Liberty St is the former **Plaza Hotel** (353 E Forsyth), built in 1904 by Robert Bexley. On the site originally stood the house of his father, Dr Augusta Bexley, chief surgeon for the Confederate Army. When it burned in the 1901 fire, Robert rebuilt a similar structure with fireproof-molded concrete blocks as a hotel. In 1913 it became his home. It has a two-story verandah and turret. *Turn left onto Liberty St, then left onto Adams St.*

The Bedell Building (101 E Adams) is the former **Jacksonville Public Library.** You can still see where its name used to be. Below the window are the words "Open To All". The Klutho-designed Classical Revival building was completed in 1905 with $50,000 in funds donated by philanthropist Andrew Carnegie. Four fluted columns are capped with 16 scholarly faces. The four visible from the street are Aristotle, Plato, Shakespeare, and Newton. On the adjacent corner is the **Central Fire Station** (39 E Adams), which originally featured Mission architecture, but was remodeled in 1944 to its current appearance. It has served downtown for more than 80 years.

There's a handsome 15-ft cast-iron and bronze **clock** on the northwest corner of Adams and Laura streets erected by Greenleaf & Crosby Company, a jewelry store. Stand next to the clock and look across at the **Barnett National Bank** (112 W Adams), **Atlantic National Bank Annex** (118 W Adams), and **Professional** (126 W Adams) buildings. The Barnett was the tallest building in the city from 1926 until 1954. Note the lion heads between the third and fourth floors. Across the street is the **Levy Building** (135 W Adams) designed by Marsh & Saxelbye with a granite base and decorative terra cotta panels featuring leaf and griffin motifs. *Turn right onto Hogan St, then right onto Monroe St.*

Though the **South Atlantic Investment Building** (37-41 W Monroe) and **Buckman and Ulmer Building** (29-33 W Monroe) have both seen better days, their original architectural beauty is still evident. Note the stylized dolphins in the arch over the South Atlantic's main entrance. Its Italian Renaissance brick neighbor has many lovely cast-stone details. Two blocks east on the opposite side of the street is the imposing Gothic

Revival style **First Presbyterian Church** (118 E Monroe). The original 1847 building, which burned in the 1901 fire, was replaced in 1902 and expanded in 1928. It has a stained-glass window over three carved double wooden doors. Before turning left onto Newnan St, look at the **Morocco Temple** (219 N Newnan) on the southeast corner of Newnan and Monroe. Though later remodelings somewhat altered Klutho's original 1910 design, his marriage of Prairie and Egyptian Revival styles remains evident. Note the lovely squat terra cotta columns with lotus leaf capitals, terra cotta sun disk ornament with cobra heads, and 12-ft tall cartouches on either side of the entrance. The interior was similarly themed. Among the events held in the 1,500-seat auditorium decorated with murals depicting Arabian scenes was an address by President William H. Taft in 1912. *Turn left onto Newnan St, then make a short detour by turning right onto Duval St.*

St Johns Episcopal Cathedral presides at the corner of Duval and Market streets. Originally constructed in 1842, it was burned by Union soldiers in 1863. New York architect Edward Potter completed a replacement in 1877, only to see it destroyed in the 1901 fire. Potter completed the current church in 1906 in a Gothic Revival style with a cruciform shape and square bell tower. It was restored again in 1984 for the parish's 150th anniversary. Farther west on Duval the Late Gothic Revival **Immaculate Conception Catholic Church** (121 E Duval) has a similar history of destruction by Union forces and fire, followed by rebuilding by a New York architect. Take a few minutes to look inside if the building is open.

Three blocks west on the left is **Hemming Plaza**, on the right the beautiful **St James Building** (117 W Duval). Though the plaza has seen many redesigns since 1866, the Confederate Monument unveiled in 1898 is the one constant. When Jacob and Morris Cohen asked Klutho to design a department store building adjacent to the park, he sold them on the idea of a mixed-use four-story, block-long building. When it was completed in 1912, it was the largest building in the city and the 9th-largest department store in the country. It's a fine example of Prairie School architecture, complete with beautiful terra cotta spiral seashell and native plant motifs and rooftop lighting. It was restored and now serves as City Hall. *Turn right onto Julia St, then right onto Church St.*

Detour momentarily up Julia Street one half block on the left to the **Thomas Porter Residence** (510 N Julia), built in 1902 and now housing an architectural firm. It was designed by Klutho and features a "Classic Colonial" style with a two-story portico with six Corinthian columns, a serpentine balcony, coffered ceiling, and mansard roof. Other stately mansions once surrounded it. *Return to Church St.*

One block east on the left are the **First Baptist Church** (133 W Church) and the **First Baptist Church Sunday School Building** (125 W Church). Klutho had a hand in designing the former, whose Romanesque style has features similar to those of Boston's Trinity Church. *Turn right onto Laura St.*

The Gothic Revival **Snyder Memorial Methodist Church** (226 N Laura), which is unchanged from its post-1901 fire construction, features carved stone detailing, a crenelated bell tower, and a rose window. Next is the elegant **Greenleaf & Crosby Building** (208 N Laura St) designed by Marsh & Saxelbye for the namesake jewelers. It features extensive terra cotta ornamentation, including motifs of griffins, eagles, urns, and flowers. Klutho's **Florida Life Building** (117 N Laura) is considered his finest example of a skyscraper and closely related to the Chicago and Prairie schools. Among the 11-story building's many details are the pilasters capped with ornate terra cotta scrollwork and broad Chicago windows. *Turn left onto Bay St.*

The six-story brick Beaux Arts **Dyal-Upchurch Building** (4 E Bay) has many firsts. It was Klutho's first Jacksonville building, the first high-rise structure built downtown, and the first to be constructed on wooden pilings. Among its current occupants is Klutho's Cafe. In the next block on the opposite side sits the **Guaranty Trust Savings Bank Building** (101 E Bay St), which served as at least four different banks, and the next door **Holmes Block** (107-117 E Bay), a group of three buildings with fine brickwork on the upper floors. Across the street is the **Herkimer Block** (136 E Bay), a three-story structure with stepped gables, dormers, and arched window openings. *Turn right onto Newnan St and walk to the waterfront.*

Seven bridges cross the St Johns River. Look left at the Isaiah D Hart Bridge in the distance. Above you is the Main Street Bridge. To the right is the Acostia Bridge, followed by the Fuller Warren Bridge in the distance. On the opposite bank is the redeveloped area called Southside, where along with hotels and restaurants is the small but intriguing Jacksonville Historical Center and several other museums. *Walk west along the riverfront and return to Jacksonville Landing.*

Lodging

While there is only one hotel downtown, there are several modern hotels on the river's south bank and numerous bed-and-breakfasts and hotels in the nearby historic districts of San Marco, Riverside, and Avondale. The Omni, Hilton, and Radisson are business hotels, so offer significant reductions and attractive weekend packages Thursday to Sunday.

Guests have three historic B&B choices in Riverside. **The House on Cherry St** ($$-$$$, 904/384-1999) features antiques, four-poster canopy beds, and fresh flowers at 1844 Cherry St. The Prairie-style **St Johns House** ($$$, 904/384-3724) has large smoke-free rooms, porches, and handmade quilts (on the beds and for sale) at 1718 Osceola St. The large verandah with Doric columns is reminiscent of a southern plantation, hence the name, **Plantation Manor Inn** ($$$-$$$$, 904/384-4630), for this lovely nine-room circa 1906 B&B with antiques, fireplaces, data ports, in-room fridge stocked with complimentary drinks, and a secluded garden at 1630 Copeland St.

Downtown's only hotel is the **Omni Jacksonville Hotel** ($$$, 904/355-6664) at 245 Water St, North Riverwalk, a few blocks from Jacksonville Landing. The 15-story building has 354 large rooms and lots of amenities. Because it's a business hotel, weekend rates are significantly lower. On the St Johns opposite bank are the very upscale **Jacksonville Hilton & Towers** ($$$, 904/398-8800) overlooking the river at 1201 Riverplace Blvd, South Riverwalk; and the moderately priced **Radisson Riverwalk Hotel** ($$, 904/396-5100), which has tennis courts and rooms with riverviews at 1515 Prudential Dr, South Riverwalk. Because the former caters to business travelers, it has very attractive weekend rates.

Arts & culture

Jacksonville has an active cultural calendar, with gallery shows, theatrical and musical performances, and museums focusing on everything from manuscripts to science.

On the second Friday of each month, member galleries in the **Jacksonville Association of Art Galleries** participate in "2nd Fridays" and stay open until 8 pm or 10 pm. Some also have artist receptions. For galleries, call 904/398-3161, ext 311. Five Points has a similar program called 1st Fridays. Call 904/381-8844.

    Chilam Balam features African-American folk art at 4315 Brentwood Ave. **Pedestrian Gallery** at 2007 Park St, Five Points, showcases local and southeastern artists. **Stillpoint Studio** at 8444 San Jose Blvd features marble, bronze, onyx, marble works of fine art. It also operates a downtown gallery called **Viscosity** that focuses on up-and-coming regional artists at One W Independent Dr.

The **Alhambra Dinner Theatre** at 12000 Beach Blvd offers a dinner buffet followed by a Broadway-style play. **Florida Theatre** hosts theater performances and concerts throughout the year at 128-134 E Forsyth. **Theatre Jacksonville** starts its 80th season at 2032 San Marco Blvd, San Marco. The **Times-Union Center for the Performing Arts**, 300 W Water St, has several stages. One of them is home to the Jacksonville Symphony Orchestra.

Cummer Museum of Art & Gardens at 829 Riverside Ave, Riverside, is noted for its collection of Old Master and American paintings as well as local interest works. The Jacksonville **Historical Center** at 100 B Wharfside B, on the South Riverwalk, captures the city's early days. **Jacksonville Maritime Museum** at 2 Independent Dr, displays models of the ships that once carried passengers and goods to the downtown docks. **Jacksonville Museum of Contemporary Art** recently moved into the Times-Union Center, 300 W Water St, while it awaits a new home. The **Karpeles Manuscript Museum** at 101 W First St, exhibits one of the largest private collections of original documents relating to history and the arts, including many about Jacksonville. **Museum of Science and History** at 1025 Museum Circle, South Riverwalk, features a permanent collection of Civil War items among its many exhibits.

B Dalton Bookseller at Jacksonville Landing has a large local-interest section. The **U.S. Government Printing Office Bookstore** is at 100 W Bay St. Across the river in San Marco there's the **San Marco Book Store** at 1971 San Marco Blvd features a large selection of new and rare books as well as maps and prints of historic Jacksonville.

Food & drink

Many downtown restaurants cater to the business community and thus are only open on weekdays for breakfast and lunch. Jacksonville Landing has inexpensive eateries in a food court as well as several restaurants. Neighboring Riverdale and Avondale have several fine restaurants serving lunch and dinner.

Klutho's Cafe ($, 904/356-8330) attracts the breakfast and lunch crowd to the historic Dyal-Upchurch Building at 4 E Bay St, for diverse salads featuring mixed greens, deli-style and grilled sandwiches, and rotisserie chicken. Also downtown is **Juliette's** ($$, 904/355-7118) in the Omni Jacksonville Hotel at 245 W Water, which has an evolving menu of fine foods, including a pasta bar and antipasto buffet. Both restaurants serve Sunday brunch. The focus is on healthy, all-natural contemporary cooking with a hint of New Orleans at the **Lavilla Grill** ($–$$, 904/355-0807) at 820 N Davis St in the historic Witschen Building, formerly a hardware store, grocery, and shoe store (now Urban League). The **Parkview Cafe** ($–$$, 904/356-3100) at 1001 N Main St serves salads, barbecue, and soups in a wonderfully fanciful 1929 Mediterranean Revival building originally built as a sandwich stand.

Just across the river are three good choices: the popular **River City Brewing Company** ($–$$, 904/398-2299), brewing its own beer to accompany seafood and beef in a waterfront setting at 835 Museum Circle; **Ruth's Chris Steak House** ($$–$$$, 904/396-6200) serving steaks as well as seafood overlooking the river in the Jacksonville Hilton at 1201 Riverplace Blvd; the **Wine Cellar** ($$–$$$, 904/398-8989), offering an impressive wine selection and a contemporary menu of American and Asian influenced dishes like ahi tuna with key lime wasabi at 1314 Prudential Dr.

Nightlife

Downtown at 45 W Monroe St is **De Real Ting Cafe,** whose DJs serve up reggae on Wednesday, Jamaican music on Fridays, and a mix of Caribbean flavors Saturdays. At the west edge of historic downtown is **Milk Bar/Paradome** at 618 W Forsyth St, the premier spot for alternative sounds with some of the coolest DJs in town. **Jacksonville Landing** has live entertainment ranging from jazz to Latin on weekends. One of the city's most popular dance clubs is **Club 5** at 1028 Park St in historic Five Points.

Events

Downtown's annual two-day **American Music Festival** salutes American culture through music and visual arts at the Times-Union Center, 300 Water St.

Timucuan Ecological and Historic Preserve

With miles of thickly wooded nature trails, grasslands, coastal marshes, islands, tidal creeks, estuaries, an ancient trash pile whose refuse yields clues about an extinct culture, a 19th-century indigo and cotton plantation, and a reconstructed fort, Timucuan Ecological and Historic Preserve is truly an eco-heritage tourist's dreamscape.

Nestled between the Lower St Johns River and the Nassau River, just 14 miles from downtown Jacksonville, the 46,000-acre preserve encompasses the National Park Service's Fort Caroline National Memorial, Theodore Roosevelt Area, Kingsley Plantation, and the Ribault Monument, as well as undeveloped tracts and islands at Cedar Point, Broward Islands, and Thomas Creek, thus providing easy access and interest to hikers, bicyclists, bird watchers, fishermen, photographers, historians, naturalists, canoeists, kayakers, and boaters.

When French explorer Jean Ribault landed on May 1, 1562, on the shores of the St Johns River, he was greeted by the Native American Timucuans. They and their prehistoric ancestors, the "People of the Shell Mounds," already had been settled there for more than 1,000 years. Today, trails traverse the huge mounds of their discarded shells and tools that evidence their long-lived culture in an area of the preserve called the Theodore Roosevelt Area.

Ribault claimed the land for the French king, Charles IX, and erected a monument on the bluffs on the south shore of the river before sailing home. The exact location of the monument is unknown, but a replica was erected on May 1, 1924, by the Florida Daughters of the American Revolution to highlight the beginnings of European colonization of Florida. It remains a cultural landmark today.

Two years after Ribault's journey, René de Goulaine de Laudonnière returned to establish Fort La Caroline as a permanent French Protestant (Huguenot) settlement on the river's south bank. The Spanish, who had already claimed Florida, dispatched Pedro Menéndez de Avilés to dislodge the French in 1565 (and establish St Augustine). He massacred the settlers, sparing only women and children. Laudonnière and 50 to 60 others escaped back to France. Today, nothing remains of the original fort, but a near full-scale interpretive rendering of the fort and a visitor center operate as Fort Caroline National Memorial.

More than 250 years later, Zepheniah Kingsley and his African wife, Anna Jai, built Kingsley Plantation, the state's oldest remaining plantation home, on Fort George Island (see Little Talbot Island Walking Tour) on the north shore of the St Johns River. In its day, the plantation yielded cotton and indigo. Today, the historic property includes an interpretive center, the original plantation house, a barn, kitchen house, ruins of 23 of the original quarters that housed the enslaved workers, and one restored quarters.

There are short hiking trails at Kingsley Plantation and Fort Caroline, but the best walking and hiking is on the three trails covering more than four miles at the 600-acre Theodore Roosevelt Area.

Information

Timucuan Ecological and Historic Preserve, Fort Caroline National Memorial, 12713 Ft Caroline Rd, Jacksonville, FL 32225; 904/641-7155, 904/221-7567. Theodore Roosevelt Area, 13165 Mt Pleasant Rd, Jacksonville, FL 32225; 904/641-7155. Jacksonville and the Beaches Convention & Visitors Bureau, 201 E Adams St, Jacksonville, FL 32202; 800/733-2668, 904/798-9111; www.jaxcvb.com.

Getting there

Jacksonville International Airport is about 20 minutes west off I-95 at exit 127 (Airport Rd). Amtrak's (800/USA RAIL, 904/766-5110) station is at 3570 Clifford Lane. Greyhound (800/231-2222, 904/356-9976) has a station at 10 N Pearl St. Timucuan Ecological and Historic Preserve is located 14 miles northeast of downtown Jacksonville. From the north, take I-95 to exit 124A (Heckscher Dr/Hwy 105) going east. After six miles, turn right onto Hwy 9A, which crosses the St Johns River. As soon as you cross the bridge, exit right onto the Southside Connector. Turn left onto Merrill Rd, which merges left with Fort Caroline Rd. The fort is about 4.5 miles on the left. From the south take I-95 to exit 99 (Southside Blvd). Drive north 11 miles, then turn right onto Merrill Rd. Continue as directed above. To reach the Theodore Roosevelt Area (TRA), instead of merging left onto Fort Caroline Rd, veer right onto Mt Pleasant Rd and continue 1.5 miles east to the preserve's TRA entrance.

First steps

The ranger station at Fort Caroline National Memorial oversees visitor information for all areas of Timucuan Ecological and Historic Preserve. Fort Caroline National Memorial is open daily 9 am to 5 pm (closed Christmas). The Theodore Roosevelt Area is open daily from 8 am to dusk (closed Christmas). The gate closes at 8 pm during summer and 6 pm in winter. Kingsley Plantation is open daily 9 am to 5 pm (closed Christmas). Admission is free to all parts of the preserve.

Fort Caroline and Its Leader ($3.95) by Charles E Bennett is a scholarly guide to the fort's history.

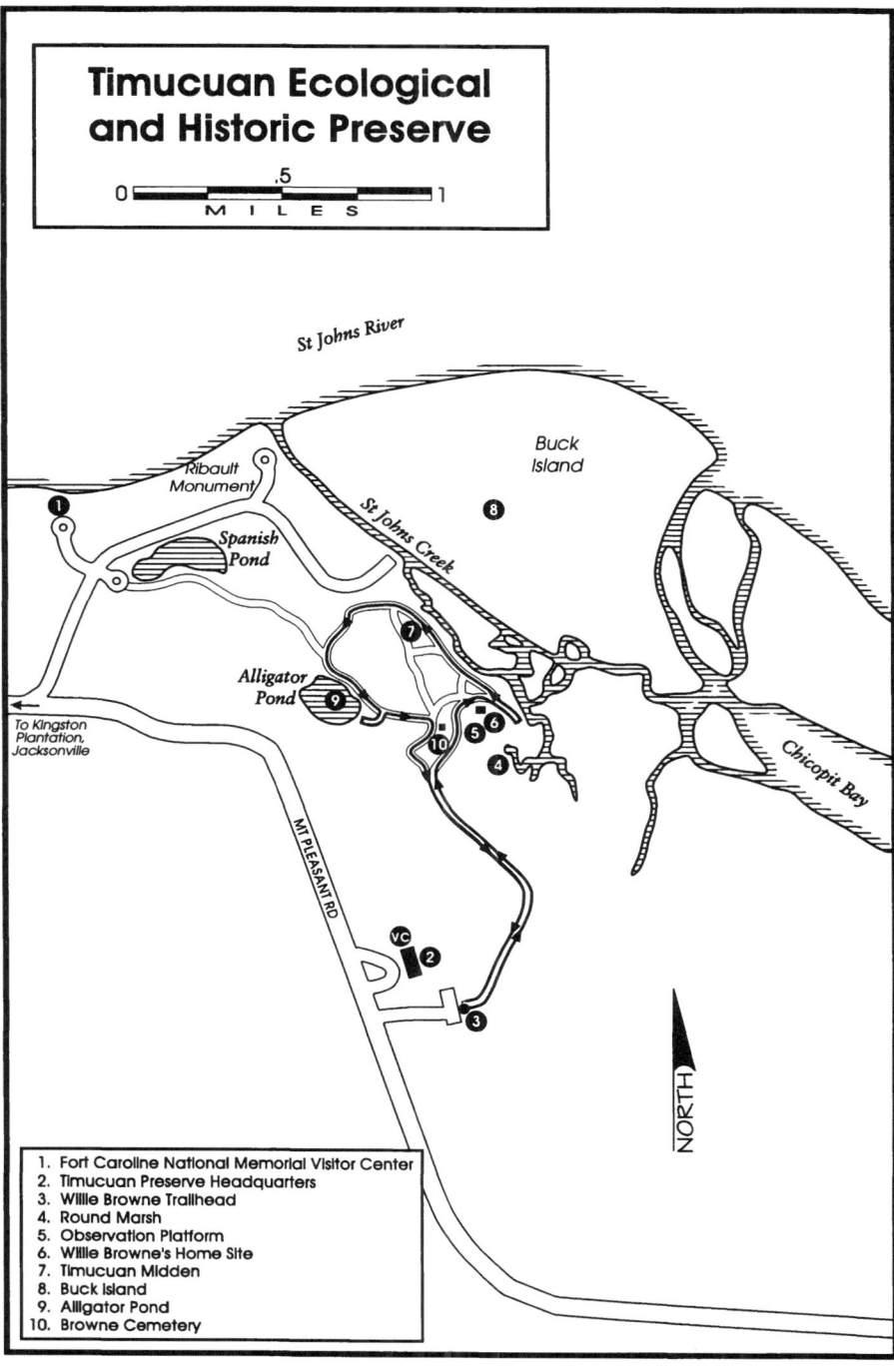

Timucuan Ecological and Historic Preserve

0 |═══════ .5 ═══════| 1
M I L E S

St Johns River

Buck Island

Ribault Monument

St Johns Creek

Spanish Pond

8

Alligator Pond

7

9

To Kingston Plantation, Jacksonville

10 5 6
    4

MT PLEASANT RD

VC 2

3

Chicopit Bay

NORTH

1. Fort Caroline National Memorial Visitor Center
2. Timucuan Preserve Headquarters
3. Willie Browne Trailhead
4. Round Marsh
5. Observation Platform
6. Willie Browne's Home Site
7. Timucuan Midden
8. Buck Island
9. Alligator Pond
10. Browne Cemetery

Walking tours

Rangers lead guided walks through the Theodore Roosevelt Area on weekends during fall and spring. With a few exceptions, all of the programs/walks are free. Ranger-guided programs on archaeology, history, and natural history combine a short walking tour on weekends at Fort Caroline National Monument. At Kingsley Plantation, daily programs on the plantation and slavery include a short walk on the plantation grounds.

Seasonal highlights

Bird enthusiasts will find the most water birds during winter and the most songbirds during the spring and fall migratory seasons.

Natural Timucuan Ecological and Historic Preserve, Theodore Roosevelt Area. *This 3-mile route covers hammock, salt marsh, Native American shell midden, Alligator Pond, and an historic home site and cemetery. Allot three hours for the walk and visit to the interpretive center.*

Begin at the Fort Caroline National Memorial Visitor Center. After viewing the extensive exhibitions that cover the cultural and natural history of the region, drive along Mt Pleasant Road to the **Timucuan Preserve Headquarters.** Pick up the **Willie Browne Trailhead** just outside the headquarters building.

The late William H. Browne III, known as Willie Browne, said, "People have to work in the cities, they can't live in the woods anymore. But they ought to have a place in the woods they can go to." Before he died, Browne bequeathed his property to the public. He had moved to Jacksonville from New York in the late 1800s and made this property his home with his brother until 1970. He dedicated the land in the name of his hero, President Theodore Roosevelt. The namesake trail, which leads to the site of his former cabin and Round Marsh, is open to hikers and bicyclists.

The trail winds through a hardwood hammock with saw palmettos (*Serenoa repens*), cabbage palms (*sabal palmetto*), thick vines of southern fox grapes (*Vitis rotundifolia*), and tread softly (*Cnidoscolus stimulosus*), similar to a stinging nettle. At 0.5 miles, the trail crosses the small Hammock Creek on a foot bridge, then forks to the Willie Browne Trail Loop. *Take the right trail.*

The fork's right leg skirts **Round Marsh**, a salt marsh that offers excellent birdwatching. At just under one mile into the walk, climb the 10 feet to the top of the new **Observation Platform**. About the size of a small bedroom, the platform overlooks Round Marsh and the tidal creeks that feed it. At low tide, the marsh appears dry and ibis and other birds that feed on the flats can be observed. *Continue on the trail, then turn right onto the Timucuan/Spanish Pond Trail.*

A marker on the right indicates **Willie Browne's Home Site**, where he lived from 1890 to 1970. The Timucuan Trail climbs the **Timucuan Midden** of primarily oyster shells discarded by the trail's namesake Native Americans. Enslaved workers on area plantations mixed the midden's oyster shells and lime derived from burnt shell with water and sand. The mixture was poured into wooden frame molds. When it hardened, the blocks of "tabby" were used to construct buildings. The origin of tabby is thought to be African because it's found in only two places, West Africa and the southeastern United States, where free and enslaved Africans lived.

The trail winds across the forested midden with glimpses of the marsh through the trees. Wild blueberries grow alongside the trail. Watch and listen for pileated woodpeckers in the trees. At the top of the trail, there's a refreshing breeze. Look down on **Buck Island** in the middle of the St Johns River. The manmade island was created from the city's dredging projects. You also can see St Johns Bluff. *At two miles, the road splits. Follow the Spanish Pond Trail signs to the left toward Alligator Pond. Turn right to the pond.*

Note the sign about active alligators. Although **Alligator Pond** is less than three acres, it's home to approximately 30 alligators, so you can always spot a few. The trail is narrow and bordered by alligator-friendly habitat on both sides. Stay alert.

The pond opens onto an expanse bordered by large live oaks (*Quercus virginiana*), saw palmettos, cabbage palms, and slash pines (*Pinus elliottii*). *Return to the Spanish Pond Trail and continue right. At the Willie Browne Trail intersection, turn right.*

The trail follows the other side of the Willie Browne Trail Loop, passing the small **Browne Cemetery** where Willie and his brother are buried. *Continue along the trail, past the loop intersection back to the preserve headquarters.*

Lodging, food & drink
See Downtown Jacksonville Walking Tour.

Events
In September, members of the Florida Military History Preservation Society join park rangers in a Living History Encampment called **Battles for the Bluff**

(904/641-7155), commemorating the battle between the French and Spanish for Fort Caroline and the Civil War battle for St Johns Bluff. In October the **Kingsley Heritage Celebration** (904/251-3537) features musical performances, living history presentations, craft demonstrations, and talks by visiting historians along with tours of Kingsley Plantation.

St Augustine

St Augustine, the nation's oldest city, sits at the end of a peninsula overlooking the San Sebastian River and the Intracoastal Waterway about 45 miles south of Jacksonville and 65 miles north of Daytona Beach. The city retains much of its historic charm. Tall trees shade the narrow cobblestone streets laid out in a checkerboard pattern more than 400 years ago. The streets are flanked by restored Colonial Spanish and English buildings that have courtyards, porches, loggias, and balconies.

St Augustine is the oldest, continuously operated European settlement in the United States. Prior to the arrival of Europeans in the late 16th century, Timucuan Indians lived nearby. After decades of failing to secure a foothold in Florida, Pedro Menéndez de Avilés established a settlement in 1565. With the Spanish came the first Africans, not as slaves, but as artisans, seamen, navigators, and adventurers. After repeated attacks by the British, the Spanish constructed the Castillo de San Marcos in 1672, the city's most conspicuous landmark.

Over the next 300 years Florida would change to British rule, then back to Spanish rule before finally becoming part of the United States in 1821. Americans were quick to migrate south. Henry M. Flagler caught on quickly, and, in the late 1880s, started building fancy hotels for northern tourists and brought them south on his railroad. This created a building boom that lasted until the railroad headed south and the rich tourists followed. St Augustine gradually built itself back up as a major tourist destination, using its cultural heritage as the attraction.

Today, efforts to preserve the Native American and European heritage are strong. However, St Augustine balances uneasily between its heritage and its commercialism. For example, St George Street, the main pedestrian thoroughfare in historic Old Town, portrays the city's different Colonial periods. But it's overly commercial. Because so much emphasis is placed on this narrow strip of commercial real estate, on weekends, holidays, in high season, and during special events, it can be uncomfortably crowded. It also means that too few visitors venture out to the dozens of blocks of equally historic and intriguing sites.

History is measured in periods in St Augustine. The First Spanish Period ran from 1565 to 1763; the British Period from 1763 to 1784; the Second Spanish Period from 1784 to 1821; the U.S. Territorial Period from 1821 to 1845; the U.S. Statehood Period from 1845 to 1888; and the Flagler Era from 1888 to 1914.

Information

St Augustine/St Johns County Visitor Information Center, 10 Castillo Dr, St Augustine, FL 32084; 800/653-2489, 904/825-1000; www.oldcity.com/vcb. There's another Visitor Center in the Government House Museum, 48 King St; 904/825-5033. St Augustine Historical Society, 271 Charlotte St, St Augustine, FL 32084; 904/824-2872.

Getting there

Take I-95 to exit 94 (Hwy 207) from the south, exit 95 (Hwy 16) from the north. Follow the signs nine miles east to US-1/Hwy A1A, then south to the Visitor Center. The closest airport is in Jacksonville (45 miles north). Amtrak's (800/USA RAIL) closest station is in Palatka (28 miles southwest). Greyhound (800/231-2222, 904/829-5401) has a station at 100 Malaga St.

First steps

Stop at the Visitor Information Center, which shows a film hourly depicting the city's history ($3). The center is open daily 8 am to 7:30 pm in summer, daily 8:30 am to 5:30 pm in winter. It also has restrooms. For more information about the houses and historic districts in St Augustine, read *America's First City: St Augustine's Historic Neighborhoods* by Karen Harvey, and *The Houses of St Augustine* by David Nolan.

Seasonal highlights

The Thanksgiving to Christmas season is a busy, magical period for St Augustine. There are special lighting ceremonies, caroling in the streets, parades, and home tours (see Events below).

Tours

Costumed guides lead an entertaining 90-minute Ghostly Experience Walking Tour (888/461-1009, 904/461-1009) through the historic district at night. Tickets cost $6. Free guided tours of Flagler College (904/829-6481), the former Ponce de Leon Hotel, depart from the restored rotunda daily on the hour from 11 am to 4 pm, May through August.

Historic St Augustine. The tour covers 2 miles and takes about two hours. You can stretch the time by visiting sites en route and stopping for lunch. It takes in commercial and residential sections of historic St Augustine.

Begin at the Visitor Center on Castillo Drive. The Visitors Center was built of coquina, a quarried native shellstone, in 1938 by the Federal Emergency Relief Administration and U.S. Civil Works Administration in

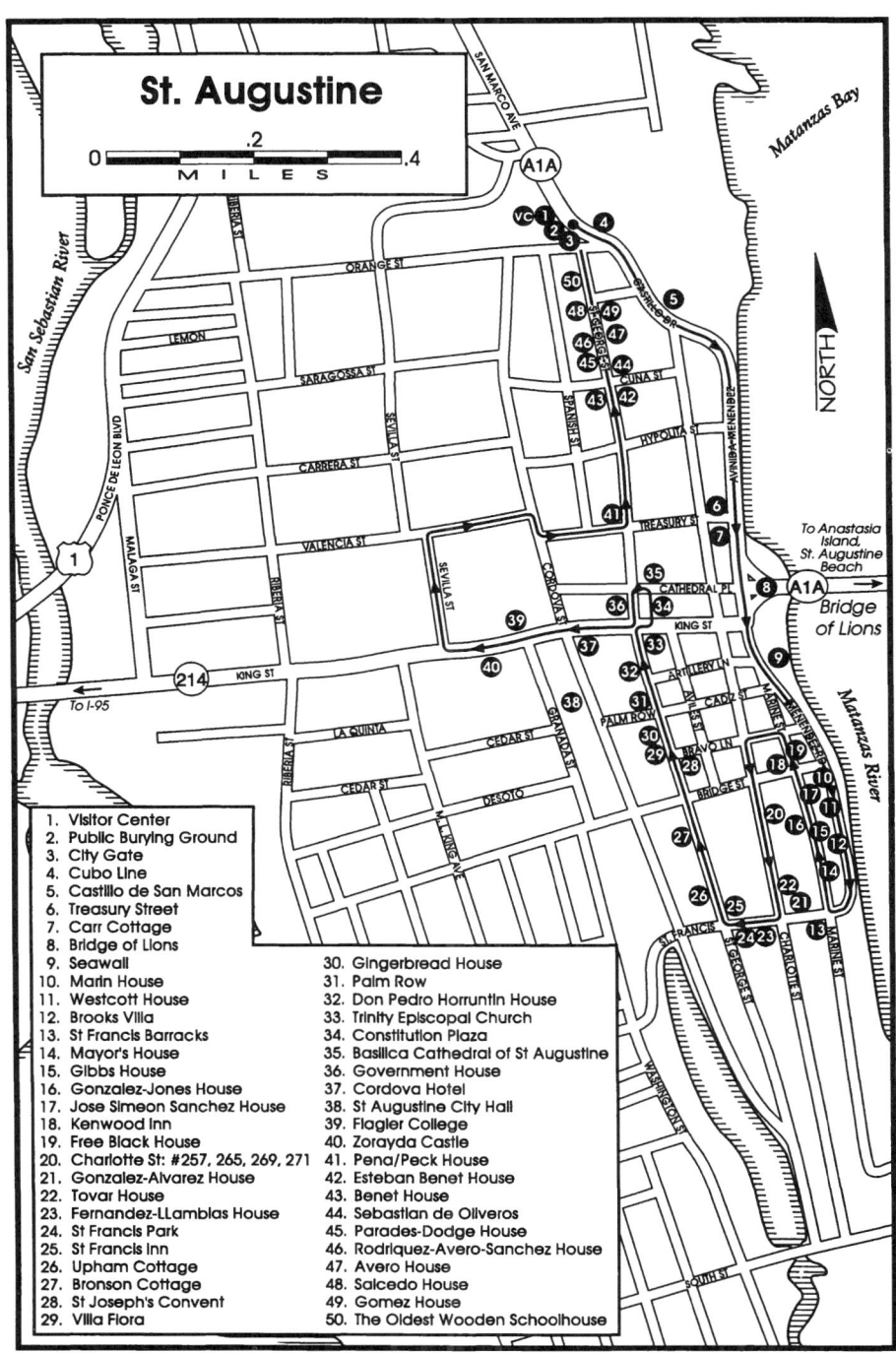

St. Augustine

0 |=====| .2 |=====| .4
M I L E S

1. Visitor Center
2. Public Burying Ground
3. City Gate
4. Cubo Line
5. Castillo de San Marcos
6. Treasury Street
7. Carr Cottage
8. Bridge of Lions
9. Seawall
10. Marin House
11. Westcott House
12. Brooks Villa
13. St Francis Barracks
14. Mayor's House
15. Gibbs House
16. Gonzalez-Jones House
17. Jose Simeon Sanchez House
18. Kenwood Inn
19. Free Black House
20. Charlotte St: #257, 265, 269, 271
21. Gonzalez-Alvarez House
22. Tovar House
23. Fernandez-LLamblas House
24. St Francis Park
25. St Francis Inn
26. Upham Cottage
27. Bronson Cottage
28. St Joseph's Convent
29. Villa Fiora
30. Gingerbread House
31. Palm Row
32. Don Pedro Horruntin House
33. Trinity Episcopal Church
34. Constitution Plaza
35. Basilica Cathedral of St Augustine
36. Government House
37. Cordova Hotel
38. St Augustine City Hall
39. Flagler College
40. Zorayda Castle
41. Pena/Peck House
42. Esteban Benet House
43. Benet House
44. Sebastian de Oliveros
45. Parades-Dodge House
46. Rodriquez-Avero-Sanchez House
47. Avero House
48. Salcedo House
49. Gomez House
50. The Oldest Wooden Schoolhouse

a Mediterranean Revival style. *Walk out the east entrance to Castillo Dr and turn right.*

Next door is the **Public Burying Ground**, also known as the Huguenot Cemetery. It opened in 1821 during the yellow fever epidemic and is supposedly haunted by the ghost of Judge John B Stickney, a local official whose body was desecrated—his gold teeth were stolen—when the body was disinterred to be reburied in Washington, D.C., where his children lived. *The road forks, bear left along the waterfront.*

On the right you'll pass the **City Gate**, the coquina block entryway built in 1808. It joined the **Cubo Line**, the palm-log defense wall that stretched from the Castillo de San Marcos to the San Sebastian River. You can see what remains of it on the left. *Carefully cross the street and continue south along Castillo Dr.*

The imposing **Castillo de San Marcos** was begun in 1672 by Ignacio Dazo, a Spanish royal engineer, to protect the strategically located military outpost. Dazo died before it's completion in 1695, but his design was sound and for the past 300 years the quarried coquina fortress has survived repeated attacks and inclement weather. It became a National Monument in 1924. *Continue along the waterfront. Castillo Dr becomes Avenida Menéndez.*

As you pass **Treasury Street** on the right, note that it retains its original width dating back to the Colonial era. The large **Carr House** (46 Avenida Menéndez) burned in an 1887 fire that destroyed most of the original Cathedral (see below), public market, and St Augustine Hotel. Its Spanish Revival design was reproduced a year later with concrete rather than the original coquina. Today it houses a restaurant.

When the beautiful Mediterranean Revival **Bridge of Lions** (on the left, end of Cathedral Place) was completed in 1927, it was hailed as "The Most Beautiful Bridge in Dixie." The two Carrara-marble lion statues—sculpted by Italian artist F Romanelli after a pair guarding the Loggia Dei Lanzi in his native Florence—were donated by Dr Andrew Anderson, a philanthropist who thought the town needed more art in public places. The bridge, which leads to Anastasia Island, St Augustine Beach, and Anastasia State Recreation Area (1340A A1A South), is at the center of a major preservation battle to replace the aging structure with a new span.

The **Sea Wall** (on the left) was built by the Spanish in 1690. It originally stretched from the Castillo to the Plaza, then was extended to the St Francis Barracks in the mid 1800s. It was a popular place for strolling for whites. A law in the late 1800s forbade "colored persons (bond or free) to use the sea wall as a place for promenading." The penalty was a large fine or beating.

Several buildings along Avenida Menéndez between Bridge Street and St Francis Street are noteworthy. The **Marin House** (#142), built in 1880, forms a complex with another house behind it on Marine St, built of coquina by Francisco Marin in the 1790s; the **Westcott House** (#146) also built around 1880, was the home of Dr John Westcott, who pushed for a railroad line nearby; and the Moorish Revival style **Brooks Villa** (#174) was constructed in 1891. Its owners have included the two handsome, socially prominent Brooks brothers, Charles and Tracy, and Senator Frederick M Sackett of Kentucky, who served as the ambassador to Germany during Adolf Hitler's early years. *Turn right onto St Francis St.*

The 17th-century St Francis monastery burned in 1702, was replaced soon after, and was later converted to the **St Francis Barracks** (southwest corner of Marine and St Francis), used by the British and Spanish. *Turn right onto Marine St.*

Marine Street's lovely, quiet block between St Francis and Bridge streets has one of St Augustine's finest collections of Colonial buildings, now mostly private residences and quaint inns. Two of St Augustine's mayors lived in the small "**Mayor's House**" (#67), built of coquina just before the Civil War. Note the coquina chimney and that the weatherboarding on the dormers runs at a 45-degree angle instead of straight across, typical of the period.

The early, prominent Gibbs family owned the **Gibbs House** (#59) from 1839 to 1870, before it was sold to a Seminole War army captain. The restored **Gonzalez-Jones House** (#56) was occupied by the Jones family for more than 100 years before it was sold in 1983. The **Jose Simeon Sanchez House** (#43, aka 7 Bridge St), and others constructed during the Second Spanish Period, was built right up to the street with a loggia, typical of houses in Spain. The family called it Bleak House after the Charles Dickens novel. *Cross Bridge St and continue on Marine St.*

In the next block, the **Kenwood Inn** (38 Marine St) has a long history of hospitality. It was built in 1865 as a private home, but became a guest house by 1886, then the Kenwood Hotel by 1911. Now it's a B&B. The Colonial building across the street is referred to as the **Free Black House** (35 Marine St) because although a slave woman and her child were traded for it in 1811, two subsequent owners were free black women, as were their families, who occupied it until the turn of the century. *Turn left onto Bravo Lane, then left onto Charlotte St. Turn right onto St Francis St.*

Before turning right onto St Francis, detour left to the **Gonzalez-Alvarez House** (14 St Francis), known as The Oldest House. Europeans have lived on the site since the early 1600s. The earliest remaining structure, a one-story, two-room coquina block building, dates from 1715. It was occupied by the Spanish, British, the Spanish again, and now is a museum run by the St Augustine Historical Society. Within the complex is the **Tovar House** (22 St Francis), now the Museum of Florida's Army. *Return to the walk.*

The **Fernandez-Lambias House** (31 St Francis) is an example of a house constructed as one story during the First Spanish Period, then converted to two stories during the British Period. Now owned by the Historical Society, it's open once a month for tours. St Francis Park (33 St Francis St) is a peaceful place to take a respite. *Turn right onto St George St.*

On Sunday afternoons from spring to fall, music wafts from the courtyard garden of the **St Francis Inn** (279 St George), built in 1791 for Gaspar Garcia, a Spanish soldier, as a one-story coquina house, then turned into a two-story boarding house where many notable literary figures—Edith Everett Taylor and Van Wycks Brooks among them—lived or visited. The house is now a B&B and has a well-documented history. Several houses in the next block have been beautifully restored, including the 1892 Queen Anne **Upham   Cottage** (268 St George), originally a winter residence for Colonel John J. Upham, a Gettysburg veteran, who entertained many visitors, including writer Henry James, Mrs Henry Flagler, and Mrs William Deering. Down the street is the **Bronson Cottage** (252 St George), another winter residence built in the late 1800s. It was designed by noted architect A. J. Davis, best known for his Gothic Revival designs.

St Joseph's Convent (241 St George) was built of coquina in 1874 for the Sisters of St Joseph. It has been extensively remodeled. Originally a winter residence, the elaborate 1898 Moorish Revival and Romanesque style **Villa Flora** (234 St George) has yellow rather than typical red bricks. It served as a winter rental, hotel, gift shop, restaurant, classroom, and finally home for young women planning to enter the St Joseph order. Attorney and public official J.D. Stanbury and his family owned the beautifully restored **Gingerbread House** (232 St George), one of the city's best examples of the Civil War era Carpenter Gothic style, from 1873 to 1941. Now a private residence, it also served as an inn until 1945.

When **Palm Row** (next street on the left) was developed in 1904, it boasted of baths, cold and hot running water, and other modern conveniences. Six of the 12 planned Victorian buildings were constructed on opposite sides of a wide paved brick walkway lined with palm trees. The houses have served as everything from residential and business rentals to a private school and legal offices.

Spanish and British officials occupied the **Don Pedro Horruntina House** (214 St George), built in the 1760s. Its most notorious occupant was Dr Robert Catherwood, who was disliked by his colleagues and charged with speculating on slaves in 1783. On the southeast corner of St George and King streets stands **Trinity Episcopal Church**, started in 1825 and expanded in 1902. One of its stained glass windows is an original Tiffany. *Turn right onto King St. Cross Constitution Plaza and turn left onto Cathedral Pl, then left onto St George St.*

St Augustine's **Constitution Plaza** was laid out with a central plaza in 1598 for official meetings, the market, and public gatherings. Typical of towns in Spain, it is surrounded by government and church buildings. Among those buildings is the **Basilica Cathedral of St Augustine** (Cathedral Place at St George St), completed in 1797 for the first parish, which was established in 1594. Its clock tower, built in 1888 as an addition following a fire the previous year, was designed by James Renwick, architect of St Patrick's Cathedral in New York. The early 17th-century **Government House** (48 King St) served as residence and headquarters for Florida's Colonial governors. It was rebuilt in 1936 and now houses a museum and visitor center. The plaza also has several monuments, including a **Constitution Obelisk**, erected in 1814 to celebrate a newly formed constitutional government in Spain; a **Confederate War Memorial** obelisk, and a **WWII Memorial Monument**. *Turn right onto King St.*

Henry Flagler purchased the Moorish Revival style **Cordova Hotel** (99 Cordova St) from developer Franklin W Smith in 1889. It had shops on the ground floor and later became the St Johns County Court House. In the next block is **St Augustine City Hall** (75 King St), the former Alcazar Hotel, one of Flagler's more moderately priced hotels, which now also houses the **Lightner Museum**. Across the street sits the Spanish Revival **Flagler College** (74 King St), originally built in 1888 as Flagler's flagship, the Ponce de Leon Hotel. The college has tours in summer. The rest of the year its beautiful rotunda is open for viewing. Along with the Cordova Hotel, Franklin W. Smith built **Zorayda Castle** (83 King St), another impressive structure on King Street. It claims two firsts: it's the city's first poured concrete building and first Moorish Revival structure. *Turn right onto Sevilla St, right onto Valencia, right onto Cordova St, then left onto Treasury. This takes you all the way around the college. Continue two blocks to St George St and turn left.*

Royal Treasurer Juan Esteban de Peña lived in the coquina **Peña/Peck House** (143 St George, southeast corner) during the First Spanish Period. It housed enslaved Africans during the Second Spanish Period. The second floor was added in 1838 by Dr Seth Peck, who practiced medicine on the first floor and lived upstairs with his family, which donated the house to the city in 1931. It's now a museum.

The next block of St George Street is a pedestrian section with original and reconstructed buildings dating from St Augustine's three earliest periods, 1565 to 1821. Note that the buildings are built right up to the street. Most are occupied by shops and restaurants. The Benet family, Minorcan merchants, occupied the **Esteban Benet House** (**#65**), and the **Benet Store** (**#62**), built in 1840, until the turn of the century. Corsican mariner **Sebastian de Oliveros** lived on the street (**#59**) with his Minorcan wife in 1795. Another Minorcan lived nearby in the **Parades-Dodge House** (**#54**), built in 1803. It was later owned by jeweler James Dodge, who claimed it was built in the mid 1500s and proclaimed it the Oldest House. He was wrong. The **Rodriguez-Avero-Sanchez House** (**#52**), built between 1752 and 1762, *is* one of the oldest surviving buildings. Ironically, it shares a common wall with the Parades-Dodge House.

During the British Period, Minorcans used the **Avero House** (**#41**) as a Catholic Church. After a period of commercial use, the Greek Orthodox Diocese purchased it and installed a shrine to St Photios. This reconstructed **Salcedo House** (**#42**) was originally built in 1784. Among its occupants was General Jorge Biassou, a black Haitian revolutionary leader. Lorenzo Gomez and his wife lived in the reconstructed board and batten wood frame **Gomez House** (**#25**) during the 1760s. Its wood frame construction stands out amid coquina and tabby neighbors. **The Oldest Wooden Schoolhouse** (**#14**), also known as the Genopoly House after Greek carpenter Juan Genopoly, one of a group of dissatisfied Minorcans who migrated north from New Smyrna in 1777, was built around 1800 and is the only surviving Second Spanish Period frame building in the city. It was touted as a tourist attraction from as early as 1907. *Pass through the City Gates and return to the Visitor Center.*

Lodging

Many of the properties are bed & breakfasts and inns located in restored houses in the historic district. Rates vary most by day of the week rather than season and are considerably lower Sunday through Thursday. There is often a two-night minimum on weekends and holidays. There are plenty of hotels/motels, too, especially along San Marco Avenue and Anastasia Blvd across the Bridge of Lions on Anastasia Island.

Bed & Breakfast, Inns: The opulent Flagler-era lifestyle is prevalent at the Mediterranean-style **Casa de la Paz** ($$/$$$, 800/929-2915, 904/829-2915) at 22 Avenida de Menéndez, where guests are treated to antique-rich decor, a verandah, sunroom, and sun-lighted courtyard with a fountain, smells of spice potpourri, and gourmet breakfasts of raspberry stuffed French toast. The **Inn at Old City House** ($$/$$$, 800/653-4087, 904/826-0113) is in a restored 1873 house built as a stable for the Ammidown Mansion at 115 Cordova St. Spacious guestrooms are decorated in antiques. Complimentary wine and cheese are served on the verandah. The three-story **Kenwood Inn** ($$/$$$$, 800/824-8151, 904/824-2116) is a B&B/hotel hybrid with wraparound porches, Victorian wicker and antique-furnished rooms and suites, a pool, and walled courtyard at 38 Marine St. Complimentary continental breakfast consists of homemade pastries and juices. The 1791 coquina-construction **St Francis Inn** ($$/$$$$, 800/824-6062, 904/824-6068), a block from "The Oldest House," has 11 large rooms and suites, a two-bedroom, two-bath cottage formerly a cookhouse/slave quarters, a pool, courtyard garden, and complimentary bicycles at 279 St George St. First floor rooms have private entrances; upper floors have balconies. Lots of extras at **Westcott House** ($$/$$$$, 800/513-8914, 904/824-4301), an elegant Victorian-era B&B, make guests feel special at 146 Avenida Menéndez.

Hotels, Motels & Resorts: Opened in 1999, the sophisticated **Anastasia Inn** ($$, 888/226-6181, 904/825-2879) has a pool and 23 guest rooms decorated with high-quality furniture at 218 Anastasia Blvd, Anastasia Island. Rooms have a coffee machine, microwave, and refrigerator. Continental breakfast is included. The **Bay Front Inn** ($$/$$$, 800/559-3455, 904/824-1681) at 138 Avenida Menéndez has a pool and pastel decor. It is one of the few hotels in the historic district. The inn is modern, except for four rooms in the historic Diego Rodriguez Jacinto House. Most rooms have a view of the Intracoastal Waterway. For location, views, and price, it's hard to beat the 18-room **Edgewater Inn** ($$/$$, 904/825-2697), which has simple, clean rooms overlooking the water at the foot of the Bridge of Lions, 2 St Augustine Blvd, Anastasia Island.

Youth Hostel: Visitors looking for a real bargain should consider the **St Augustine Hostel** ($/$, 904/808-1999), where there are clean and comfortable dorm and private rooms in the heart of Old Town, 32 Treasury St, with dorm beds for $12, private rooms from $28.

Arts & culture

St Augustine has a lively arts calendar featuring stage productions, reenactments, galleries, and art walks. You can find detailed monthly arts events on the city's web site.

The **Limelight Theater** (904/825-1164, 1681 US-1 South) is a non-profit professional theater company in historic St Augustine. It stages varied contemporary productions throughout the year on weekends. For more than 20 years, **Flagler College's EMMA Concert Series** (904/797-2800, 74 King St) has featured internationally acclaimed performers such as the Italian National Opera. The **Dance Company** (904/829-1617, 74 King St) presents dance concerts in winter and June featuring company students and guest performers from studios throughout Florida. **Jacksonville Symphony Orchestra (PA4)** (904/354-5547, 74 King St) performs with guest artists in Flagler College Auditorium.

Don't let the name fool you, **Fine Fish Gallery & Store** (904/825-4577, 137A King St) is much more than fish. It features great art in media ranging from mesquite wood to marble sculptures. **First Friday Art Walk** (904/829-0065, downtown) is a free self-guided art gallery tour with light refreshments sponsored by the Art Galleries of St Augustine (AGOSA) on the first Friday of each month from 5 pm to 9 pm. The **Gallery Contempo** (904/823-3536, 75 King St) features contemporary photographs and rare and fine antiques in the courtyard of the historic Lightner Museum. Area artists have a fun venue to exhibit their work at **Rembrandtz Gallery** (904/829-0065, 131 King St), where displays of pottery, sculpture, wall art, and hand-painted furniture change monthly. The **St Augustine Art Center (G4)** (904/824-2310, 22 Marine St), established in 1924, presents monthly exhibits showcasing regional talent. The **Temple of Great Art No Spitting** (904/825-0837, 82 San Marco Ave) is a zany art gallery featuring very original works.

The **Avenue Books** (904/829-9744, 142 King St), the largest used bookstore in St Augustine, is favored for its glossy, coffee-table books on fine, decorative, and performing arts. Although **Booktown** (904/471-5556, 4075 Hwy A1A S) carries a wide selection of paperbacks and hardcover books, it specializes in audio books. The **Dreamstreet New Age Bookstore** (904/824-8536, 64 Hypolita St), with relaxing music and comfy chairs, is a veritable shrine to new ageism, from self-help to inspirational. Old books, magazines, and prints are just the beginning of the selections to sort through at **North Country Antiques** (904/829-2129, 25 Granada St). Rocking chairs, light music, and paperbacks and hardbacks are at **Second Read Books** (904/829-0334, 51-D Cordova St). History is taken very seriously at **Wolf's Head Books** (904/824-9357, 48 San Marco Ave), where Barbara Nailler and Harvey Wolf specialize in regional Americana, military, and rare and out-of-print books.

The **Flagler Memorial Presbyterian Church** (904/829-6451, 36 Sevilla St at Valencia St) was built by Henry M Flagler in Venetian Renaissance style in 1890 as a memorial to his daughter, Jennie, who died at birth. It features elaborate terra cotta decoration, Tiffany glass, and mahogany screens and paneling. To protect the rear access to St Augustine by way of the Matanzas River, the Spanish built **Fort Matanzas** (904/471-0116, 8635 A1A S), now a National Monument, out of coquina in 1742. If you're interested in how 18th-century soldiers survived battles, illnesses, and diseases, you'll be fascinated by the **Spanish Military Hospital** (904/825-6830, 3 Aviles St), a reconstruction of a military hospital that once stood on the same site. Expand on your knowledge of early American history at the **Spanish Quarter Village** (904/825-6830, 29 St George St), a 1.5-acre, 9-building living history museum where costumed interpreters go about the daily activities of the period.

Food & drink

St Augustine offers restaurants to satisfy the palates of international visitors, as well as locals who've migrated from northern cities that have acclaimed restaurants. Expect lines on weekends, especially in winter season. Most places stay open late on weekends.

You can dine outdoors and view nature's artistry or indoors and view works by local artists at the **Florida Cracker Cafe** ($$, 904/829-0397) at 81 St George St, where the house specialties include fried shrimp stuffed with blue crab meat. The Irish serve authentic fare at two popular locations, **Murphy's Pour House** ($$, 904/826-3522) at 72 Spanish St, and **Lynch's Irish Pub** ($$, 904/810-5413) at 32 Avenida Menéndez. Both have extensive beer selections. **Fusion Cuisine** ($$, 904/823-1444) is a mixed pedigree of Far Eastern cuisines, including Japanese, Vietnamese, Thai, Chinese, and Korean at 237 San Marco Ave. The sushi is fresh, fresh, fresh. Almost 25 years ago **Le Pavillon** ($$$, 904/824-6202) opened at 45 San Marco Ave with a lot of excitement. It's still creating a stir with memorable bouillabaisse served in a big terrine and a very aromatic chicken curry "Bombay," boneless chicken breast and rice pilaf served with coconut, raisins, bananas, and chutney. The view overlooking the Matanzas Bay and the Bridge of Lions is as good as the seafood at O.C. **Whites Seafood & Spirits** ($$–$$$, 904/824-0808), a casual eatery in the historical General Fort Worth Mansion at 118 Avenida Menéndez. Don't hesitate to try the house specialty, grouper in paradise, sauteed with shallots, tropical fruits and nuts, then flambeed with coconut rum and simmered in a brown sugar cream sauce. At **Old City House Restaurant** ($$–$$$, 904/826-0781) the menu, which changes frequently, is a superb mix of traditional Old Florida/Old South fare and contemporary favorites at 115 Cordova St. For appetizers, there might be Low Country fried grits as well as baked brie. For entrees there might be certified angus beef filet mignon and Creole stew with fresh shellfish, alligator sausage and diced vegetables. The handsome **Raintree Restaurant** ($$$,

904/824-7211) combines fine food with an historic setting at 102 San Marco Ave. Menu selections like crab-stuffed mahi-mahi baked in puff pastry and brandy pepper steak are cooked to perfection. If you're looking for a quick and inexpensive bite along St George St, step into the **Spanish Bakery** ($) at 42 1/2 St George St, where $3 buys a big bowl of soup, freshly baked roll, and drink. Don't miss the heavenly sweet potato turnover.

Nightlife

St Augustine boasts a lively night scene in clubs and in restaurants. In addition, there are a few more youth-oriented hot spots on St Augustine Beach. While you won't hear the latest crazes in rap and heavy metal, you'll be entertained with live music, DJs, ethnic performers, and even karaoke.

The convivial **Conch House** presents live guitar music Thursday to Sunday at 57 Comares St. During the dinner hour on most Mondays, a live jazz band plays soothing notes at **Dunes Cracker House** at 641 A1A S. Things heat up Thursday to Saturday, when a DJ spins mostly dance tunes, except Friday, which is always reggae night. **Milltop Tavern** has a variety of live music nightly, both local and guest talent at 19 1/2 St George St. The authentic pub decor at **Murphy's Pour House** goes right along with the authentic Irish musicians who start with traditional tunes, then break into more lively party music mixed with a bit of Jimmy Buffett Thursday to Saturday at 72 Spanish St. The **Oasis Deck & Restaurant** brings a wide range of musicians, from jazz and country to light rock at 4000 A1A, St Augustine Beach. A local favorite, **Scarlett O'Hara's** turns it up with solo acts and bands on weekends at 70 Hypolita St.

Events

There are major events throughout the year, but November and December have a magical quality due to the special lights and outdoor evening events. Not surprising, most of the events have an historical theme. What follows is a partial list of events.

In February the annual **Native American Pow Wow** (904/826-4131) celebrates the heritage of Native Americans through food, music, arts, and crafts. The **Fort Matanzas Torch Light Tour** (904/829-6506) takes visitors on an evening tour of the fort along with an historic reenactment. February ends with the **Menéndez Festival** (904/825-5088), which honors St Augustine's namesake founder with entertainment, Spanish dance, and a 16th-century village festival. March opens with a **Union Encampment** (904/829-6506) for a Civil War reenactment at Castillo de San Marcos. It's followed in April by the **Historic Inns and Garden Tour** (904/829-3295) and the **Gamble Rogers Folk Festival** (904/794-0222), a three-day festival in honor of St. Augustine native, the late Gamble Rogers, a well-known folk musician. In June, there's a torch light procession called **Spanish Night Watch**

(904/825-2240) through the Spanish Quarter by reenactors in period dress, along with music and daytime living history displays. September features **Days in Spain/Founders** Day (904/825-1010) celebrating the anniversary of the city's founding with a reenactment of the landing of Don Pedro Menéndez de Avilés and a Spanish-style fiesta. October's **Cracker Day Festival** features banjos and fiddles playing bluegrass. Live entertainment kicks off the annual November **Lincolnville Festival** (904/829-8379), a celebration that chronicles the freedom of St Augustine's Lincolnville community, once called "Little Africa." It is one of the oldest black settlements in the country. The city's most popular event is **Nights of Lights** (800/Old-City), a series of evening holiday events that begins with the illumination of more than a million lights along the bay and outlining buildings in the historic district, then continues with music, theatrical performances, historical reenactments, parades, caroling, and tours. The year ends with a spectacle, the **Siege of 1702** (904/829-6506), in which the townspeople of Old St Augustine (visitors are welcome to join in) run to the Castillo de San Marcos for protection during a British attack, complete with muskets and cannon firing on the fort.

Washington Oaks State Gardens

Seemingly in the middle of nowhere—it spans the peninsula between the Atlantic Ocean and the Matanzas River on the east and west and between Daytona Beach and St Augustine on the north and south—this sparkling gem in the state park systems is worth the drive. Though only 400 acres, Washington Oaks State Gardens encompasses diverse communities, including coastal scrub, coastal hammock, and landscaped gardens. Sunrise over the boulder-strewn beach and sunset over the scenic tidal marshes are memorable experiences.

Archaeological evidence shows that Native Americans lived on the site for thousands of years. The hill at the top of the rose garden was formed by generations of Native Americans discarding oyster shells and other things onto a midden. The first documented settlement of Europeans dates from 1770. In 1818 Jose Mariano Hernandez, a St Augustine native of Minorcan descent, bought the land and named it Bella Vista. When Florida became part of the United States, he changed his name to Joseph Marian Hernandez and became a militia general during the Second Seminole War.

George Lawrence Washington, a son-in-law and descendant of the first U.S. President, built a two-story beach house, which he and his sons used for hunting, fishing, and growing citrus. The land was sold in 1923 to developers, who planned a subdivision called Hernandez Estates. Fortunately, it was saved by the collapse of the 1920s Florida land boom. New York designer Louise Powis Clark and her third husband, Owen D. Young, bought the land in 1936 and created the formal gardens. In 1964 she donated the property to the state. Their house, known as Young House, serves as the park's Visitor Center.

Information

Washington Oaks State Gardens, 6400 N Oceanshore Blvd (Hwy A1A), Palm Coast, FL 32137; 904/446-6780; matgeo@mail.state.fl.us. **Department of Environmental Protection**, Division of Recreation and Parks, 3900 Commonwealth Blvd, Tallahassee, FL 32399; 850/488-9872. **Flagler County Chamber of Commerce**, Star Route 100 & Airport Rd, Bunnell, Fla. 32110; 904/437-0106

Getting there

Take I-95 to exit 91C (Palm Coast Pkwy). Follow the signs east to Hwy A1A (Oceanshore Blvd), then north to the entrance. The closest airports are in Daytona Beach (35 miles south) and Jacksonville (75 miles north). Amtrak's (800/USA RAIL) closest station is 40 miles west in Palatka. Greyhound Bus Lines (800/231-2222,

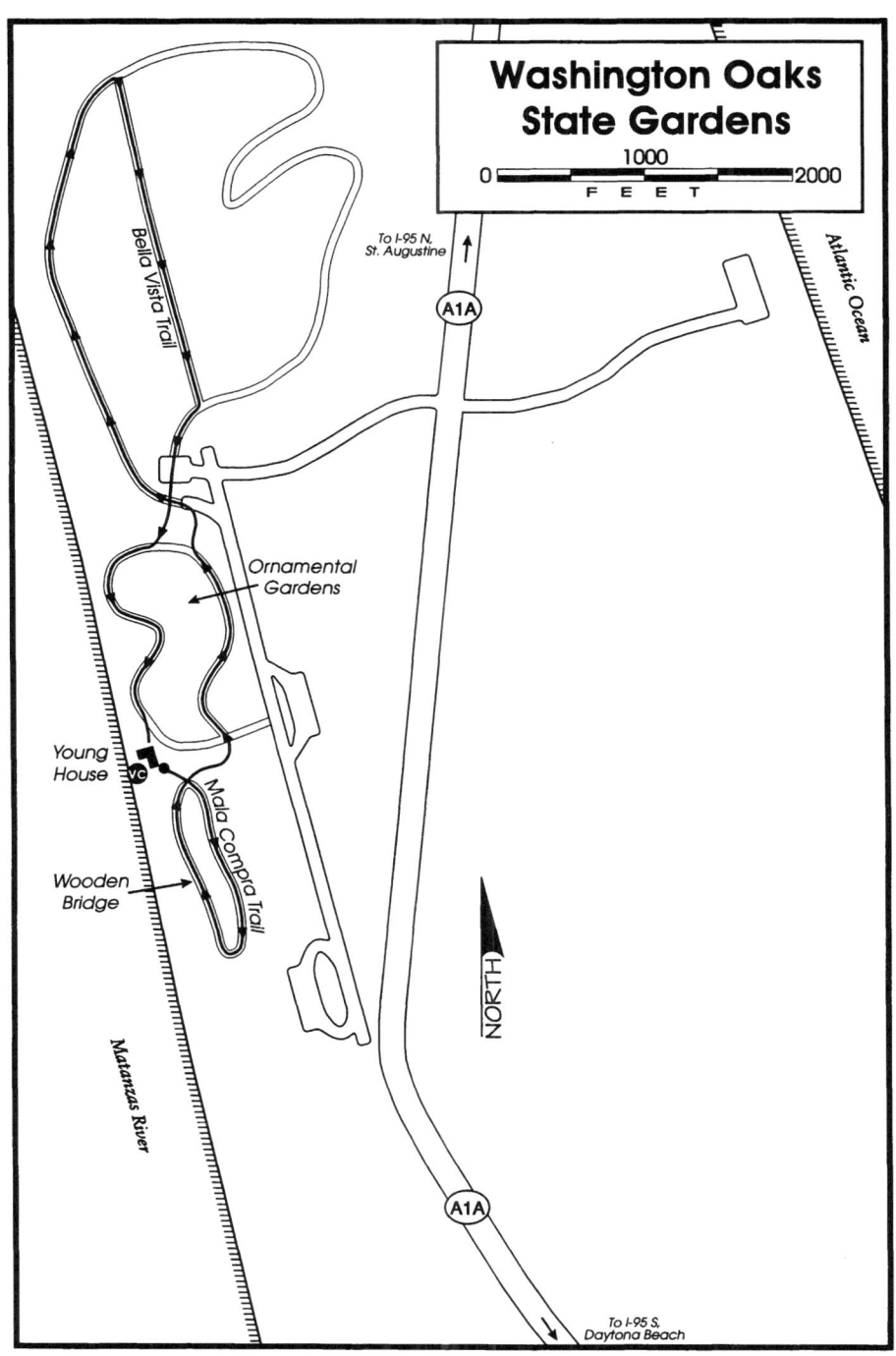

Washington Oaks
State Gardens

1000
0 ━━━━━━━━━━━━━ 2000
F E E T

Atlantic Ocean

Bella Vista Trail

To I-95 N,
St. Augustine

A1A

Ornamental
Gardens

Young
House

VC

Mala Compra Trail

Wooden
Bridge

Matanzas River

NORTH

A1A

To I-95 S,
Daytona Beach

941/385-7741) serves the town with drop-offs and pick-ups at the McDonalds on Palm Coast Hwy.

First steps
For garden information, contact **Washington Oaks State Gardens** or the Department of Environmental Protection, Park Information. The garden is open daily 8 am to sundown; the visitor center daily 8 am to 5 pm. Admission is $3.25 per vehicle. For regional maps and information, contact the Flagler County Chamber of Commerce.

Seasonal highlights
There's always something in bloom in the gardens, but spring and summer offer the most color. Look for camellias in the winter.

Tours
Ranger-guided walks are given on weekends and by request.

Natural Washington Oaks State Gardens. *Walking the park takes in three areas. You can combine them—as we have done—for a 2.5-mile route, or take the 0.5-mile garden walk; 0.5-mile looped Mala Compra walk, which passes through a coastal hammock community and returns along the river's tidal marsh; or the Bella Vista trail, which meanders through coastal hammock and coastal scrub communities.*

Begin at the Mala Compra Trail, located south of the Young House Visitor Center.

The **Mala Compra** trailhead is very enticing. Lanky red bays (*Persea borbonia*) and towering mature live oaks (*Quercus virginiana*) draped in Spanish moss (*Tillandsia recurvata*) form a dense, arching canopy over the wide, leaf-covered trail. Deep green ferns and hand-shaped fronds of cabbage palms (*Sabal palmetto*) and saw palmettos (*Serenoa repens*) add a delicate texture. The trail gently twists, so as not to reveal too quickly the pleasures that lie ahead.

Interpretive signs describe some of the plants found along the trail. Mushrooms and resurrection ferns (*Polypodiumpolypodioides*) cling to the limbs and trunks of trees. Red and white lichens appear more like paint splotches than living organisms. Other plants in the understory include American (*Ilex opaca*) and yaupon holly (*Ilex vomitoria*), both of which have bright red fruits that attract birds and animals. The latter is used for Christmas decorations. Native Americans boiled the leaves to make a ceremonial drink. The scarlet red coral bean (*Erythrina herbacea*) blooms February to June.

Butterflies are profuse, especially skippers and swallowtails. Look down and brush away some of the dry leaves covering the sand ground. There are oyster and sea shell fragments, evidence that the sea was once here. *At 0.15 mile, the trail intersects with a trail on the right marked "Fishing." Take it to loop back through the Matanzas River tidal marsh. The main trail continues a few hundred feet, ending at a picnic area and restrooms.*

You can spot the masts of sailboats beyond the tall cord grass before you can see the river. At a quarter mile, a small wooden bridge crosses a slough that runs between the trail and the river. Cross over to the beach and look out across the river and scenic tidal marsh. There's a picnic table and grill.

Return to the trail and continue along the slough, which is lined with a thicket of black mangroves (*Avicennia germinans*), their erect, pencil-like roots protruding up through the mud at the base of the trees. About 100 yards ahead, you'll have to duck to pass under a large cabbage (also called sabal) palm that arches across the trail like a windswept coconut palm (*Cocos nucifera*). Just ahead, there's a stand of large red cedars on the left.

The trail continues past more slash pines (*Pinus elliottii*), sabal palms and saw palmettos before returning to the starting point. *Cross the street and continue past the Visitor Center to the formal gardens.*

The entrance to the formal gardens is marked by shrimp plants on both sides of the path, followed by a large live oak and a sabal palm and mondo grass (*Ophiopogon japonicus*). *Take the first right fork.*

The path opens onto the site of Washington's two-story beach house and a cistern. Turn right and enter the Rose Garden. Just before leaving the Rose Garden, stop to observe the many butterflies feeding at the two lantana (*lantana spp*) shrubs at the exit.

The path continues past a pond with a patio with Adirondack chairs and benches in front of it. As it curves left, it passes a small collection of hibiscus, followed by crinum lilies, shell ginger, ferns and a bay cedar.

Stay to the right, following the path lined with mondo grass, past one of the garden's largest live oaks. A few hundred feet ahead is a collection of painted fingertip bromeliads (*billbergia spp*).

As the path bends left, there's an herb garden in raised beds. Continue, passing between the two ponds. The one on the left has a piled-rock fountain. At a quarter mile, a small wood bridge crosses the pond, flanked by ferns, giant philodendrons and variegated gingers.

When the path recrosses the pond, there's a lovely planting of heliconia and bananas, as well as giant birds of paradise. Hug the road as it veers right and return through the Rose Garden, past the house site and on to the beach, where you can rest and watch the river before returning to the Visitor Center.

To reach the Bella Vista Trail, you can either pass back through the formal garden to the right of the herb collection or drive from the main parking lot a few hundred yards to the trailhead parking lot.

This part of the walk follows the red Jungle Road Loop *(0.65 miles) and* blue Timucuan Loop *(0.95) portions of the Bella Vista Trail.*

The trail starts as an open, grass-covered path. *Go left at the first fork. It's a little confusing, because the trails aren't marked by name or color beyond the start. Then turn right at the sign that reads "Nature Trail."*

The trail narrows under a tight canopy of cherry laurel (*Prunus caroliniana*), sugar hackberry (*Celtis laevigata*), various oaks and southern magnolias (*magnolia grandiflora*). You can hear, but not see the river traffic just to the left.

The evergreen trees along the trail are southern red cedars (*Juniperus virginiana* var*silicicola*). Their powdery blue berries are an important food source for birds and their dense foliage provides them with good cover. There's a southern magnolia at 0.37 miles on the right. Its fragrant flowers bloom from April to August.

At 0.45 miles there's a blue sign. *Turn left toward the river for a view of the water.* Mockernut hickories (*Carya tomentosa*) like the one on the right at 0.54 miles soar to 115 feet. Their fruits look like a smooth-shell walnut. Their wood was used to make golf club handles and automobile wheel spokes before steel became readily available.

Take a close look at the resurrection ferns on a live oak at mile 0.58. In dry season the ferns shrivel up into a dark brown mat and appear dead. After a substantial rain they unfold into lush green, frilly fronds.

The canopy almost disappears as the trail winds past wax myrtles and saw palmettos and gives way to coastal scrub, which depends on periodic fires for their existence. The fires allow the endangered Florida scrub jays and gopher tortoises to feed.

At around 0.84 mile the trail curves and the trees start to reappear. Note the colorful lichen on the trunks. Just past the 1 mile mark on the right is a patch of coontie (*Zamia pumila*), a fern-like cycad with a short, stout trunk and a center fruit that looks like an oversized pine cone. Native Americans ground their underground stems into flour and the endangered atala butterfly uses it as a primary larval food source.

A glade of saw palmettos crowd the sides of the road at 1.25 miles. Coontie are interspersed. There's an interpretive sign at 1.47 miles describing the culinary uses of the red bay's bay leaves, which is in the same family as the equally familiar avocado.

The trail crosses the asphalt at 1.53 miles and continues to the main road. Turn left at the sign and return to the entrance.

Lodging

Palm Coast remains a fairly pristine area, but development encroaches on the area daily. The accommodations are limited. If you're willing to drive a few miles south to neighboring Flagler Beach, you'll broaden the list of waterfront bed & breakfasts and a unique historic hotel.

Accommodating guests is the mission at **The Shire House Inn** ($$–$$$, 800/345-4394, 904/445-8877) at 3398 N Oceanshore Blvd, Palm Coast, whether they want breakfast in the dining room or breakfast in bed (with or without Champagne), candlelight dinners, to fish off the dock, or just want to enjoy a quiet weekend in one of five well-appointed guest rooms, each with a whirlpool tub and queen and king bed.

The **Haborside Inn at Palm Coast Resort** ($$–$$$$, 904/445-3000) has nautical decor and a breezy, relaxed atmosphere at 300 Clubhouse Dr, Palm Coast. The 154 rooms located along exterior corridors on three floors reached by stairs face either the marina or Intracoastal Waterway. Amenities include tennis courts, boating facilities, waterfront bike and walking paths, a pool, restaurant, and entertainment lounge.

The oceanfront **White Orchid Inn** ($$$–$$$$, 904/439-4944), with wood floors, big windows, and heated pool, has a sleek deco façade and a timeless feel at 1104 S. Oceanshore Blvd, Flagler Beach. The spacious rooms are simply but elegantly decorated and have large Jacuzzi baths. Fine dining, afternoon wine and hors d'oeuvres, beach chairs, umbrellas, and bicycles are a few amenities.

A gemologist's guide describes a topaz as "symbol of love and affection, aid to sweetness of disposition." That description also applies to the **Topaz Hotel/Motel** ($$–$$$/$–$$, 904/439-3301), a modestly priced gem built in the 1920s in a mix of Prairie and Mediterranean styles at 1224 S Oceanshore Blvd (Hwy A1A), Flagler Beach. The lobby and smallish rooms in the original building are filled with very interesting antiques, thanks to the owners, who are collectors. Additional true motel rooms are alongside. There's an on-site restaurant (see below) and the beach is across the street.

Food & drink

Area restaurants tend toward the casual. The closest eateries are very casual, but the food and service are very good. As with the lodgings, there's a bigger selection in

Flagler Beach.

Almost outside the park gates is rustic **Norris' Crazy Crab** ($–$$, 904/447-5553)at 5949 N Oceanshore Blvd (Hwy A1A), Palm Coast, where the food, mostly seafood, is cooked perfectly and served with genuine hospitality. The steamed crabs are served Maryland style, spicy and tender. Just down the street are two local favorites, **Teddy's** ($, 904/445-7484), which turns out popular burgers at 5054 N Oceanshore Blvd, Palm Coast, and **Peggy's Place** ($, 904/445-9958), where the menu includes burgers, dogs, Philly cheese steaks, and budget-friendly ($6.95) pasta night and steak night at 5224 N Oceanshore Blvd, Palm Coast. **Raymond's** ($–$$, 904/446-2433), offers an eclectic menu of fish, veal, and beef, prepared many ways, plus German dishes a few miles south and inland in the Palm Harbor Shopping Village, 242 Palm Coast Pkwy, Palm Coast.

Farther south in Flagler Beach, the **Topaz Cafe** ($$–$$$, 904/439-3275) in the Topaz Hotel/Motel at 1224 S Oceanshore Blvd seems to be everyone's first choice for the marvelous homestyle meals, including freshly prepared breads and pastries, which sisters Lisa and Catherine Hampton have run since the mid-1980s.

Events

The park celebrates Earth Day in a big way with speakers, craft vendors, entertainment, interpretive programs, a civil war encampment, and food.

North Central Florida

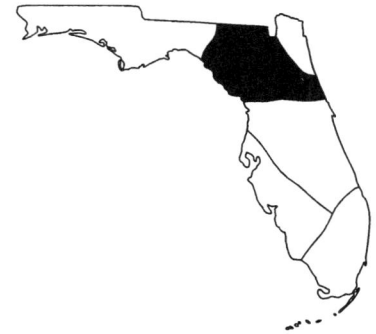

"How happily situated is this retired spot of earth! What an elisium it is! where the wandering Siminole, the naked red warrior, roams at large, and after the vigorous chase retires from the scorching heat of the meridian sun."—William Bartram from *The Travels of William Bartram*

Introduction

Alachua County occupies most of North Central Florida. It's southwest of Jacksonville, about 90 minutes from both coasts. At its heart lies Gainesville, named for General Edmund P. Gaines, who captured Aaron Burr and fought in the Seminole Wars.

Timucuan tribes occupied the region when Spanish explorer Hernando de Soto passed through in 1539. They died off from European disease and warfare within 250 years. De Soto was followed by Franciscan missionaries and then Spanish ranchers, who established in the 1650s the largest cattle ranch in the state, Rancho de la Chua, most of which is now Paynes Prairie State Park.

Under British occupation (1763–1783) naturalist William Bartram traveled through the region in 1774 and wrote, "On the first view of such an amazing display of the wisdom and power of the supreme author of nature, the mind for a moment seems suspended, and impressed with awe." Seminole Indians, descendants of Creek Indians who migrated south from Alabama and Georgia in the 1700s, escorted him through the region.

Friction between white settlers and Seminoles who refused to give up their land increased and led to the Second Seminole War (1835–1842) and raids by Native Americans on plantations in Micanopy and other settlements. By 1842, three years before Florida joined the Union, the Seminoles had been killed, deported, or driven into the Everglades.

Farming, phosphate mining, and growing citrus were the primary industries until 1906, when the University of Florida opened at Gainesville.

The town, and indeed the county, owes its prosperity to the university. Alachua County has a population of 200,000 spread sparsely over more than 900 square miles. Gainesville makes up half of the population, with nearly half of that number students.

With such a widely spread population, much of the region is still undeveloped and is home to numerous state, county, and city parks. The terrain features heavily treed gently rolling hills dotted with farms and old small towns, rivers, and springs. Paynes Prairie State Park occupies 33 square miles of the southern half of the county, stretching from Gainesville to Micanopy.

University of Florida, Gainesville

Masonry gargoyles and whimsical figures atop Gothic-style brick spires stand watch over the University of Florida, the state's oldest, largest, and most prestigious university. The lively, sprawling campus is beautifully planted with native plants and shady trees. Its burgeoning population of 42,000 students spills out onto the surrounding streets into fast-food eateries, restaurants, clubs, stores, Greek houses, and apartments.

While its academics are second to none in the state and the university ranks among the top 60 public and private universities in North America, it's probably better known as home to the Florida Gators, the collegiate football team that was ranked number one in the country after winning four consecutive Southeastern Conference Championships.

In 1906, a year after eight institutions of higher education merged, including the East Florida Seminary in Gainesville, which was established in 1853 (hence the university's founding date) the new University of Florida opened its doors with 102 male students. Women joined the student population in 1947.

The South Carolina architectural firm of Edwards and Walter was hired to design the campus. They chose Collegiate Gothic architecture, a style that expresses a new, assertive positive outlook on life. A fitting choice for the state's first university. Frederick Law Olmsted, the designer of New York's Central Park, provided the landscape design.

A cluster of 21 of the original red brick Gothic-style buildings constructed between 1906 and 1939 remains at the heart of the campus and forms the University of Florida Historic District, listed on the National Register of Historic Places. It is surrounded by buildings dating from the second construction boom of the 1940s and 1950s, as well as more recent structures. Many feature a similar red brick exterior, creating a feeling of continuity and harmony.

Information

University of Florida, Public Affairs, Tigert Hall, 1201 NW 13th St, Gainesville, FL 32611; 352/392-3261; www.ufl.edu. Alachua County Visitors & Convention Bureau, 30 E University Ave, Gainesville, FL 32601; 352/374-5231; acv acb@ns1.co.alachua.fl.us; www.co.alachua.fl.us/~acvacb.

Getting there

Major carriers serve Gainesville Regional Airport. Amtrak (800/USA RAIL, 904/766-5110) provides bus-link service to Gainesville at 104 SE 1st Ave.

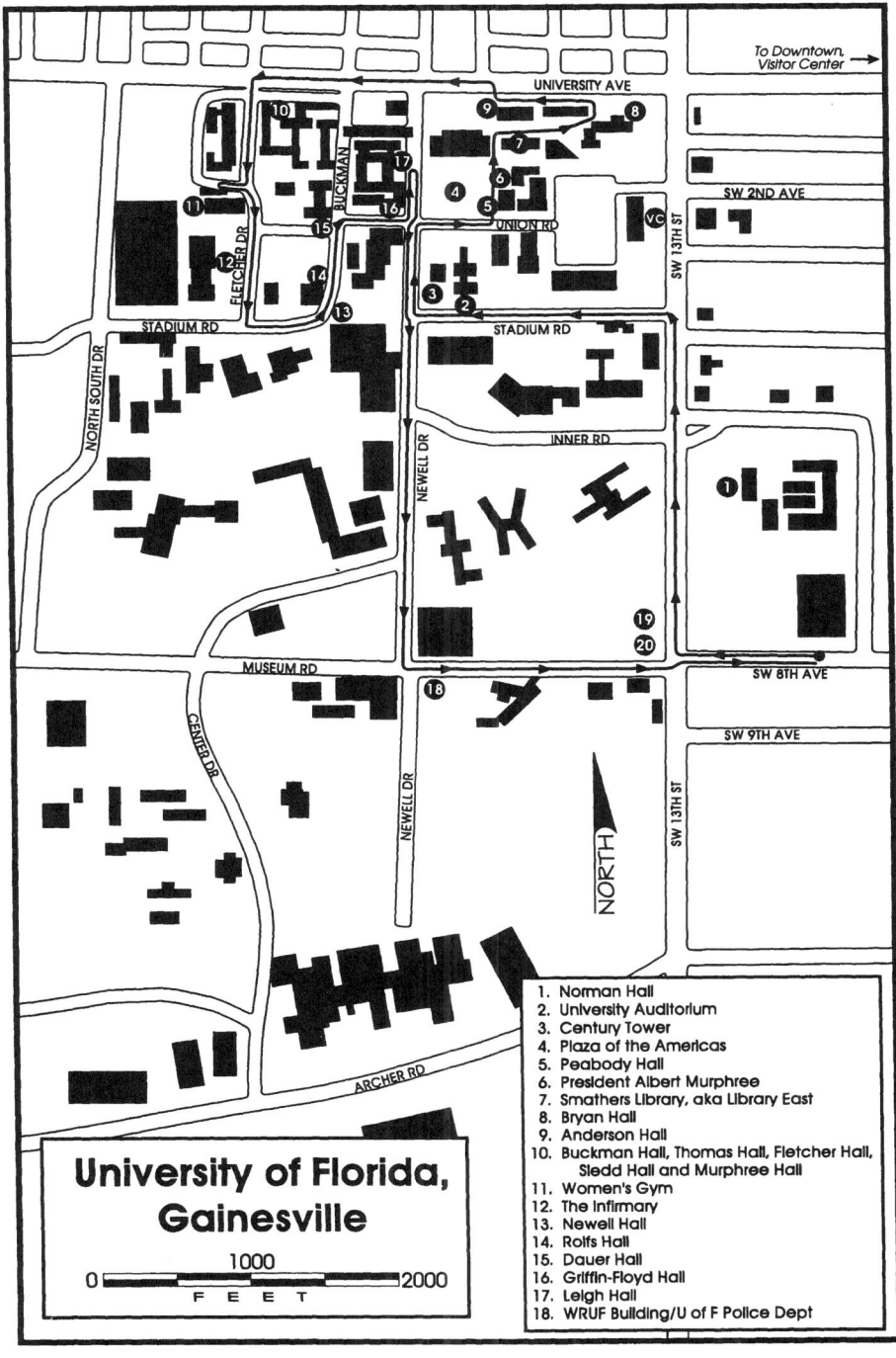

University of Florida, Gainesville

0 ⟝━━━━━ 1000 ━━━━━⟞ 2000
F E E T

1. Norman Hall
2. University Auditorium
3. Century Tower
4. Plaza of the Americas
5. Peabody Hall
6. President Albert Murphree
7. Smathers Library, aka Library East
8. Bryan Hall
9. Anderson Hall
10. Buckman Hall, Thomas Hall, Fletcher Hall,
    Sledd Hall and Murphree Hall
11. Women's Gym
12. The Infirmary
13. Newell Hall
14. Rolfs Hall
15. Dauer Hall
16. Griffin-Floyd Hall
17. Leigh Hall
18. WRUF Building/U of F Police Dept

Greyhound Bus Lines (800/231-2222, 352/376-5252) has a station at 516 SW 4th Ave. By car, the University of Florida is between SW 13th St and SW 34th St, south of W University Ave. From I-10 exit onto I-75 south, then take exit 76 (Newberry Rd). Go east five miles. Newberry Road becomes University Ave. Turn right onto SW 13th St and enter the parking lot at SW 2nd Ave.

First steps

For maps and information, contact the University of Florida's Public Affairs office. One of the best books covering the university is the *Guide to the University of Florida and Gainesville* by Kevin M. McCarthy, a member of the U of F faculty, and Murray D. Laurie, who writes about Florida's historic architecture.

Visitors can obtain a free parking permit at any of the entrances (not necessary on weekends). Unfortunately, during the regular school season parking at the university is akin to a game of musical chairs in which there are 100 players for every chair. If possible, go on a weekend, holiday, during school breaks, or in the summer. Better still, leave your car at the hotel. Many area hotels offer free shuttle service to the university. If you want to drive and try to find a parking space, Parking Garage #8 is the closest to the tour starting point. Call 352/392-PARK for more information.

Walking tours

The Florida Cicerones/Student Alumni Association offers free campus tours on a regular basis. Tours are designed to acquaint students and parents, so the tour covers many modern structures as well as some of the historic district.

Seasonal highlights

Although it can be very hot, the summer is the quietest time to visit the university.

Historic University of Florida. *This 2.25-mile route covers the University of Florida Historic District. Allot 90 minutes. However, a more leisurely trip of two or three hours will allow you to look around the interiors of some of the buildings.*

Park in Garage #8, then walk north on SW 13th St to begin the tour at Norman Hall. Originally the P.K. Yonge Laboratory School, which children attended so that teachers could learn to teach, **Norman Hall** (southeast corner of SW 13th St and SW 5th Ave) now serves as the College of Education. Though it has traditional Gothic architecture, note the whimsical architectural details created to appeal to the building's young audience. *Walk north on SW 13th St and turn left onto Stadium Rd.*

The campus crown jewel is the soaring **University Auditorium** (Newell Dr, between Union Rd and Stadium Rd). Completed in 1924, it features shaped parapets, mullions and stone tracery on the windows, and a towering spire. Go inside. On the ground floor wall are several plaques describing the building's history and construction. Then climb the steps to the second floor. The doors opposite the offices lead into the auditorium. Its striking cathedral-like interior has massive open beams with figures representing academic, professional, and athletic pursuits; a 45-foot high vaulted ceiling; gargoyles, and a magnificent organ. It's a popular venue for concerts, dramatic performances, and speeches by visiting dignitaries. The **Century Tower** rises 157 feet adjacent to the auditorium. Built in 1953 to commemorate the university's centennial, its carillon has 49 bells that are rung for important occasions and noon concerts. The carillonneur must climb 194 steps to reach the 61-key keyboard. The largest bell measures five feet and weighs more than three tons. *Head north on Newell Dr, then turn right onto Union Rd.*

The grassy swath on the left is the **Plaza of the Americas** (northeast corner of Newell Dr and Union Rd), planted in 1931 with 21 live oaks representing the Latin American countries taking part in the campus' invitational Pan American Conference. It remains a central meeting place, rally point, and spot for a respite under the shade of a tree. *Turn left onto the service road that runs on the east side of the plaza.*

On the right **Peabody Hall** (northeast corner of Union Rd and the service road) was completed in 1913 as the first College of Education. Among its other uses, the hall served as the office of *The Florida Alligator*, the campus newspaper, and the first library. A bronze statue of a seated **President Albert Murphree** was erected on the north patio of Peabody Hall. The service road ends at **Smathers Library**, aka **Library East** (east side of Newell Dr, south of W University Ave), which despite several major additions, retains much of the original 1925 detailed Gothic ornamentation. Go inside to see the wood-beam and coffered ceilings. Outside look for the parapets, red tile roof, and terra cotta details. *Walk diagonally northeast on the sidewalk, passing between the two wings of the library.*

Bas-relief ornamentation of a law book, scale of justice, and gavel decorate **Bryan Hall** (corner of SW 13th St and W University), constructed in 1914 as the College of Law. It's the alma mater of Florida governor Lawton Chiles and US Congressman Charles Bennett, among other notables. Today, it's part of the College of Business Administration. *Walk to the front of the building and turn left onto University Ave.*

Completed in 1913, four-story **Anderson Hall** (W University Ave) was originally named Language Hall. It housed the president's office, registrar, and classrooms for English, language, history, and math. Note the traditional Gothic recessed entry, gargoyle, and elaborate detailing on the door. *Continue west on University Ave.*

On the right are eateries, off-campus student facilities, bookstores, some campus buildings. On the left are **Buckman Hall, Thomas Hall, Fletcher Hall, Sledd Hall** (W University Ave, between Buckman Rd and Fletcher Dr), and **Murphree Hall** (W University Ave, west side of Fletcher Dr) . Take time to slowly walk around the buildings and observe such rich Gothic detailing as multi-story oriel and bay windows, bas-relief and carved ornamentation, the Anguished Scholar (Buckman), birds and animals (Fletcher and Sledd), seals of other universities (Sledd and Fletcher), gargoyles (Sledd), children playing (Thomas), and recessed arched entries (Murphree and Sledd) and vestibules. Courtyards and passageways connect the buildings, which are now residence halls. Thomas and Buckman, built in 1906 and 1907, respectively, are the two original campus buildings. *Turn left onto Fletcher Dr, then take the second right.*

The town of Gainesville donated the funds to complete the **Women's Gym** (Fletcher Dr) in 1919. Then-President Albert A. Murphree persuaded the New York Giants to hold spring training on campus to initiate the new building. They played exhibition games against the university team and the Boston Red Sox. Like the auditorium, it features grand Gothic features and is worth a few extra minutes to see the interior and exterior. *Return to Fletcher Dr and continue south.*

The Infirmary (on the right, Fletcher Dr) was built in 1931. Though its purpose is quite serious, the main entrance features a group of whimsical characters carved in stone, each suffering from a different ailment. *Continue south on Fletcher Dr, then turn left onto Stadium Rd, then left onto Buckman Rd.*

The handsome corner building on the right is **Newell Hall** (Buckman Dr, just northeast of Stadium Rd), named after Dr Wilmon Newell, Dean of the College of Agriculture. It opened in 1910 as the Florida Agricultural Experiment Station to bridge the state's academic and practical agricultural needs. Students had hands-on experience at the adjacent fields. Note the quatrefoil ornamentation. *Continue north on Buckman Rd.*

Almost 17 years after Newell Hall opened, **Rolfs Hall** (Buckman Dr, just north of northwest corner of Stadium Rd) was opened as the Horticulture Building to expand the university's agricultural programs. Look for the wreathed beehive plaque on one of the parapets. *Continue north on Buckman Rd.*

The first student center was built as **Dauer Hall** (northwest corner Buckman and Union) in 1937 with a basement soda fountain, lounges, meeting rooms, and a second-floor auditorium/chapel. Note the stained-glass window installed in 1938. Below them on the sidewalk is a marker about the building's namesake professor. *Turn right onto Union Rd, then left onto Newell Dr.*

The first building on the left, the first College of Agriculture, is **Griffin-Floyd Hall** (Newell Dr at Union Rd). The Newell Dr entrance features an elaborate masonry cornucopia of fruit above the doorway. The 1912 building was originally named Floyd Hall, honoring an early science professor, but was renamed after it was saved from demolition and restored by a donation from former UF student and citrus millionaire, Ben Hill Griffin, Jr, whose name also appears on the football stadium. Next door is **Leigh Hall** (between Buckman and Newell, north of Union Rd), built as the Chemistry-Pharmacy Building in 1926. Take time to study the rich detail of whimsical figures, names of scientists, and alchemical symbols for the elements on the facade. *Backtrack south on Newell Rd and go four blocks, then turn left onto Museum Rd.*

Quite a departure from the campus Gothic-style architecture, the Tudor Revival **WRUF Building** with half-timbered walls, a steeply pitched roof, and an intersecting gable, has since the 1950s served as the **University of Florida Police Department** (southeast corner Newell Dr and Museum Rd). WRUF Radio went on air in the late 1920s as the "Voice of the University of Florida." Red Barber began his sportscasting career here announcing collegiate games. *Continue east on Museum Rd and return to Parking Garage #8.*

Lodging

There are numerous inexpensive and moderately priced chain hotels and motels on SW 13th Ave. The two bed-and-breakfast establishments are downtown, about 15 minutes away. Rooms are difficult to find and rates go up during major sports events.

Built in 1885, the **Magnolia Plantation B&B Inn** ($$–$$$$, 352/375-6653) is a marvelous Second Empire mansion at 309 SE 7th St in the heart of the downtown historic district. Along with six beautifully decorated rooms with fireplaces and private baths, it has a verandah, pond, and gazebo. **Sweetwater Branch Inn B&B** ($$–$$$$, 800/595-7760, 352/373-6760) is a restored Victorian house built in 1885 at 625 E University Ave. The inn has fireplaces, an acre of lovely gardens, and eight guestrooms gracefully outfitted with antique furnishings and private baths with claw-footed tubs.

Of the major chains, the most comfortable include the **Sheraton Hotel Gainesville** ($$–$$$, 352/377-4000), which has a restaurant, spacious well-appointed rooms, and a scenic lake and nature refuge at 2900 SW 13th St; the **Marriott Residence Inn** ($$–$$$, 352/371-2101), where guestrooms feature kitchens, fireplaces, and living rooms and the grounds feature a pool and exercise facility at 4001 SW 13th St; and the **Holiday Inn University Center** ($$, 352/376-1661)at 1250 W University Ave, which promotes itself as the closest hotel to the University. It has a pool, fitness room, free newspapers, and a restaurant. Less expensive, but comfortable options include the **Comfort Inn** ($$, 352/373-6500) at 2435 SW 13th St, which offers a pool and free continental breakfast, and the larger **Cabot Lodge** ($$, 352/375-2400) at 3726 SW 40th St, which includes free continental breakfast, local calls, and evening beverages.

Arts & culture

The City of Gainesville Department of Cultural Affairs operates a 24-hour arts hotline at 352/373-ARTS (hammock.ifas.ufl.edu/arts-culture). There are bookstores galore, primarily selling new and used university required textbooks. The *Gainesville Sun* publishes "Scene Magazine," a guide to cultural events, in the newspaper's Friday edition.

A professional theater company performs at the beautifully restored historic **Hippodrome State Theatre** (352/375-HIPP, 25 SE 2nd Pl) downtown. The **Acrosstown Repertory Theatre** (352/378-9166, 619 S Main St) stages avant-garde and experimental drama throughout the year in the Baird Center. Art films and classics are shown at the **Hippodrome Cinema** (352/375-HIPP, 25 SE 2nd Pl) daily except Mondays. It has a full-service bar. **Gainesville Community Playhouse** (352/376-4949, 4039 NW 16th Blvd) presents comedies, tragedies, and musicals in the downtown theater. **Florida Players at the Constans Theatre** (352/392-1653, J Wayne Reitz Union) stages theater and dance performances presented by University of Florida students.

There's a monthly **Gallery Walk** (352/375-1911) in which downtown art galleries stay open late. **Gainesville Artisans' Guild Gallery** (352/378-1383, Greenery Square, 5402 NW 8th Ave) is a bit off the beaten track, but worth the drive. It represents numerous artists who create high-quality art, decorative items, and crafts. **Gallery of the J. Wayne Reitz Union** (352/392-2378, Reitz Union, basement level, University of Florida) features ceramics, jewelry, screen printing, stained glass, and unique gifts. The historic **Thomas Center Galleries** (352/334-2197, 302 NE 6th Ave) has two exhibition spaces with rotating shows of contemporary visual artists from Florida and beyond. It also hosts lectures in conjunction with major exhibitions.

Books Inc (352/374-4241, 505 NW 13th St) has used, collectible, and new books, as well as art exhibitions and an attractively priced vegetarian cafe.

Food & drink

Thanks to the university, Gainesville has diverse and notable dining options, from sophisticated bistros to ethnic eateries. Prices run the gamut from student cheap to haute cuisine prix fixe. Downtown, 10 to 15 minutes from the university, offers the best variety.

At **Emiliano's Cafe** ($$–$$$, 352/375-7381) at 7 SE 1st Ave the servers are friendly without being overly chummy and readily explain the exciting menu of Latin and Caribbean specialties well prepared with a twist of creativity. Dine indoors or al fresco. Located downtown next to the State Theater, **Maude's Classic Cafe** ($–$$$, 352/336-9646) at 101 SE 2nd Pl has live music, beer, wine, and an outdoor cafe, Sun Center. It's also a popular breakfast spot with the downtown business crowd. Another before theater option is **Amelia's** ($$–$$$, 352/373-1919), which serves authentic fine Italian dishes indoors and outdoors at 235 S Main St, Sun Center. If you enjoy very creative cuisine, try **Pura Vida** ($$–$$$, 352/378-3398) at 12 SW 1st St, which is difficult to classify because it offers an eclectic, but delicious menu along with organic coffees and espresso and microbrews and fine wines. Step back in time to the 1950s at **Louis' Lunch** ($, 352/372-9294) at 436 SE 2nd St. At this original burger joint, you can still buy a burger for less than a buck, a milkshake made the old-fashioned way, catfish sandwich for $2, and two burgers, with fries, and a drink for under $3 every day but Sunday.

If money is no object when it comes to fine cuisine, try either **Steve's Cafe Americain** ($$$, 352/377-8037) for exotic, artfully prepared dishes at 12 W University Ave, and **Wolfgang's** ($$$, 352/378-7850) for innovative world cuisine at 11 SE 1st Ave.

Beyond the downtown area, but still just a short drive from the university are **Saigon Cafe** ($–$$, 352/338-0023) at 1222 W University Ave for tasty authentic Vietnamese cuisine that will satisfy vegetarians and non-vegetarians, and **Our Place Cafe** ($–$$, 352/371-1172) at 808 W University Ave, the only full-service vegetarian restaurant in Gainesville. It's only open until 3 pm or 4 pm weekdays and Sunday, but has late, late hours on Friday and Saturday.

Nightlife

As expected, most of the nightlife appeals to the college-age crowd. There are pleasant exceptions, primarily downtown.

Baja Beach Club has three floors and non-stop, loud DJ music aimed at the under 25 set at 201 W University. **Eddie C's Pub** features live music four nights a week at

2106 SW 13th St. Grüv has house, dance, and hip-hop at 104 S Main St. There's a wide variety of music several nights a week at the smoke-free **Covered Dish**, which has been open for seven years, downtown at 210 SW 2nd Ave. The crowd depends upon the talent, which runs from ska bands to troubadours. National recording acts alternate nights with DJs at the **Florida Theater** at 233 W University Ave. There's live jazz and blues several nights a week at the **High Note Jazz Club** at 233 W University Ave, at **Soul House** at 15 SW 2nd Pl, and at **Stella's** at 232 SE 1st St. For a radical departure from the norm, there's Middle Eastern dance shows (belly dancing) Thursday through Saturday at the **Gainesville Elks Lodge** at 2424 NW 23rd Blvd.

Events

The **Downtown Jazz & Blues Festival** (352/372-1835) kicks off in the fall. November's **Downtown Festival and Art Show** (352/334-2197) is north central Florida's biggest fine arts and crafts festival, which also features live musical entertainment. Downtown and the neighboring historic districts light up for the December **Festival of Lights** (352/334-2197), which includes a procession of lights to the Community Plaza.

Morningside Nature Center

Gainesville is as rich in natural settings as it is in history. Within the city limits and just a few miles beyond are more than a dozen city, county, and state nature parks. Among these wild urban places is the Morningside Nature Center, a 278-acre sanctuary that is one of the few remaining longleaf pine savannas that once covered most of north Florida.

More than 130 species of birds and 175 species of wildflowers have been spotted here along with such Florida endemic fauna as gopher tortoises and Sherman's fox squirrels. Natural fires caused by lightning traditionally keep pine flatwoods from transforming into hardwood forests. The park manages a fire plan that serves the same function as the natural fires

Seven and a half miles of well-marked, well-maintained walking trails—mostly loops—cross sandy pine-oak uplands, cypress domes, tupelo gum swamps, and wet marsh. Two observation decks and a wildlife viewing blind allow visitors to get as close as possible to wildlife without intruding. Visitors also will see remnants of human history, which included logging and turpentining. The small nature center offers frequent programs and has restrooms.

On the opposite side of the park is the 10-acre Living History Farm with exhibits that recreate the self-sufficient agricultural economy that typified north central Florida in the late 1800s. There's a reconstructed log farmhouse originally built in 1880, a windmill, outbuildings, tools, a school, garden, and split-rail fenced barnyard with farm animals. On most Saturdays the costumed interpretive staff demonstrates traditional period skills.

Information

City of Gainesville, Morningside Nature Center, 3540 E University Ave, Gainesville, FL 32641; 352/334-2170; Alachua County Visitors & Convention Bureau, 30 E University Ave, Gainesville, FL 32601; 352/374-5231; acv acb@ns1.co.alachua.fl.us; www.co.alachua.fl.us/~acvacb.

Getting there

Take I-75 to exit 75 (Archer Rd/SW 13th St) or 74 (/Williston Rd/SE 11th St) northeast to University Ave and turn east. Continue 1–3 miles, depending on which exit you took, to the park entrance. Major carriers serve Gainesville Regional Airport. Amtrak (800/USA RAIL, 904/766-5110) provides bus-link service to Gainesville at 104 SE 12th Ave. Greyhound (800/231-2222, 352/376-5252) has a station at 516 SW 4th Ave.

First steps
For area maps and information, contact the **Alachua County Visitors & Convention Bureau.** It's open weekdays 9 am to 5 pm. For trail maps, park programs, and wildlife and plant lists, contact the **Morningside Nature Center.** The hours are daily 9 am to 5 pm.

Tours
Rangers lead Fall Wildflower Walks after the controlled burning. The fires bring out wildflowers, which attract lots of butterflies.

Seasonal highlights
Spring and fall are the best times to see wildflowers, migrating birds, and butterflies.

Natural Gainesville. *On the 2.5-mile Moccasin Creek and Tupelo Marsh loops, you'll pass through pine flatwoods, a cypress dome and hardwood hammock, cross a boardwalk, and stop at an observation blind.*

Start at the Nature Center. The trailhead is left of the building, but before starting, look to the right of the **Nature Center** entrance at the beautiful specimen red buckeye tree (*Aesculus pavia*).

The trail floor is pine needles and groomed grass bordered by a thick understory of saw palmetto (*Serenoa repens*), bracken fern (*Pteridium aquilinum*), horrible thistle (*Cirsium horridulum*), wax myrtle (*Myrica cerifera*), gallberry (*Ilex glabra*), and fetterbush (*Lyonia lucida*). Don't touch the pretty, white, trumpet-shaped, five-lobed flowers. It's tread softly (*Cnidoscolus stimulosus*) also called stinging nettle.

The trail forks at about 1/8th of a mile to the **Cypress Dome Boardwalk** *Continue straight. It forks again at another 1/8th of a mile. Bear left.* At about a quarter mile, it forks again, with signs pointing to the **Wildlife Blind,** a 20-ft by 5-ft, slatted-wood, thatched-roof structure with a long bench and narrow openings that look onto a clearing with half a dozen makeshift bird feeders. Sit quietly and you'll be entertained by zooming chickadees and titmice, cardinals, red-headed woodpeckers, and other birds. *Return to the trail and at the next fork bear left.*

As you approach **Moccasin Creek**, the trail becomes damp, with more ferns and moss and fewer pines. In spring, look for the small shiny blueberry (*Vaccinium myrsinites*), with half-inch elliptical leaves and one-third-inch blue-black berries that are candy sweet. *At half a mile, the trail forks again, continue straight.* The low hum of traffic beyond the creek is almost drowned by singing towhees, mockingbirds, and warblers.

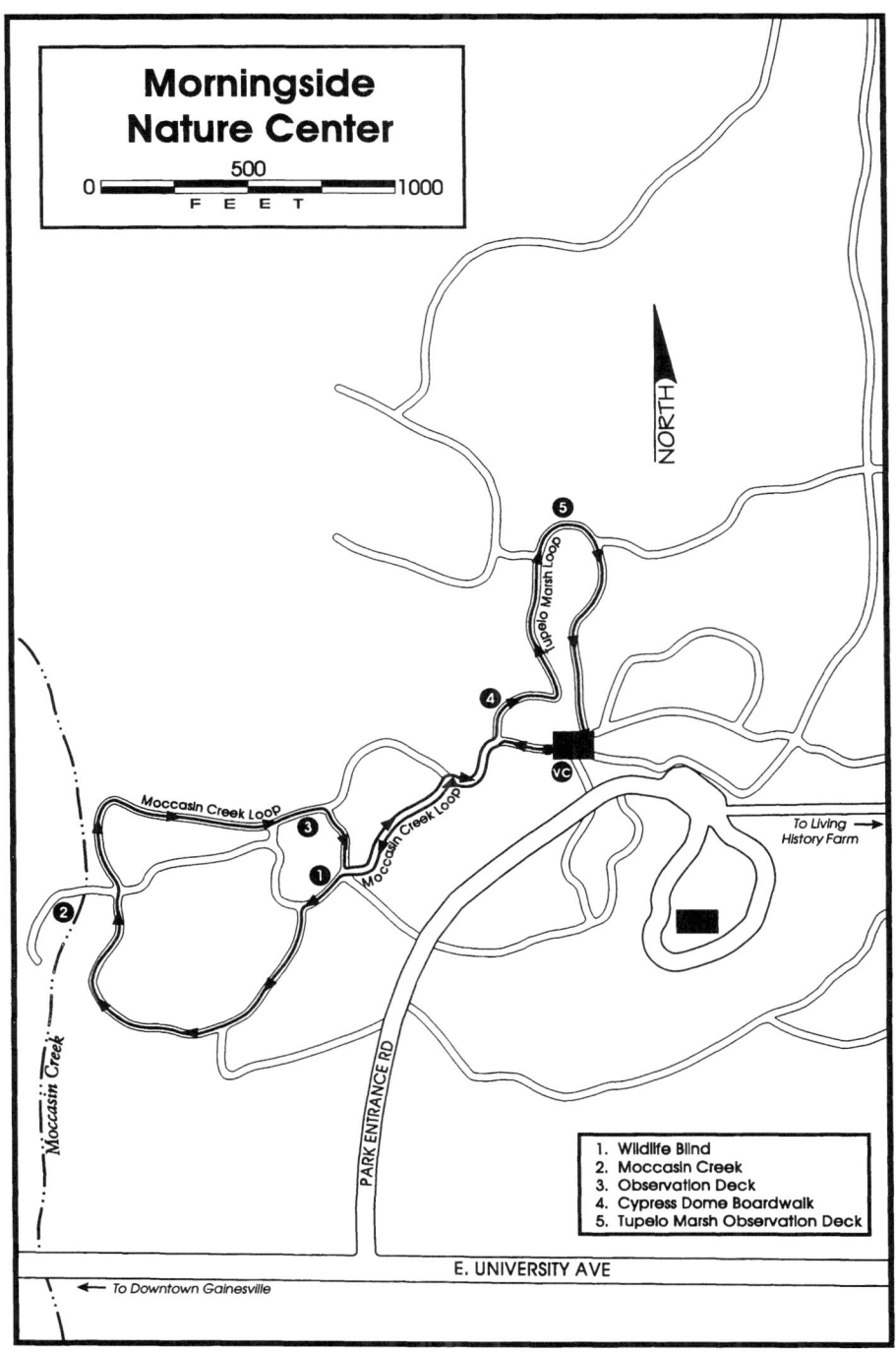

Morningside Nature Center

500
0 |===========| 1000
F E E T

NORTH

Tupelo Marsh Loop

Moccasin Creek Loop

Moccasin Creek Loop

Moccasin Creek

Moccasin Creek

VC

To Living History Farm

PARK ENTRANCE RD

E. UNIVERSITY AVE

To Downtown Gainesville

1. Wildlife Blind
2. Moccasin Creek
3. Observation Deck
4. Cypress Dome Boardwalk
5. Tupelo Marsh Observation Deck

Follow the trail as it curves right and crosses **Creek Bridge Trail** *and parallels* **Perimeter Trail.** Magnolias show up. *At just under a mile, the trail forks again. Stay right.*

At the next fork, look to the right for the marker showing the way to the **Observation Deck**, a wooden platform that overlooks wiregrasses, ferns, and small trees in front of a backdrop of towering pines. *Leave the platform and turn right, then take the next left. Either way will take you back to the Cypress Dome Boardwalk intersection, but this way you'll pass the wildlife blind for a second peak.*

At the **Cypress Dome Boardwalk** *intersection, turn left.* The railed, wooden boardwalk zig zags for only about a tenth of a mile, but the view of ferns, tall cypress, and their knees is quite beautiful. There are benches for those who want to linger.

The first right is an unmarked service road. The second right is lined with logs and leads to the Visitor Center. *Bear left to the* **Tupelo Marsh Loop,** which passes through both open pine and pine/hardwood zones. The **Tupelo Marsh Observation Deck** is half way down the trail. This smaller deck overlooks pickerelweed (*Pontederia cordata*), grasses, and black (*Nyssa sylvatica*) and water (*Nyssa aquatica*) tupelo trees. *Return to the trail, which ends behind the Visitor Center.*

Lodging, Food & drink
See University of Florida, Gainesville Walking Tour.

Events
The annual **Farm & Forest Festival** has taken place for more than 20 years on the first weekend in May.

Paynes Prairie State Preserve

The vast 21,000-acre Paynes Prairie State Preserve in north central Florida, 10 miles south of Gainesville, is comprised of the fascinating Alachua basin covered by marsh and wet prairie and surrounded by a rim of pine flatlands, hammock, ponds, and streams that supports an extensive biological diversity of plant and animal life.

Botanist-traveler William Bartram visited in 1773 and wrote excitedly about the "great Alachua Savanna" in his book *Travels.* He describes the abundant native wildlife—sandhill cranes, hawks, wading birds, turkeys, alligators, otter, bald eagles, snakes, turtles, lizards, weasels, bobcats, deer, squirrels, fox, frogs, fish—much of which still abounds here today. Add to the list such non-native species as scrub cattle and scrub horses, brought here in the mid-1600s when the largest cattle ranch in Spanish Florida operated on the north rim. In an attempt to preserve the prairie and restore it to its natural state, the Florida Park Service has reintroduced the native bison, which Native Americans, who occupied the prairie as far back as 10,000 BC, hunted for food and Bartram described as "once so numerous is not at this day to be seen in this part of the country." In addition, more than 400 plant species are found within the preserve.

The basin is a series of sinkholes formed by the solution of the underlying limestone and subsequent settling of the terrain. Rain and water from the surrounding upland creeks, springs, and streams flow down into the basin. From the basin the water flows into the Floridan (sic) Aquifer System. Several times in recorded history—including within the past five years—the basin has plugged up, flooded, and formed a lake. In 1871 the flooding was so severe and lasted so long, that people used steamboats to travel from one side to the other. Then in 1891, the basin suddenly breached and drained. Seeds sprouted and colonized and returned the basin to prairie and marsh.

In 1970 the state added the preserve to the Florida Park System, which is attempting to restore it to the way it looked more than 200 years ago, when Bartram was hosted by Seminole Indians living along the rim. Today's preserve, designated a National Natural Landmark, has a half dozen trail networks within distinct sections of the park. The Gainesville-Hawthorne State Trail, a rails-to-trails system, crosses the park between endpoints in its namesake cities. Then there is the Bolen Bluff Trail, named for an African-American family who farmed and ranched here in the 1800s, located about three miles south of Gainesville on US-441. The La Chua Trail, which crosses a former cattle ranch, is accessible from the North Rim Interpretive Center, an early 1900s bunkhouse. The main park entrance, about 10 miles south of Gainesville, has about half a dozen interconnected trails, an observation tower, and a visitor center whose unique design earned an architectural award.

Information
Paynes Prairie State Preserve, Route 2, Box 41, Micanopy, FL 32667; 352 /466-3397, 352/466-4100. Alachua County Visitors & Convention Bureau, 30 E University Ave, Gainesville, FL 32601; 352/374-5231; acvacb@ns1.co.alachua.fl.us; www.co.alachua.fl.us/~acvacb.

Getting there
Take I-75 to exit 73 (CR-234). Go east to Micanopy, where you can pick up US-441. The preserve's main entrance is about 5 minutes north. Or from Gainesville, you can take the more scenic drive south on US-441. Gainesville International Airport is about 10 miles (25 minutes) north. The closest Amtrak and Greyhound stations are in Gainesville and Ocala.

First steps
For maps and information about the preserve, contact the Paynes Prairie State Preserve. For area information, contact the Alachua County Visitors & Convention Bureau.

In the unabridged edition of *Travels of William Bartram* edited by Mark Van Doren, you can read about how the prairie looked more than 200 years ago.

Sunscreen and a hat are essential when walking across the open marsh.

Walking tours
On Saturdays throughout the year, rangers lead walking tours like the half-day, 3.5-mile Prairie Rim Ramble and the 3-mile Wildlife Walk, as well as the 6.5-mile overnight backpacking trip. Call for schedules. The Florida Trail Association also leads walks several times a year. Call 800/343-1882 or 352/378-8823 (see Practical Information, page 20).

Seasonal highlights
Depending upon the amount of summer rain, the basin may flood periodically. The degree of flooding varies considerably. Flood waters may cover low trails or even the entire basin. Winter is the best time to see alligators along the La Chua Trail. Also in winter, thousands of migratory greater sandhill cranes join the resident Florida sandhill cranes.

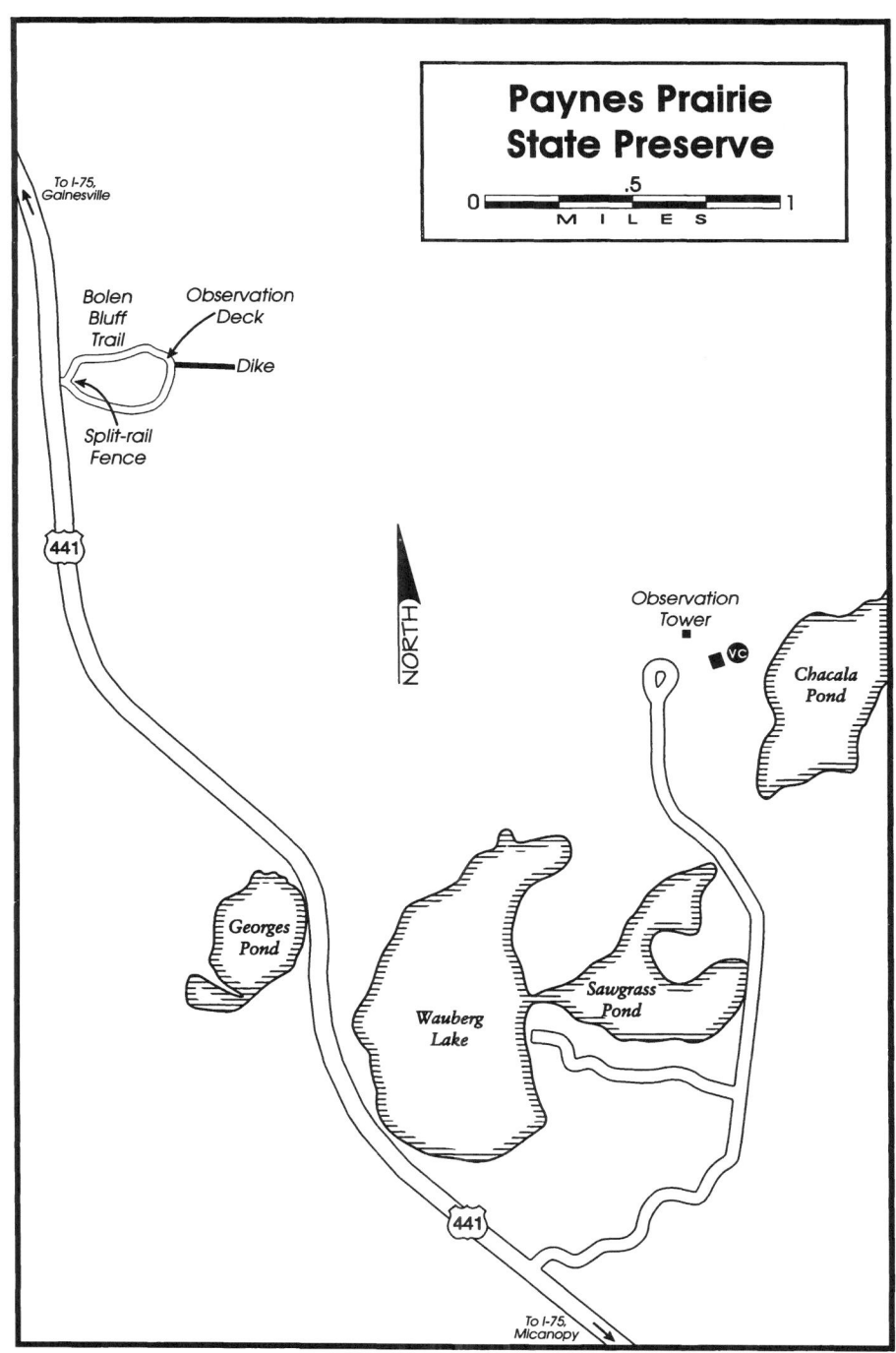

Paynes Prairie
State Preserve

0 |———————| .5 |———————| 1
M I L E S

To I-75,
Gainesville

Bolen
Bluff
Trail

Observation
Deck

Dike

Split-rail
Fence

441

NORTH

Observation
Tower

VC

Chacala
Pond

Georges
Pond

Wauberg
Lake

Sawgrass
Pond

441

To I-75,
Micanopy

Natural Paynes Prairie. *At a little more than 2 miles, this looped route covers shady hammock and open marsh habitats at Bolen Bluff. Allot a little over an hour for a leisurely walk. But first, give yourself an hour to drive about seven miles to the Visitor Center, where you can watch a video about the preserve, see exhibits on the preserve's natural and cultural history, and walk about a quarter mile to climb the 50-foot observation tower, which looks out across the prairie.*

Begin at the parking lot for Bolen Bluff, just off Hwy 441, about three miles south of Gainesville. The trail begins as a tunnel with a fine-sand floor under a canopy of oaks, hickories, turkey oaks, and maples. *At the split-rail fence, follow the road to the right.*

The scenery along the trail gradually becomes more open as it changes to a mix of pines, cabbage palms (*Sabal palmetto*), oaks, and saw palmettos (*Serenoa repens*). Squirrels and birds rustle the trees and underbrush. The numbered sign posts along the trail correspond to a tour brochure written by students at Wiles Elementary School.

The trail winds along for about half a mile in and out of canopies of large oaks interspersed with hollies. At about 0.8 miles, the trail crosses a scenic clearing encircled by large oaks heavily hung with Spanish moss. Note the stand of cabbage (or sabal) palms, the state tree, on the right.

The trail narrows again, then reaches a marker bench and observation deck at 0.85 miles. You leave the woods and find yourself on a bluff overlooking the prairie. Stand at the bench and look down onto the broad expanse of the wet prairie and marsh. It presents a stark contrast to the forest that Bartram wrote about. Suddenly, there are no trees. However, there is a constant attempt by the trees to invade the marsh, but periodic flooding raises the water level for extended periods, creating an inhospitable environment for the growth of woody plants. Depending on the extent of flooding, the dike may not be accessible. *Climb down the bluff to walk along the dike or turn around and pick up the trail on the right to loop back to the start. Note the alligator sign.*

The bluff gradually descends about 20 feet to the prairie divided by a dike that was added by early 20th-century ranchers to hold back the water and provide grazing land for herds of cattle. Moisture-loving herbaceous plants thrive on the wet prairie. Tall grasses, sedges, sundews, and rushes wave in the wind. In the wetter marsh areas, meadow beauties (*Rhexia* spp.) and blue hyssops (*Bacopa caroliniana*) grow.

Grasses and wildflowers bloom in spring and summer. Note the tall, yellow horrible thistle (*Cirsium horridulum*) growing from three to eight feet high along the dike at the convergence of the woody and marsh plants.

At about one mile, the ground on either side of the dike is covered with water on which the broad-leaved plants like spatterdock (*Nuphar luteum*) grow intermingled with rushes. The vegetation grows more and more diverse.

Walking along the dike is a highly sensory experience. The full sun beats down on the wet prairie and marsh, which can be very noisy with birds singing and frogs calling. During mating season, you also can hear alligators grunting. Look at the ground, which if slightly moist, reveals tracks of animals, birds, and alligators. There are grasshoppers, butterflies, and beetles, and surprisingly few mosquitoes in summer. Depending on the season, a warm or cool breeze blows across the prairie. *Walk out onto the dike as far as you can, then return and pick up the loop trail on the right.*

The loop trail plunges into a dense, shady overstory and understory. At about 1.75 miles on the left, there is a large oak whose trunk is split from the ground to about a foot high, then joins and splits again into two large trunks at about eight feet high.

At mile 1.90 notice the wild grape vines that twist around the trees. The vines need full sun to grow and were there before the trees, which grew up between them and carried them higher on their branches. The area has numerous visible sinkholes and the ground alongside the trail drops off sharply.

A large magnolia (*magnolia grandifolia*) grows along the right side of the trail at about 2 miles. The trail returns to the split-rail fence and the trailhead. It's a short walk back to the parking lot.

Lodging, food & drink
See the University of Florida, Gainesville Walking Tour or the Micanopy Walking Tour.

Events
In February craftsmen, artisans, and history buffs demonstrate the construction and use of tools and weapons used by the Native Americans who lived in the region thousands of years ago, at the **Paynes Prairie Annual Knap-In & Primitive Arts Festival.**

Micanopy

This pleasant little town in the shadow of Gainesville makes you want to "pull over and stay a spell." Small, tree-lined streets feed into a mile-long "Main Street" where restored 19th-century buildings house antique shops, a book store, museum, church, two restaurants, two B&Bs, and a few residences and public buildings. That's it. And that's precisely what makes it so attractive.

Its small size belies the magnitude of its history. When Hernando de Soto passed through in 1539, Timucuan Indians had already been living off the fertile soil for 10,000 years. They were killed off by European diseases by the time the Spanish transferred Florida to England in 1763. During that period, botanist William Bartram came and stayed in Cuscawilla village with the Seminole Indians, who had migrated south from Alabama and Georgia. Spain reoccupied Florida in 1783. In 1817 a land grant—the Arredondo Grant—from the king was centered around present-day Micanopy. With permission from Seminole Chief Micanopy, Edward Wanton established a trading post in the village in 1821, originally calling it Wanton, but in 1834 changing the name to Micanopy's Town. Enticed by Bartram's vivid descriptions of the county in his well-received book, *Travels of William Bartram*, more settlers moved into the area, starting farms and cattle ranches. They demanded the Seminole lands. Rather than move to reservations, the Seminoles fought what was to become the Seminole Wars.

During the second Seminole War, Fort Defiance was built and burned, then rebuilt as Fort Micanopy. It's believed that the trading post and fort were located near present day Cholokka Boulevard, Micanopy's main street, a former ancient Native American trading path.

Strict development regulations that even protect old trees assure the town's preservation. Now, the only battles being fought in Micanopy are for parking spaces when visitors from around the state pour in on busy weekends.

Information
Alachua County Visitors & Convention Bureau, 30 E University Ave, Gainesville, FL 32601; 352/374-5231; www.co.alachua.fl.us/~acvacb.

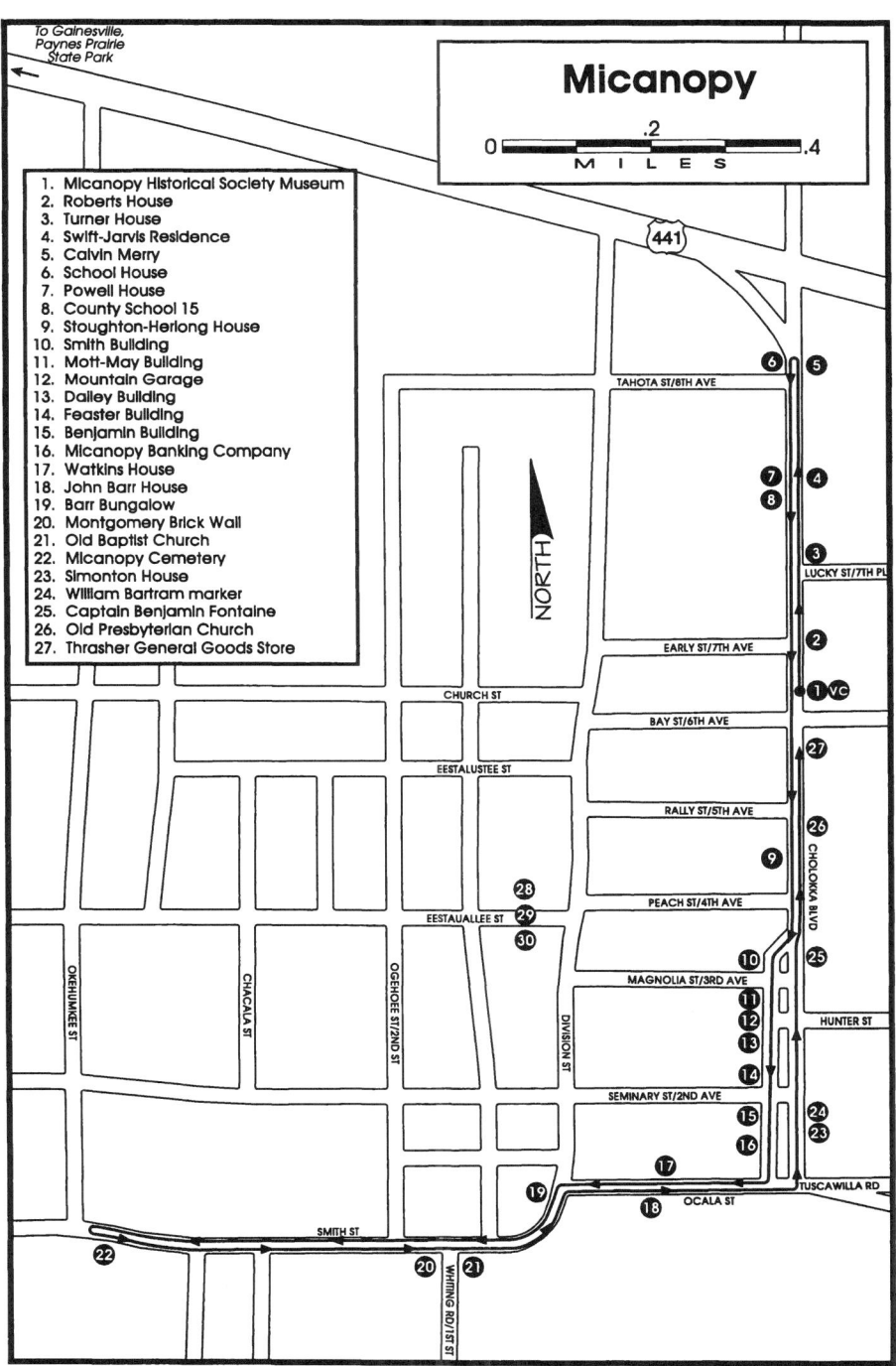

Micanopy

0 ⸻ .2 ⸻ .4
M I L E S

1. Micanopy Historical Society Museum
2. Roberts House
3. Turner House
4. Swift-Jarvis Residence
5. Calvin Merry
6. School House
7. Powell House
8. County School 15
9. Stoughton-Herlong House
10. Smith Building
11. Mott-May Building
12. Mountain Garage
13. Dailey Building
14. Feaster Building
15. Benjamin Building
16. Micanopy Banking Company
17. Watkins House
18. John Barr House
19. Barr Bungalow
20. Montgomery Brick Wall
21. Old Baptist Church
22. Micanopy Cemetery
23. Simonton House
24. William Bartram marker
25. Captain Benjamin Fontaine
26. Old Presbyterian Church
27. Thrasher General Goods Store

To Gainesville,
Paynes Prairie
State Park

NORTH

441

TAHOTA ST/8TH AVE
LUCKY ST/7TH PL
EARLY ST/7TH AVE
CHURCH ST
BAY ST/6TH AVE
EESTALUSTEE ST
RALLY ST/5TH AVE
PEACH ST/4TH AVE
EESTAUALLEE ST
MAGNOLIA ST/3RD AVE
HUNTER ST
SEMINARY ST/2ND AVE
OCALA ST
TUSCAWILLA RD
SMITH ST

OKEHUMKEE ST
CHACALA ST
OGEHOEE ST/2ND ST
DIVISION ST
CHOLOKKA BLVD
WHITING RD/1ST ST

Getting there
Take I-75 to exit 73 (CR-234). Go east to town. A more scenic drive is US-441. Gainesville International Airport is about 10 miles (25 minutes) north. The closest Amtrak and Greyhound stations are in Gainesville and Ocala.

First steps
For area maps and information, contact the **Alachua County Visitors & Convention Bureau.** It's open Monday to Friday 9 am to 5 pm. Most of the information you'll need is available at the **Micanopy Historical Society Museum**, where the tour starts, 352/466-3200; Cholokka Blvd; www.afn.org/~micanopy. It's open daily 1 pm to 4 pm. Admission is a $2 donation.

Many of the buildings do not have numbers, but none are difficult to locate. Streets crossing Cholokka Blvd have an alpha and numeric name on the signs.

Tours
The **Micanopy Historical Society Museum** leads walking tours $2 of the town the first Saturday of the month at 1 pm.

Historic Micanopy. *Walking the two-mile route takes you along Cholokka Blvd and three side streets. It takes about an hour.*

Start at the Micanopy Historical Society Museum. This treasure-trove of local history is a must stop. It's located in the Thrasher Warehouse, built in 1890 by J.E. Thrasher. Its odd shape is explained by the fact that it was built alongside the railroad tracks with service doors and a loading ramp. A Coca-Cola sign from the 1920s and the words No. 1 Thrasher Bros WHSE from the 1890s are still visible on the north side of the building. *Walk north up Cholokka Blvd.*

The **Roberts House** (#703), built around 1910, is a typical frame vernacular cabin that was constructed from the 1820s to 1920s. It has a deep metal roof over the porch. Two houses down, the 1920 **Turner House** (#707) is another frame vernacular house, but with a few decorative accents. The **Swift-Jarvis** residence at (#711) dates from 1910. The original building on the site dated from 1895. It had been constructed by Otis Feaster, who also built a three-story commercial building down the block and still has many descendants in town. **Calvin Merry** and his new wife moved into the two-story frame house partially hidden by large oaks and native plants at the corner in 1880. It's the oldest house on this side of the streets. *Cross the street and return down Cholokka Blvd.*

The small wood-frame **School House** (#802, corner of Tahota/8th Ave) provided primary education around 1920, then was moved here.

Captain Benjamin Powell returned from the Civil War in 1866 and built the two-story **Powell House** with a wrap-around porch. It's next to the brick Town Hall/Library, which originally served as **County School 15**. Its cornerstone reads, "God & Little Children."

The block's most elegant building is the two-story **Stoughton-Herlong House** (#402). It was built as a frame house in 1845 by R.S. Stoughton, but converted in 1915 by his son-in-law, Z.C. Herlong into the Classical Revival beauty it is today with 10 fireplaces, mahogany-inlaid oak floors, and leaded glass windows.

The 1920 **Smith Building** (south side of Peach/4th Ave) is one of the small commercial buildings built during the period. It has several novel features, including concrete-block columns, and a metal roof over a second-floor balcony. N.B. Mott built the **Mott-May Building** (#214) as a general store in the late 1800s. The second floor served as an undertaker's offices.

The words J.R. Mountain can still be read over one of the bays of the **Mountain Garage** (#212), which the namesake owner used as a service station from 1913 until the 1940s, when it became a bus station. Dr I.A. Dailey had his offices and a drugstore in the **Dailey Building** (south side of Seminary/2nd Ave) in the 1920s. Ornamentation of the **Feaster Building** is limited to segmental arches over the windows and corbelling at the roofline, as was typical of many turn-of-the century industrial buildings. It served as a general store, offices, and theater on the second floor.

Three shop fronts peak from under the porch roof of the brick **Benjamin Building**, which originally stood two stories and sold fancy linens and fabrics in 1885. The vault is still intact in the **Micanopy Banking Company** (last building on the street), opened in 1906 by John J. Barr. *Turn right on Ocala St.*

John J. Barr built the **Watkins House** (#104), a traditional Craftsman Bungalow, in 1916 for his daughter when she married John Watkins. It's across the street from his own house (#103), whose most interesting feature is the large oak tree that Chief Micanopy purportedly held council meetings under in the 1830s. The street dead-ends with another Craftsman Bungalow (#100 Division St) built for another Barr relative in 1923. *Turn left and continue walking around the corner as Division St becomes Smith St.*

Three structures are noteworthy on very quiet Smith St. The house that once stood behind the 1895 **Montgomery Brick Wall** (on the left) burned in the 1920s. Now an apartment building, the wood-frame **Old**

Baptist Church (#107) with a square metal bell tower was built in 1880. The Micanopy Cemetery a few houses down on the left went into service in 1826 and still operates. The older section is at the rear. The first pair of headstones as you enter the far gate are in pink granite. Francis Louise Vaughn's reads, "Life's uncertain, eat dessert first," under a bowl of food. *Return down Smith, then cross the street to the Cholokka's service road.*

The magnolia and live oak trees at the large Queen Anne Simonton House (#852, corner Cholokka and Ocala/Tuscawilla Rd) are much older than the residence built by James Simonton, in 1910. It has a wrap-around verandah and round turret, and was described in an article in *The Gainesville Sun* in 1911 as "one of the prettiest houses in Micanopy." Just past the house is a marker commemorating William Bartram's visit. Another Queen Anne house down the block was built by Captain Benjamin Fontaine (#209) in 1911 to replace the first house, which burned. Fontaine ran a phosphate business and a general store. The latter was located where the gazebo stands today. The wide wraparound porch, widow's walk, and columns with decorative capitals are interesting features. The Old Presbyterian Church built in 1870 was converted to the Mediator Episcopal Church. J.E. Thrasher conveniently located his brick General Goods Store (corner Bay/6th Ave) next to his warehouse. The words Thrasher 1923 appear just below the roofline. *Return to the museum.*

Lodging
There are only two places to stay in town, the first is the very elegant, historical Herlong Mansion ($$–$$$$, 800/HERLONG, 352/446-3322) that's filled with antiques at 402 Cholokka Blvd. The other is the more casual Shady Oak B&B ($$–$$$, 352/466-3476), which also serves as an ice-cream parlor and collectibles shop downstairs at Cholokka Blvd and Hunter St.

Arts & culture
Micanopy Historical Society Museum, (352/466-3200) at Cholokka Blvd; www.afn.org/~micanopy. It's open daily 1 pm to 4 pm. Admission is a $2 donation.

O Brisky Books (352/466-3910) in the Benjamin Building, at Cholokka Blvd and Seminary St carries new and used books.**

Food & drink
Dining is limited to two restaurants on Cholokka Blvd.

The small **Old Florida Cafe** ($, 352/466-3663) turns out tasty black beans and rice, sandwiches, soups made from scratch, and unforgettable desserts. Dine indoors or outdoors daily 10 am to 4 pm on the east side of Cholokka Blvd near Hunter/2nd Ave. **Mildred's Cottage Gourmet** ($, 352/466-0609) features sandwiches, five different scrumptious chicken salads, pasta salads, vegetarian dishes like broccoli couscous and black bean and corn salad at 102 NE Hunter Ave. Service is weekdays 10 am to 5 pm, except closed on Tuesday, and weekends 9 am to 5 pm, when breakfast is served until 11:30 am.

Ocala National Forest

Ocala National Forest lies between the St Johns and Oklawaha rivers in central Florida. It was established in 1908, making it the oldest national forest in the eastern United States. Within its 430,000-acre boundary lie central highlands, coastal lowlands, swamps, springs, streams, and hundreds of lakes and ponds. Almost half of the forest is sand pine scrub, hence its nickname, The Big Scrub. This sandy scrub habitat contrasts widely with the lushly vegetated semitropical communities around the springs.

The forest accommodates palms, pines, and hardwoods, more than 200 bird species, including bald eagles, sandhill cranes, wild turkeys, and scrub jays—rare in most of Florida, but abundant here—black bear, bobcats, white-tailed deer, gopher tortoises, and river otters.

Criss-crossing the forest are dozens of hiking trails, the longest of which is the Florida National Scenic Trail. The 67-mile Ocala section traverses longleaf pine forests, clumps of dwarf live oaks, cypress and gum swamps, and winding boardwalks. Dozens of other hikes range from one half to eight miles, some of which connect or loop across the Florida Trail. Many of these trails originate near the half dozen clear, bubbling springs, the forest's most historically significant features, which have attracted visitors to the area for their so-called medicinal healing powers since the early 1900s. Today's visitors take advantage of the waters' constant 72-degree temperatures at carefully developed recreation areas to swim, snorkel, scuba dive, canoe, kayak, and fish. They're a perfect spot to cool off after a hike.

The Visitor Center just west of Ocala on Hwy 40 has interesting exhibits of the forest's flora and fauna, and the history of man in the park, including the turpentining and lumbering industries.

The springs at Salt Springs Recreation Area have lifeguard service (May to September), new facilities, including showers, restrooms, a food concession, neighboring marina, and boat and canoe rentals. Besides the two-mile Salt Springs Trail accessed a mile south, walkers and hikers can access from the forest's marina next door a four-mile trail that connects with the Florida National Scenic Trail.

Ocala National Forest is very widely used, so the best time to come is during the week.

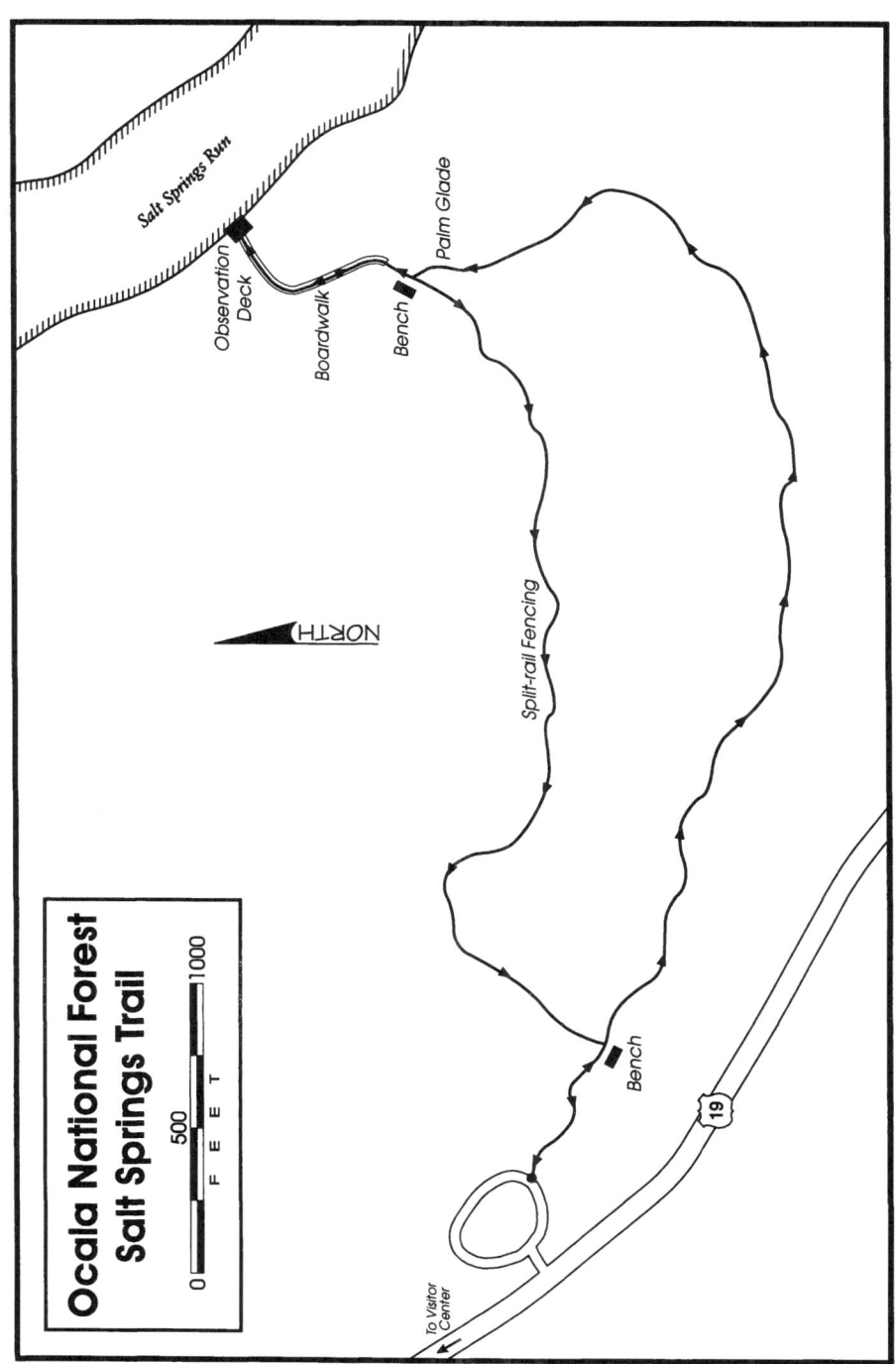

Ocala National Forest
Salt Springs Trail

Information
Ocala National Forest, Seminole Ranger District, 40929 State Road 19, Umatilla, FL 32784; 352/669-3135; Lake George Ranger District, 17147 E Hwy 40, Silver Springs, FL 34488; 352/625-2520; Salt Springs Visitor Center, 14100 Hwy 19 N, Salt Springs, FL 32134; 352/685-3070. Ocala-Marion County Chamber of Commerce, 110 E Silver Springs Blvd (Hwy 40), Ocala, FL 34470; 352/629-8051.

Getting there
Take I-75 to exit 69 (E Silver Springs Blvd/Hwy 40) east 10 miles to the first of three Ocala National Forest Visitor Centers. Salt Springs Trail is 18 miles northeast of the Ocala Visitor Center on Hwy 314. At Hwy 19, which crosses the forest from north to south, turn right and go almost a mile. The entrance, on the left, is easy to miss. Look for a small gray sign with an egret on it. Hwy 40 traverses the forest from east to west. Tampa and Orlando have the closest airports, about 60 miles away. Amtrak's (800/USA RAIL, 352/629-9863) station is at 531 NE 1st Ave. Greyhound (800/231-2222, 352/732-2677) has a station at 512 N Magnolia Ave.

First steps
For maps and information on Ocala National Forest, contact the Seminole Ranger District or Lake George Ranger District. For information about the Salt Springs Trail, contact the Salt Springs Visitor Center. All three are open daily 9 am to 5 pm. For area maps and information, contact the Ocala-Marion County Chamber of Commerce, which is open weekdays 8:30 am to 5 pm.

Tours
Ranger-led tours (352/625-2520) run once a week November to March. Call for a tour schedule.

Seasonal highlights
In spring wildflowers cover the landscape. It's also the peak birding season.

Ocala National Forest (Salt Springs Trail). *This 2-mile loop route covers sand pine and scrub habitats, hardwood hammock, sand pine flatwoods, bayheads, cypress, and a boardwalk and observation deck overlooking the Salt Springs Run.*

Start at the parking lot one mile south of the intersection of County Road 314 and US Hwy 19. It's 0.05 miles across a wood-chipped path to the Trailhead sign. The trail's white "sugar" sand floor is strewn with brown oak leaves. The canopy and understory are semi-open, providing lots of light and filtered sunshine. In the overstory look for sand pines (*Pinus clausa*) as well as an occasional oak. The understory is more diverse here, with scrub or sand live oak (*Quercus geminata*), Chapman's oak (*Q. chapmanii*), and myrtle oak (*Q myrtifolia*), as well as saw palmetto (*Serenoa repens*), and silk bay (*Persea humilis*). The latter, a small tree, is easily distinguished by silky shiny golden hairs on the underside.

The right edge of the trail is bordered by light green moss/lichen near the bench at 0.18 miles. In 100 feet the trail splits. *Take the right leg.*

There is less and less traffic noise as the trail gradually descends away from the road. The large, fragrant, creamy white flowers of the magnolia (*Magnolia grandiflora*) on the left at 0.34 miles bloom late spring through early summer.

At 0.44 miles on the right, there's a small oak with lipstick red blanket lichen (*Herpothallon rubrocinta*) coating the entire side facing the trail. Within 100 yards the habitat changes to an oak scrub characterized by much taller oaks draped in Spanish moss.

Just before the left trail leg rejoins the right trail leg, around 0.85 miles, more palms begin appearing. Stay to the right and the trail widens. For the next 100 feet there's ground lichen before the trail gradually narrows again. Ferns begin to appear along both sides of the trail around 0.94 miles. A short wooden bridge over wet ground is another indication that the sand scrub has given way to the hardwood hammock.

At one mile, the trail opens onto a bench in a clearing ringed with saw palmettos, a few tall pines, cabbage palms, and sensitive briar (*Mimosa quadrivalvis/Schrania microphylla*), whose bright pink fuzzy, spherical flowers on small leaflets close when touched. The trail narrows to a railed wood boardwalk and the overstory rises and becomes more dense with sweet gum (*Liquidambar styraciflua* L), identified by large five-lobed star-shaped leaves with rounded clusters of pendent flowers. The palms lining the boardwalk are significantly taller; the ferns denser.

The boardwalk ends in a wide observation deck with benches overlooking the Salt Springs Run, which originates about a mile up the run at Salt Springs and flows about four miles before discharging into Lake George. The large shrubs at the left rear of the deck with showing white globular, pincushion-like flowers on opposite or whorled 6-inch lanceolate to elliptical leaves are buttonbush (*Cephalanthus occidentalis*). The riverfront has lavendar-colored pickerelweed (*Pontederia cordata*), cattails (*Typha domingensis*), and maidencane (*Panicum hemitomon*). There's abundant wildlife on the run, including river otters, alligators, eagles, ospreys, and wading birds such as limpkins, several heron species, and snowy and American egrets. You're also likely to see boats and canoes plying the waters. *Return to the trail and take the right fork.*

At about 1.5 miles there's a section of split-rail fencing on the left. Twenty feet beyond it are two pines that show evidence of turpentining, the practice of extracting resin by cutting away sections of bark. It was a major industry at the turn of the century.

The tiny shiny blueberry (*Vaccinium myrsinites*) and its relative, highbush blueberry (*Vaccinium corymbosum*), line both sides of the trail for the next 100 feet. A few feet beyond, a section was removed from a log that fell across the trail. Just beyond it are more blueberries, as well as ferns, and more sensitive briar. Touch the leaves and watch them close up, but avoid the stem, which is prickly.

This leg of the trail is a pine-oak ridge with fewer pines, more oaks, saw palmettos, chinquapins, and many magnolias, especially around 1.75 miles. At just under 2 miles, the two legs rejoin. *Follow the trail back to the parking lot.*

The walk ends here, but you can enjoy the source of the run, Salt Springs, by leaving the parking lot and turning right, then right again at the intersection. Follow the road about a mile to the Salt Springs Recreation Area on the right. It's a $3 admission to swim in the springs, picnic, and use the spotless new facilities. Another visitor center is located a quarter mile farther.

Lodging

Other than a handful of historic inns and B&Bs around the forest and in Ocala, the accommodations are limited to moderately priced chains.

Without a doubt, the best place to stay close to the forest is the new 52-acre **Refuge at Ocklawaha** ($$$, 877/862-8873, 352/288-2233), an ecotourism resort with 11 one- to three-bedroom Florida vernacular style cottages with screened porches, locally made furnishings, and no TVs or phones, set among moss-draped oaks on the pristine 6,000-acre Ocklawa Prairie, a prime wildlife and bird-watching site at 14835 SE 85th St, on the southwest edge of Ocala National Forest. It has a restaurant, bar, pool, and miles of foot, bike, and horseback riding trails. The refuge is jointly partnered by the Florida Audubon Society, Pew Charitable Trusts, St Johns River Water Management District, Excel Legacy Corporation and ecotourism pioneer Stanley Selengut.

A unique place to stay within the forest is **Kerr City** ($$, 352/685-2557), a former 1880s lakefront town that was bought up by ancestors of the current owners when it went bust after the citrus freeze. They restored several two-story Florida frame vernacular cottages that are now used as guesthouses in a country setting at 22850 NE Hwy 316, three miles northwest of Salt Springs Recreation Area. The houses show a bit of age, but are comfortably furnished and have fireplaces.

In Ocala is the **Seven Sisters Inn** ($$$–$$$$, 352/867-1170), a richly decorated eight-room 1888 Queen Anne Victorian restored to better-than-new splendor and finely decorated and furnished at 820 SE Fort King St. Rooms have fireplaces, king beds, and private baths. The only thing better is the first-rate service. Another place where the innkeepers take good care of their guests is the **Heritage Country Inn** ($$, 352/489-0023), a six-room recently constructed B&B in a leafy setting at 14343 W Hwy 40. Each of the large guestrooms has a fireplace and private bath and is decorated in a different period style.

Food & drink

Dining within the park is mostly limited to concessions at the recreation areas. There are a few restaurants, some of which are open only on weekends or in winter season.

Within the park, next to the Silver Springs Visitor Center, you'll find **Leonors** ($, 352/685-0527) at 14100 Hwy 19N. It's a country diner with friendly waitresses who call you "honey" and serve substantial portions of burgers, sandwiches, fried chicken, and fish, with the usual sides of fries, greasy onion rings, fried okra, and slaw. There's entertainment Wednesday and Sunday evenings. Square Meal ($, 352/685-2288) also serves home-style dishes like chicken-fried steak, meatloaf, and open-faced roast beef sandwiches smothered in gravy a few doors down in the same complex at 14100 Hwy 19N.

Downtown Ocala has several good options, including **Petit Jardin** ($$$, 352/351-4140) at 2209 E Silver Springs Blvd. It's Ocala's finest restaurant. The menu changes weekly but always features a signature onion soup as well as several poultry, beef, seafood, and vegetarian dishes. With experience from Colorado to New York, the executive chef-owner is adept in southwestern, French, and German cooking. If dinner is too pricey, go for lunch, where the dishes are small versions of the delicious dinners at almost half the price. One of the most popular dishes at **The Bistro** ($$–$$$, 352/867-5980), an Italian restaurant at 917 E Silver Springs Blvd, is linguine à la malafemmina, which translates to something like tawdry woman's pasta, but is actually a delicious blend lobster, shrimp, and clams in an aromatic tomato sauce over pasta. Locals have been coming back to **Carmichael's** ($$, 352/622-3636) for 12 years to dine on made-from-scratch American food served three times a day at 3105 NE Hwy 40. **Harry's Seafood Bar & Grille** ($$, 352-840-0900) is a casual, fun regional chain that often is located in historic downtowns, as it is here at 24 SE First Ave.

Northwest Florida

"My own sense of history is that it belongs to human beings; they make history and are in turn affected by it whether they are noted, ordinary, or even obscure individuals."—Gene M Burnett in *Florida's Past: People And Events That Shaped The State* Volume 1.

Introduction

The Apalachee Indians occupied the Panhandle when Spanish explorer Tristán de Luna arrived in 1559 and established North America's first European settlement at Pensacola. Nearly wiped out by a hurricane, the village was abandoned after two years. There wasn't another long-lived settlement in the region until the Spanish reestablished an outpost nearby in 1698.

The region passed through Spanish, British, and French hands until 1812, when Andrew Jackson made an unauthorized capture of Pensacola in 1814. Panama City and Tallahassee—the latter designated the capital in 1824 because it was halfway between Pensacola and St Augustine—were other early cities of the region.

After the Apalachee were eliminated, Seminole Indians, descendants of Creek Indians, moved into the region. Their stay was short-lived. Even before Florida was a state, Andrew Jackson—later to become the state's provisional general and the nation's president—began systematically driving the British, Spanish, and Native Americans out of the Panhandle and eventually the rest of Florida.

Jackson's actions started the first of Florida's three Seminole Wars in 1818. By 1823, many Seminole leaders had signed the Treaty of Moultrie Creek, which required them to leave northern Florida for reservations south of Ocala. This left the region open for white settlers.

Tobacco and cotton farming, Coca Cola, fishing, and the military played major roles in the region's development. Today, tourism, fishing, farming, and the military lead the region's economy.

The Northwest region could easily hold the Florida titles of "Least Visited," "Least Developed," and "Most Different." Sandwiched between Alabama and Georgia on the north and the Gulf of Mexico on the south, the topography is markedly different from other parts of the state. Unlike most of Florida, there are scenic bluffs, steep-sided ravines, and modest hills. Here, the trees change color in autumn, the beaches have fine white sand, and the dunes are higher. A string of barrier islands runs along the coast to Apalachicola, where the coastline changes to saltmarsh. There are abundant rivers, springs, and caves.

Although most of the population resides along the seashore and new towns such as Seaside are springing up along the Gulf, there are few major cities and many large national, state, and county parks and refuges that protect the coast from overdevelopment. Two large military bases with vast open land around airfields provide additional green space.

Downtown Pensacola

Pensacola is the largest city in the Florida Panhandle. Endowed with more than 40 miles of scenic Gulf Coast shoreline, more than 400 years of history, and the Pensacola Naval Air Station, home of the Blue Angels flying team, today's Pensacola is a well-organized tourist destination that promotes its cultural, eco, and Naval heritage with great zeal. Closer to New Orleans, Birmingham, Mobile, and Atlanta than it is to Jacksonville, Orlando, Tampa, or Miami, Pensacola retains much of its Old South charms. This it combines with several centuries of influence by Spanish, French, African, and British pioneers.

It all comes together in the historic downtown, one of the Florida's best examples of historic preservation . The area has been thoroughly researched, unearthed, restored, and revitalized. Historic commercial, government, and residential buildings have been readapted to house museums, restaurants, galleries, cultural centers, nightclubs, and accommodations, keeping downtown buzzing day and night. Most everything is within a short walking distance or trolley ride.

When Spanish explorers first came ashore at Pensacola in 1559 led by Don Tristan de Luna, the area was inhabited by Panzacola Indians. The 1,400 colonists with de Luna established a short-lived settlement that was destroyed by a major hurricane. It was not until 1698 that explorers successfully established a permanent village. Aided by enslaved Africans, the Spanish built a fort on Pensacola Bay. This was destroyed by French forces from Mobile, Alabama, in 1719. A third outpost was destroyed by a hurricane in 1722. The Spanish rebuilt in 1752 and named the city Pensacola after the native residents. The British enlarged the outpost. Over the next 250 years, the city changed hands among the Spanish, French, English, Confederates, and Americans. The University of West Florida Archaeology Institute has uncovered evidence of fortifications that Spanish, British, and American soldiers occupied between 1752 and 1821 under much of what is now the Historic Pensacola Village.

It wasn't until the 19th century that the city really took off. The Navy shipyard was established in 1825 and became the Pensacola Naval Air Station, increasing jobs, industry, and population. Fishing, brick making, the railroad, and lumber were the dominant industries throughout the century. Today, tourism and the military drive the economy.

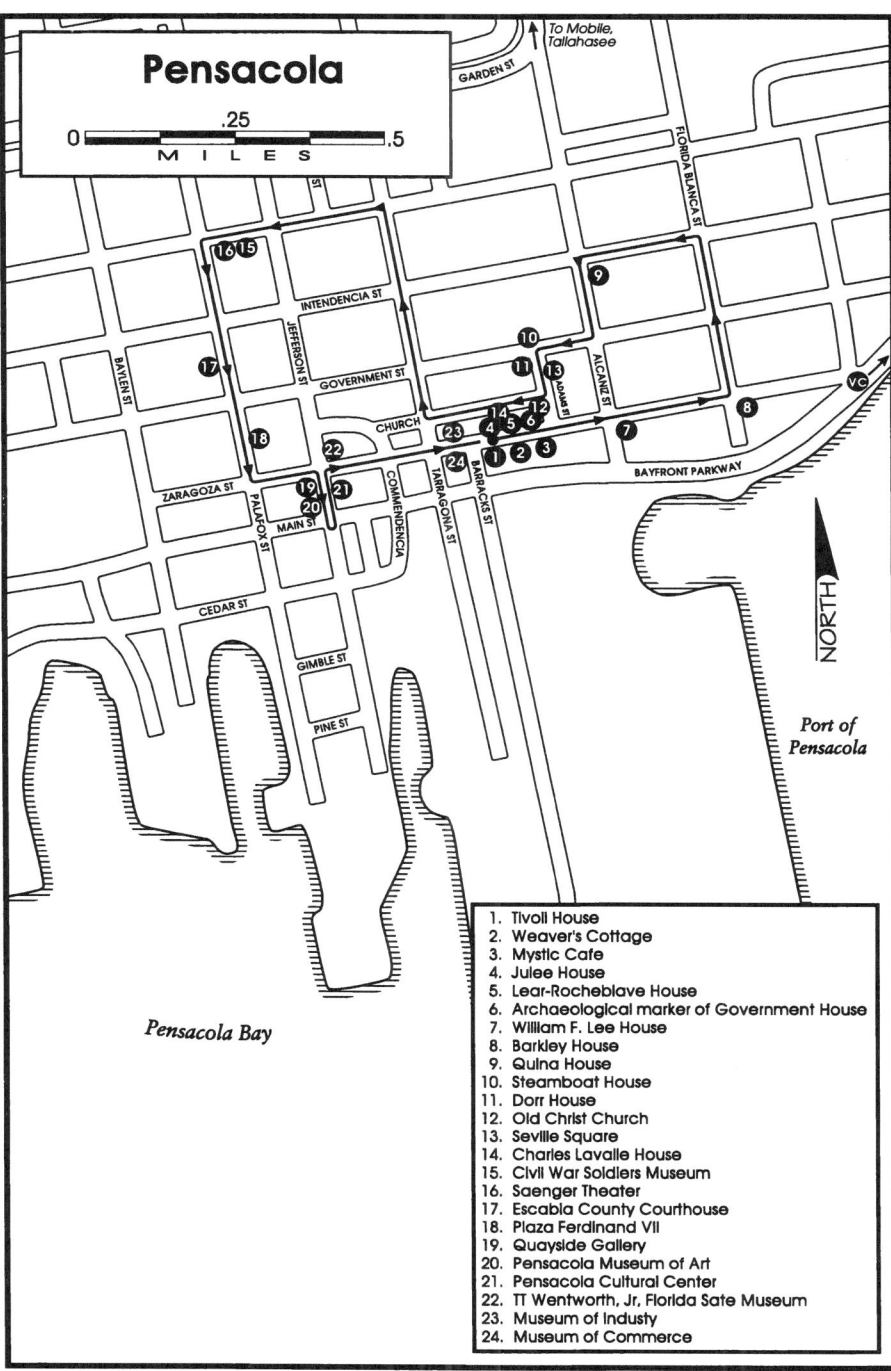

Pensacola

0 |======= .25 =======| .5
M I L E S

Pensacola Bay

Port of
Pensacola

1. Tivoli House
2. Weaver's Cottage
3. Mystic Cafe
4. Julee House
5. Lear-Rocheblave House
6. Archaeological marker of Government House
7. William F. Lee House
8. Barkley House
9. Quina House
10. Steamboat House
11. Dorr House
12. Old Christ Church
13. Seville Square
14. Charles Lavalle House
15. Civil War Soldiers Museum
16. Saenger Theater
17. Escabia County Courthouse
18. Plaza Ferdinand VII
19. Quayside Gallery
20. Pensacola Museum of Art
21. Pensacola Cultural Center
22. TT Wentworth, Jr, Florida Sate Museum
23. Museum of Industy
24. Museum of Commerce

Information
Pensacola Convention and Visitor Information Center, 1401 E Gregory St, Pensacola, FL 32501; 800/874-1234, 850/434-1234; www.visitpensacola.com. Historic Pensacola Village, 120 E Church St, Pensacola, FL 32501; 850/444-8905.

Getting there
Take I-10 to I-110 south to exit 1, follow signs to Visitor Information Center, which is about one mile east of the historic district. Pensacola Regional Airport (850/435-1745, www.flypensacola.com) is served by USAirways, Delta, Continental, and Northwest airlines. Amtrak's (800/USA RAIL, 850/433-4966) station is at 980 Heinberg St. Greyhound (800/231-2222, 850/476-4800) has a station at 505 W Burgess Rd.

First steps
For area maps and information, contact the Pensacola Convention and Visitor Information Center. Downtown streets can be confusing. Some are one-way, some are closed off. To get your bearings, board the Trolley ($.25) to familiarize yourself with the area. Two lines run through downtown and the adjoining bayfront and take 15 and 30 minutes. Trolleys have been part of Pensacola's history since 1832. Don't be confused by the varied spelling of a few streets, such as Zaragoza, which is also Zarragossa.

Seasonal highlights
Summer is high season along the Gulf Coast and rates are 20 to 30 percent higher.

Tours
Historic Pensacola Village offers interesting guided tours of the village daily. The cost is $6 for adults, $5 for seniors and military, $2.50 for children under 16 years.

Historic downtown Pensacola. *This 2-mile route covers part of the historic downtown area, specifically the Seville Historic District. Several museums and houses along the route are part of Historic Pensacola Village and require admission ($6 for all of them) payable at the Tivoli House. The tickets are good for a week, so you can visit them at your leisure. Three of the houses have guided tours at set times. See Tours above.*

Start at the Tivoli House, 205 E Zaragoza St, between Tarragona and Adams streets. The Tivoli House is a reconstruction of the original house on the site, which was a boarding and gaming house with a theater and ballroom used by early residents. Walking east on Zaragoza St, next door is a hip-roof house built in 1888 and today known as the Weaver's Cottage

(207 E Zaragoza St) for its exhibits of textile manufacturing, from spinning and dying to weaving and carding. Two doors down is the **Mystic Cafe** (221 E Zaragoza St), originally a two-room honeymoon cottage built by Francisco Moreno for one of his daughters. Across the street is the **Julee House** (204 E Zaragoza St), erected in 1790 at 214 W Zaragoza as a two-room cottage, then purchased for $300 in 1804 by a freed enslaved black woman named Julee, who lived there along with other freed enslaved people over many years. Alongside the house is a well dating from about 1815. It was uncovered during an archaeological dig. The next building is the **Lear-Rocheblave House** (214 E Zaragoza St), a two-story Victorian beauty built in 1890 by John and Kate Lear, who divorced before moving into the house. Its second namesake owner was a colorful tugboat owner who ran guns and Cubans to Cuba before the Spanish American War. He sold the house and the boat in 1910. The house later became Mrs Snowden's Boardinghouse. Anecdote-rich tours of Julee House and Lear-Rocheblave House are given by Historic Pensacola Village. Next door is another archaeological marker indicating the foundation of the three-story **Government House**, which was demolished in 1821. *Continue on Zaragoza, crossing Adams and Alcaniz streets.*

The namesake owner of the **William F Lee House** (corner of Alcaniz and Zaragoza) came to Pensacola in the 1850s as a railroad surveyor, then joined the Confederate Army, where he lost an arm. He married and built the house on Gregory St in the 1860s. To save it from demolition when the street was widened, it was moved to this location and now operates as the headquarters for a real estate organization. The exquisite **Barkley House** was built by a British merchant and customs inspector who married a woman of French descent in New Orleans. The house's design reflects both styles. While the interior is very British, the exterior is French Creole, typical of Louisiana plantation houses. It's occupied by the Pensacola Heritage Foundation, which offers tours. *Turn left onto Florida Blanca St, then left onto Intendencia St, and left onto Alcaniz St.*

Italian-born Desiderio Quina, who lived in the 1810 **Quina House** (204 S Alcaniz St), now a museum of the Pensacola Historic Preservation Society, moved to Spain and joined the Spanish Army, which brought him to Pensacola. He left the army and became a shopkeeper, then an apothecary. The house was built in a Spanish style and is one of Pensacola's oldest structures on its original foundation. It has two front doors, brick piers, and a double chimney in the center of the house. *Turn right onto Government St.*

The first two owners of the 1881 ship-shaped **Steamboat House** (308 E Government St) had bad luck. The builder, Dionicio Reache was a merchant, not a seaman, who lost his fortune and house. The second owner, a grocer, was widowed once and divorced twice during his 19-year-ownership. The third family, headed by Manuel Gonzalez of Spain, was a successful tobacco manufacturer and used his basement to cool the tobacco during his 35-year tenure. *Turn left onto Adams St.*

In 1871, following the death of one of her sons and her young husband, a lumber executive in Bagdad, Florida, Clara Barkley Dorr, daughter of the owners of the Barkley House, returned to Pensacola with her five remaining young children and built the Greek Revival **Dorr House** (311 S Adams St). Tours are given by Historic Pensacola Village. In the next block is the recently renovated and reopened **Old Christ Church**, named after Christ Church of Philadelphia, which donated funds for its construction. It is the oldest church building in the state. Hand-hewn heart pine beams cross the ceilings. Now operated as a museum by the Pensacola Historical Society, the church also served as a Union barracks, hospital, and stable, as well as a Negro Episcopal church, and library. Across the street is **Seville Square**, named after the Spanish city. As part of a fortification, the British built four guard houses and four block houses around the Public Square. The Spanish later replotted the town, keeping Seville Square open. Bricks from one of the British guardhouses on the square were used to build the church. *Turn right onto Church St.*

Tours of the **Charles Lavalle House** (205 E Church St), which is accessed through the picket fence, are given by Historic Pensacola Village. It was built as a duplex rental house in French Colonial style in 1805 on Government Street by Charles Lavalle, a real estate tycoon, and Marianna Bonifay, a married French woman who migrated from Santo Domingo during a revolt of enslaved people. It was moved here in 1968, restored, and furnished with period pieces. *Turn right onto Tarragona St, crossing Government and Intendencia before turning left onto Romana St and left onto Palafox St.*

The **Civil War Soldiers Museum** (108 S Palafox) displays the private collection of Confederate army and navy artifacts gathered by a local physician. Built in 1923 by New Orleans entrepreneur Julien Saenger, the Spanish Baroque Revival **Saenger Theater** (118 S Palafox) featured state-of-the-art facilities and elaborate decoration inside and outside. Saenger built several other theaters before going broke and killing himself during the Depression. The building that now serves as the **Escambia County Courthouse** (corner of Government and Palafox) was originally erected as a Federal building in 1854. It was so unattractive that its burning in 1880 was almost a relief. An attractive new building replaced it in 1887, until it became too small in 1937. The Federal government swapped the building for a County structure and it became the courthouse. On the left in the next block is **Plaza Ferdinand VII** (between Government and Zaragoza, Palafox and Jefferson), named after a Spanish king. Part of the original Spanish Parade Grounds, it served as the site at which Spain ceded Florida to the United States at a ceremony involving Andrew Jackson and Jose Callava, the Spanish Governor, on July 17, 1821. *At the corner of Zaragoza and Jefferson, make a short detour onto Jefferson St.*

To the right and on the right is the **Quayside Gallery** (15-17 E Zaragoza St) in a two-story building constructed in 1873 one block north of the wharves. It was the headquarters and social center for the Germania Steam Fire Engine and Hose Company, which housed the "Marie Louise," a 2.5-ton horse-drawn steam pumping engine. Next door is the **Pensacola Museum of Art** (407 S Jefferson St) in the Spanish Revival former jail building dating from 1906. The bars have come in handy to protect the artwork. Across the street is the **Pensacola Cultural Center** (400 S Jefferson St), which once housed jail cells and hospital facilities for men and women, a guard's room, sheriff's office, and a visitor's room. All of the cells faced the gallows. The north side of the Center was the Court of Record Building with a courtroom and chambers for the judge, solicitor, and jurors. The original marble staircase connecting the first and second floors of the Court of Record Building remains intact. On the northeast corner of Zaragoza and Jefferson is the commanding **T.T. Wentworth, Jr Florida State Museum** (320 S Jefferson St) built in 1907 as the City Hall in what was described as "Gulf Spanish" style, an early Mediterranean Revival construction. It featured the gas and electric fixtures as well as 200 opera-style seats so residents could watch meetings. It now contains a wonderful museum that features exhibits ranging from artwork and African-American artifacts to antique photographs and a children's museum. *Return to Zaragoza St and turn left.*

On the left is the **Museum of Industry** (200 E Zaragoza St), which houses exhibits of Pensacola's three most important early industries—brick making, lumbering, and fishing—as well as some railroad exhibits. Across the street is the **Museum of Commerce** (201 E Zaragoza St), designed as a replica of an early Pensacola streetscape. The businesses—toy store, print shop, hardware, and music store among them—from which the rich assembly of artifacts were drawn all existed along Palafox St. *Return to the Tivoli House, where is water, snacks, and restrooms.*

Lodging

Accommodations within walking distance of the historic district are limited to a handful of historic B&Bs and a few hotels, but there are lots of choices within a five-minute drive. If you're willing to drive up to 20 minutes, you can add lodgings on the beach to your list of choices. Most places offer free pickup from the airport, train, or bus station.

The **Pensacola Victorian Bed & Breakfast** ($$–$$$, 800/370-8354, 850/434-2818) has an inviting front porch with rocking chairs, homemade sweet treats, and spacious rooms in historic downtown. The **Marsh House** ($$–$$$, 850/433-4866) at 205 Cevallos St is a beautiful B&B downtown near the historic district with lots of extras, including comfortable top-of-the-line mattresses and airport pickup service. North of the downtown historic district is the North Hill Preservation District, where the early 1900s **Noble Manor Bed & Breakfast** ($$–$$$, 850/434-9544) is located at 110 W Strong St. Antique-furnished rooms, a billiard game room, lush plants, and an elegant breakfast table make for a first-class stay. The **Yacht House Bed & Breakfast** ($$–$$$, 850/433-3634) is larger than most B&Bs, but that doesn't detract from its personal appeal. The 21 antique-filled rooms are contained in two early 1900 buildings with screened porches and decks at 1820 Cypress St, near the historic Pensacola Yacht Club.

The **Pensacola Grand Hotel** ($$, 800/348-3336, 850/433-3336) was designed by L&N Railroad engineers and built in 1912 at 200 E Gregory St. The old building serves as the lobby and public areas. Modern, spacious guest rooms are in an adjoining glass high-rise. The **New World Landing** ($$, 850/434-7736) was built as a box factory in the late 1800s on land that was created by the accretion of 38,000 tons of ballast emptied by sailing vessels arriving from throughout the world at 600 S Palafox St across the street from the historic district. The large rooms are well-appointed with slightly worn upholstered furniture, an armoire, custom-made toiletries, and a phone in the bathroom.

Arts & culture

Downtown's historic buildings make perfect venues for Pensacola's active arts scene, which includes more than a dozen galleries, theater, and museums. Thrice yearly the Downtown Arts District Association (DADA) stages a **Midsummer Night's Eve Gallery Night** (850/432-9906). Two trolleys and one bus provide free transportation to the 15 member galleries, which have open house, demonstrations, hors d'oeuvres, and entertainment.

The Classical Revival **Pensacola Cultural Center** houses the Pensacola Little Theatre, a museum, offices, dance studios, exhibition/ conference rooms, a three-story atrium, library, rehearsal hall, and board room. It's home to the African American

Heritage Society, Kaleidoscope Dance Theatre and Ballet Pensacola, Communities in Schools, and the West Florida Literary Federation. Each year the **Pensacola Little Theatre** (850/432-2042) presents six main shows on its 474-seat state-of-the-art center stage, two shows for children, and four one-act plays on a small stage at 400 S Jefferson, in the Pensacola Cultural Center. The **Pensacola Opera**'s (850 /433-6737) season runs January through March with guest soloists from such distinguished companies as the Metropolitan Opera at the Saenger Theatre. The renovated **Saenger Theatre**, an elaborate Spanish Baroque Renaissance building erected in 1923 at 118 S Palafox St, hosts touring Broadway shows as well as university productions and the symphony, opera, and ballet. The **Seville Dinner Theatre** presents dinner or brunch with plays, musicals, comedies, mysteries, and late night cabaret nightly throughout the year at 241 E Garden St.

The **Adams Street Artists Gallery** features the works of several local artists at 305 Adams St. The **Muse Gallery** at 223 W Gregory St features art, furniture, and accessories created by local artists. While **Moon Dance**'s centerpiece is its large collection of beads, it also features gifts and works by local artists at 423 E Government St. **Quayside Gallery**, one of the city's finest art centers, is the largest co-op gallery in the Southeast and has an eclectic collection of art in textiles, watercolors, and other media at 17 E Zaragoza St. **Bayfront Gallery** at 713 S Palafox has a phenomenal collection of blown art glass, ranging from a four-tiered glass fountain to paperweights. Rock Hard, the artists/owner of **Rock Hard Designs** showcases handmade jewelry at 16 N Palafox. At **Twelve South Palafox Gallery** at 12 S Palafox Pl the walls and floors are lined with paintings, wood furniture, pottery, and sculptures. **Schmidt's Gallery** at 8 S Palafox St carries an exceptional collection of paintings by regional and nationally recognized artists.

In addition to the museums on the tour, don't miss the **National Museum of Naval Aviation**, one of the largest aviation museums in the world at 1750 Radford Blvd, Naval Air Station Pensacola. It's loaded with exhibits of airplanes as well as a moving Vietnam POW exhibit and an IMAX Theater. Also noteworthy are the eight-acre **Historic St Michael's Cemetery**, which has been in use since 1781 and is open to the public with a free self-guided walking tour brochure, at the corner of Garden and Alcaniz streets, and the **University of West Florida Archaeology Institute** with exhibits of pre-Columbian, colonial and post-colonial artifacts taken from northwest Florida sites, in the Margaret Jane Smith Archaeology Institute Bldg, UWF main campus, 11000 University Pkwy. Free guided tours are given Wednesdays (850/474-3015).

Food & drink

There are many dining options, from small lunch eateries to fine restaurants, within Pensacola's downtown historic district that cater to the neighboring business community, locals who return to downtown at night, and a large number of visitors. Prices run from inexpensive to moderate, with a sprinkling of expensive choices.

The Cajun Experience ($, 850/432-4848) at 424 E Government St serves Louisiana-spiced homestyle cooking, including po-boys for lunch and dinner. **Frank Bennett's** ($$–$$$, 850-435-0930) serves innovative lunches starting at $4.50 and more pricey dinners with entertainment in a sophisticated setting at 25 S Palafox St. Wine connoisseurs who visit Pensacola make a point to stop at **Jamie's Wine Bar & Restaurant** ($$–$$$, 850/434-2911)at 424 E Zaragoza, which has been recognized by The Wine Spectator and other publications for its fine selection of wine and delicious dishes like grilled portabello mushroom and escargot with roasted garlic and cabernet sauce. **Jackson's** ($$–$$$, 850/469-9898) combines Southern style with haute cuisine in a white tablecloth setting at 400 S Palafox St. The quality is just as fine, but the food is much more creative—such as sesame crusted grouper with tempura fried zucchini and sweet potato drizzled with cranberry glaze and basmati rice—at **Dharma Blue** ($$–$$$, 850/433-1275), which also has a sushi bar at 300 S Alcaniz. The atmosphere is laid-back, the seafood is prepared in dishes like ginger grouper, and the sushi is fresh at the **Fish House Dockside Bar & Grill** ($$, 850/470-0003) at Palafox and Gregory streets. The **Nautical Steam Shack** ($$, 850/456-8070) at 3050 Barrancas Ave is probably the only place where you'd want to eat a Garbage Bowl. This house specialty features a huge bowl of steamed crabs, oysters, shrimp, and vegetables. At the **Palace Oyster Bar** ($$–$$$, 850/434-6211) the seafood is prepared with a dash of creativity and a huge dollop of skill at 130 E Government St in Seville Quarter.

There are numerous places to stop for a quick, inexpensive bite of lunch. Among them are **Breezes Coastal Cafe** ($, 850/GET-FOOD), which serves fresh salads and hot entrees at 304 S Alcaniz St; **Ever'man Natural Foods** ($, 850 /438-0402), whose deli prepares healthful foods at 315 W Garden St; **Mystic Cafe** ($, 850/432-5200)at 221 E Zaragoza St, where the gumbo is good and hot, the daily specials include red beans and rice and jambalaya, and the cookies, fresh from a local bakery, are served soft and warm.

There are also several noteworthy choices across the bridge on Pensacola Beach, including **Chan's Gulfside** ($$–$$$$, 850/932-3525)at 2 1/2 Via de Luna, which has two restaurants: one is an award-winning fine dining establishment and the other has casual outdoor seafood dining. While the indoor and outdoor beach setting with entertainment may be very rustic at **Peg Leg Pete's** ($$–$$$, 850/932-4139) at 1010 Fort Pickens Rd, the large portions of well-prepared seafood seem to come straight out of a New Orleans kitchen.

Nightlife

Pensacola's nightlife ranges from evening concert series to clubs and bars that feature live entertainment, both local and touring groups. There's something for every age, including teens.

Pensacola's best blues club is the **Blues Angels Club,** where local and guest acts perform inside the Seville Dinner Theatre complex at 241 E Garden St. Another night spot that rates a superlative is the **Seville Quarter,** a complex of seven clubs/bars/restaurants that feature different types of music and dancing nightly at 130 E Government St. The laughs keep coming Fridays and Saturdays at the **Comedy Zone** in the Palafox Restaurant & Trolley Lounge, 11 S Palafox St. The Pensacola Heritage Foundation presents the annual free **Evenings in Olde Seville Square** series of Thursday evening outdoor concerts throughout the summer at Seville Square, between Adams and Alcaniz and Government and Zaragoza streets. **Sluggo's** attracts a younger crowd for the live performances by local and visiting bands at 130 S Palafox St. The **Cigar Brewery** is noted for its variety and quality, featuring blues and rock groups and solo acts as well as acoustic solos at Zaragoza St. If it's the blues you're looking for, look no farther than **Kooter Brown's West,** which serves it up several times a week at 7601 W US 98. The **Jazz Society of Pensacola** (850/433-8382) presents inexpensive concerts at various venues in town. Ditto the **Blues Society of Northwest Florida** (850/505-9878). Over on Pensacola Beach, there's another series of free summer evening concerts at Quietwater Beach Boardwalk or the Gulfside Pavilion.

Events

Pensacola has an extensive events calendar featuring arts and cultural celebrations. For information about the listed events, call 800/874-1234.

March is a cultural feast featuring the annual **Festival of the Arts Downtown** and **Pensacola Music Festival,** and **Pensacola Jazz Fest.** Beginning in May, the **Evenings in Olde Seville** concert series takes place every Thursday through August. June hosts the city's biggest celebration, the **Fiesta of Five Flags,** which celebrates the five countries—Spain, France, Britain, the Confederacy, and the United States—that have flown flags over the city. The town goes crazy eating crab cakes, crab claws, crab chowder, crab salad, and any other crab dish they can concoct during the annual three-day **Crabfest** (850/434-6211) in July. This happens just after the **Blue Angels Air Show.** September and October feature the **Blues on the Beach Concert Series** and the **Latin Heritage Festival,** respectively. The **Great Gulfcoast Arts Festival** attracts artists and art lovers and is held in November. So is the **Frank Brown International Songwriters Festival.** The year closes with the annual New Year's Eve cultural festival called **First Night Pensacola.**

Seaside

Seaside, the forerunner of the New Urbanism movement, is a 1980s recreation of an old-fashioned small beach town made up of architecturally charming wooden houses with wide porches and picket fences on small lots lining narrow brick lanes. Nearly 300 "cottages" are spaced out on 80 acres at the water's edge. Everything—the beach, shops and galleries, restaurants, town square, post office, and recreational facilities—is within walking distance.

The idea was to develop a community reflecting the regional building tradition that would create "coherence, cohesion, and a strong sense of place." It would once again give residents a feeling of belonging, a sense of community. It would alleviate sprawl.

It works beautifully. People talk to one another. People know one another. The architecture is beautiful and the streets are comfortable, safe, and pleasant to walk. It's a great place for families. Children safely play in the streets and ride their bikes around town unchaperoned. The pace is slow. There are day and evening recreational and cultural activities for young and old.

That said, critics say it's too much like Disneyworld, contrived. They say that it really isn't a community, because people live in their communities year round, and most of Seaside's houses are vacation rentals part of the year. They say that though great efforts go toward maintaining an architectural mix, there is an inescapable homogeneity. As examples, they site the white picket fences in front of almost every house. Though of different design, they create uniformity. Most fences feature a similar white sign with blue lettering indicating the house's name (if it has one), the owner's name, and the owner's original hometown. They point out that on the beach, all of the umbrellas and chairs have the same design and royal blue color—a few green ones at the eastern end—and are lined up at the same distance from the sea. There is no industry. They claim that it lacks ethnic diversity as well, too.

In Steven Brooke's *Seaside*, founder Robert Davis grants that Seaside is "an idealized vision of a town, and...as a holiday town...does not contain a full complement of human activities." But he believes that "Its idealized vision can be translated to 'real' cities. And the compromises necessary in the translation will likely produce a result which, in the end, is more satisfactory than the 'ideal.'"

Pros and cons aside, Seaside remains an interesting place, a place worth experiencing if only as food for thought. Few communities have so

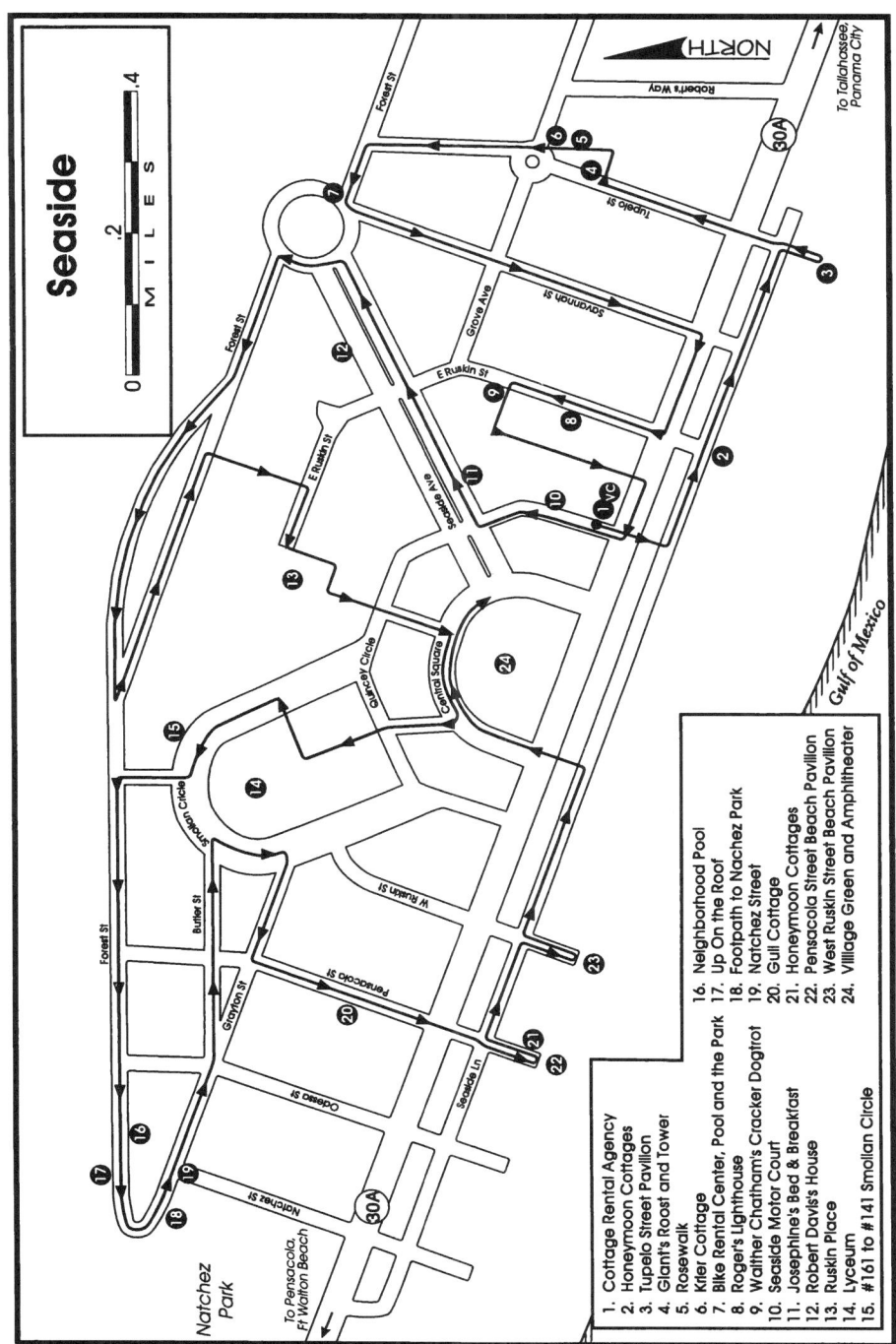

Seaside

1. Cottage Rental Agency
2. Honeymoon Cottages
3. Tupelo Street Pavilion
4. Giant's Roost and Tower
5. Rosewalk
6. Krier Cottage
7. Bike Rental Center, Pool and the Park
8. Roger's Lighthouse
9. Walther Chatham's Cracker Dogtrot
10. Seaside Motor Court
11. Josephine's Bed & Breakfast
12. Robert Davis's House
13. Lyceum
14. Ruskin Place
15. #161 to #141 Smollan Circle
16. Neighborhood Pool
17. Up On the Roof
18. Footpath to Nachez Park
19. Natchez Street
20. Gull Cottage
21. Honeymoon Cottages
22. Pensacola Street Beach Pavilion
23. West Ruskin Street Beach Pavilion
24. Village Green and Amphitheater

many exceptional architectural designs. More importantly, it is the harbinger of one of the most significant trends in America: a change in the pattern of urban and suburban growth. Since the first buildings were erected in 1982, dozens of similar communities have been developed across the country as an antidote to endless sprawl.

Information

Seaside Visitors Bureau, Hwy 30-A, PO Box 4870, Seaside, FL 32459; 888/SEA-SIDE; seasideinfo@seasidefl.com; www.seasidefl.com. Seaside Cottage Rental Agency, east side of Central Square; 800/277-8696. Beaches of South Walton Visitor Information Center, corner of Hwy 98 and Hwy 283, PO Box 1248, Santa Rosa Beach, FL 32459; 800/822-6877, 850/267-1216.

Getting there

Take I-10 to exit 14 (Hwy 331 south). Go east at Hwy 98, then south on Hwy 283, and east on Hwy 30-A to Seaside. It's about seven miles from the Beaches of South Walton Visitor Information Center on the corner of Hwy 98 and Hwy 283. The closest major airports are Panama City Airport (850/763-6751) 40 miles east, Pensacola Regional Airport (850/435-1745, www.flypensacola.com) 70 miles west, and Tallahassee Airport 110 miles northeast. Amtrak's (800/USA RAIL) closest stations are in Crestview, about 60 miles northwest, and Chipley, about 60 miles northeast. Greyhound's (800/231-2222) closest station is in Fort Walton Beach.

First steps

For area maps and information, stop in the Beaches of South Walton Visitor Information Center. Stop at the Seaside Cottage Rental Agency for maps, information, and walking tour brochures. Architectural photographer Steven Brooke's coffeetable book, Seaside ($20), is an insightful and colorful portrait of this unique community.

Seasonal highlights

Summer is high season along the Gulf Coast and rates are considerably higher.

Seaside. *This 2-mile route covers the original and new sections of Seaside. Allow about 90 minutes which includes a little time for gazing out at the beautiful sea.*

Start at the Cottage Rental Agency, located on the east side of the Central Square. Cross County Road 30-A and walk west along the sandy footpath that parallels the shore.

The Cottage Rental Agency is designed as a traditional dog-trot, one of the earliest styles used by Florida pioneers in north Florida. On the right are the **Honeymoon Cottages**, rising two stories out of beachfront dunes. They were designed after Thomas Jefferson's Cottage at Monticello. *At Tupelo St, turn right and walk out to the Tupelo Pavilion that overlooks the sea, then return across the street and walk north on Tupelo St.* Seaside streets empty onto Hwy 30-A across from the beach. Each neighborhood has its own beach and pavilion. The latter serve as gateways to the sea. The Tupelo Street pavilion is the town's logo. Tupelo Street was the original Seaside street and thus has more mature landscaping, all of which is required to be native. Architect Deborah Berke designed the tower of **Giant's Roost and Tower** (#109) as a small vacation getaway in 1983. Years later, the main house was added.

Turn right through the round arch between #107 and #109 Tupelo St to enter the Rosewalk. The **Rosewalk** is a neighborhood within a neighborhood. Its 14 houses, among the first constructed in Seaside, are built around lush native landscaping with a natural sand path connecting them. *As the path forks, bear left and exit along the steps onto Grove Ave, then turn left, then right onto the north half of Tupelo St.*

Note that the street ends in a circle with a gazebo, the way most Seaside streets end. Take a moment to view the lofty **Krier Cottage** (#115). Each floor has only one room, the one bedroom on the ground floor, the living room on the second, and the studio/temple with a library and fabulous views on the third. It features a loggia on the first and second floors. *Turn left onto Forest St.*

On the right are the Bike Rental Center, Pool, and the Park, a natural area connected by footpaths. *Turn left onto Savannah St. Turn right onto Hwy 30-A, then right onto E Ruskin St.*

There are two exceptional houses on Ruskin. With a skeletal wood frame exterior, **Roger's Lighthouse** (#110), designed by architect Victoria Casasco, appears to have its insides out. Walther Chatham's futuristic update on a classic Cracker dogtrot style features two peak-roofed houses (#116) on separate wood platforms joined by a wood deck. The walls on the deck side can be opened. There's a footpath on the left between houses at #114 and #116. Footpaths like this were designed throughout the community to give easy access to the public areas and different neighborhoods. It might remind you of cutting through your neighbors' yards to get to a friend's house when you were a kid. *Take the footpath, then turn left again when the footpath forks. Follow the footpath back to Hwy 30-A and turn right, then right again onto Quincy Circle.*

Quincy Circle passes between shops on the left and the rental office and restaurants on the right. Halfway up Quincy Circle on the right is the

Seaside Motor Court, a reinvented classic motor hotel of the 1940s and 1950s. Rooms were furnished in part with authentic period pieces from the region. *Turn right onto Seaside Ave.*

Seaside Avenue, the community's grand thoroughfare, is a broad avenue with street lights, brick sidewalks, and a median of natural vegetation. It runs from the village green to the Park. The large-scale houses along it have two-story porticos. **Josephine's Bed & Breakfast** (#101) was designed as an antebellum plantation house with front and side porticos, a metal roof, and rooftop patio. It has seven fireplaces. If you're wondering what kind of house the visionary of Seaside would live in, stop in front of **Robert Davis's House** (#204), a two-story, 3,500-square-foot, house with clapboard siding, two porches, and a widow's walk. *Follow Seaside Ave to Forest St and turn left. As Forest St splits around a green space, take the right fork. When the two roads meet again, turn east and return on the lower fork of Forest St. Turn Right onto the footpath between #112 and #114. Follow it south to East Ruskin St and turn right.*

East Ruskin Street empties into **Ruskin Place,** an artists' enclave of three-story row houses reminiscent of an old Italian town. Many have galleries, shops, or eateries downstairs with living space upstairs. Though of varied design, they all have second-floor balconies. The centerpiece of Ruskin Place is a green used for exhibitions, concerts, and other events. *Turn left and follow the path to the Central Square and turn right. At the first path, turn right again, crossing Quincy Circle.*

By definition, a lyceum is a hall in which public lectures, concerts, and similar programs are presented. That's exactly how Seaside's **Lyceum** is used, along with a school for children and adults. *At the path on the right, turn left out of the Lyceum grounds onto Smolian Circle.*

The houses on the right, numbered #161 to #141, have towers with widow's walks. *Turn right after you pass #141, then a quick left onto Forest St.*

Notice that the houses along this end of Forest St lack porches that face the street, rather, some are paired with the porches facing each other. On the west end of Forest, the style changes again to front porches. To the left is the neighborhood pool. House #852 is a wonderful blend of styles, with large white piers modeled after Craftsman style. The road makes a hairpin turn and changes its name to Grayton St.

Notice the footpath just after the turn next to house #882. It allows residents at this end to reach Natchez Park and to cut to the beach. At Natchez Street, pause a moment to look right to the unique Natchez Street

Beach Pavilion. It's made of locally harvested juniper and is modeled after a beach umbrella and waves. *When the road forks, bear left onto Butler St. Turn right onto Smolian Circle, then another quick right back onto Grayton St. At Pensacola St turn left.*

On Pensacola Street the **Gull Cottage** (#43), designed by Warrior Group, is reminiscent of a ship. *Continue south on Pensacola St, then turn left onto Hwy 30-A.*

The walk along Hwy 30-A passes more Honeymoon Cottages and two interesting pavilions. At the end of Pensacola Street, Tony Atkin designed the **Pensacola Street Beach Pavilion** with a large illuminated pelican on top. The **West Ruskin Street Beach Pavilion**, designed by Michael McDonough, features a whimsical design of multiple-masted sailing ships. On the right is the OBE District, short for obelisk and beach. It has a fair-like quality and features shops and restaurants. *Turn left onto the Central Square.*

On the right is the Village Green and Amphitheater, surrounded by kiosk shops and two-, three- and four-story stores and restaurants. It is the lifeblood of Seaside. Cultural events, food and wine tastings, Christmas carolers, films, kite flying, and people watching bring residents and vacationers together here. *Return to the starting place.*

Lodging

Privately owned rental cottages are the primary accommodations in Seaside. Plan ahead in summer, and especially summer holidays, when cottages fill up very quickly. There also are a few beds available in several B&Bs in Seaside and neighboring Grayton Beach. After Labor Day and before Memorial Day rates go down and there are attractively priced packages. Staying three or more nights significantly reduces the per night cost.

Seaside Cottage Rentals (800/277-8696) works as a clearinghouse and service provider for the hundreds of different individually decorated and designed, fully furnished cottages ranging from one to six bedrooms. Summer rates for one night run from $150 to $1,365. Winter rates are 10 to 20 percent lower. In addition, there are some charming motel-style accommodations that start at $145. Contact them at PO Box 4730, Hwy 30-A, Seaside, FL 32459.

Its position in the heart of Seaside makes **Josephine's French Country Inn** ($$$–$$$$, 800/848-1840, 850/231-1940) a favorite with vacationers. You'll certainly be pampered in this Georgian-style plantation house that has 15 rooms and suites with private baths, phones, TV/VCRs, microwaves, coffee makers, refrigerators, and fireplaces in most. The inn has its own award-winning restaurant.

To say that **Just Rite** ($$$, 850/231-1790) practices the "art" of good living is a play on words, as this second-floor studio efficiency adjoins the Studio 210 art gallery at 210 Ruskin Place. Its view is spectacular and it has all the conveniences of home plus you can wake up and smell—and indulge in—the delicious coffee and pastries from Studio 210.

Guests instantly feel right at home at **Hibiscus Coffee & Guesthouse** ($$–$$$, 850/231-2733) five minutes west of Seaside in Grayton Beach at 85 Defuniak St. Hidden among trees is a two-story bed and breakfast with a serene courtyard, herb garden, screened porch, popular vegetarian cafe, cozy library, and four bedrooms furnished in an Old Florida style. Just west of Grayton Beach in Blue Mountain Beach, Hibiscus also rents a two-bedroom, loft, and two-and-a-half-bath vacation home called the **Funky Magnolia** ($$$–$$$$, 850/231-2733), so named for its unusual design as a 60-foot-long trapezoid set on an angle with every room (including a huge lower porch and upper deck) facing the beach. Contact the Hibiscus Coffee & Guesthouse for reservations.

Arts & culture

While there are no performing arts companies, museums, or historic sites, there are lots of planned cultural activities. Many activities are held outdoors in public spaces and have no charge. Other activities, such as film festivals, wine tastings, concerts, and theater productions, have an admission charge. Unless noted, the contact information number for all cultural activities is available from the Seaside Visitor Bureau (888/SEASIDE).

The **Merchants of Seaside** organization (850/231-5424) sponsors various cultural activities, including Storyteller hours, a Summer Film Series for kids, a Foreign Film Festival (850/231-5424) for adults, a Sunset Serenade Series, and dance and music concerts.

At the **Ruskin Place Artist Colony** at Ruskin Place, the weekly Music in the Artist Colony series (850/864-7800) fills the evening air with varied concerts.

The **Seaside Institute** (850/231-2421) sponsors cultural and community programs throughout the year at various locations. Cultural programs include **An Evening at the Opera**, the **Little Art Festival** of children's art, visiting master storytellers, and a **Fall Concert Series**. The community programs focus on community enhancement, the built and natural environment, urban planning, and architecture.

Sundog Books (850/231-5481), the only bookstore in town, carries everything from literature to kid's books to bestsellers at Central Square.

Around the green at Ruskin Place, in the heart of Seaside, is the **Ruskin Place Artist Colony** (850/231-5424), named after 19th-century British writer and art critic John

Ruskin. This collection of interesting galleries and studios features a wide range of artists. Among the galleries are **Cara Roy Artworks** (850/231-2535), which features tropical watercolors, prints of Seaside, and posters. Carol Bass Hawkins and Charlotte Arnold sell their impressionistic watercolors at **Hawkins & Arnold Fine Art At Seaside** (850/231-2840). An interesting mix of paintings and sculptures by more than a dozen American artists are exhibited at the **J. Proctor Gallery** (850/231-1091). **Keramikos** (850/231-5564) carries whimsical and contemporary ceramics, porcelain, and raku artwork. Seaside's oldest gallery, **Newbill Collection** (850/231-4500), focuses on American contemporary art and crafts, including jewelry. It's not surprising that viewers find the style of photographs at **The Photography of Michael Belk** (850/231-3995) familiar. His fashion shots have appeared in major publications for more than 20 years. **Studio 210** (850/231-1790) sells cappuccino, espresso, sinful desserts, and contemporary and traditional art in a setting that invites you to linger day and night.

Outside of Ruskin Place are a few galleries, including the very popular **Fusion** (850/231-5405), a gallery of decorative and functional glass art.

Food & drink

Seaside has a handful of casual restaurants serving everything from pizza to Greek cuisine. This is a resort community, so expect higher-than-average prices for average food. Fortunately, several of the state's best bliss-inducing—though wallet-busting—restaurants are also within a 10-minute drive of Seaside.

Seaside's premier restaurant is **Josephine's French Country Inn** ($$$, 850 /231-1940), which starts the day with casual, healthy breakfasts. By dinner, diners have returned in more sophisticated garb to dine on eclectic seafood dishes, crab cakes, rack of lamb, and filet mignon in a romantic setting at 101 Seaside Ave. It's difficult to categorize **Bud & Alley's** ($$, 850/231-5900) on Cinderella Circle because the menu features American fare like steaks and seafood, as well as dishes with Mediterranean and Gulf Coast influences. The wine selection is extraordinary. For a quick bite or a noon or sunset picnic, **Modica Market** ($, 850/231-1214) has terrific deli choices, wines, produce, and icy cold thirst-quenching fresh lemonade in summer at Seaside Central Square. The international offerings include Greek entrees at **Cafe Bouzouki** ($–$$$, 850/231-2700) for lunch and dinner at Quincy Circle, and Italian specialties served in the casual beachfront setting of **CafeSpiaggia** ($, 850/231-1297) at Hwy 30-A.

When you're in the mood for something ethnic, **Borago** ($$$, 850/231-9167) satisfies with seafood prepared with the taste of Asia and the Southwest at 80 E Hwy 30-A, Grayton Beach. **Criolla's** ($$$, 850/267-1267) at 170 E Hwy 30-A in Grayton Beach is a handsome restaurant with a hip chic that matches Chef Johnny Earles creative French Creole cuisine, an imaginative blend of African, French, and Spanish gastronomy. Servers are skilled, knowledgeable, and attentive. It is consistently one of the best. **Hibiscus Coffee & Guesthouse** ($, 850/231-2733) offers a vegetarian menu of baked goods, fresh fruit, toasted waffles topped with peanut butter and fresh fruit, pancakes with chocolate chips or fruit, quiche, and frittatas for breakfast. Lunch is equally appealing with homemade soups served with corn muffins, Michigan potato salad, fresh fruit with pecans and coconut, sandwiches, pitas, and veggie burgers.

Events

Seaside Institute sponsors events throughout the year. In April, architecturally significant houses are open for personalized tours during the **Spring Architects' House Tour**. There's another tour in the fall. In October, the annual **Florida International University/Seaside Institute Writers' Conference** features some of the country's most talented and celebrated authors as faculty.

The Merchants of Seaside host several annual events, including a **Cajun Music Concert** in February, **Seaside Spring Wine Festival** in May and the annual **Seeing Red Wine Festival** in October. In February and October, their annual Seaside Yard Sale is a big hit.

Torreya State Park

While northerners smirk at the concept of hills in Florida, visitors to Torreya State Park who have traveled around the state will be impressed by the park's changing elevation—up to 250 feet—and the high bluffs—up to 150 feet—that overlook the scenic Apalachicola River.

For centuries the river has carved and shaped the park's bluffs and deep ravines that are forested by hardwood trees more commonly found in the Appalachian Mountains of Georgia than in Florida. There are also river swamps and high pinelands.

The park, which has a plant checklist of more than 30 pages, draws its name from the endangered torreya tree, endemic to the bluffs, ravines, and slopes of the Apalachicola River. Once plentiful, the species was almost eliminated by disease in the 1960s. Two other rare plants in the park are the Florida yew tree and the US Champion winged elm. Visitors will be amazed by the variety of ferns and wildflowers.

Also of great interest are the more than 140 birds that live or visit the area along with more than 60 reptiles and amphibians, including the rare Barbour's map turtle.

Archaeologists have found several sites indicating that Native Americans lived within the park's boundaries. Had they still been here in the early 1800s, they would have been run off by the notorious Indian killer, General Andrew Jackson, who crossed the river here with his army.

The river served as an important interstate highway during the 1800s, when steamboats plied the waters and the first government road across north Florida ended here.

During the Civil War, the river overlook was protected by a six cannon battery. Though none remain today, interpretive markers along the trail indicate the location. What remains from that era is the Gregory House, built in 1849 as a plantation house on the other side of the river. It was moved to the park in 1935 by the Civilian Conservation Corps, which developed the park.

Information
Torreya State Park, Rte 2, Box 70, Bristol, FL 32321; 850/643-2674. Department of Environmental Protection, Division of Recreation and Parks, 3900 Commonwealth Blvd, Tallahassee, FL 32399; 850/488-9872.

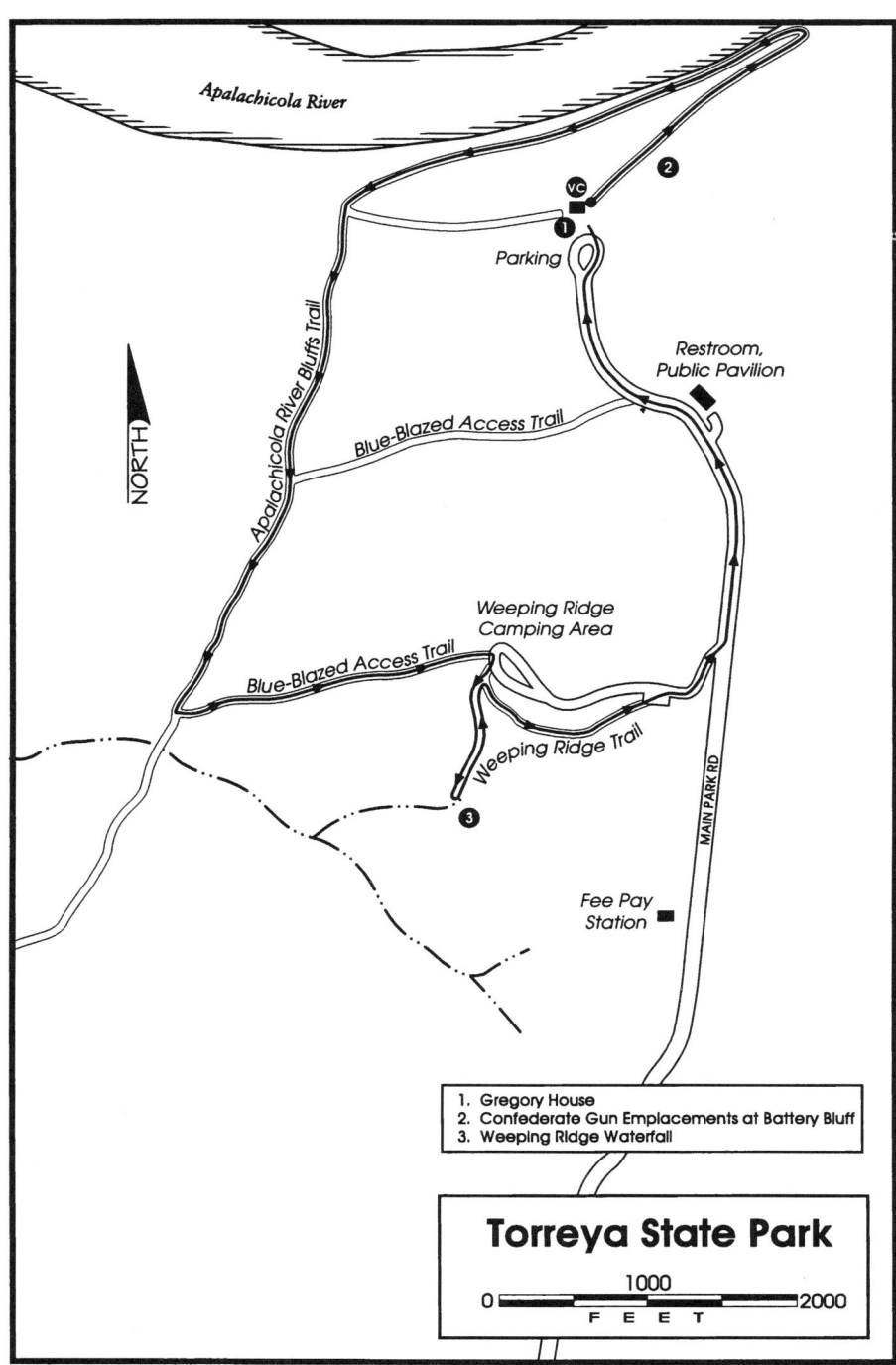

Apalachicola River

Parking

VC

Restroom,
Public Pavilion

Apalachicola River Bluffs Trail

Blue-Blazed Access Trail

NORTH

Weeping Ridge
Camping Area

Blue-Blazed Access Trail

Weeping Ridge Trail

MAIN PARK RD

Fee Pay
Station

1. Gregory House
2. Confederate Gun Emplacements at Battery Bluff
3. Weeping Ridge Waterfall

Torreya State Park

0   1000   2000
F E E T

Getting there
Take I-10 to exit 25 (Hwy 270) south towards Greensboro, then turn left (west) onto Hwy 12. Turn right (south) onto County Road 1641. From there it's seven miles to the park. Starting at Hwy 12, there are plenty of park signs. Tallahassee Airport is 30 miles east on I-10 at exit 28 (Hwy 263, Capital Circle). The closest train and bus depots are in Tallahassee and Quincy.

First steps
For park information, contact **Torreya State Park** or the **Department of Environmental Protection**. Admission is $2 per car with up to 8 people; $1 for pedestrians and bicyclists. There's an additional $1 charge to tour the Gregory House.

Tours
Rangers lead tours ($1, plus park admission) of the historic Gregory House weekdays at 10 am, weekends and state holidays at 10 am, 2 pm, and 4 pm.

Seasonal highlights
Because of the many hardwood trees, the park probably has the best fall color in the state.

Natural Torreya State Park. *This three-mile walk passes Confederate gun emplacements, river overlooks, ravines, and the park's only waterfall. It can be lengthened up to seven miles.*

Start with a tour of the Gregory House. Jason Gregory ran a plantation that used enslaved African laborers to produce cotton and other crops during the mid 1800s at Ocheesee Landing, across the river. His house was built on five-foot brick piers to protect it from flooding. He lost everything in the Civil War and moved to Gainesville. However, his daughter returned in 1895, paid the property taxes and lived in the house until she died in 1916. In 1935, the house was moved to this site. *After the tour, walk behind the house for a view from the bluffs above the Apalachicola River.*

A park bench shaded by tall oaks hung with Spanish moss tempts you to linger near the bluffs. Look down river to see Ocheesee Landing. *The trailhead is about 200 feet on the right.*

Begin walking on the blue-blazed access trail that joins the seven-mile Apalachicola River Bluffs Trail. This part of the trail passes through a hardwood hammock of broad-leaved trees. You'll see southern magnolias (*Magnolia grandiflora*), laurel oaks (*Quercus laurifolia*), mockernut hickories (*Carya tomentosa*), and American beeches (*Fagus grandifolia*) towering above the American holly (*Ilex opaca*), hop hornbeams (*Ostrya virginiana*), needle palms (*Rhapidophyllum hystrix*), and oakleaf hydrangeas (*Hydrangea quercifolia*). About a hundred feet into the walk is an interpretive sign for a southern magnolia; a fine specimen stands behind it. Also look for torreya trees (*Torreya taxifolia*), Florida yews (*Taxus floridana*), both of which look like small Christmas trees.

The trail begins with a gradual descent. The steepest parts of the trail are stepped with wooden slats, which can be slippery when it rains.

The first of three gun emplacements is on the right at Battery Bluff, at 0.1 miles. An interpretive signs explains that it was placed there in 1863 and describes the battery's components.

Sounds along the trail include cicadas, song birds, river traffic, and the rhythmic slap of boat wakes hitting the river bank.

At 0.2 mile there's an interpretive sign about the Apalachicola River, a resting bench, and the intersection with the main trail. *Turn left.*

As the trail descends and switches back, you can catch glimpses of the river through the trees. Look for orange blazes as the trail runs along the edge of the bluff over the river. The ground here is closer to the river and saturated with water that runs off the bluff above. Not surprisingly, there are cuts and ravines filled with ferns, blue phlox (*Phlox divaricata* Linnaeus), white monkey flower (*Mimulus alatus* Aiton), mushrooms, and moss, especially in the summer.

The floor of the trail is uneven and covered with a fascinating web of exposed tree roots. Watch your step. Stop occasionally to look for small tree lizards and tiny frogs whose camouflage matches the tree bark.

At 0.25 mile, there's an interpretive sign for a needle palm, named for the dense cluster of pointed spikes protruding from its base. There are also several magnolias. At 0.27 mile, there's a confusing sign with a yellow arrow at a fork. *Bear left.* Numerous side trails lead to the river bank.

The trail makes a sharp descent at 0.3 mile, then curves, levels out, and plunges into deep shade, with a tight, low canopy lined with bamboo. At 0.35 mile an interpretive sign describes the Apalachicola River, the largest in Florida.

After the short wooden bridge at 0.4 mile, the trail runs between two creeks and moves away from the river. At 0.5 mile the road intersects the blue-blaze access trail that returns to the Gregory House. *Continue on the right, following the orange-blazed trail toward the Primitive Sites.*

From there, the trail crosses a creek and climbs, then follows a ridge with lots of bamboo and magnolias. At 0.6 it intersects with an access trail to the High Pine Picnic Area. *Continue right.*

Soon, the landscape widens and is dotted with pine trees. Their needles litter the ground. The trail descends from the high pinelands to a river swamp, distinguished by its water-loving cypress trees surrounded by knees.

Leaving the river swamp, the trail climbs again through another pineland, then curves left along another ridge. The understory is scattered with palms, grasses, and blue common spiderwort (*Tradescantia ohiensis*). The vista to the right from 0.85 mile to 1 mile is of a glen of trees and brilliant green grasses.

At 1.25 mile the trail intersects the blue-blazed access trail marked Campground. *Leave the orange-blazed trail and take the access trail.*

From 1.25 to 1.5 mile, the trail gradually climbs up a smooth hill with magnolias alongside. The trail is wide and open and has a ravine on the left. Just after it steepens, the trail crests at 1.53 miles and intersects with the Weeping Ridge Trail. *Bear right and take the Weeping Ridge Trail. Ignore the sign that estimates the time at 1 hour and 44 minutes. It won't take nearly that long to reach the waterfall. Two hundred feet beyond, bear right again for the waterfall.*

The wide-open trail gradually rolls up and down, bordered by magnolias, spruce pine (*Pinus glabra*), and white oaks (*Quercus alba*) that provide broken shade. At 1.8 mile, the small waterfall is visible with a drop of about 20 feet. Though unimpressive in size, the setting is tranquil. During the rainy summer season, water seeps out of the ground, creating the falls. Note the large tree on the right side of the trail. It's riddled with woodpecker holes from about one foot up to as far up as you can see. There's also a Torreya tree next to it. *Return to the Weeping Ridge Trail intersection and take the trail's right fork to the parking lot.*

At 2.25 miles the Weeping Ridge Trail parking lot, which has a pay phone, intersects the main park road on the right. *At the road, turn left and follow it back to the Gregory House.*

From the road, you have a clear view of many birds, deer, trees, and plants that can be difficult to see within the forest. It passes the High Pine Picnic Area at 2.5 mile on the right. The facilities include grills, covered pavilions, soda machines, and a playground. The road gradually rises, falls, and curves back to the Gregory House.

Lodging

Campgrounds within the park are the nearest accommodations. For hotels, you'll have to travel 15 miles to Quincy, 30 miles west to Marianna, or 30 miles east to Tallahassee. For Quincy lodgings, which include three bed and breakfasts, check with the Quincy Walking Tour. Marianna and Tallahassee lodgings, which are listed below, include a bed and breakfast, an historic hotel, and several chain motels and hotels. You can find a comfortable room in both cities for less than $60.

The refined bungalow style **Hinson House Bed & Breakfast** ($$, 850/526-1500) features decorative Italian tiles, French doors, five spacious antique-filled guest suites, antique claw-foot bath tubs, and ceiling fans. It's decorated for Christmas year round at 4338 Lafayette St, Marianna.

The **Hampton Inn** ($$, 850/526-1006) is conveniently located near the highway and features 70 comfortable rooms along exterior corridors at 2185 State Road 71S, Marianna. Nearby is the **Comfort Inn** ($–$$, 850/526-5600) with comparable rooms at a slightly lower rate at 2175 State Road 71S, Marianna. Both have a pool.

The stately 40-room **Governors Inn** ($$$–$$$$, 850/681-6855) at 209 S Adams St, in Tallahassee's historic district, is deeply entrenched in Florida history, from the rooms—named after former Florida governors—converted from hardware stores and warehouses to the antique-furnishings.

Of the chain properties, the most relaxing is probably the country inn-style **Cabot Lodge** ($$, 850/386-8880) with 160 rooms, a screened porch, pool, and exercise room situated on six landscaped acres at 2735 N Monroe St, Tallahassee. The best value is probably the **Comfort Inn** ($–$$, 850/562-7200) with an outdoor pool and continental breakfast at 2727 Graves Rd, Tallahassee. Also in Tallahassee, the **Doubletree** ($$–$$$, 850/224-5000) at 101 S Adams St, the **Hilton Garden Inn** ($$, 850/385-3553) at 3333 Thomasville Rd, the **La Quinta Inn** ($$, 850/385-7172) at 2905 N Monroe St, and the **Radisson Hotel** ($$–$$$, 850/224-6000) at 415 N Monroe St, all have more than 100 rooms and offer above average comfort and amenities.

Food & drink

As with accommodations, most dining options are found nearby in Chattahoochee (six miles north), Quincy (see Quincy Walking Tour), Marianna, and Tallahassee.

Northside Seafood ($, 850/663-4031) is seasoned with local color at 10 Main St, Chattahoochee, where the fish and shrimp are fried traditional style, crisp on the outside and flaky and flavorful on the inside. It also has burgers, sandwiches, and a salad bar. The **Jones House Restaurant** ($–$$, 850/663-8464) at 35 S Main St, Chattahoochee, serves steaks, seafood, and Italian specialties in a 1919 Sears & Roebuck catalog building that has a large welcoming porch and five fireplaces.

One of the finest places to eat in Tallahassee is **Chez Pierre** ($$, 850/222-0936)at 1215 Thomasville Rd, where authentic French entrees, chocolates, cookies, wines, and pâtés are served in an indoor/outdoor French country setting. The menu, which changes frequently, features regional cuisine with a hint of contemporary Louisiana and California, at **The Mustard Tree** ($–$$, 850/893-8733) at 1415 Timberlane Rd. It offers an excellent choice of fine wines by the glass.

The Southwest meets the Gulf of Mexico at the **Red Canyon Grill** ($, 850 /482-4256), where authentic Southwestern cuisine is served in a regional setting at 3297 Caverns Rd, Marianna.

Events

In May the park conducts **Candlelight Tours of the Gregory House** with heritage music, candle dipping, hearth cooking, and living history and Civil War demonstrations.

Downtown Quincy

The tranquil, tree-lined Quincy of today belies its late 19th- and early 20th-century importance as the hub of north Florida's tobacco industry and home to Quincy State Bank, whose visionary president encouraged depositors to invest in a fledgling enterprise, the Coca Cola Company.

Gone are the international salesmen and frenetic farmers who tore down their outhouses so every inch of land could be put to tobacco. It's no longer a bustling town by anyone's imagination. However, what it lacks in excitement it makes up for in quiet charm, most of which is found in dozens of restored mansions, warehouses, and packing houses in a 36-block National Historic District.

Native Americans were the first to farm the region. Mounds found near Chattahoochee indicate that from 1450 to 1650 Muscogee Indians occupied the western part of Gadsden County. In the middle of that period, Seminole and Creek Indians migrated from Alabama and the Carolinas, and remained in the region until the 1800s, when they were forcibly evicted or killed under the Indian Removal Act. Spanish explorers and missionaries arrived in the late 17th century.

Quincy became the government seat for Gadsden County, the fifth county formed after the United States acquired Florida from Spain in 1821. In 1828, five years after the county was established, farmers who had migrated from Virginia and the Carolinas with their enslaved African laborers founded the town of Quincy, naming it after then Secretary of State, John Quincy Adams.

The town was then, and remains today, agricultural. As the depressed cotton market swept across the South, Floridians looked for another crop. They chose tobacco, and Quincy became the center of the tobacco culture. By 1842 European and Northern buyers were flocking to the town to buy the region's spotted hybrid tobacco leaves that made good cigar wrappers. Production jumped from 75,000 pounds in 1839 to 1.2 million pounds by 1860.

When the first census was taken in 1825, enslaved people made up 41 percent of the population. As tobacco grew in value, that number rose. At the height of the tobacco rush, more than 57 percent of Quincy's population was enslaved people working the tobacco fields.

With the Civil War came the loss of slave labor. The industry was crippled and did not recover until the 1880s and 1890s. Just after the turn of the century, Quincy farmers developed a shade method for growing tobacco that improved its color and texture and made it highly

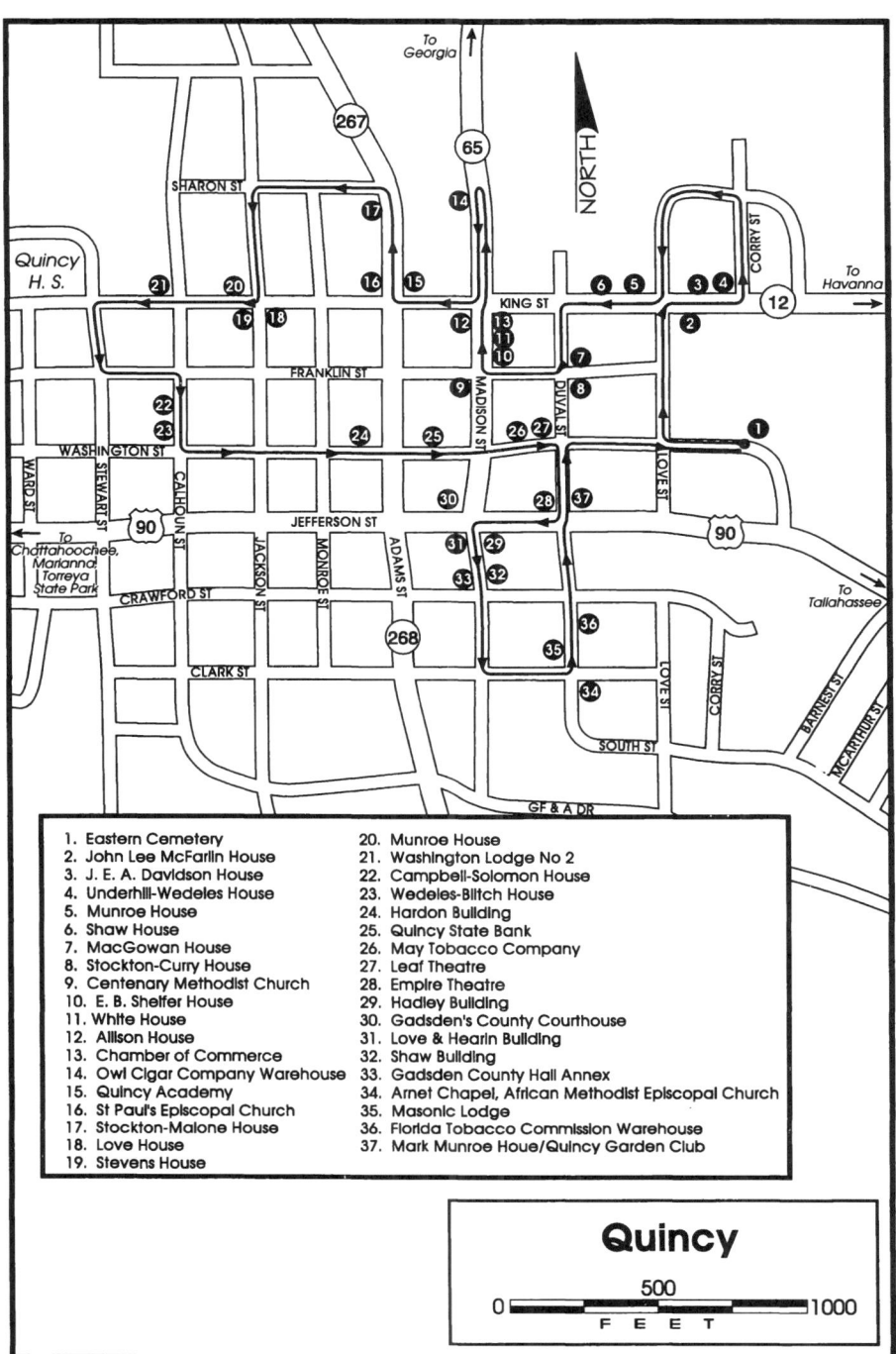

1. Eastern Cemetery
2. John Lee McFarlin House
3. J. E. A. Davidson House
4. Underhill-Wedeles House
5. Munroe House
6. Shaw House
7. MacGowan House
8. Stockton-Curry House
9. Centenary Methodist Church
10. E. B. Shelfer House
11. White House
12. Allison House
13. Chamber of Commerce
14. Owl Cigar Company Warehouse
15. Quincy Academy
16. St Paul's Episcopal Church
17. Stockton-Malone House
18. Love House
19. Stevens House
20. Munroe House
21. Washington Lodge No 2
22. Campbell-Solomon House
23. Wedeles-Blitch House
24. Hardon Building
25. Quincy State Bank
26. May Tobacco Company
27. Leaf Theatre
28. Empire Theatre
29. Hadley Building
30. Gadsden's County Courthouse
31. Love & Hearin Building
32. Shaw Building
33. Gadsden County Hall Annex
34. Arnet Chapel, African Methodist Episcopal Church
35. Masonic Lodge
36. Florida Tobacco Commission Warehouse
37. Mark Munroe Houe/Quincy Garden Club

Quincy

0 ▬▬▬▬ 500 ▬▬▬▬ 1000
F E E T

desirable as a wrapper for premium cigars. The plants were grown under cheese cloth and harvested by hand.

Less expensive tobacco and wrappers coming out of Latin America signaled the final decline of the industry in the county by the 1960s.

Quincy's second golden period came in the early 1920s, when banker Mark "Pat" Munroe recommended that his customers and friends buy stock in a nearby Atlanta soda company called Coca Cola. The stock skyrocketed and turned Quincy into the richest town per capita in the United States. Among its population of 8,000, it claimed 25 millionaires and dozens of others who were worth almost that much. At one time, the town's residents were the company's largest group of stockholders.

Information
Gadsden County Chamber of Commerce, 221 N Madison St, PO Box 389, Quincy, FL 32353; 800/627-9231.

Getting there
Take I-10 to exit 25 or 26 north to Hwy 90 east to downtown. Tallahassee Airport is about 20 minutes east on Hwy 90 or I-10 at exit 28 (Hwy 263, Capital Circle). Amtrak's (800/USA RAIL) closest station is in Tallahassee. Greyhound (800 /231-2222, 850/627-7413) has a station at 106 E Jefferson.

First steps
For area maps and information, contact the **Gadsden County Chamber of Commerce**, which is open weekdays 8:30 am to 4:30 pm. Request a copy of the free "North Florida Art Trail" brochure.

Downtown Quincy. *This four-mile route covers the downtown historic district. Allow about two hours, a little longer if you stop to see the interiors of the bed and breakfasts or any of the commercial buildings.*

Start at the Eastern Cemetery at the east end of Washington St, one block east of Love St. The **Eastern Cemetery** was first used in the 1820s by Quincy's pioneer families and today has numerous memorials and headstones of interest. *Walk west on Washington St and turn right onto Love St, then right onto King St.*

The **John Lee McFarlin House** (305 E King) is the most exuberant example of Victorian architecture in Gadsden County. It was built in 1895 for the namesake owner, one of the most influential tobacco growers in Florida and Georgia. Across the street is the **J.E.A. Davidson House** (306 E King), former home of one of Florida's state senators. The 1905

Underhill-Wedeles House (318 E King) is named for the original owner, G.M. Underhill, and Max Wedeles, a member of one of the county's oldest tobacco families. *Turn left onto Corry St, left onto Sharon St, left onto Love St, then right onto King St.*

George D. Munroe helped his brother, Pat, found the Quincy State Bank, the first chartered state bank of Florida. He had the Victorian **Munroe House** (234 E King) with stained glass windows built in 1898. Next door is the **Shaw House** (222 King St), originally built in 1840 as a two-story house by Arthur Foreman, a prominent tobacco grower who, as the first to the region's hybrid tobacco abroad, created the boom that launched the product as a cigar wrapper. *Turn left onto Duval St.*

The attractive **MacGowan House** (203 N Duval) was originally a one-room dentist's office. A series of successful businessmen lived in the antebellum Classical Revival **Stockton-Curry House** (121 N Duval, southeast corner of Duval and Franklin). The first occupant in 1836 was Pennsylvanian Phillip Stockton, who came to Florida to operate a mail coach line between Florida and Alabama, but later became an attorney and lived in the house until 1879. In 1883 James E. Broome, later a state senator, purchased the house. By 1902 the house had changed hands again to C.H. Curry and his brother-in-law Alexander Shaw, who helped develop the unique shade growing process used by Panhandle tobacco farmers. *Turn right onto Franklin St.*

On the southwest corner of Franklin and Madison is the **Centenary Methodist Church** (122 N Madison), built in 1918 and noted for its beautiful stained-glass windows, two of which were designed by the Tiffany Studio in 1896. *Turn right onto Madison St.*

During Quincy's second tobacco boom, successful shade tobacco grower E.B. Shelfer built the **E.B. Shelfer House** (205 N Madison), a two-and-a-half story Victorian with a front and side wraparound porch. The Greek Revival two-story **White House** (212 N Madison) was purchased by Judge P.W. White, who served in the Civil War as Chief Confederate Commissary Officer for Florida. His wife headed up the Ladies Aid Society, which nursed sick and wounded Confederate soldiers after the battles of Olustee and Natural Bridge. Though the exterior of the **Allison House** (215 N Madison) has little in common with the Georgian style house it was originally built as, it is important as the former home of A.K. Allison, who was a general during the Indian Removal era, a territorial legislator, speaker of the Florida House and president of the Florida Senate before the Civil War, then governor of Florida, and an attorney in his last years. *Continue to the end of Madison.*

On the left side is the brick **Owl Cigar Company Warehouse** (404 N Madison), where tobacco was cured and Quincy's own brands of cigars, White Owl and Robert Burns, were manufactured. *Return south on Madison. Turn right onto King St, then right onto Adams.*

The brick Federal **Quincy Academy** (303 N Adams) was a private school, public school, library, and meeting house. It's now a church community center. Across the street, on the northwest corner of King and Adams, **St Paul's Episcopal Church** (10 W King) is Quincy's oldest church building, built in 1892 and enlarged in 1914 and 1928. Over the years, very little has been changed on the 1892 **Stockton-Malone House** (326 N Adams St), whose namesake owner was Col William Tennent Stockton, a West Point graduate, and officer in the Confederate Calvary. *Turn left onto Sharon St, then left onto Jackson St.*

Two houses on Jackson Street are relatively unchanged classic Georgian style with two rooms flanking a broad central hallway. The 1831 **Love House** (219 N Jackson), named for Edward Love, a planter, lawyer, and politician, and the 1842 **Stevens House** (220 N Jackson), after Samuel Stevens, an early wealthy resident. *Turn right onto King St.*

Little has changed in the Classical Revival **Munroe House** (210 King St), purchased for Thomas Munroe in 1850 and still in the Munroe family today. After a hurricane in 1832 destroyed the wood frame headquarters of local Masons, members moved into the safer **Washington Lodge No 2** (304 King St) building, whose walls are three bricks thick. Over the years, the building also has been home to the Quincy Women's Club, Gadsden Historical Society, and Quincy Historic Preservation Commission. *Turn left onto Stewart St, left onto Franklin St, then right onto Calhoun St.*

The 1843 **Campbell-Solomon House** (118 N Calhoun St) is a rare example in Quincy of Creole Cottage architecture more typically found along the Gulf Coast. Max Wedeles lived in the **Wedeles-Blitch House** (302 W Washington, northwest corner of Calhoun) at the turn of the century. His Chicago-based company helped develop Quincy's shade tobacco industry. *Turn left onto Washington St.*

In 1899, William Hardon, an African American entrepreneur, built and owned one of Quincy's first ice and electric plants, both run by steam, in the **Hardon Building** (16 W Washington). It later became a stable and veterinary office. Today, it's an office supply store. The **Quincy State Bank** (22 E Washington) operated in this building until 1961. Although originally built in 1906 for a grain company, by 1920 it was headquarters for the **May Tobacco Company** (104 E Washington). Today, it's a mixed-use building, with commercial businesses downstairs and residences upstairs. The **Leaf Theatre** (118 E Washington) was named and colored green and brown in tribute to the mighty tobacco leaf. It closed in 1980, but was reopened and restored in the mid-1980s and now is the Quincy Music Theater, a performing arts center. *Turn right onto Duval St, then right onto Jefferson St.*

In 1910, the Quincy Fire Department built the **Empire Theatre** (112 E Jefferson) as an opera house, which served as a center for traveling and local performing arts groups. Beautifully decorated with details, the 1840 **Hadley Building** (107 E Jefferson) was owned by Nathan Hadley, an African-American barber. **Gadsden's County Courthouse** (10 E Jefferson), built in 1913, sits in the middle of the square bounded by Madison, Adams, Washington and Jefferson streets. Across the street, on the southwest corner of Madison and Jefferson streets, is the **Love & Hearin Building** (21 E Jefferson). Originally built in 1894 as store selling dry goods and hardware, today it's a jewelry store. *Turn left onto Madison St.*

As you turn the corner, note the Coca Cola mural on the side of the Love & Hearin Building. The beautiful **Shaw Building** (9 S Madison) housed the C.R. Shaw Ford Motor Co in the early 20th century. It remains mostly unchanged and today is a furniture store. Across the street is the attractive **Gadsden County Hall Annex** (16 S Madison), which has served as a municipal government building since it was built in 1914. *Turn left onto Clark St.*

Near the corner of Duval and Clark stands the **Arnett Chapel, African Methodist Episcopal Church** (209 S Duval). It was founded in 1866 and the present wood structure was built in 1898, making it the oldest surviving African-American church in the county. In 1940 a brick chapel was built. *Turn left onto Duval St.*

In the early 1870s officials built the simple, two-story frame building as Dunbar High School for black students. In 1907 it became a **Masonic Lodge** (122 S Duval) for black Masons, who still meet there, though the building has been moved from its original site and was remodeled in 1976. Down the street is the **Florida Tobacco Commission Warehouse** (105 S Duval), which was built as offices and a processing and storage center for "Shade Leaf" tobacco. On the northeast corner of Duval and Jefferson is the large Victorian **Mark Munroe House/Quincy Garden Club** (204 E Jefferson), built by the president and co-founder of the Quincy State Bank in 1893. It was purchased by John Welch Bates in the 1970s and donated to the city. It's home to the Quincy Garden Club, which maintains a formal rose garden. *Turn right onto Washington St and return to the start.*

Lodging
There are three lovely bed and breakfasts in historic houses along the walking tour and one in Havana, about 10 minutes northeast. A little farther away are several comfortable chain motels. See Torreya State Park Walking Tour for accommodations in Tallahassee and Chattahoochee.

Rooms are romantically decorated with antiques and 1.5 acres of gardens and trees surround the beautiful, three-story Queen Anne style **McFarlin House B&B Inn** ($$–$$$, 850/875-2526) at 305 E King St. Service and breakfast are memorable. Elegant English country charm best describes **The Allison House Inn** ($$, 850/875-2511)at 215 N Madison St, which has spacious high-ceiling rooms filled with antiques, crisp linens, and modern conveniences in an altered brick Georgian style house built in 1843. The innkeeper, antique book dealer Susan Mick, is as delightful as the cozy, intriguing, artistically and informally furnished two-story **Quincefield Inn** ($$, 850/627-2196) built in 1892 at 121 N Jackson

In neighboring Havana, a major destination for Old South charm and antique seekers, there's the restored 1907 **Gaver's Historic Havana House B&B** ($$–$$$, 850/539-5611), built by the town's first mayor at 301 E Sixth Ave. It features dramatic 12-foot ceilings, two tranquil guest rooms furnished in antiques and original art, a fireplace and ceiling fans, a screened porch, and garden pergola.

The two closest non-B&B or chain lodgings are the **Quincy Motor Lodge** ($, 850/627-7175) at 368 E Jefferson (Hwy 90) with a pool, and the 40-room **Holiday Inn Express** ($$, 850/875-2500) just off I-10 at 75 Spooner Rd, on the outskirts of town.

Arts & culture
The North Florida Art Trail is a self-guided brochure tour of Gadsden County's art galleries, artisan's studios, outdoor murals, and other artistic and historic venues.

Quincy Music Theatre (850/875-9444) at 118 E Washington St stages four Broadway shows annually, along with concerts, comedies, and shows for children. **Gadsden Arts** (850/875-4866) is a cultural and educational facility with art galleries and exhibition space at 407 N Adams St. The **Quincy Gallery** (14 E Washington St) is an artists coop featuring the work of local artists, including architect and watercolorist Joel Sampson, who frequently paints historical local buildings. Individual nationally recognized artists such as Mark Lindquist (850/875-9809) operates **Lindquist Studio** in a renovated shade tobacco warehouse at Glory Rd. He uses native trees to create wood sculptures. His work is featured at the Smithsonian Institution and The White House. Bob and Jo Ann Bischoff create stained, leaded, and beveled glass and architectural decorative arts at **Bischoff Studios** (850/875-3184) at 902 Solomon Dairy Rd.

In Havana, the **Florida Art Center & Gallery** (850/539-1770) showcases the work of local artists, including gallery owner and watercolorist Lee Mainella at 208 First St NE. The **Gallery-In-Between** (850/539-3800) has studios and galleries as well as changing exhibitions of works by regional artists in The Cannery at 115 E 8th Ave. Betts Overstreet (850/539-9070) creates traditional watercolor and black-and-white sumi-e Chinese brushwork art at Rich Bay Road.

Food & drink
It's the oddest thing. This fairly affluent town has very few restaurants. There is a handful of others in neighboring Havana. Most locals who want to go out to dinner make the 20-minute drive to Tallahassee. (See Torreya State Park Walking Tour for restaurants in Tallahassee and Chattahoochee.)

Located next to the Leaf Theatre in an 1820s carriage factory, **Alice's Carriage Factory** ($–$$, 850/875-1735) at 104 E Washington offers lots of well-prepared seafood specialties like blackened grouper, traditional catfish, and shrimp, as well as Black Angus steaks, and barbecue.

Nicholson Farmhouse Restaurant ($$–$$$, 850/539-5931) was built on Highway 12 between Quincy and Havana in 1828 as a residence for Dr Malcolm Nicholson. Four generations of Nicholsons lived there through the 1960s, when they turned the farm into a very popular restaurant, entertainment, and shopping complex. The family-style restaurant specializes in steaks, but also serves grilled chicken and pork chops. Besides the farm, there's the converted outbuildings and several historic buildings that have been relocated here.

In downtown Havana, there are several popular choices, including **Dolly's Expresso Cafe** ($, 850/539-6716) at 206 First St NW whose local lunch (open until 5 pm) favorites include Greek salad, Cuban sandwiches, and black beans and rice. **The Cannery**, located in a former canning factory at 115 E 8th Ave, has a lunch restaurant, **Tailgatz** ($, 850

/539-6222), for quick sandwiches and salads, and a full-service lunch and dinner (Friday and Saturday) restaurant called **Shade** ($-$$, 850 /539-8401), which specializes in Old South specialties like buttermilk fried chicken with mashed potatoes, iron skillet pork chops with sausage cornbread stuffing.

Events
For events information, contact the Gadsden County Chamber of Commerce. In March, the **Havana MusicFest** features three days of jazz, blues, swing, gospel, reggae, plus food, and vendors. The **Florida Art Center National 100**, a competition that features the work of artists from around the world, takes place in the fall in Havana. Also in fall, Gadsden Arts sponsors **Art in Gadsden**, a juried art show featuring the works of more than 50 local and regional artists, in Quincy.

Southeast Florida

"(Carl) Fisher was the first man to discover that there was sand under the water...that could hold up a real estate sign. He made the dredge the national emblem of Florida."—Will Rogers

Introduction

The development of Florida's east coast is inextricably tied to Henry Morrison Flagler. From the late 1800s to 1912, his Florida East Coast Railroad pushed Florida's frontier south from Jacksonville to Key West. In its wake arose prosperous resort towns with Flagler-owned luxury hotels.

In 1893, Flagler, a partner in Standard Oil, drove his railroad south along the coast from St Augustine. At Stuart the fledgling pineapple industry boomed when the railroad provided a way to take fruits quickly to market. Pressing on to Palm Beach, Flagler built the Royal Poinciana Hotel to hold 1,500 guests, more than the city's population.

Julia Tuttle and William Brickell, large Miami landowners, persuaded Flagler to continue the railroad—and the accompanying tourist boom—70 miles south. The railroad arrived and Flagler built the Royal Palm Hotel. Miami's boom was born. A year later, in July 1896, the city incorporated.

Flagler pressed southward achieving an engineering marvel of bridging the scores of islands between Miami and Key West in what was initially termed "Flagler's Folly." In 1912, the first train rumbled into Key West.

While Flagler was building his Overseas Railroad, Carl Fisher, who had made millions in the Midwest auto industry, came to Miami. He dredged Biscayne Bay and dropped the sand onto a barrier island off Miami, creating Miami Beach.

South Floridians started draining the Everglades along Miami's and Fort Lauderdale's western boundary and cutting the Miami Canal to divert water from the Everglades into Biscayne Bay and create arable land for housing and farming.

Miami boomed again from 1920 until 1926, when the heavily speculative market crashed and a hurricane ripped through the city, bringing the Depression to South Florida a few years early.

By the mid-1930s, things were booming again. New Art Deco hotels sprang up on Miami Beach to accommodate the re-emerging tourist industry. Since then, other than a few stumbling periods, South Florida has never stopped growing as a region and major tourist destination.

South Florida's explosive growth had a devastating effect on the environment. In 1947 Marjorie Stoneman Douglas published *The Everglades: River of Grass*, drawing attention to the importance of the Everglades as the major watershed for South Florida and as a unique ecosystem. Draining land, changing the natural water flow, and polluting the water with agricultural chemicals were killing the Everglades and the wildlife.

That same year, Everglades National Park was created to protect part of the unique subtropical wilderness. The draining and polluting continued. Not until the 1990s, when the water of Florida Bay and the coral reefs around the Florida Keys showed serious signs of problems, did South Florida take action to abate the destruction.

Today, despite unbridled development, natural remnants survive in Southeast Florida in places like Everglades National Park, more than a score of state parks, as well as beaches and the coral reefs off the Florida Keys.

Stuart

Architects, historians, city planners and visitors rave about Stuart's renewed historic downtown. The 10-year revival of this pretty, well-to-do little waterfront town located between the St Lucie and Indian Rivers, about 40 miles north of Palm Beach, has brought a cultural, social, and economic renaissance. Stuart preserved its rich architectural history by converting its historic buildings into workplaces, shops, restaurants, residences, and recreational areas, all within easy walking distance. There are fine examples of Wood Frame Vernacular, Art Deco, Mediterranean Revival, and Colonial Revival architecture. So too, remain several waterfront mansions built along "Millionaire's Row" by those who prospered from the pineapple industry, which began in 1880 and gave the town its first boom when the Florida East Coast Railroad pushed south through Potsdam (later renamed Stuart) in 1895. By the mid-20th century, the pineapple industry had died out, replaced by tourism and recreational fishing. Today, Stuart's lively main streets are the same ones used by farmers to bring their pineapples to the downtown loading docks in its heyday.

Information

Stuart/Martin County Chamber of Commerce, 1650 S Kanner Hwy, Stuart, FL 34994; 561/287-1088, 800/524-9704; fax 561/220-3437; enjoy@goodnature.org; www.goodnature.org. Stuart Heritage, Inc, Stuart Heritage Museum, 161 SW Flagler Ave, Stuart, FL 34994; 561/220-4600. Historical Society of Martin County, Elliott Museum, 825 NE Ocean Blvd, Hutchinson Island, Stuart, FL 34996; 561/225-1961.

Three books worth reading for historical background are *Martin County, Our Heritage* by Caroline Pomeroy Ziemba, whose grandparents were among the first pioneers in Stuart, and *History of Martin County* by the Historical Society of Martin County, and *Treasure Coast Black Heritage: A Pictorial History* by Annie Kate Jackson, Andrea V. Moore, et al.

Getting there

From I-95, take Exit 61 and follow SR-76/Kanner Hwy north for seven miles to downtown. The more scenic Hwy A1A also runs through downtown.

Major airlines serve West Palm Beach International (PBIA), about 30 miles south of Stuart. From the airport, you can travel by rental car or Greyhound bus to Stuart. Stuart's Greyhound (800/231-2222, 561/287-7777) station is at 1308 S Federal Hwy. By the year 2000, Amtrak (800/USA RAIL) will open a new station in downtown Stuart.

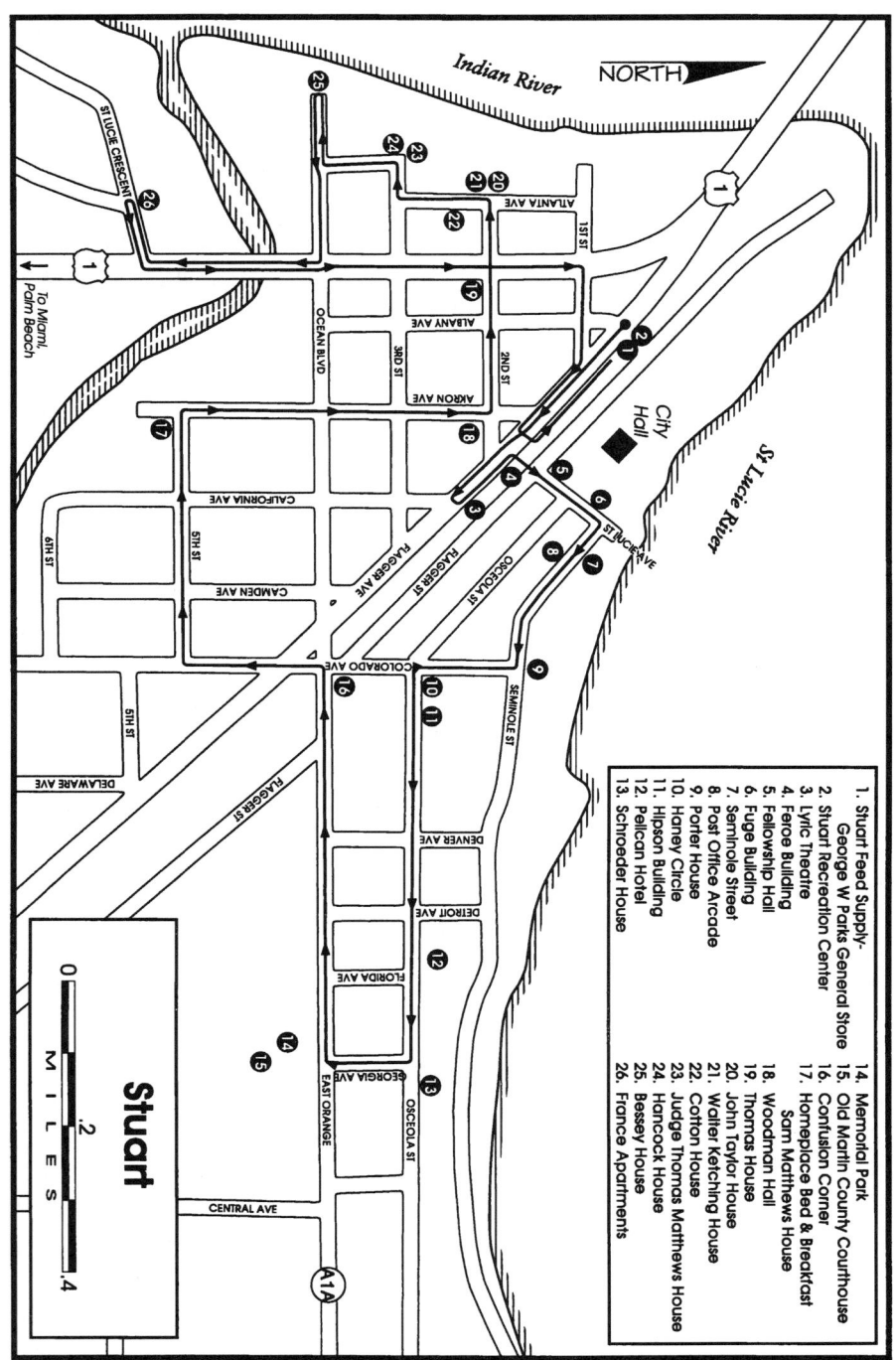

1. Stuart Feed Supply-
   George W Parks General Store
2. Stuart Recreation Center
3. Lyric Theatre
4. Feroe Building
5. Fellowship Hall
6. Fuge Building
7. Seminole Street
8. Post Office Arcade
9. Porter House
10. Haney Circle
11. Hipson Building
12. Pelican Hotel
13. Schroeder House
14. Memorial Park
15. Old Martin County Courthouse
16. Confusion Corner
17. Homeplace Bed & Breakfast
    Sam Matthews House
18. Woodman Hall
19. Thomas House
20. John Taylor House
21. Walter Ketching House
22. Cotton House
23. Judge Thomas Matthews House
24. Hancock House
25. Bessey House
26. France Apartments

Stuart

First steps

For maps and information, contact the **Stuart/Martin County Chamber of Commerce**. For historical information, contact **Stuart Heritage, Inc.** The latter operates the Stuart Heritage Museum.

The Stuart News is a local daily newspaper with community events and nightlife information.

Seasonal highlights

The busiest and most expensive season runs from December to April. Summers, spring break, and weekends are also popular.

Historic Stuart. *This three-mile route covers downtown Stuart and Millionaire's Row along Atlanta Ave. The tour can be walked comfortably in three hours, but it's more entertaining to allot a full day to see the interiors of some of the buildings and to stop for lunch at one of the downtown restaurants.*

Begin at Stuart Feed Supply, housed in the George W. Parks General Store (161 SW Flagler Ave). Pioneer families depended on ships such as Walter Kitching's trade boat, the *Merchant*, to receive supplies and ship goods before the arrival of the railroad in 1895. Once the railroad arrived, Kitching, George W. Parks, Harry E. Feroe and other pioneers built a business district, railroad dock, and depot along the river. Among those remaining is the **George W. Parks General Store**, constructed in 19th-century Wood Frame Vernacular style with a false front and gabled tin roof. Parks and his family lived upstairs and served customers downstairs. It's now home to the Stuart Heritage Museum, a must-see attraction. It houses more than 10,000 artifacts, from early maps, paintings, and photographs to household goods, newspapers, and equipment. (The museum will have reduced hours while undergoing renovations from fall 1999 to spring 2000.) *Leave the store and turn right.*

Enter the yellow and white tin-roofed art deco **Stuart Recreation Center**, built in 1943 by the Army Corps of Engineers as a serviceman's club for soldiers from nearby Camp Murphy. Though a few alterations were made, the original building's façade, roof, and walls remain. Note the original Dade pine beams and cypress joints. *Turn left and walk past the Stuart Heritage Museum.*

Cross St Lucie Avenue and stop at the **Lyric Theatre** (59 SW Flagler Ave), one of three that John C. Hancock opened starting in 1913. This third Mediterranean Revival building cost $100,000 and opened in 1926 as a silent-movie house. If the ticket window is open, stop inside to see the refurbished 600-seat theater, which has excellent acoustics, a stage, balcony, lobby, entrances on two streets, and a coffee bar. *Leave the building and walk back to the corner of Flagler and St Lucie avenues.*

In 1913 Sam Matthews built the **Feroe Building** (73 W Flagler Ave) in "rock-face" masonry block and cast-iron front columns for Harry E. Feroe to house a drugstore and post office downstairs, offices upstairs. Located across from the train depot, it quickly became a central gathering point, where people waited for mail and passengers. *Turn right onto St Lucie Avenue.*

The building at **204 St Lucie Ave** was originally constructed with a bell tower in 1912 by Sam Matthews. It has housed a bank, city hall, and police department. Today it serves as Fellowship Hall.

The **Fuge Building** (61 SW Osceola St) occupies the corner of Osceola Street and St Lucie Avenue. Now a restaurant, it was built in 1912 by several businessmen to house the town's first bank and five stores. The bank, headed by E.A. Fuge, was once robbed by the notorious Ashley Gang, which committed crimes in the area from 1911 to 1924.

One block up is **Seminole Street.** Before the street was created, the homes and businesses here, which front the St Lucie River, were accessed by boat. Starting at the corner is a wood frame vernacular building called The Annex. It housed 14 units of the St Lucie Hotel, once located across the street. Today, the street is lined with lovely restored waterfront cottages, most of which are businesses. *Stop mid-block a*t the **Post Office Arcade** (23 SW Osceola St), unmistakable for its Mediterranean Revival architecture with decorative blue and white "icing" above the entryway. Built in 1925 by Sam Matthews, it has entrances on Seminole and Osceola streets to allow airflow through the building. The post office is gone, but the refurbished building contains shops and restaurants. *Continue to Colorado Ave and turn left.*

Four ship's prow corner gables top the **Porter House** (100 Colorado Ave), also known as the Owl House. The style is supposed to have enabled the 1904 structure to withstand hurricane-force winds. *Return along Colorado St to the corner of Osceola St.*

Porter's widow, Ethel, donated the land at this intersection to the town and called it **Haney Circle** in honor of her friend Cynthia S.B. Haney, a local prohibitionist, suffragist, and newspaper columnist. The French bronze statue of a woman in the circle is called *Abundance. Turn left on Osceola* St.

The **Hipson Building** (33 E Osceola St) is a fine example of streamline art deco architecture. Note the horizontal wraparound eyebrow sunshades, courtyard garden, and mirrored porthole windows. Up the block, the large Mediterranean Revival **Pelican Hotel** (221 E Osceola St) with white stucco and a red barrel tile roof is now called Waterside Place and houses a law firm. It was popular among wealthy visitors. In the next block, the **Schroeder House** (319 E Osceola St) was built in 1908 in a Wood Frame Vernacular style for Curt Schroeder, the town's first historian and an original council member. Note the wide porch on three sides. It now houses a restaurant and several businesses. *Turn right onto Georgia St, then right onto E Ocean Blvd.*

When **Memorial Park** was created in the 1940s by the Woman's Club of Stuart, 225 trees were planted, each representing a Martin County World War II veteran. The **Old Martin County Courthouse** (80 E Ocean Blvd) is now headquarters for the Martin County Council for the Arts. Downstairs are gallery exhibits. On the staircase landings are interesting historic photos of the original schoolhouse building, its 1925 courthouse conversion, and the final 1937 WPA renovation.

At the intersection of East and West Ocean Boulevard, Flagler Avenue, and Colorado Avenue lies **Confusion Corner**, a dizzying traffic circle. It was here that thoroughfares used by pineapple farmers to bring their crop to town converged and then led northwest to the railroad loading docks. *Turn left onto Colorado Ave, then right onto West 5th St.*

At the corner of West 5th Street and Akron Avenue, the restored Homeplace Bed & Breakfast (501 S Akron Ave) occupies the wood frame vernacular **Sam Matthews House**, built in 1913. Massachusetts-born Matthews helped build Henry Flagler's famous Royal Poinciana Hotel in Palm Beach before moving to Stuart and constructing scores of buildings throughout Martin County. *Turn right onto Akron Ave.*

Woodman Hall (217 S Akron Ave), another Matthews construction, was erected in 1914 for the Woodman of the World Fraternal Insurance Organization. From 1916 to 1959, the Palm Beach Telephone Company and Southern Bell used the first floor as the town's telephone exchange. The second floor has been used almost continuously for meetings, including one in which William Jennings Bryan was the speaker. *Turn left onto West 2nd St.*

Much of the **Thomas House** remains as it was when carpenter/cabinet maker George Thomas built the Wood Frame Vernacular structure in 1901 at the corner of Albany Avenue (#200). Note his turned porch posts, Dade pine wainscoting, windows, and the second-floor balustrade. *Continue on W 2nd St across Hwy 1 and turn left onto Atlanta Ave.*

Sam Matthews was one of the finest builders in the state. Wealthy Stuart residents hired him to build their houses on the west side of Atlanta Avenue, with their fronts facing the river. It was Stuart's first residential neighborhood. Among these are the Craftsman Bungalow **John Taylor House** (#206), built in 1914 as a wedding present for Walter Kitching's daughter and her husband, John Taylor. Next door is the **Walter Kitching House** (#210) built in 1894 by Cocoa contractor Bob Jones (before Matthews arrived in Stuart). The original Queen Anne Victorian was the first house to have running water. Across the street, on the less exclusive east side of Atlanta Avenue, were smaller Matthews-built houses, such as the one-story Wood Frame Vernacular **Cotton House** (#203), constructed for Mrs. Kitching's seamstress. Note the interesting roof line. Back on the west side, Matthews spared no expense building the **Judge Thomas Matthews House** (#218) in a Colonial Revival style with classical columns and a pediment above the front entrance.

The road takes a slight jog before passing the **Hancock House** (#300), built in 1908 for John C. Hancock, owner of the Hancock Insurance Agency and the Lyric Theatre. *Turn right onto West Ocean Boulevard.*

Susan Corbin Bessey, wife of Stuart's first settler, built the classic American Bungalow **Bessey House** (601 W Ocean Blvd) in 1933, using lumber from the Danforth House hotel, which the Besseys had owned before it was destroyed by a hurricane. Among its notable guests were actor Joseph Jefferson and four presidents, including Grover Cleveland. Note the low-pitched gable roof, front porch and original windows. The house, which is under restoration, originally faced the river, but was moved in 1959 by new owners. *Cross over Atlanta Avenue, turn right onto Hwy 1, then right onto St Lucie Crescent.*

The last building on the tour is the Mediterranean Revival **France Apartments** (524 SW St Lucie Crescent), built in 1927 by AW France as a residential hotel. It had a garage below, common lounge areas, fireplaces, solariums connecting the two wings, and a boathouse on the river. *To return to the starting point, go back to Hwy 1 and turn left. Turn right onto West 1st St. Cross the tracks at St Lucie Ave and turn left onto Flagler Ave.*

Lodging

Stuart has a limited number of accommodations, especially in or near the historic district. Your best bet is one of the two historic bed and breakfasts. The next best option is one of the waterfront resorts across the river on Hutchinson Island. Prices are significantly higher from December through mid-April.

There's history, a beautiful Victorian setting with private baths, gardens and a pool, large breakfast, and enthusiastic owners at **The Homeplace Bed & Breakfast Inn** ($$–$$$$/$$–$$$$, 561/220-9148, www.homeplace.com), located in the Sam Matthews House at 501 Akron Ave. The third night is free Sunday–Thursday, May 1–November 30. Elegantly cozy describes the rooms, suites, and cottages at the **HarborFront Inn Bed & Breakfast** ($$–$$$$/$$–$$$$, 561/288-7289, www.harborfrontinn.com) located at 310 Atlanta Ave, overlooking the St Lucie River near the historic Kitching and Hancock houses.

The **Indian River Plantation Marriott Resort** ($$$$/$$$, 561/225-3700) at 555 NE Ocean Blvd is an upscale 298-room resort complex built in a Florida plantation style between the river and ocean. Amenities include golf, tennis, and water sports. The 120-room **Ramada Inn** ($$/$$, 561/287-6900) at 1200 S Federal Hwy has exterior corridors, a pool, restaurant, and complimentary continental breakfast. It's about a mile from the historic district.

Arts & culture
The Martin County Council for the Arts publishes a schedule of events, activities, and list of cultural groups in and around Stuart.

The **Lyric Theatre** (561/286-7827, 59 SW Flagler Ave) presents theatrical performances, concerts, recitals and bands. The **Barn Theatre** (561/2874884, 2400 SE Ocean Blvd), is a well-respected community theater that stages productions year round.

The **Elliott Museum** (561/225-1961, 825 NE Ocean Blvd, Hutchinson Island) covers the inventions and patents of inventor Sterling Elliott and his son as well as turn-of-the-century life through tools, toys, costumes, automobiles, and autographed memorabilia of Baseball Hall of Fame members. It's open daily 10 am to 4 pm, except some holidays. Admission is $4.00 for adults, $0.50 for children 6-13. The oldest structure in Martin County is **Gilbert's Bar House of Refuge Museum** (561/225-1875, 301 SE MacArthur Blvd, Hutchinson Island). It was built in 1875 as one of 10 houses commissioned by the U.S. Life-Saving Service to provide haven for shipwrecked sailors and travelers along Florida's east coast. The museum has nautical and marine history, aquariums, and a boat house with early lifesaving equipment. It's open daily 10 am to 4 pm, except some holidays. Admission is $2.00 for adults, $0.50 for children 6-13.

Besides the gallery in the **Court House Cultural Center** in the Old Martin County Courthouse, there is a gallery with changing exhibits in the **Elliott Museum** (see above).

What the **Arcade Book Nook** (561/220-9465, 31 Osceola St) lacks in space, it makes up for in a knowledgeable staff, good selection, and good resources. **Flagler News & Tobacco** (561/223-8119, 5 Flagler Ave) is a good source for newspapers and magazines.

Food & drink

Stuart is taking the lead in preserving its history by renovating its downtown. Restaurants have opened in many of the historic structures. There are parks with picnic benches and restrooms next to the Stuart Recreation Center (201 SW Flagler Ave) and the Bessey House (601 SW Ocean Blvd).

The theme at **Bubba's Fish Camp** ($–$$, 561/220-3747), located in a restored 1949 Standard Oil Service Station at 421 S Federal Hwy, is an early 20th-century Florida fishing camp. It serves Creole- and Cajun-style seafood, gumbo, collards, and sandwiches on the screened porch and inside under open-beam ceilings at lunch and dinner, plus breakfast on Sunday.

Damiano's ($$–$$$, 561/781-5009), located in a beautifully restored 1913 tin-roof house at 18 Seminole St, describes its cuisine as transcontinental. Translate that to fusion of many cultures, which Anthony and Lisa Damiano do quite well, having worked at Maxim's in Paris, the Russian Tea Room in Manhattan, and other worldly spots.

David's in the Courtyard ($$–$$$, 561/219-4446), located in the Post Office Arcade (23 Osceola St) has a piano lounge, plus white-tablecloth service. The menu has many grilled items accompanied by polenta, arugula, sauteed spinach, and fresh roma tomatoes. Reservations are suggested.

The Flagler Grill ($$–$$$, 561/221-9517) at 47 SW Flagler Ave in historic downtown offers a dinner-only menu featuring innovative New World cuisine in a turn-of-the-century building decorated with art work.

Nature's Way Cafe ($, 561/220-7306) in the Post Office Arcade (25 Osceola St) is big on healthy sandwiches, soups, pastas, and green salads and fresh squeezed juices and smoothies. Eat in or take out.

There's no smoking at the small bistro-style **Riverwalk Cafe** ($–$$, 561/221-1511), where the lunch and dinner menus feature salads, sandwiches, seafood, lamb shank, and pasta dishes at 201 SW St Lucie Ave.

Nightlife
Stuart has a small selection of bars and clubs, but all are located outside of the historic district. For live music, try the **Java Joint** at 201 S Federal Hwy on Friday nights or **The Refuge** at 2196 SE Ocean Blvd, which specializes in blues. **Rocking Horse American** at 1580 SE Federal Hwy is a country dance club with free lessons and live entertainment Tuesday-Saturday. **Groucho's Comedy Club** at 950 S Federal Hwy and **Jake's Retreat Sports Bar** at 2908 SE Waaler St are both exactly what their names imply.

Events
Stuart Heritage, Inc, stages an annual **Historic Homes Tour** in mid-February. The cost is $10. The Martin County Black Heritage Association presents an annual **Martin County Black Heritage Festival** in late February.

Miami Beach

They say that you can't reheat a soufflé. Fortunately, Barbara Capitman wasn't aware of the cliché when she visited Miami Beach in the 1970s and fell in love with its forgotten treasure-trove of 1920s-1940s Art Deco architecture. Watching helplessly as many of the decaying structures with their jutting towers, streamlined curves, window eyebrows, parallel straight lines, zig-zags, chevrons, and neon fell to the wrecking ball, she helped found the Miami Design Preservation League. Together with other preservationists they worked to have a one-square mile area on the southern end of Miami Beach—South Beach—listed on the National Register of Historic Places.

As a result of their efforts, South Beach contains nearly 800 fascinating, intact Art Deco buildings, the largest collection in the country. Almost every block offers architectural delights, ranging from Art Deco and Zig Zag Moderne to Streamline and Depression Moderne, as well as sections of Mediterranean Revival.

It all started at the turn of the century, when John Collins, a Quaker farmer, unsucceessfully tried growing citrus on a mangrove-covered island off Miami. Midwesterner Carl Fisher, who had made his money in the automobile industry, came down in 1910. A few years later he purchased part of the island from Collins and began dredging sand from Biscayne Bay and dumping it on the island. Fisher created a large sandbar, man-made beach, and what was to become "America's Riviera."

Colorful publicity extravaganzas attracted land speculators. Elegant homes went up for wealthy northerners seeking winter relief on the warm beach. Miami Beach became THE place to be. *Life Magazine* wrote in 1947, "Each winter it becomes the mecca for stage stars, songwriters, playboys, labor leaders, big-money executives and big-money gamblers." Throughout the 1920s, 1930s, 1940s, and into the early 1950s, the building went on and the people came, slowed only by the 1926 hurricane and land-boom bust, and then the Depression.

The scene changed in the late 1950s and 1960s as development moved north on the island with the construction of the Fontainebleau and American, the new mega-resorts. South Beach's Art Deco hotels slowly closed or became long-term, low-income residences to the area's aging population.

Not until the late 1970s when the bulldozers were on the move to make way for the new condo revolution did Miami Beach's fate change. Enter Barbara Capitman and the Miami Design Preservation League, who stood up against turning the beach into a "Condo Canyon" in the late 1970s. Enter also designer Leonard Horowitz, credited with the "Deco Revival pastel palette" according to Capitman, that gave the previously mostly white buildings their distinctive Miami Beach Art Deco style.

While the 1980s heralded Miami Beach's comeback, the 1990s renamed it "America's Riviera" as preservationists and savvy business dealers invested hard work and hundreds of millions of dollars into converting many of the old vacation hotels and apartments into glamorous hotels, swish apartments, trendy restaurants, racy clubs, and tony boutiques.

Today, South Beach is again a landmark destination where New York escapees, fashion and film moguls, curious tourists, Europe's elite, South American investors, gays and lesbians, Hasidic Jews, and Cuban immigrants live and play. Day and night, it's awash in activity ranging from strolling the cafe-lined Ocean Drive, in-line skating, dancing until dawn, dining al fresco, people watching, kite flying, shopping, star gazing, and touring the architectural treasures.

There's no need for a car. Everything is within walking distance. The district runs from 6th Street north to 23rd Street and Lenox Avenue east to the Atlantic Ocean.

Information

Greater Miami Convention & Visitors Bureau, 701 Brickell Ave, Suite 2700, Miami, FL 33131; 305/539-3063, 800/283-2707; fax 305/539-2911; www.miamiandbeaches.com. **Art Deco Welcome Center**, 1001 Ocean Dr, 305/531-3484. **Miami Beach Chamber of Commerce**, 1920 Meridian Ave, Miami Beach, FL 33139; 305/672-1270; fax 305/538-4336.

Getting there

Major carriers from around the world fly into Miami International Airport, NW 36th St and Le Jeune Rd. Greyhound (800/231-2222, 305/871-1810) operates three stations in Miami, none in Miami Beach. The closest stations are at 4111 NW 27th St and 700 Biscayne Blvd. Amtrak (800/USA RAIL, 305/835-1221) offers train service to Miami at 8303 NW 37th Ave.

By car, five causeways span Biscayne Bay to link Miami Beach to mainland Miami. All of them can be accessed from I-95. In addition, Hwy A1A is a coastal route connecting the island to northern barrier islands.

First steps

For area maps and information, contact the **Greater Miami Convention & Visitors Bureau**. The **Art Deco Welcome Center** is run by the Miami Design Preservation

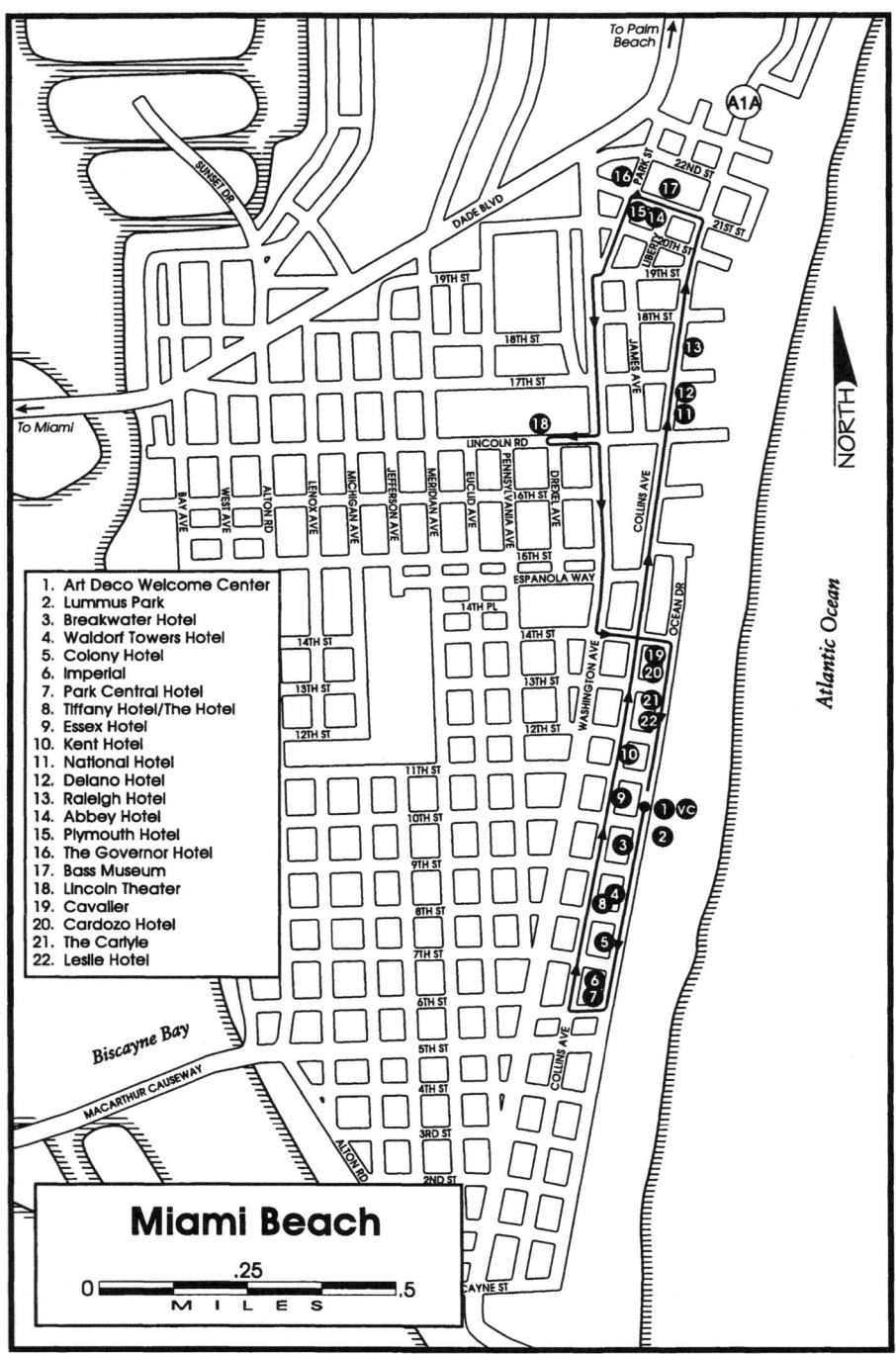

1. Art Deco Welcome Center
2. Lummus Park
3. Breakwater Hotel
4. Waldorf Towers Hotel
5. Colony Hotel
6. Imperial
7. Park Central Hotel
8. Tiffany Hotel/The Hotel
9. Essex Hotel
10. Kent Hotel
11. National Hotel
12. Delano Hotel
13. Raleigh Hotel
14. Abbey Hotel
15. Plymouth Hotel
16. The Governor Hotel
17. Bass Museum
18. Lincoln Theater
19. Cavalier
20. Cardozo Hotel
21. The Carlyle
22. Leslie Hotel

Miami Beach

0   .25   .5
M I L E S

League and is a must stop for information and tours of the historic district. It's open daily from 11 am to 6 pm, later in high season. **Miami Beach Chamber of Commerce** has maps, information, accommodations, and info about local services and businesses.

Deco Delights: Preserving the Beauty and Joy of Miami Beach Architecture ($22) by Barbara Baer Capitman, the woman who started the Miami Beach renaissance, is a fascinating read and look at America's first 20th-century historic district. *The Life and Times of Miami Beach* ($45) by Ann Armbruster takes you from the beginning, from a mangrove-studded island to a glitterati playground. Laura Cerwinske captures the past and future of Miami Beach in *Tropical Deco: Architecture and Design of Old Miami Beach* ($18).

Walking tours

The **Miami Design Preservation League** (305/672-2014) operates several tours, including the popular 90-minute Art Deco Historic District Walking Tours ($10), which depart Saturday at 10:30 am and Thursday at 6:30 pm from the Art Deco Welcome Center on Ocean Drive, 1001 Ocean Dr. They also give tours ($5–$10) to special areas of the district.

Seasonal highlights

January is high season in terms of crowds and prices. It's also the month with the most happening, from the Art Deco Weekend to the annual Art in Miami Week to the Original Miami Beach Antique Show.

Historic Miami Beach. *This 3.75-mile route covers the historic hotels along two of South Beach's main north-south streets—Collins Avenue and Ocean Drive. Allot 90 minutes. However, a more leisurely trip of three or four hours will include stops inside a few buildings, a museum, and sidewalk cafes.*

Begin at the Art Deco Welcome Center. After browsing the Miami Design Preservation League's information about the historic district, walk south along Ocean Drive. On the left side of the street is **Lummus Park**, a broad, patterned sidewalk and landscaped area that stretches almost the length of the district along the wide white-sand beach. This is LA's Venice Beach, Rio's Copacabana, and France's Riviera all rolled into one. The scene is a whirl of tanned bodies, bikini- and shorts-clad skaters, super jocks posing and playing volleyball, little old ladies toting umbrellas and handbags, and tourists in awe of it all.

It's hard to decide when the **Breakwater Hotel** (940 Ocean), designed by Anton Skislewicz in 1939, is more beautiful. By night, its two-faced blue neon name in vertical letters between vertical blue neon stripes stretches toward the black sky. By day, the pastel yellow and blue accents on white seem to shimmer in the sunlight.

Albert Anis designed the three-story **Waldorf Towers Hotel** (860 Ocean) with an oceanfront sun porch, continuous sunshade above the windows, and a circular corner lighthouse-style tower that wears a blue ring of neon light at night. The tower was torn down in 1981, but rebuilt by the hotel's new owner a few years later. The **Colony Hotel** (736 Ocean) was an early work of Henry Hohauser, one of the fathers of Miami Beach's Art Deco movement. Take a moment to look at the lobbies of both hotels.

In the next block, the white **Imperial** (650 Ocean) with lavender and green trim features many decorative elements such as sunshades over the windows, vertical bars of floral plaques, and three circular ornaments on the parapet. Next door in the same colors is the **Park Central Hotel** (640 Ocean), designed in 1937 by Henry Hohauser, a New Yorker who brought ideas of the new modern movement south to Miami Beach. Like most of the district's buildings that mostly date from the 1920s to 1940s, with a few from the 1950s, the hotel did not have air-conditioning. Architects designed in an abundance of windows, sunshades over windows, and windows on two sides of corner apartments to allow the natural ocean breezes to cool and ventilate. Today, the hotel is one of the National Trust's Historic Hotels of America. Step beyond the metal balustrade onto the porch, through the doors set in Vitrolite, and into the hotel's vast lobby for a view of the beautiful terrazzo floors. *Turn right onto 6th St, then right onto Collins Ave.*

Corners gave architects the opportunity to expand a building's streamlined look with a smooth curving sweep, as in the case of L Murray Dixon's 1939 **Tiffany Hotel/The Hotel** (801 Collins). Its original name still rockets skyward in neon, but after a lawsuit by the famous New York jewelry store following the hotel's renovation, the property changed its name to The Hotel.

Local architects interpreted the movement to fit Miami Beach. Along with the usual Art Deco and Moderne themes, they incorporated nautical, marine, tropical plant, and bird elements. Hohauser's 1938 **Essex Hotel** (1001 Collins) is a fine example, recalling a streamlined ocean liner, complete with porthole windows, circular ornaments resembling portholes, and its name in neon rising at the corner like a ship's smokestack.

Except for sprucing up interior rooms, very little has changed on L. Murray Dixon's modest 1938 **Kent Hotel** (1131 Collins). The lobby's stylish terrazzo floors and recessed lighting are worth a look inside.

Buildings on this end of Collins are larger and topped with more elaborate towers. Among these is Roy France's 1940 **National Hotel** (1677 Collins), whose beautifully restored sleek monument to the movement has a silver dome topping a cupola with Moorish arches. The pool is a must-see. Another spectacular pool is found at Robert Swartburg's white-on-white **Delano Hotel** (1685 Collins), which wears an Aztec-style headdress that made it the most "outrageous" building of its time. Philippe Starck's cutting-edge redesign in 1995 for Ian Schrager, who started Studio 54, assured that the outrageous description would stick.

Ribbons of glass windows run horizontally around L Murray Dixon's **Raleigh Hotel** (1777 Collins Ave), anchored at the corner of 18th St and Collins Ave with its name in script and capital letters above the entrance and an "R" monogram on the roof. Go inside and wander through the lobby and bar, then stop by the pool, which *Life Magazine* described in a 1940 article as the most beautiful pool in the world. *Continue north on Collins Ave, then turn left onto 21st St.*

On the corner of 21st St and Liberty Ave is the **Abbey Hotel** (300 21st), an Albert Anis design. Among its notable features are the corner tower that rises over the entrance with a curved eyebrow, matching spires that end in stylized tulips, and a center relief sculpture of a reptile and flowers.

Up the street, Anton Skislewicz's abstract 1940 **Plymouth Hotel** (336 21st) seems to skyrocket from the pavement. According to Barbara Capitman in *Deco Delights*, "it is astonishingly reminiscent of the Trylon and Perisphere, the central symbol of the 1939-1940 New York World's Fair. Like that icon of the Deco world, the Plymouth features two impressive sculptural elements: a pylon towering over a rounded entry... This impressive central shape is the center from which wings flow on either side, and the whole is a powerful, unornamented study in concrete." Today, the building is a residence for musicians of the New World Symphony. Across the street is **The Governor Hotel** (435 21st), another Hohauser building, similar to his Cardozo Hotel (see below). The elaborate interior, as striking as the detailed exterior, is worth a peak.

The **Bass Museum** (2121 Park) started out as the Miami Beach Library and Art Center in 1930. It was designed in 1930 by Russell Pancoast, grandson of John Collins, the founder of Miami Beach. The building leaves no doubt that the Art Deco movement has its roots in Mayan architecture. Take a close look at the keystone carvings by Gustav Bohland above the entrances. The left panel features three early explorer ships; the center has a stylized pelican and other natural elements; the right has elements of modern Miami, boats, planes, radio towers, railroad and automobile bridges, and the skyline. *Turn left onto Park Avenue, which at 19th St connects to Washington Ave. Continue south on Washington Ave, then turn right onto Lincoln Road for a short detour.*

Lincoln Road is a seven-block pedestrian mall with chic boutiques, galleries, cafes, and tourist shops. In its heyday, five movie theaters lined the street. Today, the best preserved of these is the **Lincoln Theater** (541 Lincoln), home of the New World Symphony. The parapet and pilasters feature beautiful bas-relief stylized palm fronds. *Return to Washington Ave and continue south. Turn left onto 14th St, cross Collins, then turn right onto Ocean Dr.*

Roy France's 1936 **Cavalier** (1320 Ocean) speaks Art Deco from its carved name in the façade to the carved Mayan style ornamentation above and below the windows. Next door, the **Cardozo Hotel** (1300 Ocean), designed by Hohauser in 1939, is a beautiful blend of Art Deco and Streamline Moderne. It was the first of Barbara Capitman's hotel restoration projects. About 15 years later, it was purchased by musician Gloria Estefan and her husband Emilio and again restored. Today, the hotel and restaurant are a hot spot for music and dining. Note the balustrade and supporting porch columns, which were constructed of native limestone rock.

The smooth, curving sweep of **The Carlyle** (1250 Ocean) designed by Kiehnel and Elliott in 1941 exemplifies Art Deco giving way to Streamline Moderne. Vertical piers contrast with rounded eyebrows. Even the balustrade is a blend of circles and straight lines. Contrast this with the classic Art Deco style **Leslie Hotel** (1244 Ocean) next door, designed by Albert Anis four years earlier. *Return to the Art Deco Welcome Center.*

Lodging

You might as well pick your favorite color when choosing accommodations in South Beach, because so many hotels offer great service, oodles of amenities, great views, and beautiful rooms in landmark buildings. In addition, there are three National Trust hotels. Rates, which are generally well over $100 for a standard double, are higher from December through April.

Island Outpost (800/OUTPOST, 305/531-8800) owns half a dozen of the best restored landmark hotels in South Beach. Choosing one is a matter of style: elegant, hip, funky, or chic. Here's a quick run down: The **Tides** ($$$$) at 1220 Ocean Dr is the group's high chic flagship in a 1936 Art Deco jewel with 45 big, big suites, each decorated in smooth beige, white, and sand tones and featuring a breathtaking ocean view, state-of-the-art telecommunications, TV/VCR, mini-bar, service and more service, and black-out curtains and double-pane windows to block out Ocean Drive's all-night party. Imagine a sophisticated hotel in Indonesia at the height of Colonial occupation and you'll have a picture of the understated glamour that is the **Casa Grande** ($$$$) at 834 Ocean Dr. The colorful all-suite **Marlin** ($$$$) at 1200 Collins Ave is nicknamed the "rock 'n' roll hotel" because it's favored by music industry folks and has a state-of-the-art recording facility. Colorful batik interiors decorate the **Cavalier** ($$$), where a more affordable rate gives you a catbird seat with good service, pool privileges at The Tides, mini-bar, and a TV/VCR/CD in a restored 1936 classic hotel at 1320 Ocean Dr. Fashion and production companies that come to South Beach like **The Kent** ($$$) because of its affordable rates and great service, location, and amenities. It has 54 rooms and suites with restored original mahogany wood accents, classic terrazzo floors, tropical rattan furnishings with batik fabrics, and a garden one block west of the ocean at 1131 Collins Ave. **The Leslie** ($$$$), featured in *Ace Ventura Pet Detective* and *Birdcage*, looks like a birthday cake with white icing trimmed with bright yellow accents at 1244 Ocean Dr. It has a sunny beachfront porch and sidewalk cafe, 39 rooms decorated in screaming colors and 4 suites in natural wood and beige. More major renovations are scheduled for 2000.

Todd Oldham designed the interiors at the National Trust's 1939 **The Hotel** (formerly the **Tiffany Hotel**) ($$$$, 305/531-2222, 800/678-8946), which features 52 rooms and suites with bathroom floors airbrushed to resemble the ocean, tie-dyed bathrobes, in-room VCR/TV/CD and mini-bar, plus a rooftop pool, popular contemporary restaurant, fitness room, and twice-daily maid service at 801 Collins Ave. Architect Henry Hohauser, one of the fathers of South Beach's Art Deco movement, designed the **Park Central Hotel** ($$$–$$$$, 305/538-1611, 800/678-8946). Today, this elegant National Trust Hotel offers 125 pretty pastel-colored rooms and suites, ocean views, a rooftop sun deck, pool, ocean-front patio dining, two bars, and service galore at 640 Ocean Dr.

The restored 1936 **Indian Creek Hotel** ($$–$$$, 305/531-2727, 800 /491-2772) faces Indian Creek and is a block from the Atlantic Ocean at 2727 Indian Creek Dr. It offers one of the best values on the island. The 61 rooms are pleasantly outfitted with period furnishings and mini-refrigerators. A landscaped garden surrounds the pool and a promising cafe and cozy bar offer places to linger. Bargain hunters can experience South Beach in Art Deco surroundings at the **Ocean Surf Hotel** ($$, 305/866-1648), a restored family-owned 1940s boutique-style hotel across from the ocean with 49 rooms decorated in period pieces. Continental breakfast on the front porch or in your room is included at 7436 Ocean Terrace, just north of South Beach.

Young travelers can find both private and dormitory-style rooms at **Hostelling International Miami Beach-Clay Hotel** ($–$$, 305/534-2988, 800/379-2529), located two blocks from the beach in an historic Mediterranean Revival style building with a cafe, comfortable facilities, and good service. Ditto at **Banana Bungalow** ($–$$, 305/538-1951, 800/7-HOSTEL), a member of a popular national hostel chain at 2360 Collins Ave. Facilities and services include a large pool, restaurant, bar, theater, billiards room, open kitchen, laundry, Internet room, tours, volley games, and water sports equipment.

Arts & culture
Miami Beach has earned a reputation as a major arts and cultural center. On any day of the week there is usually a choice of plays, ballets, dance and musical concerts, art films, and exhibitions.

The refurbished Art Deco **Jackie Gleason Theater** (305/673-7300, 1700 Washington Ave) is the stage for the International Ballet Festival, classical concerts, Broadway series, and performances by various dance companies. The **Lincoln Theatre** (305/673-3330, 541 Lincoln Rd) is home to the New World Symphony Orchestra and presents performances by the Miami City Ballet, Florida Philharmonic Orchestra, individual classical performers, and the New World School of the Arts. **North Miami Beach Performing Arts Theater** (305/948-2990, 17011 NE 19th Ave, North Miami Beach) presents live theater and dance productions. The **Colony Theater** (305/534-9924, 1040 Lincoln Rd) hosts the Ballet Flamenco La Rosa and off-off Broadway productions. The **Performing Arts Network** (305/672-0552, 555 17th St) hosts everything from dance and music concert series to theater for children to La Rosa Flamenco Theatre.

Miami City Ballet (305/532-4880) performs classical and contemporary works. Traditional Spanish dance takes on a broader perspective with performances by **Ballet Flamenco La Rosa** (305/757-8475). **New World Symphony** (305/673-3330) performs chamber music and full-orchestra concerts.

Alliance Cinema (305/531-8504, 927 Lincoln Rd) presents art films, film festivals, and independent films. The **Edge Theater** (305/531-6083, 405 Española Way) stages a season of classic dramas and new plays such as *The Final Hours of Norma Jean*. Nearby, the **Area Stage** (305/673-8002, 645 Lincoln Rd) presents contemporary American and British classics.

More than 70 artists welcome visitors to watch them work in their studios at the **Art Center South Florida** (305/674-8278, 800 Lincoln Rd). The center also features three exhibit spaces. When collectors want cutting-edge works of art, they head for the **Española Way Art Center** (305/531-9600, 405 Española Way). The works of pop artist Romero Britto are sold at **Britto Central** (305/531-8821, 818 Lincoln Rd).

Books & Books (305/532-3222, 933 Lincoln Rd) is one of the best bookstores in Miami. It offers signings, talks, and a coffee bar.

Along with touring exhibitions, the **Bass Museum of Art** (305/673-7530, 2121 Park Ave) presents outdoor sculptures, a permanent collection of Old Master paintings, sculptures, textiles, and furnishings, as well as works by 18th to 20th-century European artists. The Belgian and Flemish tapestries are particularly worth seeing. The **Sanford L. Ziff Jewish Museum of Florida** (305/672-5044, 301 Washington Ave), housed in a beautifully restored 1936 synagogue, features exhibits covering Miami's Jewish heritage. More than 70,000 European and American design elements and works of art dating from 1885 to 1945 are on display at **The Wolfsonian/FIU** (305/531-1001, 1001 Washington Ave) in a Mediterranean Revival building. You'll find everything from a 1929 movie theater window grill to a 1910 French iron balustrade.

Food & drink

What can one say about a town that has everything from fast food to haute cuisine to trend-setting chefs. Prices vary as widely as the menus, with rarely anything as stratospheric as you'll find in Los Angeles or New York. Dine early for a table anywhere. Wait until 9ish if you want to be part of the scenery.

Some folks go to **Mezzanotte** ($$$, 305/673-4343) at 1200 Washington Ave for the sleek Italian dishes, others say it's for the unexpected show by celebrity patrons. For serious Italian cuisine without the unexpected floor show, there's the elegant **Osteria del Teatro** ($$–$$$, 305/538-7850) at 1443 Washington Ave.

Ask connoisseurs of Chinese food for the best Szechuan and Pekinese food in Miami and **Chrysanthemum** ($$$, 305/531-5656) at 1256 Washington Ave will pop up again and again. Another Asian favorite is **Thai Toni** ($$–$$$, 305/538-8424) at 890 Washington Ave, serving memorable upscale Southeast Asian cuisine in a mellow Asian setting. Be sure to try the fish. If you can stand the din, the inexpensive Asian food at **Noodles of Asia** ($$, 305/925-0050) at 801 Lincoln Rd will satisfy your appetite and soul. If you're looking for fresh, fresh sushi try **Toni's Sushi** ($$$, 305/673-9368) at 1208 Washington Ave.

In some towns, serious gourmets wouldn't go near a hotel dining room except for breakfast. Not the case in South Beach, where you need to stay a week to dine at the best of these, then another week to hit the next tier. Start at the **Blue Door at the Delano** ($$$, 305/674-6400) at 1685 Collins Ave, where a reservation will reward you with an elegant atmosphere, magical service, and excellent food that's a blend of the best of France and the Caribbean. Also at the top of the list is **Astor Place** ($$$, 305/672-7217) in the refined Astor Hotel at 956 Washington Ave. The food is creative, thoughtful, beautifully presented, and memorable to your palate. At **1220 at The Tides** ($$$, 305/604-5130) at 1220 Ocean Dr you must leave room for dessert, no matter how much you've stuffed yourself with wonderful, inventive appetizers and roasted lamb chops or sauteed soft shell crabs with morels . For more relaxed, good food in an artsy setting with live jazz upstairs, there's the **Van Dyke Cafe** ($–$$, 305/534-3600) in the historic 1924 Van Dyke Hotel at 846 Lincoln Rd.

For around-the-clock dining, there's the landmark, everybody-goes-there **News Cafe** ($–$$, 305/538-6297) with light meals, good wines, some of the best people-watching, and indoor and outdoor seating at 800 Ocean Dr. You'll find more locals than tourists at the budget-friendly **Eleventh Street Diner** ($–$$, 305/534-6373) in an Art Deco style dining car at 11th St and Washington Ave.

Joe's Stone Crab ($$$, 305/673-0365) at 227 Biscayne St is a Miami Beach institution that does stone crabs in a big way, with lots of side dishes, in season (mid-October through August). Tip: be at the door 30 minutes before it opens and you can avoid the three-hour lines!

Nightlife

In South Beach, there's nightlife for everyone—martini bars, cigar bars, lounges, drag shows, concerts, and on and on and on. Clubs range from intimate enclaves with a live jazz or blues performer to 10,000-square-foot mega hangouts with multiple dance floors or three or four different rooms catering to different crowds. You can literally club crawl all night in South Beach, as many clubs don't close until 5 am, just as others are opening. For who and what's on for the week, check out *The Miami Herald*'s "Weekend" section on Fridays.

Clubs come and go, but **Amnesia** has managed to stay around for years, catering to many tastes with open-air dance floor, bars, and restaurants at 136 Collins Ave. There are "beautiful people" galore at **Bash**, a celebrity hangout with theme nights, the hippest DJs, reggae, salsa, and fashion shows at 655 Washington Ave. You'll want to get into the swim of things at **Club Deep** at 621 Washington Ave, where you dance above a 2,000-gallon aquarium. For really late-night party folks, **Fabrik** opens its doors at 627 Washington Ave at 4 am with a different DJ spinning the latest each night. Ditto **Pump** at 841 Washington Ave. **Groove Jet** at 323 23rd St is one of the mega clubs (10,000 sq ft) with three dance floors, indoor and outdoor play areas, and "bass-heavy house music [that] thumps until the early morning." **Score** is always jam-packed with gay groovers at 727 Lincoln Road Mall.

On the smoother side is **Jazid**, a local favorite for live jazz at 1342 Washington Ave. If that's too crowded, try the intimate **Van Dyke** with live jazz above the popular restaurant at 846 Lincoln Rd. For a Latin beat, there's **Yuca** of restaurant fame with jazz and dancing at 501 Lincoln Rd. The crowd and atmosphere are gay and sophisticated at **821** at 821 Lincoln Rd. For an uptown and very classy night on the town, there's nary a match for the **Bar Room** at 346 Lincoln Rd.

Events

The year starts with the spectacular **Art Deco Weekend** (305/672-2014), with tours, antiques, vendors, and entertainment and the huge **Original Miami Beach Antique Show** (305/754-4931). That's followed by the outdoor **Miami Beach Festival of the Arts** (305/673-7730) in February. **South Beach Film Festival** (305/532-1233) hits the screen in April. That runs at the same time as the **Miami Gay and Lesbian Film Festival** (305) 534-9924. Get your taste buds ready for some of the best South Florida cuisine at the annual **Taste of the Beach Festival** (305/672-6050) in April. The silver screen lights up in April for the annual **Miami Beach Gay & Lesbian Film Festival** (305/534-9924). **The International Hispanic Theatre Festival** (305/445-8877) gets under way in June.

Everglades National Park

Marjory Stoneman Douglas immortalized the Everglades in her book, *The Everglades: River of Grass*. She opens with the emphatic statement, "There is no other Everglades in the world." It encompasses a slow-moving rain-fed sheet of water that flows from Lake Okeechobee to the southern tip of the Florida mainland. Though it is the largest subtropical wilderness in the continental United States, its 1.5 million acres cover only about one-seventh of the original Everglades. The rest has been cut off from the natural flow by canals and dikes to accommodate development.

Native Americans called it *Pahayokee* or "grassy waters" for the vast sawgrass prairies that cover much of the Everglades. Along with these are coastal mangrove and subtropical and tropical hardwood hammock communities that support an abundance of wildlife, especially birds and alligators.

The park has eastern, western and northern entrances. The eastern entrance has numerous trails, campgrounds, and the park's headquarters and main visitor center.

The Anhinga Trail, a few miles west of the eastern entrance, is the park's most popular trail. There's a good reason for that. The easily accessible trail is a half-mile elevated boardwalk that runs over marshy Taylor Slough, a deep depression in the oolite rock where water remains year round. During the dry season, when many freshwater sources in the Everglades dry up, birds, fish, and animals converge at the slough. The trail passes right through the middle of this wildlife "happening." Many of the animals are so used to seeing visitors that they stand within a few feet of the boardwalk as you pass. Please do not approach them.

The paved, half-mile Gumbo Limbo Trail has far fewer visible animals, but is another favorite among visitors because of its dense, jungle-like setting. The juxtaposition of the two trails is especially striking.

Information
Everglades National Park, 40001 State Road 9336, Homestead, FL 33034; 305/242-7700; website: www.nps.gov/ever. **Tropical Everglades Visitor Association**, 160 Hwy 1, Florida City 33034; 305/245-9180 or 800/388-9669. **Greater Homestead--Florida City Chamber of Commerce**, 43 N. Krome Ave, Homestead 33030; 305/247-2332 or 888/352-4891.

Getting there
Many major airlines serve Miami International Airport (MIA), about 30 miles northeast of the main park entrance. Greyhound (800/231-2222, 305/247-2040)

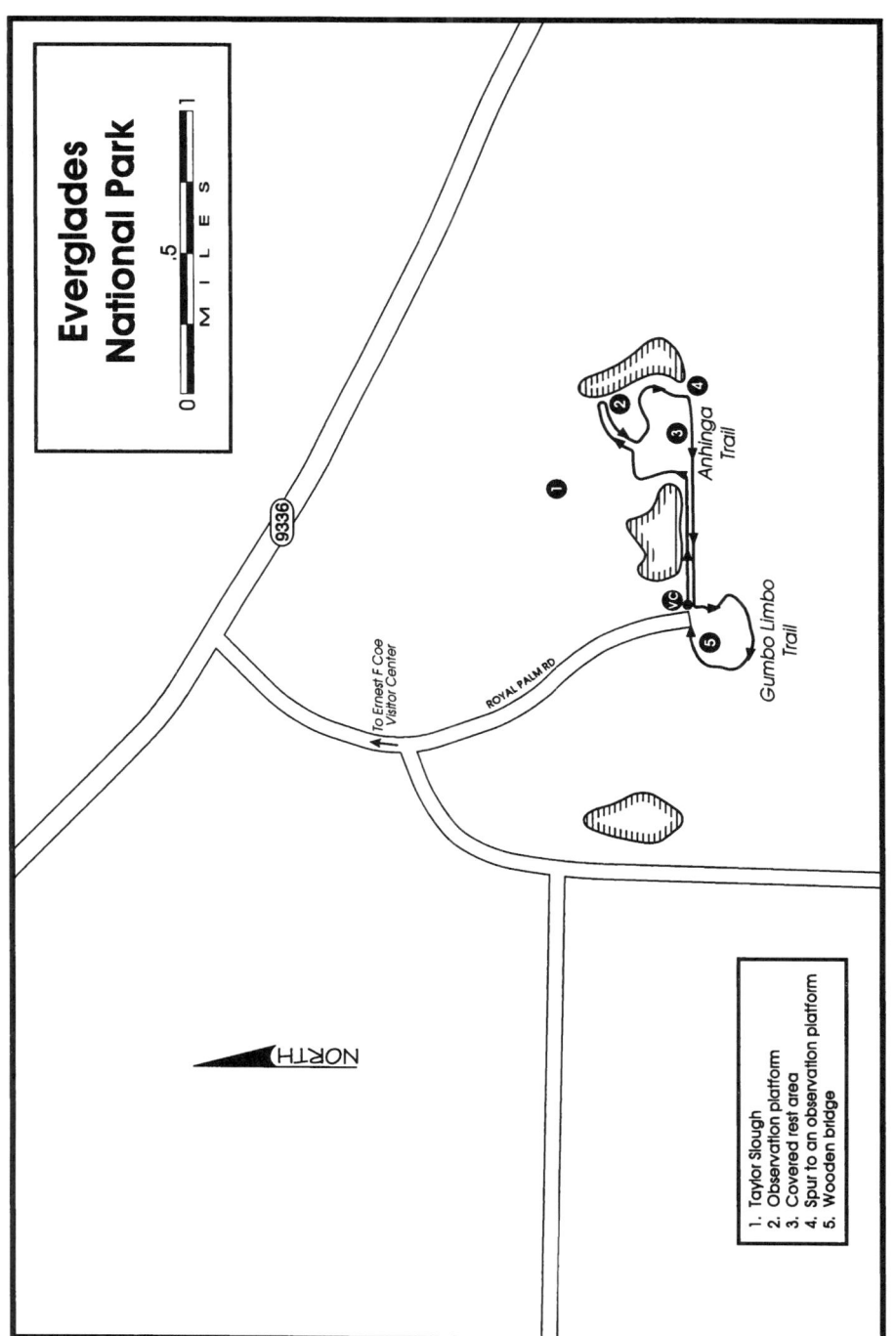

Everglades
National Park

0   .5   1
MILES

9336

To Ernest F Coe
Visitor Center

ROYAL PALM RD

Anhinga
Trail

Gumbo Limbo
Trail

NORTH

1. Taylor Slough
2. Observation platform
3. Covered rest area
4. Spur to an observation platform
5. Wooden bridge

operates service into Homestead at 5 NE Third Rd, from where you can take a taxi to the park for about $20. Amtrak (800/USA RAIL) trains run to Miami, but get no closer than that. To reach Everglades National Park's main entrance and the Ernest F. Coe Visitor Center, drive south on the Florida Turnpike, which ends at Florida City. Turn west on State Route 9336 in Florida City (the first traffic light after the turnpike ends), which leads to the park entrance. From Florida City, the Ernest F. Coe Visitor Center is about 15 miles away. The main entrance, where you have to pay a fee, is two miles beyond.

First steps

For maps and information, contact **Everglades National Park**. Admission is $10 per car, $5 per bicycle or pedestrian. It's valid for seven days at all three park entrances. The main park entrance is open 24 hours a day. Make your first stop the Ernest F. Coe Visitor Center, the park's main visitor center and museum. It's open daily 8 am to 5 pm. The Royal Palm Visitor Center, from which the two following walks depart, is open 8 am to 4:15 pm. The trails are open 24 hours. **Tropical Everglades Visitor Association** has general information about the region.

Numerous publications cover the Everglades and Everglades National Park. Among them is the 103-page *Everglades Wildguide* by Jean Craighead George, published by the National Park Service ($7.95). It gives an easy-to-understand overview of the ecosystem, including plants and animals.

Walking tours

Ranger-led tours are offered on a regular basis from November to April. Check schedules at the Ernest F. Coe Visitor Center or the Royal Palm Visitor Center.

Seasonal highlights

Mid-October to mid-May is the best time to visit the park. The trails are near sources of freshwater, a scarce commodity in winter. There are also more park activities. Once the summer rains start, the birds and other wildlife move farther away from the trails. If you come in summer, early morning and early evening are the best times for viewing. Mosquitoes and heat are the biggest summer detractors.

Natural Everglades National Park. *This 1-mile walk covers two half-mile trails, the Anhinga Trail and the Gumbo Limbo Trail. Allot one hour for both. However, you'll want more time, especially in winter, when there are hundreds of birds and scores of alligators along the trails.*

Begin at the Ernest F. Coe Visitor Center to learn about the Everglades and the park, then drive two miles to the main entrance. Turn left at the sign and continue to the Royal Palm Visitor Center. Both trails start behind it. A two-foot high rock wall behind the visitor center runs along the edge of

Taylor Slough, a slow-moving channel of water flowing through the sawgrass marsh. Peer into the water and around the edge for alligators, garfish, turtles, and frogs. To the right is the trailhead for both trails. The **Anhinga Trail** begins as a paved road, which was part of the old Ingraham Highway roadbed, constructed in 1916 by early visitors. They worked to establish Royal Palm State Park, the first protected area of what later became Everglades National Park.

The trail derives its name from the anhinga, generally a freshwater bird that dives for a fish, spears it, surfaces, then flips it into the air, catches it, and swallows it head first. When not swimming with its snakelike neck protruding above the water, it can be seen on a rock or branch with outstretched wings. Despite popular belief, the anhinga is not drying its wings. Rather, it's posing to raise its body temperature after swimming.

The boardwalk crosses **Taylor Slough** and a **sawgrass marsh.** Both communities support an abundance of fish and aquatic invertebrates—alligators, gambusia (mosquito fish), sailfin mollies, bream, bass, and garfish among them. The dominant vegetation includes submerged and floating aquatic plants—bladderwort (*Utricularia foliosa*), spatterdock (*Nuphar luteum*), floating heart (*Nymphoides aquatica*), white water lily (*Nymphaea odorata*), and sawgrass (*Cladium jamaicense*) among them, punctuated by trees like pond apples (*Annona glabra*) and willows (*Salix caroliniana*). *At 0.1 miles, the boardwalk starts. The trail, which is shaped like the lowercase letter "q," divides. Take the left fork.*

Mere inches determine what grows where. Sawgrass grows along this part of the trail, where the water ranges from one to two feet in the wet season. Alligators frequently build their nests in this dense sawgrass habitat. Reach down and gently rub a blade of sawgrass. Note the saw-like ridges that give the grass its name. Look north across the marsh to the visitor center. Because it sits on a 70-acre mound slightly elevated above the surrounding glades, it supports a tropical hardwood hammock of gumbo limbos (*Bursera simaruba*), live oaks (*Quercus virginiana*), and royal palms (*Roystonea elata*). *At 0.25 mile turn left and follow the spur to an observation platform.*

The observation platform overlooks reeds and deeper water with more spatterdock, purple-flowered pickerel weed (*Pontederia cordata*) and cattails (*Typha latifolia*). Note the charred flower spike on some of their tips. As you return along the spur back to the trail, you'll see a large pond apple tree on the right at 0.3 mile. It's overgrown with such epiphytes as bromeliads, orchids, and airplants. *Turn left back onto the trail.*

As the trail winds on, the vegetation grows taller and closer. There are more pond apple trees with epiphytes. The landscape opens again with views to open water surrounded by tall vegetation. The trail widens to accommodate the people who linger to see the birds and alligators that congregate here. A covered rest area with an interpretive sign overlooks the slough a few yards ahead. *Continue along the trail.*

The next spur runs left to an observation platform overlooking the slough. Look closely near the water's surface for dark "logs," which are often partially submerged alligators. Also look in the branches of small dead trees along the edge of the sawgrass. You often can see bird nests. In winter, they're likely to have eggs or visible fledglings. *Return to the trail and follow it back to the trailhead.*

The **Gumbo Limbo Trail** begins on the left a few yards beyond the Anhinga Trail trailhead. You'll feel as though you're entering a jungle as you take your first steps on the narrow paved footpath below a dense canopy of tree limbs and vines. Because the land here is about three feet higher than the marsh and slough, it supports hardwoods. The most obvious is the gumbo limbo, for which the trail was named. It's nicknamed the "tourist tree" for its peeling red bark. Native Americans supposedly called it "naked Seminole."

Poisonwood (*Metopium toxiferum*) is another obvious hammock plant, recognized by its splotched bark. Many people are highly allergic to it, so don't touch. At 0.75 mile on the right is a solution hole, a small, steep depression in the limestone bedrock. Because such holes are deep, they are one of the last places for animals to find water in the dry season, hence its a popular spot for wildlife viewing. Go quietly.

Far fewer animals are visible here, but there are lizards, owls, raccoons, butterflies, Florida tree snails (*Liguus fasciatus*), spiders, and other insects.

Resurrection ferns (*Polypodiumpolypodioides*) form a large mat on the trunk of a fallen tree on the left at mile 0.88, just before the large live oak with an interpretive sign for tree snails on the right. A few hundred feet farther on the right is a strangler fig (*Ficus aurea*), which entwines a host tree, which it will eventually kill by cutting it off from sunlight.

For the rest of the trail, dense ferns blanket the edge of the trail. At 0.95 mile, the path crosses a grassy road and a wooden bridge. Linger on the bridge looking for birds, alligators, and turtles. *Continue to the end of the trail.*

Lodging

The Flamingo area of Everglades National Park, about 38 miles west of the Royal Palm Visitor Center, has a comfortable lodge. The next closest accommodations are in Florida City, outside of Everglades National Park. You also can stay in the Upper Keys (40 minutes south) or Miami (40 minutes north) on Hwy 1. The park also has campgrounds.

Rooms in the **Flamingo Lodge, Marina & Outpost Resort** ($$, 941/695-3101, 800/600-3813) at 1 Flamingo Lodge Hwy are basic but comfortable with contemporary furnishings and prints of birds. There are also cottages with kitchenettes. Reservations are essential in winter. The two-story **Best Western Gateway to the Keys** ($$, 305/246-5100) at 1 Strano Blvd is built in a contemporary island style and sits off the highway away from the noise. Standard rooms have two queen-size beds or one king-size bed. It comes with complimentary Continental breakfast. Spacious rooms at the **Hampton Inn** ($$, 305/247-8833 or 800 /426-7866) at 124 E Palm Dr have lots of creature comforts like upholstered chairs, coffee makers, irons, free local calls and continental breakfast

Food & drink

Flamingo Lodge has the only restaurant in the park. Florida City, Homestead, the Upper Keys and Miami have lots of options.

Big picture windows in **Flamingo Restaurant** ($–$$, 941/695-3101) afford a picturesque view of Florida Bay. The menu features seafood, pasta, and grilled foods. It's only open in high season. The marina store, on the other hand, is open all year for pizza, sandwiches, and salads.

Friendly family members serve generous portions of well-prepared Mexican food at **El Toro Taco** ($$$, 305/245-8182) at 1 S Krome Ave, Homestead. Desserts are limited to the traditional flan and *tres leches*, a cake soaked in evaporated milk, sweetened condensed milk, and heavy cream. It's open for breakfast, lunch, and dinner. Although the **Mutineer Restaurant** ($$–$$$, 305/245-3377) at 11 S E 1st Ave (Hwy 1 and Palm Dr) has a nautical decor, its menu features ribs and steaks along with seafood. There's live music Friday and Saturday evenings .

Pigeon Key National Historic District

Pigeon Key lies a few miles southwest of Marathon, midway between Key Largo and Key West. Clear, bluish green waters surround the quiet island that's dotted with about a dozen historic buildings. The closest most people come to it is in their cars, looking down at it as they drive south on the new Seven Mile Bridge, which parallels Pigeon Key and the old Seven Mile Bridge. Yet this seemingly insignificant five-acre island played an important role in South Florida's history; both the island and the old Seven Mile Bridge are on the National Register of Historic Places.

There's no evidence of occupation until 1906, when Pigeon Key became the central construction camp for workers on the Key West Extension of the Florida East Coast (FEC) Railway's "Overseas Railroad," one of the greatest engineering feats in American history. Six years later, the first train rumbled by on January 22, 1912.

During Pigeon Key's "Construction Period," from 1908 to 1912, work began on the Seven Mile Bridge and more than 400 people lived and worked on the island. All but two of the island's remaining buildings date from 1912 to 1935, the "Railway Maintenance Period". The population dropped to 40 painters, maintenance crewmen, and bridge tenders. On Labor Day in 1935, a strong hurricane hit the Keys and destroyed the tracks 40 miles northeast in Islamorada. Still reeling from the Depression, the railroad sold the right-of-way to the state, which built the "Overseas Highway" on the remaining railbed.

During the 1938-to-1950 "Highway Maintenance Period," Pigeon Key's buildings served as the Overseas Road and Toll District's headquarters. From 1950 until the 1980s, the island was all but abandoned. In the 1980s the University of Miami used it for marine research, and in 1992 it was turned over to the non-profit Pigeon Key Foundation.

Information

Pigeon Key Foundation, PO Box 500130, Marathon, FL 33050; 305/289-0025 or 305/743-5999; pigeonkey@aol.com; www.pigeonkey.org. **Greater Marathon Chamber of Commerce and Visitor Center**, MM 53.5 Bay Side, 12222 Overseas Hwy, Marathon 33050; 800/262-7284 , 305/743-5417, Marathoncc@aol.com; www.florida-keys.fl.us/marathon.htm; or the **Florida Keys & Key West Visitors Bureau**, 402 Wall St, Key West, FL 33040; 800/352-5397; fax 305/294-7806; www.fla-keys.com. Two good reference books are *Pigeon Key & the Seven Mile Bridge 1908–1912* by Dan Gallagher, Pigeon Key's Director of Education and

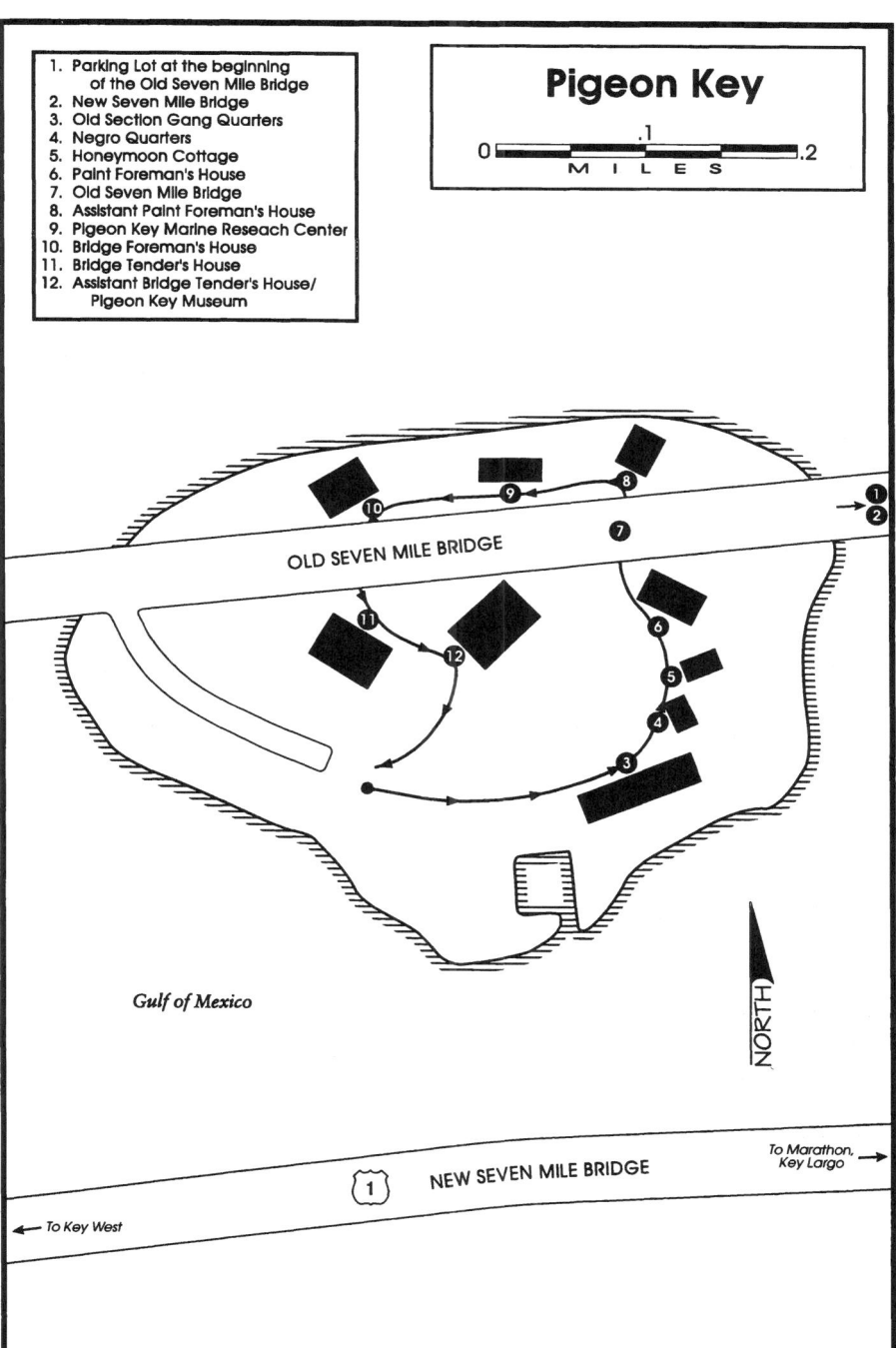

1. Parking Lot at the beginning
   of the Old Seven Mile Bridge
2. New Seven Mile Bridge
3. Old Section Gang Quarters
4. Negro Quarters
5. Honeymoon Cottage
6. Paint Foreman's House
7. Old Seven Mile Bridge
8. Assistant Paint Foreman's House
9. Pigeon Key Marine Reseach Center
10. Bridge Foreman's House
11. Bridge Tender's House
12. Assistant Bridge Tender's House/
    Pigeon Key Museum

Pigeon Key

0 ⊢─────────.1─────────⊣.2
        M I L E S

OLD SEVEN MILE BRIDGE

Gulf of Mexico

NORTH

NEW SEVEN MILE BRIDGE

To Marathon,
Key Largo →

← To Key West

Museums, and *The Bridge Stands Tall* by Priscilla Coe Pyfrom, who lived on the island during the bridge's construction.

Getting there

Pigeon Key is halfway between Key Largo and Key West, on US-1 (the Overseas Hwy), the 126-mile road that links the Keys to the mainland at Florida City, south of Miami.

Many major airlines serve Miami International Airport (MIA), about 100 miles north of Marathon. From the airport, you can travel by rental car, Greyhound Bus, or commuter plane to Marathon.

The Marathon Airport is served by shuttle flights from Miami operated by American Eagle (800/433-7300). Greyhound Bus Lines (800/231-2222, 305 /296-9072) runs a bus four times a day from Miami International Airport. The fare is $26 one way, $51 round trip. Amtrak (800/USA RAIL) trains run to Miami and Fort Lauderdale, but get no closer than that.

First steps

Adult admission is $7.50; children 5–12 years are $5. It's open daily 9 am to 5 pm. Stop at the **Pigeon Key Foundation's Visitor Center**, an old train car on Knight's Key, on the south side of US-1, just before the new Seven Mile Bridge, MM 47. Then drive north across US-1 to the parking lot. For maps and information, contact the **Greater Marathon Chamber of Commerce and Visitor Center**, which is open weekdays 8 am to 5 pm; or the **Florida Keys & Key West Visitors Bureau**, which is open daily 8 am to 6 pm.

The Keynoter covers local news and events twice a week. The *Miami Herald* publishes a Keys edition with listings of local events.

Walking tours

Docents lead free walking tours of the island throughout the day.

Seasonal highlights

The busiest and most expensive season runs December to April, especially February and April during the Pigeon Key festivals and Seven Mile Bridge Run. Summer, spring break, and weekends are also busy and more expensive.

Historic Pigeon Key. *At 4.5 miles, this route covers a two-mile portion of the old Seven Mile Bridge, a tour of the island, and a two-mile return on the old bridge.*

Start at the parking lot at the beginning of the old Seven Mile Bridge. At the time of its construction, the Seven Mile Bridge was the longest bridge in the world; exact length is 35,720 feet.

Visible to the south is the new Seven Mile Bridge, built in 1982 to replace the old bridge. Fishing and pleasure boats head out across the Atlantic Ocean. In the distance is the Sombrero Reef Lighthouse. To the north side is the Gulf of Mexico, dotted with mangrove-covered islands and tree trunks stuck in the flats, where they drifted after Hurricane Georges in September 1998. In the shallow water near the island, you often can see schools of rays and tarpon feeding. The dark-colored sea grass beds are a major ecosystem in the Keys.

At about two miles, a road descends from the bridge to the island. Just beyond the island is a gap cut out of the bridge to allow large vessels to pass. It was filled in and later dismantled during the filming of the movie *True Lies.*

Start your counter-clockwise tour of the island at the restored Old Section Gang Quarters, one of two buildings remaining from the Construction Period and one of four bunkhouses used to house up to 64 men. The next stop is the elevated single-pen style **Negro Quarters**, where African-American workers, primarily cooks, lived during the Construction and Maintenance periods. The house is on the National Black Heritage Trail and today is used to house students. *Walk to the right.*

The **Honeymoon Cottage** supposedly derives its name from the 1960s, when the president of the University of Miami had the house built for his daughter's honeymoon. In reality, the house was built decades earlier for the maid of the manager of the Overseas Road and Toll District. To the left is the restored **Paint Foreman's House,** built in the Construction Period as the cook house. *Walk to the bridge.*

As you pass under the old Seven Mile Bridge, note the railings made from old rail tracks. Portions of the original bridge are painted blue. Gone from the spot where you're standing are the railroad station and stairs that passengers climbed to board the train. *Continue beyond the bridge to the first building.*

The restored **Assistant Paint Foreman's House** was built in 1920 and today serves as the offices of the Pigeon Key Foundation. To the left is the **Pigeon Key Marine Research Center,** where researchers from the **Mote Marine Laboratory** conduct experiments in culturing live coral. Next is the **Bridge Foreman's House,** built in 1916 in four-square Georgian style. Nearby there used to be a school, two houses and a cement warehouse used during the Construction Period. *Stroll out to the pier, then walk back under the bridge to the facing house.*

Rumor is that the **Bridge Tender's House,** built during the Construction Period, is haunted by the wife of one of the tenders. Supposedly, she was having an affair and was so guilt stricken that she hung herself on the porch. It's the only two-story house on the island. *Continue left.* The tour ends at the **Assistant Bridge Tender's House** (1909). It contains the **Pigeon Key Museum**, which is chock full of post cards, photographs and exhibits. Especially compelling are the construction displays and the exhibit about C.S. Coe, the resident engineer in charge of building the Seven Mile Bridge, and Mrs Priscilla Coe Pyfrom, his daughter. At the age of 100, Mrs Pyfrom helped the museum with its interpretation and cut the ribbon for its opening in 1997. *Walk back to the parking lot or catch the train.*

Lodging

There are no visitor accommodations on the island. Nearby Marathon has numerous hotels, motels, and resorts. Make reservations early for the December to April high season. Rates are slightly higher then.

Seascape Ocean Resort ($$$/$$$, 800/332-SEAS, 305/743-6455) is a posh, but unpretentious little oceanfront resort originally built as a private villa in the early 1950s at 1075 75th St, Marathon. Artist Sara Stites and photographer Bill Stites converted the five-acre estate into nine artistically decorated no-smoking rooms (three with kitchens), gardens, a pool, dock, art gallery, and little areas for whiling away the day. **Faro Blanco Marine Resort** ($$$/$$, 800/759-3276, 305/743-9018) at 1996 Overseas Hwy, MM 48.2, Marathon, is one of the oldest resorts in the Keys. Its large marina, a favorite among the boating and yachting crowd, sets the tone for the resort's breezy atmosphere. Accommodations include rooms, cottages, houseboats, condos, and lighthouse apartments.

Other options a little north of Marathon include the **Yellowtail Inn Motel & Cottages** ($$/$$, 800/605-7475, 305/743-8400) at 58162 Overseas Hwy, MM 58.3, a small oceanfront hideaway with 11 clean and comfortable efficiencies and cottages, and the **Little Valhalla Resort at Curry Hammock** ($$/$$, 305/289-0614) at 56223 Ocean Dr, Crawl Key, MM 57.5, a simple little inn with one room, four efficiencies, and the natural outdoors—including a state park—right at the doorstep.

Arts & culture

Most of the noteworthy galleries and theaters in the Keys are located 50 miles south in Key West or 40 to 50 miles north in Islamorada and Key Largo.

Marathon Community Theatre (305/743-0994, 5101 Overseas Hwy) stages a half dozen productions throughout the year.

The small **Museums of Tropical Crane Point Hammock** (305/743-9100, 5550 Overseas Hwy, MM 50.5) complex features a one-mile nature trail, the Museum of Natural History of the Florida Keys, the Florida Keys Children's Museum, and the restored George Adderly House, once part of a prosperous black Bahamian village.

Along with the usual hardbacks and paperbacks, **Food for Thought** (305/743-3297, 5800 Overseas Hwy, MM 51) keeps a well-stocked section of books covering the history, culture, and ecology of the Keys.

Food & drink

While none of the restaurants are historically significant, many reflect the unique culture of the Keys, both in atmosphere and menu selections.

At 50 to 60 years old, **Herbie's** ($–$$, 305/743-6373) at 6350 Overseas Hwy, MM 50.5, and the **7 Mile Grill** ($–$$, 305/743-4481) at 1240 Overseas Hwy, MM 47, are considered Keys classics. Both of these laid-back waterfront eateries serve up oodles of color along with reasonably good, casual, local fare. Clearly, the best restaurant in Marathon is the **Barracuda Grill** ($$–$$$, 305/743-3314) at 4290 Overseas Hwy, MM 49.5. It's an intimate bistro-style restaurant with an eclectic dinner-only menu that features lots of fresh seafood, but also beef, pasta, and poultry. It's fresh and innovative. The **Island Tiki Bar & Restaurant** ($$, 305/743-4191) is the new kid on the block at 12648 Overseas Hwy, MM 54. While it screams commercial and tourist, the setting is prime waterfront and the food is well prepared at lunch and dinner.

Events

Pigeon Key hosts two big events every February, the **Pigeon Key Arts Festival**, followed by the **Pigeon Key Jazz Festival**. In April, a local running club hosts the **Seven Mile Bridge Run**.

Key West

Key West, situated at the end of the 126-mile road that links the Florida Keys to the mainland, enjoys a frost-free tropical climate, laid-back island mentality, rich history, restored historic homes that serve as elegant guesthouses and museums, a multitude of bars that stay open until the weeist of hours, and a large gay population. The island, which measures 2 miles wide by 4 miles long, is divided into two sections. The Old Town, west of Eisenhower Drive, is where the town was first settled. Its narrow, crowded, streets lined with many historic sites, fine restaurants and hotels seem tailor-made for walking and biking tours. New Town, east of White Street, has more chain eateries and motels and modern trappings such as the airport and shopping strips. It also has the best beaches.

Starting in the early 1800s, Key West flourished as a center for recovering ships wrecked on the surrounding coral reefs. It became the richest city per capita in the United States. From their profits, wealthy ship captains, bankers, warehouse owners, auction house merchants and wreckers built grand houses, incorporating fine woods and craftsmanship. For their families, ship's carpenters built tight, shiplike houses reminiscent of the homes they left in New England and the Bahamas. Cuban cigar makers constructed simple, shotgun houses when the town became a large cigar manufacturing center. The military also played a large part in shaping Key West's architecture, building forts and complexes. When the railroad arrived from the mainland in the early 1900s, grand hotels were built for wealthy visitors. More than 2,500 of these historic buildings remain, creating one of the largest collections of pre-Victorian and Victorian houses in the country.

Information

Greater Key West Chamber of Commerce, 402 Wall St, Key West, FL 33040; 305/294-2587, 800/527-8539, 800/352-5397; fax 305/294-7806; www.fla-keys.com; or the Florida Keys & Key West Visitors Bureau at the same location

Getting there

Key West is at the end of US-1 (the Overseas Hwy), the road that links the 126-mile stretch of Keys to the mainland S of Miami.

Many major airlines serve Miami International Airport (MIA), about 150 miles north of Key West. From the airport, you can travel by rental car, Greyhound bus or commuter plane to Key West.

The Key West International Airport is served by shuttle flights from American (800/433-7300), Cape Air (800/352-0714), Delta (800/354-9822), Continental

(800/525-0280), and US Airways (800/428-4322). Greyhound Bus Lines (800/231-2222, 305/296-9072) runs a shuttle bus four times a day from Miami International Airport. The fare is about $32 one-way, $60 round trip. Amtrak (800/USA RAIL) trains run to Miami and Fort Lauderdale, but get no closer than that.

First steps

For maps and information, contact the Florida Keys & Key West Visitors Bureau/Greater Key West Chamber of Commerce, which is open daily, 8 am to 6 pm. To learn more about Key West, its people and its architecture, read *Forgotten Legacy: Blacks in 19th Century Key West* by Sharon Wells and *The Houses of Key West* by Alex Caemmerer.

Solares Hill publishes a weekly paper filled with wit and controversy. It's loaded with local events and entertainment information. To keep in touch with the Keys and world events on a daily basis, pick up the *Key West Citizen*. The *Miami Herald* publishes a Keys edition with listings of local events. Once a month *Southern Exposure* covers news, entertainment and events of special interest to gays and lesbians.

Walking tours

Sharon Wells served as the Florida state historian in Key West for almost 20 years. Now, she publishes the free "Walking and Biking Guide to Historic Key West," which contains 10 self-guided tours. The guide is available free at guest houses, hotels, and Key West bookstores. Her company, Island City Strolls, offers one- to two-hour walking and biking tours of the island's gardens, architecture, and history for $13 to $18, as well as personalized tours for $25 an hour. For information, write or call PO Box 56, Key West, FL 33041; 305/294-8380; www.see keywest.com.

The Old Island Restoration Foundation publishes "Pelican Path," a free walking guide to Key West's Old Town history and architecture. Copies are available at the Greater Key West Chamber of Commerce.

The Key West Literary Seminar (888/293-9291, 305/293-9291) leads a Writers' Walk, a one-hour guided tour of the residences of prominent authors who have lived in Key West—Elizabeth Bishop, Robert Frost, Ernest Hemingway, Wallace Stevens, and Tennessee Williams, among others. The fee is $10. Tours depart Saturday at 10:30 am from Heritage House Museum at 410 Caroline St and Sunday at 10:30 am from the Hemingway House at 907 Whitehead St.

In addition, the Historic Florida Keys Foundation publishes several good historic walking guides of Key West and conducts walking tours of the City Cemetery on Tuesday and Thursday at 9:30 am. Contact them at 510 Greene St, Old City Hall, Key West, FL 33040; 305/292-6718.

For a more spirited tour, there's David Sloan's Ghost Tours of Key West, a

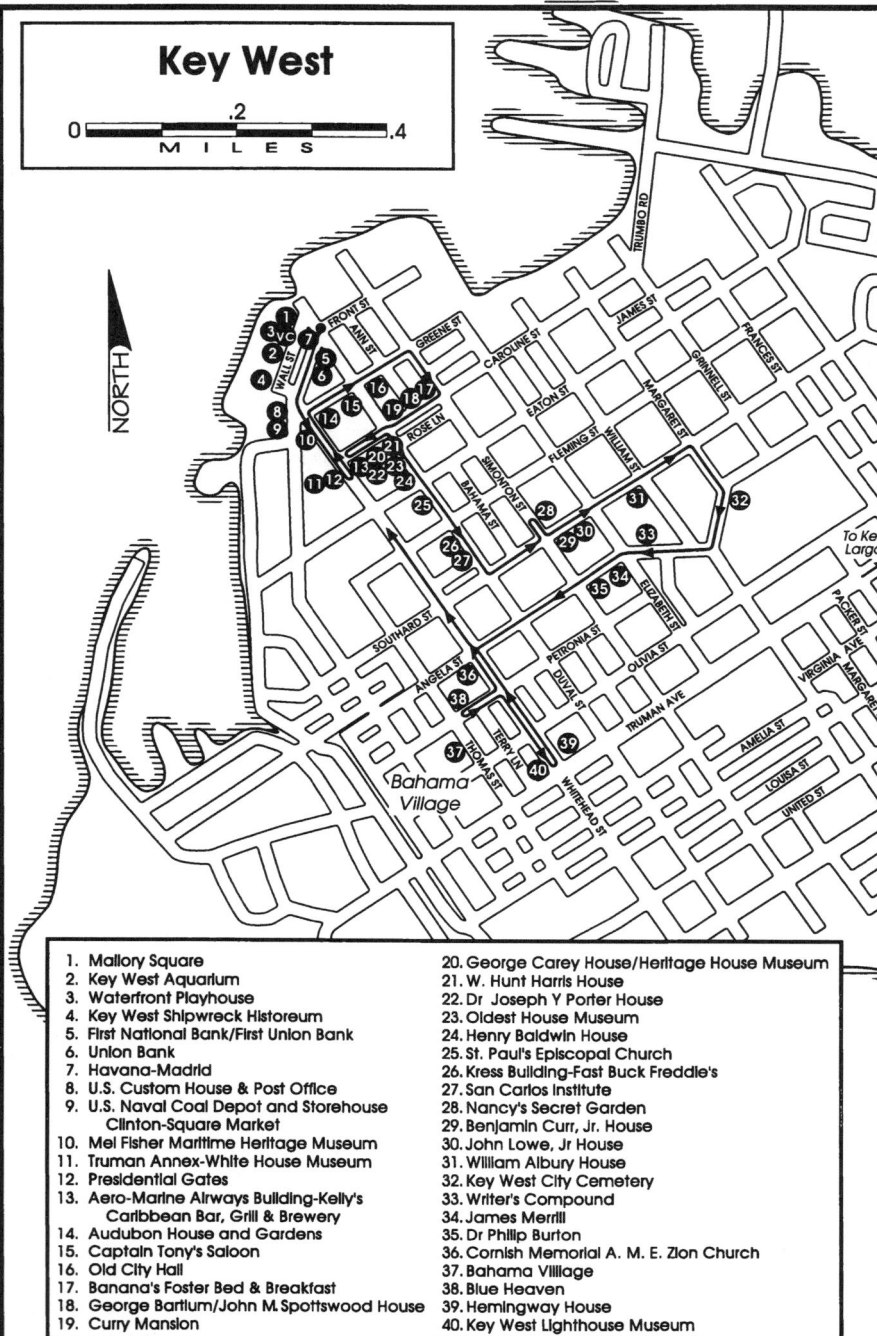

Key West

0 |======| .2 |======| .4
M I L E S

NORTH

To Key Largo

Bahama Village

1. Mallory Square
2. Key West Aquarium
3. Waterfront Playhouse
4. Key West Shipwreck Historeum
5. First National Bank/First Union Bank
6. Union Bank
7. Havana-Madrid
8. U.S. Custom House & Post Office
9. U.S. Naval Coal Depot and Storehouse
   Clinton-Square Market
10. Mel Fisher Maritime Heritage Museum
11. Truman Annex-White House Museum
12. Presidential Gates
13. Aero-Marine Airways Building-Kelly's
   Caribbean Bar, Grill & Brewery
14. Audubon House and Gardens
15. Captain Tony's Saloon
16. Old City Hall
17. Banana's Foster Bed & Breakfast
18. George Bartlum/John M. Spottswood House
19. Curry Mansion

20. George Carey House/Heritage House Museum
21. W. Hunt Harris House
22. Dr Joseph Y Porter House
23. Oldest House Museum
24. Henry Baldwin House
25. St. Paul's Episcopal Church
26. Kress Building-Fast Buck Freddie's
27. San Carlos Institute
28. Nancy's Secret Garden
29. Benjamin Curr, Jr. House
30. John Lowe, Jr House
31. William Albury House
32. Key West City Cemetery
33. Writer's Compound
34. James Merrill
35. Dr Philip Burton
36. Cornish Memorial A. M. E. Zion Church
37. Bahama Village
38. Blue Heaven
39. Hemingway House
40. Key West Lighthouse Museum

one-mile, one-and-a-half-hour tour of Old Town's haunted hideaways. The cost of the tours, which depart nightly at 7 pm, is $18 adults/$10 children under 12 years, but there are $3 discount coupons available in tourist brochures. For information, call 305/293-8009.

Seasonal highlights
The busiest and most expensive season runs from December to April. Summers, spring break, and weekends are also popular and more expensive. During the very popular Fantasy Fest in late October, there's little chance of finding a room without a reservation made months earlier.

Historic Key West. *This 3-mile route covers the waterfront and streets that feature the largest collection of historic architecture. Allot at least three hours to see everything. However, a more leisurely trip of one to two days will allow you to tour some of the houses and sites and take breaks at good restaurants.*

Begin at Mallory Square, opposite the Visitors Center (402 Wall St). It was along Old Town's waterfront that Key West sprang to life in the early 1800s as the treasures of the sea lured captains, merchants, and wreckers. The Greek Revival structure at **Mallory Square**, at the foot of Duval Street, served as a ticket office for the Mallory Steamship Line during the days when the square's auction houses, piers, and chandleries bustled with activity from the profitable wrecking business. Today, it is the ultimate place to people-watch. Each evening thousands gather for sunset in a celebration reminiscent of a seventies happening, with street performers, artisans, animals, skaters, bikers, and food vendors. It also has such attractions as the **Key West Aquarium** (1 Whitehead St), the first open-air aquarium. Opposite the square on Wall Street are the **Waterfront Playhouse**, the former Tift's Warehouse where salvaged goods were stored before auction in the 1800s, and the **Key West Shipwreck Historeum** (1 Whitehead St), a museum that chronicles the island's wrecking era. Climb to the top of the reconstructed Lookout Tower for the same view that wreckers had in the 1800s. The square was named after Key West's Stephen R. Mallory, a U.S. Senator and Confederate Secretary of the Navy. *Leave Mallory Square and walk one block over to Front St.*

Front Street claims several of Key West's most significant landmarks. When money changed hands at Mallory Square's auctions, buyers and sellers had only to walk one block away to make deposits and withdrawals at the **First National Bank/First Union Bank** (#422). A fine example of polychromatic brickwork, the bank was financed by wealthy Cuban cigar manufacturers and constructed of yellow and red bricks in 1897. Its neighbor (#423) housed the former **Union Bank** and is admired for its beautiful grillwork. At the turn of the century, the banks shared Front Street with bars, strip joints, gambling halls, and brothels. The **Havana-Madrid** building was one such establishment. Noted plume fan dancer Sally Rand performed at the Havana-Madrid Nightclub, a partially open-air patio club that regularly showcased Cuban and local orchestras.

The **U.S. Custom House & Post Office** (corner of Front and Greene streets) dominates the area. The three-and-a-half story brick masonry structure built in the Romanesque Revival style was completed in 1891 at a high cost of more than $100,000. In 1898 the U.S. Court of Inquiry investigated the sinking of the *USS Maine* here. One hundred years later, the building reopened as a museum after complete restoration. Nearby landmarks include the oldest brick building on the island, the **U.S. Naval Coal Depot and Storehouse** (200 Greene St), built between 1856 and 1861 as a supply depot and coaling station. During the Civil War, it served as the East Coast Blockading Squadron. Today it houses the **Clinton Square Market** shopping arcade and **Mel Fisher Maritime Heritage Museum** (200 Greene St), home of the incredible treasures salvaged from the 17th-century Spanish galleon *Atocha*.

Enter **Truman Annex** at Front and Caroline streets. Along with a score of buildings that were part of the Key West Naval Station is a two-story, wooden frame residence that was originally the Commandant's Quarters and is now the **Little White House Museum** (111 Front St). President Harry Truman frequently stayed here during his presidency from 1946 to 1952. In 1991 the house was completely restored to its Truman-era look. During their terms, Presidents Eisenhower and Kennedy also came here. The rest of the annex, which was deactivated in 1974, is a combination of military buildings dating from 1845 to 1923 and private houses and condominiums. *Leave the annex and walk up Caroline St.*

One block up at the corner of Caroline and Whitehead streets are the ceremonial **Presidential Gates** (1906), originally opened only for presidents and dignitaries. Across the street is the **Aero-Marine Airways Building** (301 Whitehead St), former headquarters for the air carrier that flew mail between Key West and Havana in the 1920s. By the end of the decade, Pan American Airways had moved in as the first international airline. Today, it's the site of **Kelly's Caribbean Bar, Grill & Brewery** (see Dining), owned by actress Kelly McGillis. *Turn left on Whitehead St and walk one block.* At the corner of Greene Street is the two-and-one-half-story wood frame **Audubon House and Gardens**

(#205), where ornithologist John James Audubon was a guest of Captain John Geiger in 1832. Take a self-guided taped tour of the gardens and house, where you'll see original Audubon prints. *Turn right onto Greene St.*

Key West has long been known for its bars and the interesting personalities who ran them. The tradition continues at the very popular, sometimes rowdy **Captain Tony's Saloon** (#428), which Ernest Hemingway frequented in the late 1920s and early 1930s when it was called The Blind Pig and the original Sloppy Joe's. He met his third wife, Martha Gellhorn, here. It takes its name from former owner Tony Tarracino, a craggy charter boat captain (see Nightlife). In 1937, owner Joe Russell moved the original **Sloppy Joe's** to the corner of Duval and Greene streets, the site of the former Victoria Restaurant, an elegant Cuban eatery. It remained a favorite hang-out for Ernest Hemingway, who portrayed Joe as the character Freddy in *To Have and Have Not*. Further along the block sits the brick towered **Old City Hall** (#510), a restored Victorian Italianate structure built in 1891 that still houses city government offices. *Turn right on Simonton St, then right on Caroline St. Continue the walk on the right side of the street.*

Caroline Street is a 19th-century who's who of wealthy merchants, bankers and ship captains who built their mansions along this elegant tree-lined thoroughfare. It showcases the best examples of West Indian Colonial architecture on the island. The restored **Banana's Foster Bed & Breakfast** (#537) is a fine example of Greek Revival architecture. President Harry S. Truman and his wife, Bess, were frequent visitors to the **George Bartlum/John M. Spottswood House** (#531). The namesake Spottswood was a state senator and close friend of the president. The most elegant house on the block is the Beaux Arts **Curry Mansion** (#511), built in 1905 by Milton Curry on the original homestead site of his father, William Curry, Key West's first millionaire. The house is now a museum and guesthouse. *At Whitehead St, cross over and come back up the other side of Caroline St.*

The **George Carey House/Heritage House Museum** (#410) was built in 1834 by George Carey, but is better known for its later resident, Jessie Porter Newton or Miss Jessie, a fifth-generation Key Wester who spearheaded Key West's first restoration movement and held social gatherings with such notables as Pauline and Ernest Hemingway, Katie and John dos Passos, Tallulah Bankhead, Tennessee Williams, and poet Robert Frost. Take time to tour the house and the garden cottage, where Frost frequently wintered.

Down the street are the **W. Hunt Harris House (#425)** and **Dr. Joseph Y. Porter House (#429).** The namesake owner of the latter was Miss Jessie's grandfather, a prominent physician and Florida's first Public Health Officer, who helped eradicate yellow fever. The two-story wood frame house's unique design features a mix of styles that include a mansard roof with gabled dormers, porches on both floors, and wrought-iron balconies. Dr. Porter gave the land next door to his daughter, who married W. Hunt Harris, a politician and judge. Before the house was completed, the navy occupied it during the Spanish-American war. The current unrelated owners restored it to its original splendor. *Turn right onto Duval St.*

Walk down Duval Street, the mile-long commercial pulse of Key West. Lined with bars, T-shirt shops, dance clubs, restaurants, art galleries, and a parade of eager tourists, Duval Street seldom sleeps. Setting itself apart from the rowdier lower end of Duval, Upper Duval Street, between South and Petronia streets bills itself as the "Upscale End of Town," where the shopping, dining, and partying are said to be more tasteful.

History lies behind the commercial hype of Duval Street. Among it's architectural treasures are the **Oldest House Museum (#322),** the oldest dwelling in the Keys and now a museum dedicated to Key West's wrecking business; the Classical Revival **Henry Baldwin House (#363),** one of the oldest houses and the first schoolhouse in Key West; **St. Paul's Episcopal Church (#401),** a Gothic Revival church dating from 1919; the **Kress Building,** once a five-and-dime store and now home to two of Key West's modern institutions, **Fast Buck Freddie's** department store, and **Margaritaville,** Jimmy Buffett's Cafe and Store; and the **San Carlos Institute (#516),** originally a cultural center for Cuban exiles in 1871 and the headquarters for the 1890s independence movement led by patriot José Martí. The current building, rebuilt in 1924 after a fire, was funded by private donations and the Cuban government. *Turn left on Southard St.*

Many of the original Key West settlers came from the Bahamas and became known as Conchs. There are three notable houses on Southard Street between Duval and Margaret streets that were built by these early Bahamians. But first, at Simonton Street, turn left for a quick detour. Halfway down the block is a short street on the right, Free School Lane. At the end of it is **Nancy's Secret Garden,** a lush, tropical rain forest planted over the course of 30 years. It features rare, native and tropical palms, cycads, orchids, and more and is the perfect place to stop with a bag or take-out lunch.

Back on Southard, a seventh-generation relative still lives in the

Benjamin Curry, Jr, House (#610), built in 1850 as a gabled frame house. The namesake builder of the impressive **John Lowe, Jr, House** made his fortune in sponging and lumber. He used lumber from the city's first sawmill, which he owned, to construct this house, a fine example of Classical Revival Bahamian style, with 12-foot ceilings, widow's walks, verandahs on three sides and two-story square columns. Notice the wrap-around porch and captain's walk at the **William Albury House** (#730), built in the 1880s and still owned by an Albury. *Turn right at Margaret St.*

The **Key West City Cemetery** (corner of Margaret St and Passover Ln) was moved here to higher ground in 1846 after a hurricane's flooding disinterred most of the bodies at the old waterfront cemetery. Streets are named throughout the cemetery. On Palm Avenue are two memorials, one to Cuban martyrs of the 1868 insurrection against Spain, the other to sailors who died on the *U.S.S.* Maine in 1898. On tours of the cemetery, guides point out some of the more unusual epitaphs such as "I Told You I Was Sick," "Devoted Fan of Julio Iglesias," and "Good Citizen for 65 of his 108 Years." *Leave the cemetery and walk south down Angela St.*

As the road bends into Windsor Lane, look to the right. Behind the high wall is a **Writer's Compound** (713-727 Windsor Lane) that has been home to such prominent writers as Richard Wilbur, John Hersey, and Ralph Ellison among others. The intersection of Elizabeth Street is called Solares Hill, the highest point on the island. The literary connection continues into the next two blocks, where Pulitzer Prize-winning poet **James Merrill** (702 Elizabeth St) lived until his death in the mid-1990s. He's most remembered for his epic poem *The Changing Light at Sandover*. In the next block, noted Shakespearean scholar **Dr. Philip Burton** (608 Angela St) lived until 1995 and was visited by his adopted son, actor Richard Burton, and his daughter-in-law, actress Elizabeth Taylor. *Turn left at Whitehead St.*

Sandy Cornish, a former slave and one of the first to grow fruits and vegetables on the island, helped organize the First African Methodist Episcopal Church in 1865. The current frame building, now called the **Cornish Memorial A.M.E. Zion Church** (#702), was built in 1894 in Gothic Revival Style. Sunday services feature a lively gospel choir. Thomas Street, parallel to and one block west of Whitehead, runs through the heart of **Bahama Village**. Historically inhabited by Bahamians and Cubans of African descent who worked as spongers, nurses, salt processors, and charcoal burners, it's beginning to feel the restoration efforts well underway in the rest of Old Town. An oft visited spot here is **Blue Heaven**

(#729) for breakfast, lunch, or dinner. Ernest Hemingway came here to dine, box, and gamble. His house, the island's number-one tourist attraction, is located one block east and two blocks back on Whitehead Street. **Hemingway House** (#907) is the restored house where Hemingway wrote the majority of his life's work, including *For Whom the Bell Tolls*, and lived with his second wife, Pauline. The 30-minute guided tour explores the pool, house, writer's studio, and is rich with cats and anecdotes—some of which are disputed—about the author and his family. Afterwards, you can stroll the house, gardens, and grounds surrounded by a high brick wall on your own.

End the tour across the street at the **Key West Lighthouse Museum** (#938). Yes, you may—and should—climb the nearly 90 steps to the top, where there's the same commanding view of Old Town and the surrounding waters that sharp-eyed wreckers had from their observatories as they searched the horizon for ships that had wrecked on the reef. Then whisper the words that excited the whole island, "Wreck A-shore."

Lodging

Key West has big-city charm and variety when it comes to accommodations. Sprinkled among the myriad guesthouses in restored historic buildings are cottages, large chains like Hyatt and Hilton, large independents, and even a youth hostel and campground. Among them are numerous gay-friendly guesthouses and hotels. Prices are significantly higher from December through mid-April and during Fantasy Fest in late October and other special events. Many places offer a discount if you stay a week or longer and when it's slow. Be sure to ask.

Guesthouses: There are so many fabulous guesthouses in Key West, that it's hard to make a short list. On the low-cost end is the popular **Merlinn Inn Guesthouse** ($$$/$$ 305/296-3336) with a pool and lovely secluded garden at 811 Simonton St. Physically challenged guests, children, and pets will find it especially welcoming. Key West's oldest exclusively gay guesthouse is the **Curry House** ($$$/$$, 305/294-6777) at 806 Fleming St in a renovated Victorian-style house with nine rooms, seven with private bath. There's a pool, Jacuzzi, continental breakfast, and afternoon wine. Jody Carlson, owner of **Popular House/Key West Bed & Breakfast** ($$-$$$/$$-$$$, 305/296-7274, 800/438-6155) has decorated the place with lots of local art. The less expensive rooms in the nine-room house share a bath. The other rooms are very private, large and well appointed. She serves a very generous continental breakfast.

At the top of the guesthouse list are two stellar properties. At 511-512 Caroline St is the **Curry Mansion Inn** ($$$/$$$, 305/294-5349, 800/253-3466), which is also a historic tourist attraction (see tour). It's noted for exceptional service and rooms and suites with fine furnishings in the main house and annex. Guests enjoy continental breakfast, happy hour with an open bar and live piano music, and beach privileges at the Pier House Beach Club and Casa Marina. The **Heron House** ($$$/$$$, 305/294-9227) offers almost every amenity known to mankind in a complex of four buildings centered around a pool and surrounded by a high coral fence at 512 Simonton St. Service and accommodations are superb. A lavish continental breakfast and complimentary wine and cheese are included.

Inns & Cottages: A compound of old cigar maker's cottages has been turned into bright little jewels that sleep two to six people and include a generous continental breakfast at the **Center Court Historic Inn & Cottages** ($$$/$$-$$$, 305/296-9292, 800/797-8787). Within the garden setting are a pool and Jacuzzi, sun deck and exercise room. At **Travelers Palm Garden Cottages** ($$$/$$-$$$, 305/294-9560) each of the five cottages has its own private garden with a small patio. Located at 815 Catherine St, it also has apartments and studios. It's been popular ever since Charles Kuralt praised it in his book *Charles Kuralt's America*. The service suggests expensive, but the rates are reasonable for the efficiency cottages at **Casa Alante Guest Cottages** ($$$/$$, 305/293-0702), a one-acre complex at 1435 S Roosevelt Blvd, opposite the beach. The spacious studios, suites, and two-bedrooms at the **Speakeasy Inn** ($$$/$$, 305/296-2680, 800/217-4884) come with simple, tasteful furnishings. It's on the upper, quieter end of Duval Street (#1117) with some units over the Key West Havana Cigar Co. Guests have beach and pool privileges at the Wyndham Reach.

Hotels, Motels, Resorts: On the high-end there are two historic gems. Built during the 1920s tourism boom, the **Historic Holiday Inn La Concha Hotel** ($$$/$$$, 305/296-2991, 800/745-2191) at 430 Duval St served as the way station for well-to-do travelers going from the mainland via train to Key West, then on to Havana by steamship. At seven stories, it was the tallest building on the island. It remains a classy enclave, though the rooms are smallish. Even more elegant is **Wyndham's Casa Marina Resort** ($$$/$$$, 305/296-3535), which stretches out on 13 quiet acres on the ocean at 1500 Reynolds St. It was built by railroad baron Henry Flagler as a way station hotel for affluent travelers. He died before it was completed. Everything about it was—and still is—first class, from the polished lobby to the well-appointed guest rooms, some with French doors and balconies. It has two restaurants and two pools, spa services, children's programs, tennis courts, and a health club.

Visitors looking for good value need look no farther than the **Harborside Motel & Marina** ($$$/$$, 305/294-2780) at 903 Eisenhower Dr, and the **Southwinds** ($$-$$$/$$-$$$, 305/296-2215) at 1321 Simonton St. Both are owned by the same people and offer simple, safe, clean rooms as well as a pool and coin laundry. In addition, the Harborside has four stationery houseboats and the

Southwinds is a block from the beach. Management really keeps up the **Best Western Key Ambassador Inn** ($$$, 305/296-3500, 800/432-4315) at 3755 S. Roosevelt Blvd in New Town, where bright Caribbean-style furnishings fill large rooms that overlook the 7-acre grounds, deck, pool and neighboring ocean. Rooms have a small refrigerator and a screened balcony. Continental breakfast and a weekday newspaper are complimentary. Visitors who want to be in the thick of the action should consider the **Pier House** ($$$/$$$, 305/296-4600, 800/327--8340), located at 1 Duval St, just off Mallory Square. The architecture and decor are decidedly tony Caribbean with many balconied rooms that offer great views. There's a thatch-roof tiki bar, three restaurants, bars, pool, spa facilities, and a beach. The **Hilton Resort & Marina** ($$$/$$$, 305/294-4000, 800/HILTONS) at 245 Front St is another front-seat resort complete with oodles of amenities, boat slips, waterfront dining, a beach, sunset happy hour, deck bar, and coveted off-street parking. Becoming ever more popular are its condos and cottages on the private Sunset Key, an offshore island.

Youth Hostel: The staff at the **HI Hostel International Key West & Seashell Motel** ($/$$, 305/296-5719) at 718 South St is friendly and the dorm beds and motel rooms for members and non-members are neat and clean. It's a great bargain, especially since dinner is included for another $2 and they provide discounts on snorkeling and other excursions.

Camping: Located on neighboring Stock Island, **Boyd's Key West Campground** ($, 305/294-1465) at 6401 Maloney Ave bills itself as the "southernmost campground." Amenities include a pool and game room. Pets are welcome. **Jabour's Trailer Court** ($, 305/294-5723) at 223 Elizabeth St has tent and RV sites in a pleasant setting in the middle of Old Town.

Arts & culture
Long a haven for writers and artists, Key West has numerous galleries, theaters, and bookstores, all but a few of which are in Old Town.

The small company that performs in the **Red Barn Theater** (305/296-9911, 319 Duval St) presents well-known dramas, comedies, and musicals as well as new works. The **Tennessee Williams Fine Arts Center** (305/296-9081 ext 5, Florida Keys Community College, 5901 College Rd, on Stock Island) is the islands premiere center for local and big-name concerts, plays and events, including the Key West Symphony Orchestra under the direction of the very talented Sebrina Maria Alfonso. The season runs November to April. In the mid-1850s, the **Waterfront Playhouse** (305/294-5015, Mallory Sq) served as a wrecker's warehouse. Today, it's a 180-seat, non-Equity community theater. The curtain goes up for drama and comedy December to June.

Scores of galleries have opened—and closed—in Key West, the oldest private art gallery being the **Gingerbread Square Gallery** (305/296-8900, 1207 Duval St), which focuses on big-name Keys artists. **Glass Reunions** (305/294-1720, Duval at Olivia street) carries an eclectic collection of art glass, including paperweights, jewelry, blown glass, and kaleidoscopes. Owned and operated by women, the **Guild Hall** (305/296-6076, 614 Duval St), co-operative features works by more than a score of men and women who create wearable and display art, including sculpture and photography. It's in a restored 1919 wood frame building. You'd have to travel to the Caribbean to find a more extensive collection of Haitian art than at **Haitian Art Co.** (305/296-8932, 600 Frances St). The owners buy direct from the artists, which keeps the prices attractive. While they bring back some works by newcomers, many pieces are by highly regarded artists. Once located on Duval, the **Lucky Street Gallery** (305/294-3973, 1120 White St) moved and reclaimed its position as a prominent showcase for high-end contemporary paintings, watercolors, jewelry, and crafts by some of Key West's most talented artists. Exhibits change every two weeks. Ernest Hemingway found the setting at the **Pelican Poop** (305/296-3887, 314 Simonton) stimulating enough to write *A Farewell to Arms* while he lived in the complex apartment. The soothing courtyard setting aside, the reasonably priced Caribbean art is still the main reason to come here. Potters Charles Pearson and Timothy Roeder specialize in porcelain stoneware and raku-fired vessels at **Whitehead St Pottery** (305/294-5067, 1011 Whitehead St).

Flaming Maggie's (305/294-3931, 830 Fleming St) caters to the gay and lesbian market, carrying books, magazines, and artwork by or about local authors. Pick up a book and pull up a chair at Maggie's coffee bar. Local writers come to the **Key West Island Bookstore** (305/294-2904, 513 Fleming St) for book signings and to browse. The selection features new, used, and rare titles. **Miss Marbles Parlor** (305/296-6939, 502 Olivia St) is a tongue-in-cheek tribute to the mystery genre. In the evening it becomes a mystery theater.

Food & drink

In low season, some restaurants close for a week to a month or cut back on hours or lunch. Call ahead to avoid disappointment.

While the food is good, it's the freshly brewed beer and the namesake owner, actress Kelly McGillis, who draw the crowds at **Kelly's Caribbean Bar, Grill & Brewery** ($$-$$$, 305/293-8484) at 303 Whitehead St, in the original Pan American Airways building. The menu features the usual pasta, seafood, and poultry dishes (see tour). Hemingway was at **Blue Heaven** ($$-$$$, 305/296-8666) at 729 Thomas St, in the heart of Bahama Village, both to box and watch matches. History and personality aside, its natural and West Indian-style food served indoors and outdoors under huge trees has made it a local institution. The owners of the award-wining Cafe des Artistes opened **Duffy's Steak & Lobster House** ($-$$$, 305/296-4900) next door at 1007 Truman Ave. The theme is President Harry Truman, who was a frequent visitor to the island. While Cafe des Artistes is all white table cloths and candles, Duffy's is surf and turf in a casual, fun setting.

Drink in the atmosphere at the popular bar or wait for a dinner table at **Alice's on Duval** ($$$, 305/292-4888), where Alice Weingarten serves innovative seafood, game, beef, pork, and poultry dishes that always hint of the islands or the Far East. Dinner only is served here on the quiet end of Duval Street at #1114. Wake up and smell the coffee with locals at **Breakfast Anytime** ($, 305/292-2023) at 934 Truman Ave. It's okay if you're not an early riser, breakfast is served into the early evening. It's a toss up whether **Camille's** ($-$$, 305/296-4811) at 703 Duval St is more popular at breakfast, lunch, or dinner. You can't lose at anytime. Prices are very reasonable for hearty servings of soups, sandwiches, and omelets. Joining Blue Heaven in Bahama Village as a popular dining spot is this small newcomer **Caribe Soul** ($-$$, 305/296-0094) at 320 Petronia St that prepares home-style Caribbean and soul food served indoors and outdoors and for take-out with free delivery throughout Old Town. Their new cookbook, *Using What You've Got* is sold alongside other southern and Caribbean cookbooks. The cuisine at **Dim Sum's Far East** ($$$, 305/294-6230) in the rear of 613 1/2 Duval St is a marriage of Oriental and French style. Dishes are innovative; the service is excellent. It's also open for lunch from Christmas to April. Otherwise, you'll have to wait for dinner. There's usually a lot of chaos at **El Siboney** ($-$$, 305/296-4184), which offers home-style Cuban cuisine to a dedicated following of gringo and Cuban locals and tourists at 900 Catherine St.

Louie's Backyard ($$$, 305/294-1061) is one of those names that you're just as likely to hear in St. Louis or New York as in Key West. Everybody who has been to Key West and loves good food has been to Louie's. The waterfront setting at 700 Waddell Ave is wonderful, so is the seasonal menu prepared by Doug Shook and Annette Foley. If you want the best but can't afford it, come at lunch, when the menu is considerably cheaper. Besides, that's when the view is the best, too. Pasta and wine, pasta and wine. Repeat those words. That's what **Mangia Mangia** ($$$, 305/294-2469) at 900 Southard St does best, and that's what's on the menu. If you like cozy little restaurants that serve true French bistro-style food, go directly to **Mo's Restaurant** ($$$, 305/296-8955) at 1116 White St for dinner only. The special menu, which changes according to the day of the week, is the best deal at **Pepe's Cafe and Steak House** ($$-$$$, 305/294-7192) at 806 Caroline St. It's open for three squares, serving everything from barbecue and meat loaf to seafood and sandwiches. You'll be disappointed if you walk into **Waterfront Market** ($, 305/305/294-8418 or 305/296-0778) at 201 William St craving artery-clogging food. The offerings here run to health and gourmet foods, salads, baked goods, organic produce, and beer, wine, and juice.

Nightlife

Bars are the main evening event in Key West, and Duval Street is the main drag. Join the crowds hopping from one to the other in what's become known as the "Duval Crawl." Several locations serve up history along with a good time.

There's good, live jazz nightly, including jam sessions on some evenings at **Flager's Lounge** at the **Casa Marina** at 1500 Reynolds St. The hotel was built by Henry Flagler to house wealthy visitors who rode his railway from Miami to Key West. **Sloppy Joe's** (see tour) at 201 Duval St moved here when the rents got too high. Hemingway and other loyal fans followed owner Capt. Joe Russell. The place is decorated with Hemingway memorabilia. There's live entertainment nightly. **Capt. Tony's Saloon** (see tour) at 428 Greene St is synonymous with Hemingway, who came often when it was the original Sloppy Joe's, and Jimmy Buffett, who got his start here. There's music, drinks, and a rowdy good time.

Dance the night away at **Club Epoch** at 623 Duval St, where a spirited crowd is not afraid to take its cues from the house dancers who groove to hip local and celebrity spin masters. You can dance Wednesday to Sunday. Every night you can drink, hang out on the terrace, and people watch. After the sunset celebration, folks move into the **Havana Docks Lounge** at the Pier House at 1 Duval St. There's live music nightly in season and live dance music Friday and Saturday nights year round.

The **Afterdeck Bar at Louie's Backyard** at 700 Waddell St has one of the nicest settings on the island, especially on a breezy, balmy night. **Wine Galley** at the **Pier House** at 1 Duval St is an elegant piano bar with nightly entertainment. Cocktails are served into the very early morning hours. Jimmy Buffett's **Margaritaville Cafe** at 500 Duval St draws a young and not-so-young crowd of die-hard fans for nightly live entertainment, rarely by Buffett himself. **Rick's** at 202 Duval St and **Durty Harry's** at 208 Duval St make up a popular entertainment complex that features live rock 'n' roll, disco and karoke almost until the sun comes up. The **Schooner Wharf Bar** at 202 William St hosts live music nightly. Groups run from blues to country.

Events

The big event here is Fantasy Fest, a 10-day island-wide festival that climaxes on the last Saturday of October. It's not for the overly sensitive or overly inhibited. There's everything from a pet's and a children's parade to the grande finale Twilight Fantasy Parade. The latter is a Mardi gras-style anything-goes parade with floats and costumes and many participants wearing nothing but body paint. And very artful body paint it usually is. Hotels fill up months in advance. In November or December there's the annual **International Gay Arts Festival** that focuses on the artistic talents of gay and lesbian writers, artists, and performance artists. It usually includes a tour of homes. The roar of motorcycles is almost deafening the third weekend in September when the **Florida Keys Poker Run** comes to town, benefiting a children's charity. The **Key West Literary Seminar** showcases some of America's best known writers of today and the past the second week in January. The event features tours, lectures, and workshops.

South Central Florida

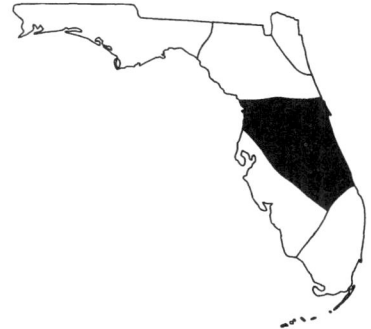

"All people need to know their heritage. A person who doesn't know where he's been has little chance of charting where he or she is going. I do believe that people live in direct relation to the heroes and she-roes they have, always and in all ways."—Maya Angelou in a National Public Radio interview with Benjamin D. Brotemarkle, as written in his book, *Beyond the Theme Parks: Exploring Central Florida.*

Introduction

The St Johns River flows northward 273 miles from its headwaters near Lake Okeechobee through South Central Florida to the Atlantic Ocean near Jacksonville. Jim Robison and Mark Andrews wrote of the river's significance to the region's development in *Flashbacks: The Story of Central Florida's Past*: "The St Johns River had the greatest influence on the early days of Central Florida. Ancient tribes followed its course inland from the coast. Later, Spanish missionaries ventured along the river. The British later established plantations along the river. Members of Southeastern tribes and runaway plantation slaves seeking sanctuary migrated south along the river."

Its importance continued after statehood as homesteaders poured inland by steamboat. They cultivated food crops and citrus. The railroads arrived in 1880 and allowed citrus growers to ship fruits quickly. The population and citrus industry exploded. Black settlers were recruited to move to the region and build more railroad tracks. Cattle ranches boomed in Kissimmee and tourism budded around lake cities like Mount Dora, Sanford, Orlando, Winter Haven, and Lakeland.

Killer freezes in 1894 and 1895 nearly wiped out the industry and sent the economy into a tailspin. Recovery was slow. The citrus industry rallied and remains one of the region's major industries, along with tourism and cattle ranching.

The construction of good roads gave tourism its first big jump in the late 1890s, then catapulted it into the fantasy stratosphere in the 1960s. "Orange County's favorable highway network was the key to attracting a project that would change the face of Central Florida forever," wrote Robison and Andrews, referring to 1964, when Walt Disney searching for a site to build Disney World, looked out his airplane's window and saw the junction of Interstate 4 and Florida's Turnpike.

Real launches to the stratosphere came in 1949, when President Harry Truman established a missile proving ground at Cape Canaveral. Ten years later NASA began launching lunar probes from the site.

South Central Florida is both temperate and tropical. Coastal habitats of tropical coastal hammocks, maritime forests, salt marshes, and beaches are found in Merritt Island National Wildlife Refuge and adjoining Canaveral National Seashore. In the interior, at Highlands Hammock State Park, the habitat shifts to a unique ecosystem of deep sand scrub on a narrow ridge. The sand is evidence that in prehistoric times the seas were higher. The majority of Florida's endemic plant and animal species and more than half of Florida's lakes are associated with the ridge.

Tourism remains the major attraction for South Central Florida, which has theme parks, the Space Industry on the coast, and outdoor recreation on the St Johns River, beaches, parks, and lakes.

Mount Dora

Less than an hour northwest of Orlando, this attractive New England-style town situated on gently rolling hills overlooking Lake Dora, has many fine examples of Victorian Revival buildings—one of them, the Alexander House, still serves as a popular resort, now called the Lakeside Inn. Along with antique and crafts shops, Mount Dora's waterfront parks and year-round arts, boating, and outdoor activities draw tourists from around the country.

Mount Dora was originally called Royellou, a name created by taking the first few letters from the names of the three children of the town's original postmaster. Its current name came from Dora Ann Drawdy, who befriended federal surveyors and let them camp in her yard, cooked dinner for them, and washed their clothes in 1846. When the surveyors returned to Washington, they named the lake after her. Transportation, more than any other force, shaped the town.

The region was home to the Seminole Indians before the Seminole Indian Wars. They were replaced by white farmers from Georgia and free blacks from the north. Wealthy northern vacationers traveling down the St Johns River on steamboats saw the potential for tourism and wealth in the pleasant climate and picturesque lake setting. They bought land, built lavish lakefront homes and resorts, and began farming citrus. But it wasn't until the railroads arrived that Mount Dora and surrounding communities really blossomed. The railroads brought thousands of tourists and took away tons of citrus. The town was almost lost in the 1920s citrus freeze, but tourism revived it and brought about another boom.

Preservation took a major step in 1991 when resident Dave Felts tacked up flyers and sat with a collection jar on the steps of an historic house that was going to be torn down if funds couldn't be raised to move it. Through contributions made by Felts, like-minded residents, and the historical society, as well as donated time by city and state workers, the house was moved. Today, it is known as the Unity House, for the cooperative efforts that went into its preservation, and it serves as a museum and headquarters for Historic Mount Dora Inc.

The city has an Historic Preservation Board and two preservation organizations, Historic Mount Dora Inc and the Mount Dora Historical Society, that actively promote the city. Lucretia Freed-West, president of the former, recently defined her organization's role, "The city is the museum and we are there to showcase the city." And what a beautiful city they have to showcase.

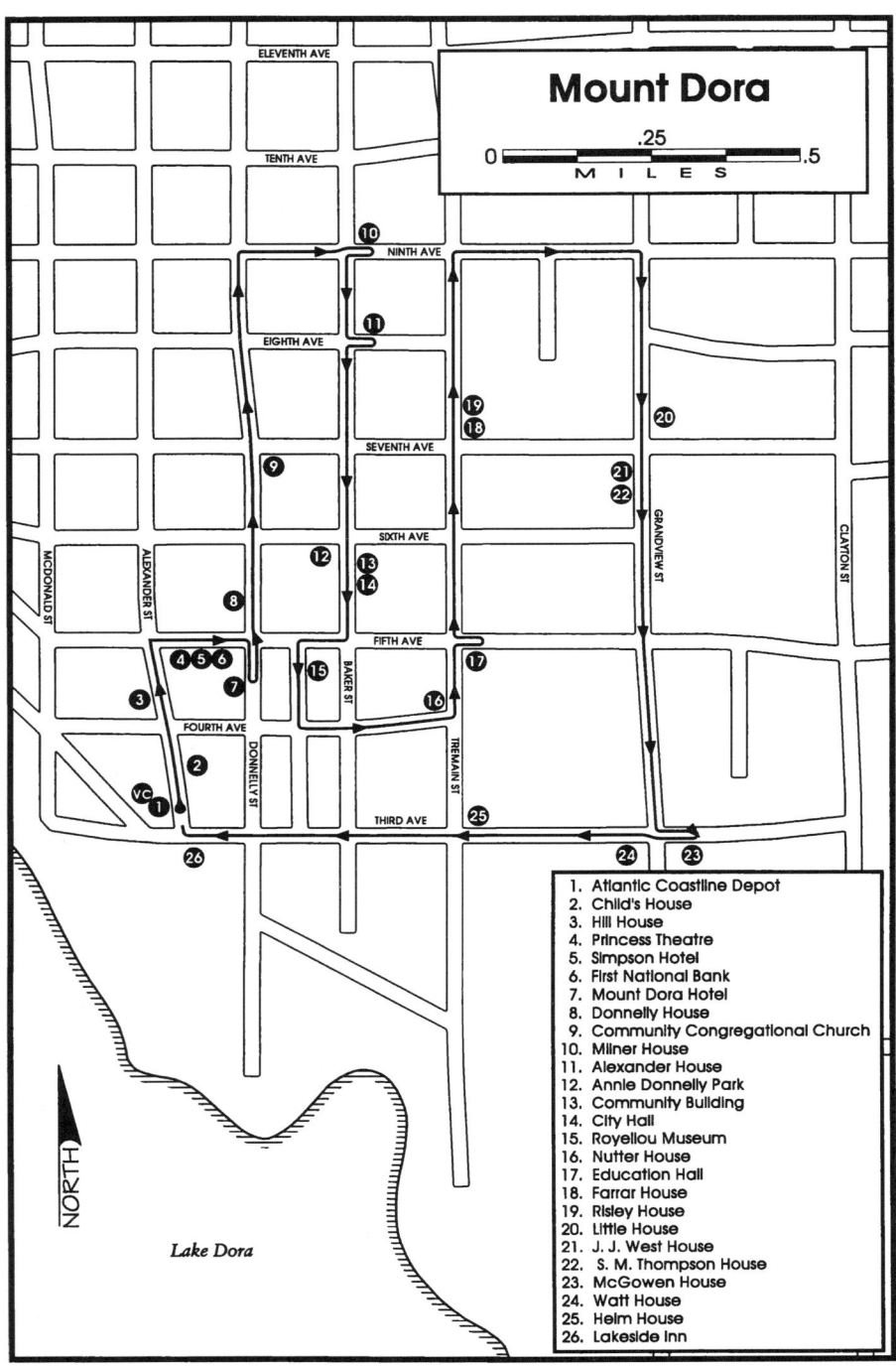

Mount Dora

.25
0 |=====|=====| .5
M I L E S

1. Atlantic Coastline Depot
2. Child's House
3. Hill House
4. Princess Theatre
5. Simpson Hotel
6. First National Bank
7. Mount Dora Hotel
8. Donnelly House
9. Community Congregational Church
10. Milner House
11. Alexander House
12. Annie Donnelly Park
13. Community Building
14. City Hall
15. Royellou Museum
16. Nutter House
17. Education Hall
18. Farrar House
19. Risley House
20. Little House
21. J. J. West House
22. S. M. Thompson House
23. McGowen House
24. Watt House
25. Helm House
26. Lakeside Inn

Information
Mount Dora Chamber of Commerce, 341 N Alexander St, Mount Dora FL 32757; 352/383-2165; 352/383-1668; chamber@mt-dora.com; www.mt-dora.com.

Getting there
From I-75 take Hwy 44 east to Hwy 441 east, which runs through Mount Dora. From the Florida Turnpike or Orlando, take I-4 to Hwy 441 west or Hwy 46 west to Mount Dora.

The closest Greyhound (800/231-2222) stations are in Tavares, about 15 minutes west, and Orlando, about 30 minutes southeast.

Amtrak's (800/USA RAIL) closest station is in Orlando.

First steps
Contact the Mount Dora Chamber of Commerce. It's open Monday to Friday 9 am to 5 pm, Saturday 10 am to 4 pm.

Historic Mount Dora. *This 2-mile route covers downtown Mount Dora and surrounding neighborhoods. Allot 90 minutes. However, a more leisurely trip of 3 hours includes stops at a cafe for a bite to eat and to visit two museums.*

Begin at the Chamber of Commerce on the corner of Alexander St and Third Ave. The chamber operates out of the **Atlantic Coastline Depot** (341 Alexander), which was constructed in 1914. Four daily trains arrived with passengers, mail, and freight and departed with citrus wrapped in tissue paper bearing a bass symbol and an offer for free information on Mount Dora. After passenger service ended in 1950 and freight service in 1973, it was taken over by the chamber, which made major changes to the interior and exterior. The Arts and Crafts **Child's House** (352 Alexander) was built from a Sears & Roebuck kit in 1922. It is named after Stanton Childs, the third owner, a wealthy industrialist from New York who donated the land next to the train depot to the city for a park. It's now an interior design firm. The Englishman who built the **Hill House** (425 Alexander) was a partner in Mount Dora's first hardware store. Now the clapboard house with a white brick chimney is an insurance firm. *Turn right onto Fifth Ave.*

Six years after it opened in 1922 at this location, a fire destroyed the façade of the **Princess Theatre** (127-137 W Fifth). It was rebuilt in a Spanish Revival style and showed movies until 1972. In 1925 well-known architect James Gamble Rogers designed the three-story **Simpson Hotel** (115–117 W Fifth) as a rental property for James Simpson, president of the First National Bank. His tenants included a realtor and vineyard owner, Western Union, a dentist, photographer, chapters of the Knights of Phythias and Phythian Sisters, and the Mount Dora Cafe. Rogers also designed the two-story **First National Bank** (100 W Fifth) for Simpson. Its lavish appointments of Alabama marble, mahogany, brass, and bronze raised its construction price to $30,000. The bank, which operated in the building until 1965, featured a private room for women to do their banking and a vault with 300 safe deposit boxes. *Take a short detour by turning right onto Donnelly St.*

During Florida's 1920s land boom, Monroe Patterson of Ohio built the **Mount Dora Hotel** (413 Donnelly), the only hotel constructed during that period. Today it's The Renaissance building. *Cross back over Fifth Ave and go north on Donnelly St.*

When Pittsburgh developer and two-time mayor John Phillip Donnelly married Annie McDonald Stone in 1893, he presented the **Donnelly House** (535 Donnelly) to her as a wedding gift. The lavish 2.5-story house features a wraparound porch, Carpenter decorations, and an octagonal turret in a blend of two Victorian styles, Steamboat Gothic and Queen Anne. John Donnelly donated the land for the **Community Congregational Church** (650 Donnelly), another marvelous Victorian Revival structure with a wood frame, octagonal bell cupola, and an elongated steeple. It was organized in 1883 and built in 1887. President and Mrs Calvin Coolidge attended services while vacationing at the Lakeside Inn. There are several other interesting homes along Donnelly St, including a brick Bungalow (#748) and a white Colonial Revival house (#851) built in 1896. *Turn right onto 9th Ave. Cross Baker St for a short detour.*

On the left side is the yellow **Milner House** (206 E 9th), known as Sunshine Corner, built in 1918 for Dr Duncan Milner, a Civil War soldier, Presbyterian minister, and author who supported Prohibition and civil rights for African Americans. The house's appearance has been significantly altered. *Return to Baker St and turn left. At Eighth Ave turn left for another short detour.*

Attorney, developer, and one of Mount Dora's most influential pioneers John Alexander built the **Alexander House** (207 E Eighth) around 1889. He homesteaded large tracts, enticed affluent friends from Kansas to settle in Mount Dora, loaned money, built the town's first store, layed out the African-American neighborhood called East Town, helped found the Methodist Church, donated money to missions in Asia, and reportedly transported his own tombstone—which reads simply "J.M. Alexander Missionary"—to the cemetary in a wheelbarrow. *Return to*

Baker St and turn left.

On the right, **Annie Donnelly Park** (508 Donnelly, corner of Baker) sits on land purchased from John Donnelly in 1924 with the agreement that it would be named for his late wife. Across the street is the 1929 **Community Building** (520 Baker) designed by architect H.M. Griffin of Daytona Beach in a Mediterranean Revival style at a cost of $5,000 for the land and $35,000 for the building made of reinforced concrete, steel, and stone tile. Although **City Hall** (510 Baker) was built in the style of an old house that once stood on the site, the building dates to 1964. *Turn right onto Fifth Ave, then left down the alley at Royellou Lane.*

The **Royellou Museum** (450 Royellou Lane) has a colorful history, originally serving as a fire station, then later as a jail, police station, public restrooms, a traffic department sign shop, and then finally in 1977 the Mount Dora Historical Society's headquarters and museum. It was refurbished in 1999 to remove the jail cells. Take time to visit the museum. *Continue down the alley, then turn left onto Fourth Ave.*

Ironically, the builder and original occupants of one of Mount Dora's oldest structures, the **Nutter House** (221 E Fourth), are unknown. Named after a family that lived in the house for 20 years until 1958, it's now the Mount Dora Inn. *Turn left onto Tremain St and detour right onto Fifth Ave.*

Education Hall (308 E Fifth) served from 1912 to 1923 as a private school for the children of winter visitors. The public library started in the basement in 1917, but was soaked whenever it rained. In 1929 the city bought the building and the library moved upstairs until a new one was built in 1977. *Return to Tremain St and turn right.*

In the next block is another of Mount Dora's oldest houses, the **Farrar House** (714 N Tremain), built in 1884 for the namesake family, which owned a 10-acre citrus grove east and south of the house. After his step-father died, Carl Risely, who was born in 1889 in Mount Dora, but had moved to Sanford with his family, returned to Mount Dora in 1910 and opened a concrete business in the back of the **Risley House** (742 N Tremain). His factory supplied concrete for most of the town's sidewalks. *Turn right onto Ninth Ave, then right onto Grandview St.*

The town's best example of a Craftsman Bungalow is the **Little House** (750 Grandview), which was originally located at 323 Tremain St. Note the "elephantine" columns supporting the porch. Its namesake owner, who ran the Little and Little dry goods store, built the house as a rental. In the next block, J.J. West, the city's first licensed real estate agent, built two identical houses in "Transitional Craftsman" style of double-walled terra cotta "Egyptian block" for himself, the **J.J. West House** (647 N

Grandview), and his sister, the **S.M. Thompson House** (618 N Grandview). The first child born in Mount Dora lived in the **McGowen House** (SE corner of Third and Grandview), built in 1882. *Turn right onto Third Ave.*

On the southwest corner is the **Watt House**, built in 1909 by the inventor of corrugated cardboard. The house is still in the family. Now the Magnolia Inn, the Spanish Revival **Heim House** (347 E Third) was built by the namesake owner, developer of Sylvan Shores. *Continue on Third Ave, then turn left onto Alexander St.*

The town's most distinguished guests, including U.S. presidents, have stayed in the **Lakeside Inn** (100 N Alexander St, corner Third and Alexander), started in 1883 by John Alexander, John McDonald, and Annie McDonald Stone, as the Alexander House, a "resort hotel for fishing, birding, and snake hunting" and added onto in 1926 and 1929. It consists of five buildings and an Olympic-size pool and was recently restored to its 1920s appearance. *Re-cross Third Ave, and return to the Atlantic Coastline Depot/Chamber of Commerce.*

Lodging

There is no shortage of cozy bed and breakfast establishments in restored turn-of-the-century houses. Along with these is the historic Lakeside Inn. There's also a handful of chain hotels and motels on the outskirts of town. Rates are higher for festivals, holidays, and weekends.

Lakeside Inn ($$–$$$, 800/556-5016, 352/383-4101), listed on the National Register of Historic Places, has beautifully decorated accommodations, a fine-dining restaurant, Sunday brunch on the verandah with an occasional ensemble playing light tunes, and rocking chairs on a porch overlooking the lake at 100 N Alexander St. The **Magnolia Inn** ($$$–$$$$, 800/776-2112, 352/735-3800) has four rooms and an adjacent suite, each beautifully decorated in antiques and coordinating wall coverings and linens with hardwood floors, ceiling fans, oriental carpets, CD/FM stereos, TVs, and hair dryers at 347 E Third Ave. A shoe merchant from Michigan built the **Farnsworth House B&B** ($$–$$$, 352/735-1894) in 1886 at 1029 E Fifth Ave. It became a seven-unit apartment house in 1944. Today it features three suites with kitchens, sitting rooms, antiques, and relaxing pastel decor on the second floor of the main house and two modern-style efficiencies with kitchenettes on the ground floor of the Carriage House. **The Mount Dora Historic Inn** ($$–$$$, 800/927-6344, 352/735-1212), in the historic Nutter House, features beautifully appointed rooms filled with antiques, old-style bathtubs, quilts, and lace at 221 E Fourth Ave.

Step back to the 1950s at the **Dora Way B&B** ($$$, 352/735-5994), a three-room inn overlooking Lake Dora at 1123 Dora Way, where the owner's collection of vintage jewelry, clothing, and accessories lend a personal air to the comfortable, light-filled rooms, public areas, and lanai. The **Darst Victorian Manor B&B** ($$$–$$$$, 352/383-4050) is a replica Queen Anne house authentically designed and decorated down to the lace curtains and bed quilts on two acres at 495 Old Hwy 441. Fresh flowers, breakfast and afternoon tea, fluffy robes, lake views or fireplaces, and terraces make the six guestrooms very inviting. Formerly a boarding house, **Simpson's Bed & Breakfast** ($$–$$$, 352/383-2087) now features five individually decorated suites with kitchenettes and attractive furnishings in the heart of downtown at 441 N Donnelly St.

Arts & culture
Mount Dora has an active performing arts company and fine arts center. During the warm, lazy summer months, music from free concerts fill the air.

The **Mount Dora Theatre Company** (352/383-4616, 1100 N Unser St), more than 50 years old, performs year round at the **Ice House Theatre**, a former ice house. **Arbors & Eyebrows** (352/735-0334) hosts a summer series of free outdoor Sunday afternoon concerts, from folk to jazz.

The non-profit **Mount Dora Center for Arts** (352/383-0880, 138 E Fifth Ave) exhibits contemporary fine arts of all media. Each February it hosts the Mount Dora Arts Festival, an outdoor show with an annual attendance of over 300,000. **Baker Street Gallery** (352/383-4199, 421 Baker St) features arts, fine crafts, and collectibles.

Dickens-Reed (352/735-5950, 140 W Fifth Ave) carries new books and gifts. **Old Towne Bookshop** (352/383-0878, 127 W Fifth Ave) sells used hardback books, from best sellers to collectibles.

The frame vernacular **Charles and Alfida Simpson House** (2015 N Donnelly), built around 1900, serves as the historical museum for Historic Mount Dora Inc. Downstairs the house is decorated in period furnishings and has rotating exhibitions.

Food & drink
The number of restaurants is limited, but there are excellent choices.

Bacco Italian Restaurant & Pizzeria ($$–$$$, 352/735-3544) at 421-B Baker St starts with very traditional appetizers like bruschetta and caprese, then follows with pastas, seafoods, pizzas, and wonderful handmade desserts.

At the tiny **Goblin Market** ($$$, 352/735-0059) at 331-B Donnelly St New Age music fills the two book-lined dining rooms and tree-shaded courtyard where they serve sophisticated fare like Snapper St Martin, a red snapper sauteed with kiwi and banana with an orange amaretto sauce, and filet portabella, an eight-ounce tenderloin of beef crowned with brie and portabella over puff pastry with sauce Bernaise and Bordelaise. Reservations are suggested.

At **Gourmet To Go** ($–$$, 352/735-0155) at 321-1 Donnelly St you can eat inside, outside, or take-out a full dinner of items like barbeque pastrami, seafood and curry salads, twice-baked potatoes or any of six to eight daily specials of seafood, including tender crab cakes, and on the weekends, prime rib. Fine wines and microbrewery beers round out the menu.

Seafood features prominently on the menu at **The Gables Restaurant** ($$–$$$, 352/383-8993) at 322 N Alexander St, where the chef prepares a popular tagliatelle with Cajun seafood ragout as well as Maryland style crabcakes.

The chefs at Lakeside Inn's **Beauclaire Restaurant** ($$$–$$$$, 352/383-4101) at 100 N Alexander St turn traditional favorites into creative New World dishes like Maryland crab cakes on a bed of baby greens with lemon-chive dressing and Zellwood corn fritters, Georgia chicken sautéed in honey bourbon glaze and pecans served with wild rice pilaf, and grilled filet mignon with blue cheese crust in a pool of rosemary-port sauce.

Nightlife
Nightlife is almost non-existent in Mount Dora. Orlando is about 30 minutes away and offers many choices. (See Ybor City and Lake Cherokee Historic District walking tours.)

The Mexican food in the downstairs family area of **Eduardo's Station** at 100 E Fourth Ave is only so-so, but the music and entertainment upstairs provide an amusing evening out.

Events
The annual **Arts Festival** (352/383-0880) unfolds displays of art with vendors and entertainment the first weekend in February. Sunday after Thanksgiving is the traditional **Light-Up Mount Dora** (352/383-2165). It's closely followed by **Mount Dora Christmas Weekend** (352/383-2165), which features a downtown stroll, parade, and lighted boat parade, the first weekend in December.

Lake Cherokee Historic District, Orlando

Decades before Walt Disney was born, Orlando was a thriving community, where settlers had been building homes and businesses since the 1800s. Today, the city has five historic districts, among them the Lake Cherokee Historic District.

In 1884, Sinclair's Real Estate Agency used a drawing of Lake Minnie—as Lake Cherokee was called at the time—to sell the virtues of Orlando to northern visitors. The drawing shows only trees surrounding the lake. Six years later, the agency's advertising material shows half a dozen properties on and near the lakeshore.

It started with four newly wed couples building houses along Lake Minnie. The lakefront was quickly nicknamed "Honeymoon Row." All of the houses were built in the standard L-plan that was popular in the 1870s and 1880s.

The district grew and now has brick streets and a gracious mix of more than 150 historic houses. Some of the earliest residences in Orlando are on the north and west sides of the lake. They were built in the 1880s as wooden houses. The Mediterranean style houses on the east and south sides of the lake were built during the 1920s boom.

Information

Orlando/Orange County Official Visitor Center, 8723 International Dr, Suite 101, Orlando, FL 32819; 800/643-9492, 407/363-5872; www.Go2orlando.com. To learn more about Orlando's historic neighborhoods and architecture, read *Orlando: History in Architecture* ($15) by the Orlando Historic Preservation Board, City Hall, 400 S Orange Ave, Orlando, FL 32801; 407/246-3350.

Getting there

Take I-4 to Orlando, exit 38 (Anderson St), go east to Delaney Ave and turn south (right), then left onto Cherokee Dr. The next left is Cherokee Circle. Park at the corner, across from Lake Cherokee and adjacent to Lake Cherokee Park. Orlando International Airport (407/825-2142) is off I-4 at exit 28 (Beeline Expwy). The Amtrak (800/USA RAIL, 407/843-7611) station is about a mile from the Lake Cherokee Historic District at 1400 Sligh Blvd. Greyhound's (800/231-2222, 407/292-3422) terminal is at 555 N John Young Pkwy.

First steps

For area maps and information, contact the Orlando/Orange County Convention & Visitors Bureau.

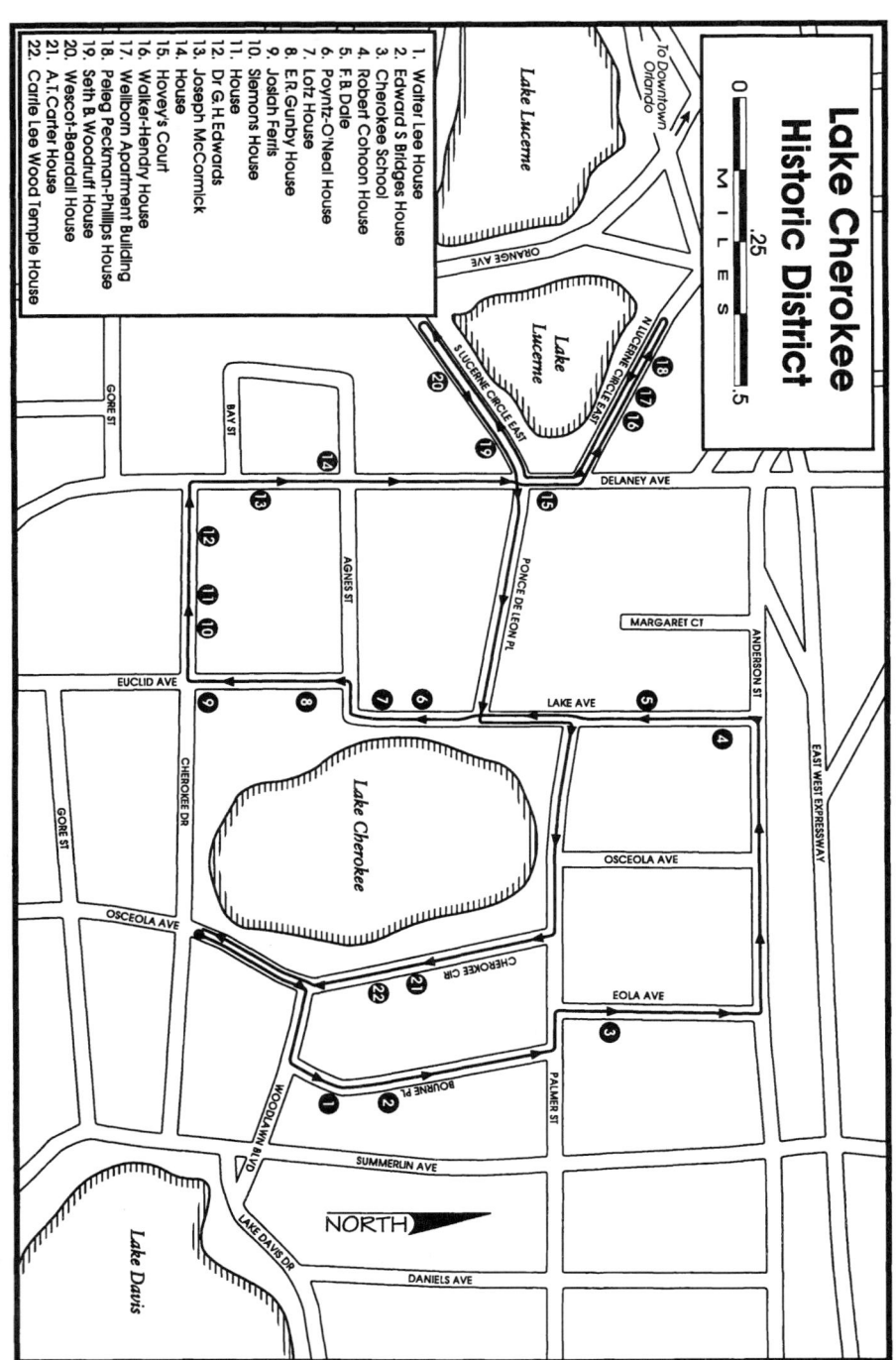

Lake Cherokee Historic District

1. Walter Lee House
2. Edward S Bridges House
3. Cherokee School
4. Robert Cohoon House
5. F.B. Dale
6. Poyntz-O'Neal House
7. Lotz House
8. E.R.Gunby House
9. Josiah Ferris
10. Siemons House
11. House
12. Dr G.H.Edwards House
13. Joseph McCormick House
14. House
15. Hovey's Court
16. Walker-Hendry House
17. Wellborn Apartment Building
18. Peleg Peckman-Phillips House
19. Seth B.Woodruff House
20. Wescot-Beardall House
21. A.T.Carter House
22. Carrie Lee Wood Temple House

Tours

Historic Lake Cherokee. *This 3.25-mile route covers the district's residences and two lakes. It will take about two hours.*

Start at the south end of Lake Cherokee, around the intersection of Cherokee Dr and Cherokee Circle. Follow Cherokee Circle north along the lake's eastern shore. Turn right onto Woodlawn Blvd, the left onto Bourne Place.

The **Walter Lee House** (635 Bourne Pl) was built in 1936. Its corbelled chimney on the front façade makes it appear taller than it really is. The Classical Revival **Edward S. Bridges House** (647 Bourne Pl) was originally located on Cherokee Circle with its portico facing the lake. The owners moved it here in 1925 and changed its orientation so the side and chimney face the street, requiring them to transform the side door into a front door. *Turn left onto Palmer St, then right onto Eola Ave.*

Even schools fell under the spell of the 1920s love affair with Mediterranean style design. Built in 1926 by architect Howard M. Reynolds, the beautiful **Cherokee School** (525 S Eola Ave) features a stucco façade with two square towers with pyramid clay tile roofs flanking the loggia of paired columns. The façade is highlighted with graceful polychromatic glazed tile inserts and decorative bas-relief.

Most of the houses on the other side of Eola Ave are Craftsman Bungalows. Extremely popular from 1900 to 1920, the style emphasizes the skills of craftsmen rather than the industrialization and urbanization of the late 1800s. Notice that stylistic variations drew upon many schools, but all were typified by one-and-a-half stories, multiple roof lines, groupings of windows, exposed rafter tails and trim, an irregular footprint, and a broad front porch supported by large columns. *Turn left onto Anderson, then left onto Lake Ave.*

A revival of European architectural styles was another fad of the early 20th century. The **Robert Cohoon House** (513 S Lake Ave) was no exception. It was designed in a Classical Revival style in 1911. The Cohoon family operated a turtle canning factory, which changed to equipment manufacturing and remains one of the oldest businesses in Orlando. New York developer **F.B. Dale** had his house (536 S Lake) built as a winter getaway in 1910. Its hip roof, wide verandah, and shady oak tree make it ideal for Florida's climate. In the next block, the **Poyntz-O'Neal** **House** (614 S Lake Ave) is the grande dame of Lake Cherokee. Built in 1887 by a banker, it is one of the two surviving original "Honeymoon Row" houses built on Lake Minnie. It remained in the second owner's family until Mabel O'Neal died in 1975. At risk of being razed for a modern structure, a preservation group bought it. Next door, the powder blue **Lotz House** (626 S Lake) is new, but was built in a style compatible to the original honeymoon house that had to be replaced. *Turn right onto Agnes St, then left onto Euclid Ave.*

On the left side just after you turn the corner is the **E.R. Gunby House** (709 Euclid Ave). Gunby, an attorney, and his wife were one of the original "Honeymoon Row" newlyweds who built houses on Lake Minnie, which in 1887 was on the far outskirts of growing downtown Orlando. He distinguished himself as a city councilman, delegate to the 1888 GOP National Convention, and Tampa tax collector, before leaving Florida for Atlanta in 1900. In 1923-1924, **Josiah Ferris**, founder of the *Independent* newspaper and private secretary to Senator Park Trammell, built this Neo-Classical house (733 Euclid Ave) to suit the Florida climate. The broad overhangs provide shade and transoms increase air circulation. *Turn right onto Cherokee Dr.*

With the exception of the broad roof overhang—an adaptation to Florida's climate—the corner 1924 **Slemons House** (339 Cherokee Dr) is a good example of American Tudor Revival design. The **house** (331 Cherokee) next door captures a Spanish flavor, one of the district's many Mediterranean Revival designs. Note the front entrance columns with polychromatic capitals. **Dr G.H. Edwards** began practicing medicine in Orlando in 1909 and helped organize the Orlando Clinic in 1914. Ten years later, he built this Colonial Revival brick house (309 Cherokee Dr) with full Ionic porticos on the east and west sides. *Turn right onto Delaney Ave.*

Lumberman **Joseph McCormick** built the elegant taupe-colored Mediterranean Revival house (713 S Delaney Ave) in 1924, and actress Delta Burke grew up in it. The details are numerous: driveway columns topped by bowls of fruit, faces on parapets, a red barrel-tile hip roof, small iron balcony, arched windows, and a porte-cochère. Five bays and a turned balustrade distinguish the brick **house** (710 S Delaney Ave) that was built in 1923. The walkway down the middle courtyard of **Hovey's Court** (545 S Delaney Ave), a cluster of nine two-story bungalows, draws focus to Lake Lucerne. Originally constructed from 1913 to 1919 as apartments, the buildings are now an office complex. They have been beautifully restored. *Across from Hovey Court is a small street with a sign that reads No Outlet and another that reads Historic Inn. To the right of it is a one-way street with traffic coming toward Hovey Court. Walk up the No Outlet street, which is N Lake Lucerne Circle E.*

The fancy-cut wood shingles, steeply pitched gables, a wrap-around porch, and turned balustrades and trim exemplify the pure Victorian style of the lovely **Walker-Hendry House** (125 N Lucerne Circle E), built in 1894, moved for the second time to this location in 1981, and then restored to its original appearance. It's part of the B&B known as the Courtyard at Lake Lucerne. The two-tone salmon-colored 1947 **Wellborn Apartment Building** (203 N Lucerne Circle E) is sandwiched between two houses of the Courtyard at Lake Lucerne. Its zig-zag layout connecting a series of cubes exemplifies Art Deco design. The colorful Victorian **Peleg Peckman-Phillips House** (135 N Lucerne Circle E) was built in 1893 for Colonel Peleg Peckman, a prominent seasonal resident. When Dr P. Phillips, a successful citrus grower, bought it in 1912, it was an excellent example of Queen Anne and Shingle styles. Phillips replaced the two-story porch with the Neo-Classical portico with Ionic columns. It's now a B&B. *Return to Delaney St and turn right. Follow the lake. Stop at the house on the corner before walking half way up S Lucerne Circle E.*

Frank Lloyd Wright's Prairie School influenced many Florida architects, including Murray S. King, who in 1936 built the **Seth B. Woodruff House** (236 S Lucerne Circle E). The namesake owner—an early cattleman, citrus grower, and politician—was a member of the Florida Secession Convention before the Civil War. It's now a legal office. It's not surprising that King was also the architect for the 1912 **Wescot-Beardall House** (214 S Lucerne Circle E), another Prairie School brick house. Note the rectilinear Chicago-style ornamentation on the parapet edges and the low-pitched hip roof with a wide overhang. *Return to Delaney and cross over to Ponce de Leon Pl. Make a short left onto Lake Ave. Following the north end of the lake, turn right onto Palmer St, then right onto Cherokee Circle.*

The imposing brick Colonial Revival **A.T. Carter House** (627 Cherokee Circle) is impossible to miss with its massive Ionic columns. The pastel-colored **Carrie Lee Wood Temple House** (615 Cherokee Circle) was built in 1922 two years before the death of the owner, the widow of a successful industrialist and former mayor of Winter Park. It is a skillful adaptation of Spanish Colonial Revival. *Continue south along the lake and return to the start.*

Lodging

The Lake Cherokee Historic District has one B&B, with two others on the outskirts. Neighboring downtown hotels cater to the business community. To accommodate the millions of theme park visitors, the options throughout the rest of Orlando are all but limitless.

If you're looking for immersion in local history, you can't beat the **Courtyard at Lake Lucerne** ($$–$$$$, 407/648-5188), where 30 rooms are spread among four historic buildings at 211 N Lucerne Circle E. Now totally renovated, the inn features antiques, fresh flowers, fireplaces, whirlpool bathtubs in many rooms, a grand piano, tropical gardens, and attentive service.

Pet-friendly **Maggie's Bed & Breakfast** ($$–$$$, 407/425-9175) at 314 E Anderson St, in neighboring downtown, features suites, a deck and spa, and disabled access. Four historic houses comprise the recently renovated **Veranda Bed & Breakfast** ($$–$$$, 407/849-0321) at 115 N Summerlin Ave, downtown, on the edge of the historic district. The nine rooms, suites, and two-bedroom cottage have been decorated in a rich, European style.

Spacious rooms filled with antiques, fresh flowers, and complimentary wine await guests at the **Fortnightly Inn Bed & Breakfast** ($$–$$$, 407/645-4440) at 377 E Fairbanks Ave, Winter Park, 10 miles north of the historic district.

Downtown, there's plenty of charm and luxury at the 891-room **Peabody Orlando** ($$$$, 407/352-4000), a large, superbly run hotel loaded with amenities and resident ducks that parade through the hotel twice a day.

North of downtown, there's the 40-year-old, 220-room **Langford Resort Hotel** ($$, 407/644-3400) in a garden setting, with a restaurant, pool, and evening entertainment at 300 E New England Ave, Winter Park.

Arts & culture

If you plan to spend a lot of time enjoying the arts, consider parking the car and hopping on **CultureQuest** (800/327-5254, 407/855-6434), round-trip transportation from five hubs to 15 cultural sites in greater Orlando. The cost is $10 to $18 for adults, $8 to $12 for children.

Downtown, **The Wildlife Gallery** specializes in wildlife and Florida scenes using conservation framing at 1219 N Orange Ave. The **William Moseley Gallery** deals exclusively in 18th, 19th, and early 20th-century oils and watercolors at 1221 N Orange Ave. North of downtown in Maitland, the **Maitland Art Center**, listed on the National Register of Historic Places, has exhibits, tours, gardens, and a museum store at 231 W Packwood Ave.

Downtown has several venues for performances, including **Civic Theatre of Central Florida** (407/896-7365), which presents Broadway and off-Broadway plays at 1001 E Princeton St; and **Theatre Downtown** (407/841-0083) with weekend performances at 2113 N Orange Ave.

Loch Haven Park, located just north of downtown, is home to several major museums, including The **Orange County Historical Museum** (407/897-6350) at 812 E Rollins St, which tells the story of Orlando from prehistoric times to the present, and the **Orlando Museum of Art** (407/896-4231) at 2416 Mills Ave, which has a small permanent collection of 19th- and early 20th-century masters and contemporary art, a terrific hands-on children's section, and major traveling exhibitions such as "Imperial Tombs of China."

There are two very special art museums in neighboring Winter Park. The **Charles Hosmer Morse Museum of American Art** (407/645-5311) at 445 Park Ave N specializes in objets of the Arts and Crafts Movement, especially Rookwood pottery and Tiffany works. There's an exquisite collection of 6,000 American and European paintings, sculptures, and decorative arts at the **Cornell Fine Arts Museum** (407/646-2526) at 1000 Holt Ave, Rollins College campus.

Chapters Bookshop & Cafe buys, sells, and trades hardcovers and paperbacks and has a restaurant, the Bread & Books Cafe at 717 W Smith St, downtown. Other downtown bookstores with large regional interest sections include **B. Dalton** at 55 W Church St and **Barnes & Noble** at 2418 E Colonial Dr.

Food & drink

It makes sense for a town that receives hundreds of thousands of international visitors a year to have cuisine to match every taste. Prices are equally varied, with many good values.

Downtown restaurants include **Cafe Europa** ($, 407/872-3388), serving tasty Eastern European specialties in a stylish setting at 55 W Church St. **Manuel's on the 28th** ($$$, 407/246-6580) features an elegant rooftop setting and a seasonal menu of contemporary cuisine in the NationsBank Center at 390 N Orange Ave. Guests feel right at home and get great value at **Le Coq au Vin** ($$–$$$, 407/851-6980), a family-run French-style bistro at 4800 S Orange Ave.

In the theme park area, there's the flavor of the Caribbean at the popular, attractively priced **Bahama Breeze** ($–$$, 407/248-2499) at 8849 International Dr.

A little north of downtown in Maitland is the pricey French **Nicole St Pierre Restaurant** ($$$, 407/647-7575), with live entertainment, located in an early 19th-century building surrounded by large oaks and beautiful landscaping at 1300 S Orlando Ave.

Nightlife

Downtown's historic Church Street area offers lively entertainment for a wide age group. The International Drive area also has many options. Disney and Universal both have outstanding multi-themed entertainment complexes.

Downtown has the **Cheyenne Saloon and Opera House**, a tri-level saloon with country and western music at Church Street Station, 129 W Church St. Using horror movie themes, **Terror On Church Street** scares the pants off young and old at 135 S Orange Ave.

Blazing Pianos Rock & Roll Piano Bar at 8445 International Dr is a large piano bar with three grand pianos played by musicians who take requests and put on quite a show.

Disney's Pleasure Island features eight night spots ranging from a comedy club to a disco in Lake Buena Vista at I-4 exit 25A or 25B or U S Hwy 192.

Universal Studio's Citywalk, Orlando is the area's newest entertainment mega-plex with restaurants, nightclubs, movie theaters, and concerts at 1000 Universal Studios Plaza and S Kirkman Rd, I-4 exit 29B and 30A.

Harry P. Leu Gardens, Orlando

The Harry P. Leu Gardens encompass nearly 50 acres of formal gardens on a gently rolling hillside overlooking Lake Rowena. Concrete pathways and wooden bridges connect the plant collections, which include the largest camellia collection in the South, the largest formal rose garden in Florida, butterfly and herb gardens, an aquatic/wetland garden, as well as collections of day lilies, palms, bamboos and cycads, annuals, and towering live oaks laced with Spanish moss.

The Leu House Museum is the focal point of the garden. Now listed on the National Register of Historic Places, the house was begun in 1888 by John Thomas Mizell, the son of the property's first owner. It was completed in 1906 by the third owner, John Woodward, and became the residence of the fourth and final namesake owner in 1936. Harry P Leu and his wife donated the home and surrounding gardens to the city in 1961.

Information
Harry P Leu Gardens, 1920 N Forest Ave, Orlando, Florida 32803; 407/246-2620; www.ci.orlando.fl.us/departments/leu_gardens. Orlando/Orange County Official Visitor Center, 8723 International Dr, Suite 101, Orlando, FL 32819; 800 /643-9492, 407/363-5872; www.Go2orlando.com.

Getting there
Take I-4 to Orlando, exit 43 (Princeton St). Go east to N Mills Ave and turn south. Turn left onto N Virginia Dr, then left onto N Forest Ave, then left into the parking lot. The closest airport is Orlando International Airport (407/825-2142), about 15 minutes south. The Amtrak (800/USA RAIL, 407/843-7611) station is at 1400 Sligh Blvd. Greyhound's (800/231-2222, 407/292-3422) terminal is at 555 N John Young Pkwy.

First steps
For garden information, contact Harry P Leu Gardens, which is open daily 9 am to 5 pm. During Daylight Savings Times, the garden is open Monday to Saturday 9 am to 8 pm, Sunday 9 am to 6 pm. Adult admission is $4.00; children grades K-12 are $1. For area maps and information, contact the Orlando/Orange County Convention & Visitors Bureau's Official Visitor Center.

Seasonal highlights
Spring and fall are the most pleasant months to visit. It's cooler and there are fewer insects. The camellias bloom October to March and peak in January. The roses are the most showy May to September. Winter temperatures can dip into the 30s and

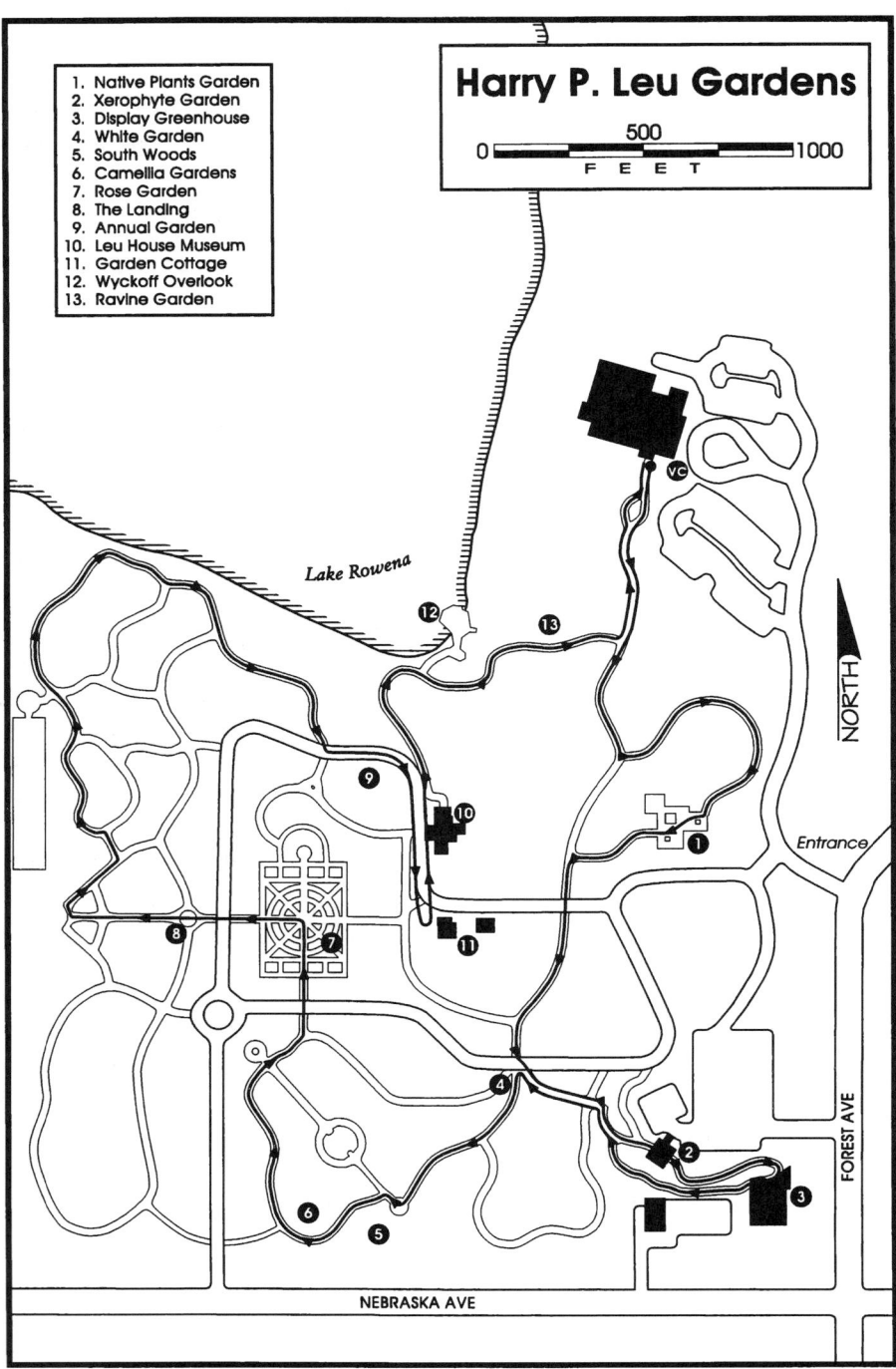

Harry P. Leu Gardens

1. Native Plants Garden
2. Xerophyte Garden
3. Display Greenhouse
4. White Garden
5. South Woods
6. Camellia Gardens
7. Rose Garden
8. The Landing
9. Annual Garden
10. Leu House Museum
11. Garden Cottage
12. Wyckoff Overlook
13. Ravine Garden

500

0 ▬▬▬▬▬▬▬ 1000
FEET

Lake Rowena

NORTH

Entrance

FOREST AVE

NEBRASKA AVE

40s when cold fronts move south from Canada. The garden is open at night for the annual Spring Moon Stroll in May.

Natural Harry P. Leu Gardens. *At approximately 2 miles, this route covers the major areas of the garden. Allow yourself two hours for a leisurely trip. Bring a lunch and sit on the boardwalk overlooking Lake Rowena.*

Start behind the Garden House Visitor Center. The walk on the concrete path starts with a little gasp as you open the door to imposing oak trees gracefully draped with Spanish moss. Lake **Rowena** sits on the right just beyond the courtyard. A wood bridge crosses over a creek whose banks are covered with spathyphyllum, monstera, ferns and croton on the left and sentinel-like birds of paradise on the right. *Take the left fork toward the Flowering Tree Garden.*

Almost any time of year there's something blooming here, such as the many varieties of Cleredendrum. The **Native Plants Garden** at 0.25 miles highlights indigenous vegetation. Look to the right at the floss silk tree (*chorisia speciosa*), whose trunk is covered with large thorns. *Cross the street and continue on the path.*

Before entering the **White Garden**, detour left to the **Xerophyte Garden** and **Display Greenhouse**, which have opposite environments. The lush, green foliage of the ferns, bromeliads, and orchids in the greenhouse gives way to a parched, rocky desert landscape strewn with boulders in the Xerophyte Garden, ideal for cactus and succulents. There are public restrooms here. *Return to the intersection and turn left.*

The White Garden derives its name from the many plants with white flowers and variegated white and green foliage. Among them are pinwheel and beautiful shell gingers, which bloom spring to fall. This section also features camellias, both white and pink varieties, and towering native slash pines (*Pinus elliottii*). *Follow the path along the south side of the White Garden, then turn left.*

Follow the path past the **South Woods** and one of the two **Camellia Gardens** that form a collection of more than 2,000 specimens. *Cross the road and enter the Rose Garden.*

The formal European style **Rose Garden** displays more than 1,000 heirloom and hybrid roses, a fountain, gazebos, and arbors. *Continue straight to the landing.*

The landing overlooks beds of day lilies and a **Floral Clock** that keeps accurate time. To the right is a veritable tropical garden of 250 species of palms, bamboos, and cycads. They're part of an experiment to test their cold hardiness in Central Florida, where winter temperatures can drop into the 30s when cold fronts push south. In the far northwest corner is the second camellia collection. *Follow the road east past the North Woods, down a few steps, then turn left onto the street.*

The **Annual Garden** on the right is a riot of color year round. The street curves right to the **Leu House Museum**, where tours are conducted on the half hour. You can wait on the broad porch of the frame vernacular house for the next tour or take a quick look at the **Garden Cottage** just beyond the house. It has a butterfly garden and an herb garden. The latter features plants used for medicinal, culinary, and fragrance purposes. *After the tour, follow the path north.*

The **Wyckoff Overlook**, a boardwalk and gazebo, juts out into **Lake Rowena**, where recreational boaters skim the waters. Houses and piers dot the opposite shore. The lake shore near the overlook is planted with ornamental and native wetland plants that serve as food and cover for birds, fish, and wildlife, including alligators. *Continue on the path.*

The path crosses a small waterway before reaching the **Ravine Garden**, another tropical oasis planted with bananas, gingers, tree ferns, palms, flowering vines, and birds of paradise. *Turn left at the crossroads and return to the Visitor Center.*

Lodging, Arts & culture, Food & drink, and Nightlife
See Orlando, Lake Cherokee Historic District

Merritt Island National Wildlife Refuge

Merritt Island National Wildlife Refuge and the adjoining Canaveral National Seashore prove that nature and technology can coexist. The refuge and seashore are located on a barrier island on Florida's east coast between Daytona Beach and Cocoa Beach. One is administered by the US Fish and Wildlife Service, the other by the National Park Service, but the land on which they are located is owned by the National Aeronautics and Space Administration (NASA) to serve as a buffer for the Kennedy Space Center launch facilities.

On Merritt Island wildlife flourishes in the shadow of launch pads, a shuttle landing strip, and vehicle assembly plants. It's not uncommon to see bobcats, white-tailed deer, otters, armadillos, manatees, gopher tortoises, sea turtles, fish, alligators, snakes, and myriad raptors and shore, water, song, and wading birds.

Sandwiched between the Intracoastal Waterway/Indian River and the Atlantic Ocean, the 140,000-acre refuge supports a wide variety of habitats, ranging from freshwater impoundments to vast saltwater estuaries to brackish marshes. There are hardwood hammocks and pine flatwoods, too. Together, they support some 1,045 species of plants and 310 species of birds.

The island has not always been isolated. For thousands of years, Native Americans harvested oysters and clams and discarded their shells in mounds or middens. They also left burial mounds. European explorers visited from the 16th to 18th centuries. In 1830 Douglas Dummett planted an orange grove that began the Indian River citrus industry. However, most citrus farmers abandoned the area due to storms, frosts, mosquitoes, and isolation.

During the 1950s engineers divided part of the marsh into impounded pools to control water levels, salinity, and saltmarsh mosquitoes. The environment attracted new wildlife. In the 1960s NASA began acquiring the land for the Kennedy Space Center. Three years later it turned over land to create the Merritt Island National Wildlife Refuge and the Canaveral National Seashore. In the 1990s, a marsh restoration project began to reconnect some of the impounded pools to the Indian and Banana rivers in order to create greater wildlife diversity in the refuge's salt marshes.

Highlights of Merritt Island National Wildlife Refuge include the six-mile Black Point Wildlife Drive. From there, walkers and hikers can access the five-mile Cruickshank Trail. There are also two shorter trails—Oak Hammock Trail (0.5 miles) and Palm Hammock Trail (2 miles)—about a mile east of the visitor center. The visitor center has interesting exhibits and a helpful support staff and volunteers.

The Canaveral National Seashore has a 25-mile natural beach with hiking trails, campgrounds, sea turtle nesting sites, and Native American shell middens.

Information

Merritt Island National Wildlife Refuge, PO Box 6504, Titusville, FL 32782; 321/861-0667. Canaveral National Seashore, 7611 S Atlantic Ave, New Smyrna Beach, FL 32169; 904/428-3384 (information center) or 308 Julia St, Titusville, FL 32796 (headquarters); 321/267-1110. Titusville Area Chamber of Commerce, 2000 S Washington Ave, Titusville, FL 32780; 321/267-3036.

Getting there

By car, take I-95 from the north or south to exit 80 east (Hwy 406/402/Garden St). You can also take Hwy 1 or A1A from the north to Hwy 406/402. From Orlando and other points west, take the Bee Line Expwy (Hwy 528). Orlando International Airport (407/825-2142), about 35 miles west of Titusville, is the closest airport served by major carriers. Greyhound (800/231-2222, 407/267-8760) operates service to 1220 S Washington Ave, Titusville, near the Chamber of Commerce. The closest Amtrak trains (800/USA RAIL) pull into Orlando, 30 miles west.

First steps

For refuge information, stop at the Merritt Island National Wildlife Refuge, which is four miles east of Titusville on Hwy 402. For seashore information, visit the Seashore Visitor Information Center, seven miles south of New Smyrna Beach on Hwy A1A. For area maps and information, contact the Titusville Area Chamber of Commerce.

Drink plenty of water and bring along a bottle. There's very little shade on the trail. Portable toilets are located at the trailhead. If you don't own a bird book, consider picking one up at the visitor center. More than 310 species of birds have been spotted here.

The refuge is open every day during daylight hours only. The visitor center is open Monday to Friday 8 am to 4:30 pm, Saturday and Sunday 9 am to 5 pm. Note: It's closed Sundays April to October.

There's a $2 donation requested at the beginning of Black Point Drive.

Walking tours

The refuge staff schedules walks throughout the year. From about November to April there are birding tours at 10 am on Thursdays. April is especially busy, with walks and speakers highlighting Florida's scrub jay, as well as events for warblers

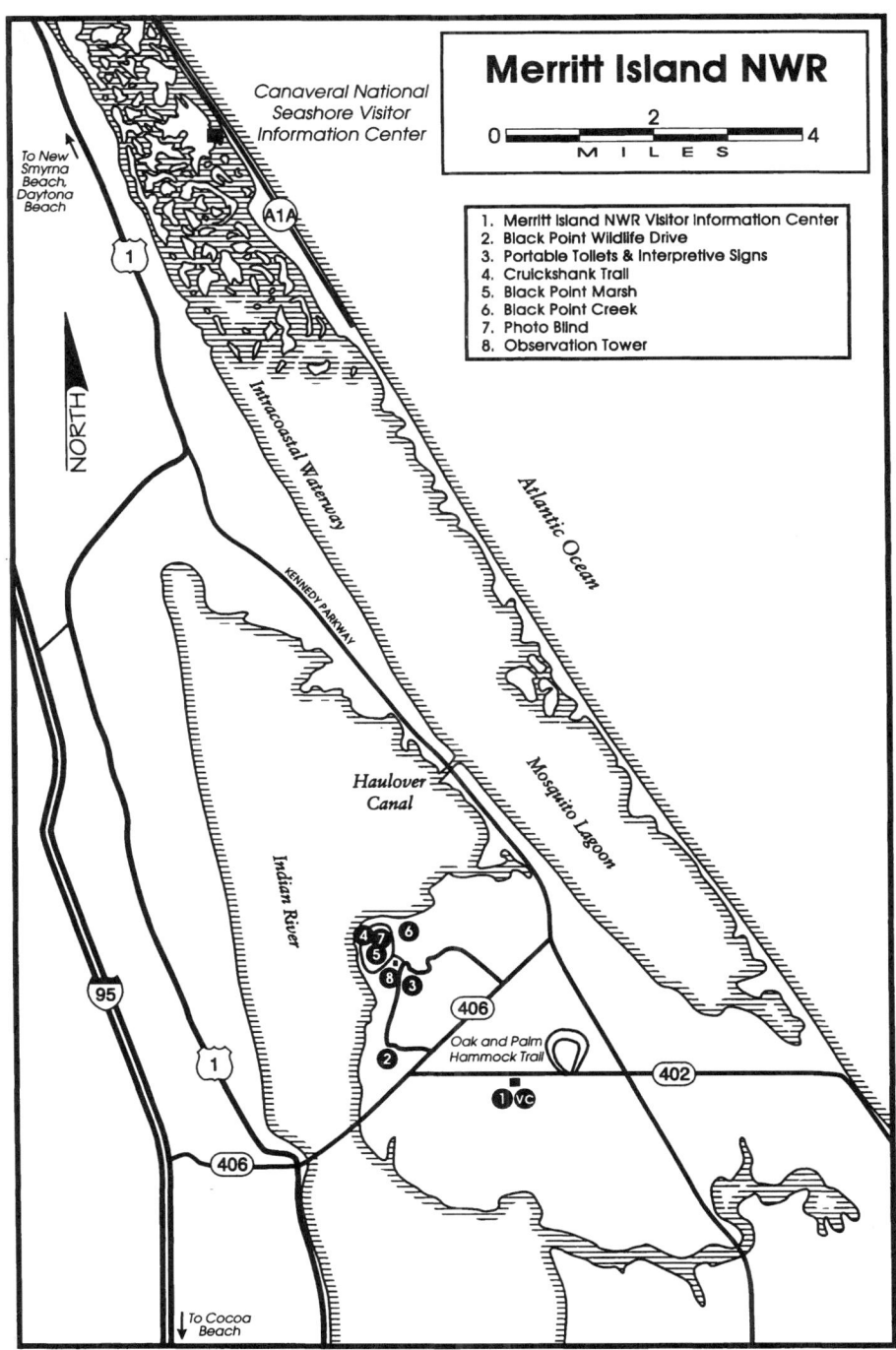

Canaveral National
Seashore Visitor
Information Center

To New
Smyrna
Beach,
Daytona
Beach

Merritt Island NWR

0 |———————— 2 ————————| 4
M I L E S

1. Merritt Island NWR Visitor Information Center
2. Black Point Wildlife Drive
3. Portable Toilets & Interpretive Signs
4. Cruickshank Trail
5. Black Point Marsh
6. Black Point Creek
7. Photo Blind
8. Observation Tower

NORTH

Intracoastal Waterway

KENNEDY PARKWAY

Atlantic Ocean

Haulover
Canal

Mosquito Lagoon

Indian River

95

1

406

Oak and Palm
Hammock Trail

402

406

To Cocoa
Beach

and shorebirds. On the second weekend in November there's a walk for the fall Fly Away.

Seasonal highlights

Wildlife populations are highest in spring, fall, and winter. From June to August it's hot, likely to rain, and likely to have biting bugs. Alligator sighting is best in the cooler months, when the reptiles bask in the sun. Bald eagles return in September, followed by a hundred thousand other migratory birds in October and November. In December, Audubon affiliates conduct the annual Christmas bird count.

Due to flooding, Black Point Wildlife Drive can be closed during and after periods of heavy rain. Cruickshank Trail may be closed in summer when female alligators nest alongside it.

Natural Merritt Island National Wildlife Refuge. *This 5-mile route covers the Cruickshank Trail, which circles a shallow water marsh. This is a birders paradise. Allot two to three hours. If you're a serious bird or wildlife watcher, plan to spend four to five hours for the walk and the drive. There are pullovers along the drive. Don't forget to bring binoculars.*

Begin at the Merritt Island NWR Visitor Information Center, about 3.5 miles east of the turn off for the Black Point Wildlife Drive/Cruickshank Trail. After viewing the exhibits, drive to the Black Point Wildlife Drive. At Stop #8, park at the Cruickshank Trailhead.

At the trailhead there are portable toilets and interpretive signs. The loop trail was named for Allan D. Cruickshank, a wildlife photographer, writer, and naturalist who frequented the area and worked to establish the Merritt Island NWR. It follows a mosquito control dike, forming a ring around Black Point Marsh, an excellent place to observe marsh and wading birds.

Be thankful for the dikes. They, along with other aggressive water management techniques, control the 23 species of mosquitoes found on the refuge. Of these, the saltmarsh mosquitoes are the most determined. The Public Lands Interpretive Association's *Merritt Island National Wildlife Refuge* book reports that "Department of Health documentation shows that prior to mosquito control, mosquitoes would land on you at the rate of 500 a minute."

The trail floor is sand with patches grass. As you head out, look right or left and you'll probably spot a green heron or white ibis. The best birding is on the right about the first mile, along Black Point Creek, where three habitats converge: salt marsh, marsh stream, and interior impoundments.

The trail is bordered by tall grasses and mangroves. Interspersed on the right bank are ferns and wild cactus, as well as small stands of palms on both sides. Scan the open marsh and creek for birds and wildlife. Also look up for birds and glance at the trail floor for tracks and droppings. The damp edge of the trail is an ideal place to observe tracks.

At about a half mile on the left, wildflowers bloom in spring and summer along the left bank. Just beyond them a narrow, rustic, winding wooden dock leads to a photo blind in the middle of the water-filled marsh. If the sign says "In Use," don't enter. If it's not in use, walk out and sit for awhile. Depending on the season and time of day, you'll be rewarded with sightings of many different kinds of birds, possibly a few of the eight species of herons and egrets that frequent the refuge. The best times are early morning and early evening fall to spring. *Return to the trail.*

As you continue, you'll pass trampled areas in the tall grasses on either side of the trail. This is where animals, especially alligators and raccoons, have passed. Look down into the water on the creek side to see horseshoe crabs. You'll find some overturned, most likely beached, and then eaten by raccoons. This is also an area where you'll find people catching blue crabs.

As the trail continues, it curves left away from the creek toward the open water of the Indian River. The right side of the trail becomes thick with mangroves. The left is the open marsh.

For the next three miles, you can glimpse sail and power boats as they cruise past through openings in the vegetation. The Intracoastal Waterway turns to the right here as it leaves the Indian River, passes through Haulover Canal, and enters the Mosquito Lagoon. If you're lucky, you'll see manatees in the open water areas on their way to the Haulover Canal, a popular spot to observe them. (Reach Haulover Canal by car by driving northeast on Hwy 406.) *Continue along the trail.*

At around 3.5 miles, the trail follows a small peninsula at the intersection of the river and another creek. This is another good area to spot birds. On the last mile, the trail winds considerably and opens with wide views of the marsh and impound pools.

Near the 4.75 mile mark, there's an observation tower on the left. Climb the 16 steps for a refreshing breeze and panoramic view of the marsh and impounds. *Climb down and continue along the trail to return to the trailhead.*

Lodging

Accommodations in Titusville are pretty limited, but if you're willing to drive north or south 15 to 25 minutes, you'll find more variety in picturesque New Smyrna Beach and the surfer's paradise, Cocoa Beach.

Best Western Space Shuttle Inn ($$, 321/269-9100) is a sprawling family-oriented motor inn with a swimming pool, basketball courts, playground, continental breakfast, standard comfortable rooms on two floors, lots of friendly service, and it's only a minute from I-95 at 3455 Cheney Hwy, Titusville. Vacationers looking for a clean, comfortable place to stay in town while watching the space shuttle will find everything they need here at the riverfront **Holiday Inn Kennedy Space Center** ($$–$$$, 321/269-2121) at 4951 S Washington Ave, Titusville, where they have a catbird's seat to the launch. The **Ramada Inn Kennedy Space Center** ($$, 321/269-5510) is just off I-95 at 3500 Cheney Hwy, Titusville, making it just minutes away from the Kennedy Space Center, Merritt Island National Wildlife Refuge, and Canaveral National Seashore.

Drive along Flagler Avenue and you'll be charmed into stopping at the **Riverview Hotel** ($$–$$$, 800/945-7416, 904/428-5858) at 103 Flagler Ave, New Smyrna Beach. It gets better inside. The beautifully restored 1885 bridge tender's house sits on the Intracoastal waterway. Most rooms have either poolside private patios or landscaped balconies with water views. It's the little things that make the biggest impression, such as evening turn-down service with a chocolate on your pillow, as well as a bathrobe on your bed, and continental breakfast served in your room with a newspaper. The hotel's seafood restaurant, Riverview Charlie's, is a favorite among locals and guests.

Old World charm meets New Age technology at the **Night Swan Intracoastal Bed & Breakfast** ($$–$$$, 800/465-4261, 904/423-4940) at 512 S Riverside Dr, New Smyrna Beach, where comfortable, well-decorated rooms with cable TV, private baths, and telephones with modems overlook either the lovely grounds or the Indian River. There are two turn-of-the-century houses, the second has more expensive rooms with private baths that have whirlpool tubs.

An 1883 riverfront estate house has been converted into the **Little River Inn** ($$–$$$, 904/424-0100), where you can unwind in a rocking chair on the verandahs or stroll the oak-dotted two-acre landscaped grounds at 532 N Riverside Dr, New Smyrna Beach. The views are equally beautiful from the rooms, which overlook the Indian River and a nature preserve. There are private and shared baths, bicycles, a tennis court, and a wonderful breakfast.

There's 750-feet of beachfront to walk along in front of the 50-room **Inn at Cocoa Beach** ($$–$$$, 800/343-5307, 321/799-3460) at 4300 Ocean Beach Blvd, Cocoa Beach. There's also a pool and beach chairs and umbrellas. Inside, French Country furnishings, Oriental rugs, and charmingly decorated ocean-view rooms go hand in hand with pampering service. Continental breakfast and afternoon wine and cheese are part of the package.

Food & drink
Food selections run toward family-style restaurants offering seafood or barbecue dishes. Prices are low to moderate. There's nothing fancy or pretentious here, just good food.

In 1890 the Denham Department Store opened in what 100 years later became **Kloiber's Cobbler & Eatery** ($–$$, 321/383-0689) at 337 S Washington Ave (Hwy 1) in Titusville's downtown historic district. In its nearly 10 years, the restaurant has become famous for its tasty fruit cobblers as well as healthy dishes like vegetarian black beans and rice. It's open for breakfast and lunch Monday to Wednesday and three meals Thursday to Saturday .

If you can't find it, just ask. Everybody in town knows **Fat Boys Bar B Que** ($–$$, 321/267-3468) at 4280 S Washington. Not only does it have the best barbecued beef, pork, and poultry in town, but its walls are lined with a wonderful collection of historical photos and it's one of the best spots in town to watch a shuttle launch. Things are also smokin' down the street at **Paul's Smokehouse** (321/267-3663) at 3665 S Washington Ave, which specializes in oak- and hickory-smoked meats served as sandwiches, plates, and combinations. It also offers a full menu of salads, soups, steaks, prime rib, seafood, and a lot of desserts.

Sweet, hard-shell rock shrimp are the specialty at **Dixie Crossroads** ($–$$, 321/269-5510), a popular family-style seafood restaurant with a rustic nautical theme at 1475 Garden St. It's family owned and operated by commercial fishermen and boat builders. There's more well-prepared seafood and casual dining on the Indian River at **Steamers Riverside** ($$–$$$, 321/269-1012) at 801 Marina Rd, in the Titusville Marina.

Events
Earth Day is the big event here with walks, talks, and big fun.

Munn Park Historic District, Lakeland

Lakeland lies in lake-studded central Florida halfway between Tampa and Orlando. The fresh appeal of this small, lively community owes itself to an active preservation program that has encouraged restoration of numerous early buildings over the last 10 years, creating an ambiance of civic pride and revitalizing a once dead downtown. Don't be fooled by the five o'clock exodus from downtown. By 6:30, the streets and parking lots start filling up, restaurants buzz with customers, and stage lights go up, especially on weekends. The renaissance is especially notable, because the focal point remains Munn Park, the original town square.

Lakeland began as a railroad outpost. In 1881, Abraham Munn, a businessman from Kentucky, purchased 80 acres in Polk County in anticipation of the Kissimmee to Tampa railroad line that would pass through three years later. He drew up a commercial subdivision, built a train depot, and sold off lots near the railroad line. By 1903 the population was 1,000. Ten years later it had soared to 8,000, as settlers came to mine phosphate and farm citrus and strawberries on rich agricultural lands.

In 1885, Lakeland erected its first hotel, The Tremont, which was replaced by The Terrace Hotel in 1924. It recently reopened to its 1924 splendor. Like other Florida cities, the 1920s led to a construction boom. Up went many expensive Mediterranean and Victorian Revival residences, as well as Classical Revival banks and commercial buildings. With a population of 25,000 by 1926, buildings were erected at a rate of three every 24 hours.

Another focal point is the Lake Mirror Promenade, built in 1928 as a backdrop to the urban skyline during Florida's City Beautiful Movement. A new amphitheater, enhanced pedestrian walkways, and additional parking are part of downtown's renaissance.

Today, Lakeland has 77,000 residents and serves as a college town and visitor hub, with antique shops, galleries, restaurants, cafes and professional centers. Its main industries remain the production of oranges and phosphate.

Information

Lakeland Area Chamber of Commerce, 35 Lake Morton Dr, PO Box 3607, Lakeland, FL 33802; 941/688-8551; fax 941/683-7454; chamber@lakeland.net; www.lakeland.net/chamber. The chamber is in the lakefront 1926 Mediterranean style Park Trammell Building that was once the town library. Parking is in the rear.

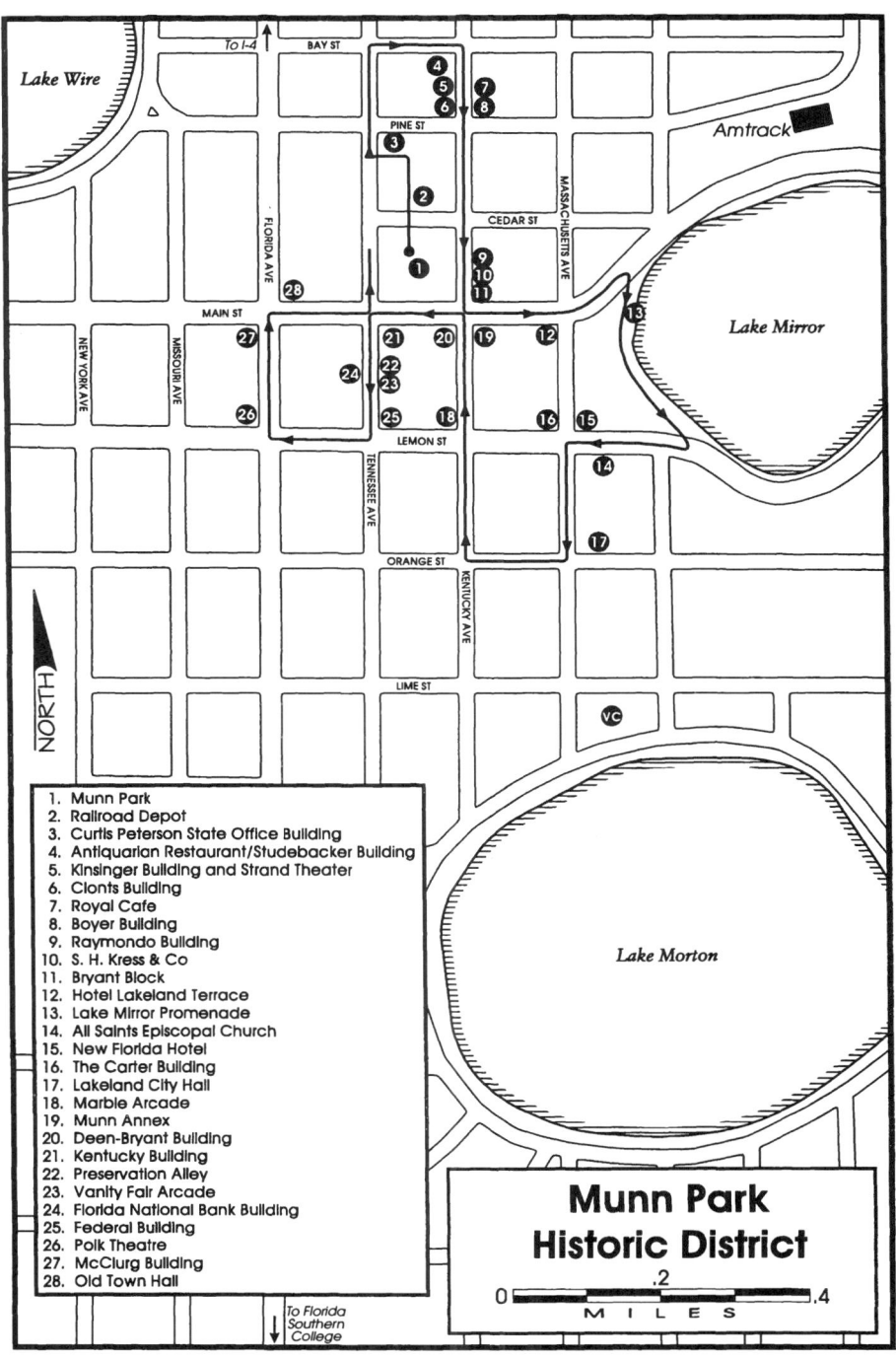

1. Munn Park
2. Railroad Depot
3. Curtis Peterson State Office Building
4. Antiquarian Restaurant/Studebacker Building
5. Kinsinger Building and Strand Theater
6. Clonts Building
7. Royal Cafe
8. Boyer Building
9. Raymondo Building
10. S. H. Kress & Co
11. Bryant Block
12. Hotel Lakeland Terrace
13. Lake Mirror Promenade
14. All Saints Episcopal Church
15. New Florida Hotel
16. The Carter Building
17. Lakeland City Hall
18. Marble Arcade
19. Munn Annex
20. Deen-Bryant Building
21. Kentucky Building
22. Preservation Alley
23. Vanity Fair Arcade
24. Florida National Bank Building
25. Federal Building
26. Polk Theatre
27. McClurg Building
28. Old Town Hall

**Munn Park
Historic District**

Central Florida Visitors and Convention Bureau, 1339 Helena Rd, Winter Haven, FL 33884; 800/828/7655, 941/298-7565; www.cfdc.org/tourism.

Getting there

Take I-4 to exit 18 (Florida Ave/Hwy 98) south, then left onto Pine St, right onto Kentucky Ave, then right into the municipal parking lot just after you cross the railroad track. The closest airports are in Tampa and Orlando, about an hour away. Amtrak's (800/USA RAIL, 941/683-6368) station is at 600 Lake Mirror Dr, downtown. Greyhound (800/231-2222, 941/682-3107) has a bus station downtown at 303 N Massachusetts Ave.

First steps

For area maps and information, contact the Lakeland Area Chamber of Commerce or the Central Florida Visitors and Convention Bureau. Both are open Monday to Friday 9 am to 5 pm. For history about the area, write Historic Lakeland, Inc, PO Box 3347, Lakeland, FL 33802.

Munn Park Historic District. *This 1.5-mile route covers the historic district's most significant structures, including Munn Park and the Lake Mirror Promenade.*

Start at Munn Park. When the Confederate monument was erected in Munn Park in 1910, the park had been in use since 1884 for concerts, political speeches, and meetings. The Railroad Depot opened on the north side of the park across Cedar Street in 1883, so the park would be the first thing passengers saw when they arrived. *Leave the park on the north side, cross Cedar St and walk up Tennessee Ave.*

Preservationists are pleased that the new brick Curtis Peterson State Office Building (corner Cedar St and Tennessee Ave) was constructed to complement the surrounding historic buildings. Before you cross Pine St, look right at the buildings at 206-208 E Pine, early storefronts built around 1910 of patterned and rusticated concrete block. *Turn right onto Bay St.*

The Antiquarian Restaurant (211 E Bay) is housed in the old Studebaker Building with a parapet. Between Bay St and Lemon St and Florida Ave and Massachusetts Ave lies the busy Antiques District. *Turn right onto Kentucky Ave.*

Retailers, theater-goers, and hotel guests have used the Mediterranean Style Kinsinger Building and Strand Theater (236-240 N Kentucky) since 1926. Across the alley is the brick Richardsonian Romanesque Clonts Building (228 corner E Pine and N Kentucky), constructed in 1923 with a corner conical tower, arched windows, and parapet. Along with making cigars here, tenants have sold dry goods and clothing over the years. On the opposite side of the street are the **Royal Cafe** (207-211 N Kentucky) and **Boyer Building** (201-205 N Kentucky). The former was built in 1917 as a restaurant and hotel. The latter a hotel and stores. Note its wooden storefront. *Cross the railroad tracks and continue along Kentucky Ave.*

This second half of the block opposite the park is a conglomeration of disparate, but complementary styles. More than half of the Italianate **Raymondo Building** (115 N Kentucky) was demolished to squeeze in the beautiful Renaissance Revival **S.H. Kress & Co** (109 N Kentucky) building, constructed 24 years later in 1929 as a chain store. Today, it's the new home of the Explorations V Children's Museum. Its neighbor is the dark red Neo-Georgian **Bryant Block** (105 N Kentucky). *Turn left onto Main St.*

On the right is the 1924 **Hotel Lakeland Terrace** (329 E Main St), an ornately detailed combination Mediterranean and Classical structure that was the city's grand hotel during the Florida boom. The hotel reopened in fall 1999 after a beautiful restoration. *Continue ahead to Lake Mirror.*

The grand **Lake Mirror Promenade** (Lemon St and Lake Mirror Dr) was built in 1928 as the Frances Langford Promenade, after the namesake native actress. It has graceful staircases, Corinthian columns, finely detailed concrete walls, and a vaulted arched loggia overlooking the lake. Current restoration and enhancements that include an amphitheater should be completed by late 1999. *Walk south along the lake, then turn right onto Lemon St.*

The church moved to this site in 1892 and constructed the Spanish style **All Saints Episcopal Church** (southeast corner of Lemon and Massachusetts) in 1923 during the Mediterranean Revival stage. Additional buildings have been added as recently as the early 1990s in the same style. Architectural detail abounds at the 1926 **New Florida Hotel** (northeast corner of Lemon and Massachusetts) a combination retail center and hotel. The builder lost money during the 1926 bust, so the hotel wasn't completed until 1935. In 1985 the city celebrated its centennial with numerous murals. The one on **The Carter Building** is a collage of downtown's historically significant structures. *Turn left onto Massachusetts Ave.*

Built in 1926, just before the bust, the Mediterranean Revival **Lakeland City Hall** (228 S Massachusetts) is lavishly detailed with an exterior cornice fresco, ornate pilastered pediment, a tower, and equally fine interior work. It's worth a look inside. *Turn right onto Orange St, then right onto Kentucky Ave.*

Lakeland's first "skyscraper" was the **Marble Arcade** (129 S Kentucky Ave), built in 1926 in a Sullivanesque style with offices on the upper floors and an arcade on the lower level. In the next block, on the right and left, respectively, are two early Lakeland buildings (1917 and 1912). The Italianate **Munn Annex** (108 S Kentucky) once housed the Postal Telegraph offices. Across the street, the Italianate **Deen-Bryant Building** (105 S Kentucky) was a storefront and office complex. Note its tile mansard roof and contrasting tan and red bricks. *Turn left onto Main St.*

Abraham Munn housed his agents opposite Munn Park in the Italianate **Kentucky Building** (205-209 Main St), name after his home state. Built in 1903, it was the first masonry building south of the tracks. *Turn left onto Tennessee Ave.*

Several downtown blocks feature east-west alleys that allowed the streets to be uncluttered and unclogged by delivery vehicles. One such thoroughfare was **Preservation Alley** (between Lemon and Main, Tennessee and Kentucky), which featured horse stables and rear entrances. Bordering the alley is the **Vanity Fair Arcade** (114 S Tennessee), built in the 1920s with shops. Its Art Deco façade is the result of a 1940s redesign. Across the street is the 1942 **Florida National Bank Building** (113 S Tennessee Ave), an Art Deco gem worth a peek inside. The **Federal Building** (124 S Tennessee Ave) was built in 1917 as the city's first full-scale post office. *Turn right onto Lemon St. Before turning right onto Florida Ave, look at the sculpture garden that runs along Lemon St.*

Stars twinkle across the ceiling of the restored Mediterranean interior of the **Polk Theatre** (127 S Florida), built in 1927 by a Tampa architect as an Italian Renaissance style stage theater. Everything from the Palladian window above the marquee to the decorative ceiling soffits to the parapet has ornate detailing. If the walls of the **McClurg Building** (101 S Florida) could talk, they would have interesting tales from their days starting in 1917 as a grocery, then offices, a Masonic Hall, and several banks. *Turn right onto Main St.*

On the left corner is the Italianate **Old Town Hall** (100 E Main St), which has held city offices, the fire department, and a jail. *Turn left onto Tennessee Ave and return to Munn Park.*

Lodging

Visitors have a choice of accommodations in restored historic buildings or modern hotels in and near the historic district. There's also the option to stay in a lovely Victorian B&B in a nearby town.

The newly restored 1924 **Lakeland Terrace Hotel** ($$–$$$, 888/644-8400, 941/688-0800) at 329 E Main St exudes charm and luxury in its 88 spacious rooms and suites that are loaded with modern appointments and conveniences. The historic downtown hotel features the club-like Terrace Bar and fine dining in the Terrace Grille that overlooks Lake Mirror.

No sign announces that you've found the **Lake Morton Bed & Breakfast** ($$, 941/688-6788) at 817 South Blvd. City ordinances forbid it, but the owners, Bryce and Mary Ann Zender, give easy directions to their pair of authentically restored 1925 Bungalows conveniently located between Florida Southern College and the Munn Historic District. The former apartments are now spacious, comfortable guest suites with period furnishings.

Properties in non-historic settings include the 139-room **Four Points Hotel by Sheraton** ($$–$$$, 941/644-0467) with a pool, restaurant, health club, and lounge aimed at business travelers at 4141 S Florida Ave, south of downtown; **Wellesley Inn & Suites** ($$, 941/859-3399) has comfortable rooms and a pool at 3520 N Hwy US 98, north of downtown.

In Bartow, 20 minutes south of downtown Lakeland, the turn-of-the-century Victorian **Stanford Inn** ($$, 941/533-2393) has four queen-bed rooms, a carriage house with a kitchen, and a two-story cottage at 555 E Stanford St. All are finely decorated with antiques and have private baths, phones, and fax machines.

Arts & culture

There's more than just art at **Arts on the Park Center for the Creative Arts** (941/680-ARTS). There are also gallery concerts (October to April), shows, outdoor festivals, and 11 exhibits a year at 115 N Kentucky Ave. **Bay Street Gallery** (941/682-1059) features works by regional artists hung on the walls of the Antiquarian Restaurant in the historic Studebaker Building at 211 E Bay St. **Griner Waters Gallery** (941/686-8280) specializes in collectible photographic art at 118 Pine St.

The **Imperial Symphony Orchestra** (941/688-3743) presents classical, outdoor pops, young artist, and holiday concerts at the **Lakeland Center** (941/499-8100), which also hosts a Broadway series and other events at 700 W Lemon St. The historic **Polk Theatre** (941/682-7553, 941/682-8227 24-hr entertainment line) was built in 1927 during the picture-palace era as a vaudeville stage and movie house and now serves as a center for films and performing arts (November to March) downtown at 127 S Florida Ave. The **Florida Dance Theatre** (941/667-1327) has a subscription series and spring performances staged at various sites. The **Pied Piper Players** (941/648-3284), Lakeland's 12-year-old community theater, stages a five-show season from October to June at the Lake Mirror Theatre at 707 E Lemon St, downtown.

Polk Museum of Art (941/688-7743) offers a permanent collection of Asian, Colombian, European, and American fabrics, paintings, ceramics, silver, and artifacts, as well as alternating contemporary and historical exhibits at 800 E Palmetto St, southeast border of downtown. At **Explorations V Children's Museum** kids learn about Asian culture, finance, television news, and the arts in a hands-on setting at the restored S.H. Kress Building at 109 N Kentucky Ave, across from Munn Park.

The collection at the **Sun 'n' Fun Air Museum** (941/644-2431) includes home-built, antique, military, and ultralight aircraft as well as memorabilia and exhibits at Lakeland Linder Regional Airport, 4175 Medulla Rd.

Downtown's **Mosswood Bookshop** at 230 N Kentucky Ave specializes in Floridiana, regional fiction and children's books, but also carries current fiction.

Food & drink

New restaurants popping up in restored old buildings are drawing people downtown. Choices run from homey staples to eclectic American cuisine. Prices are moderate to high.

Downtown's growing short list includes the New American cuisine à la carte or from a prix-fixe menu served in a setting of art and antiques at **Antiquarian Restaurant and Bay Street Gallery** ($$$, 941/682-1059) in the historic Studebaker Building at 211 E Bay St. A siren-like saxophone player standing outside **Harry's** ($$, 941/686-2228) coaxes passers-by inside this popular spot featuring tempting seafood prepared with a New Orleans accent at 101 N Kentucky Ave. The food and ambiance are a lively Gaelic at **Molly McHugh's Irish Pub & Restaurant** ($$, 941/686-6231) at 111 S Kentucky Ave. The **Landmark Restaurant** ($, 941 /682-7691) keeps customers returning by serving down home cooking with a smart twist at 228 E Pine St in an antique-filled setting in the historic Clonts Building. For light fare there's **Crisper's** ($, 941/682-7708) at 217 N Kentucky Ave, where the menu features sandwiches and a choice of 10 salads and 11 soups daily.

There are two good options just outside downtown. The ever popular 1934 **Reececliff** ($, 941/686-6661) at 940 S Florida Ave is an inexpensive small-town diner with motherly waitresses serving heaping plates of home-style food. They bake their own pies, which you can buy by the slice or whole. The **Texas Cattle Company** ($$, 941/686-1434) is a here's the beef spot at 735 E Main St.

Nightlife

Florida's easy-going lifestyle along with four-year and two-year college ensures Lakeland a fun-filled nightlife. Downtown favorites include **Molly McHugh's Irish Pub** at 111 S Kentucky Ave and **Lillian's Music Store**, with live entertainment and dancing at 215 E Main St.

Events

Artists, residents, and visitors gather at Lake Morton and Munn Park for the annual—now more than 25 years old—two-day **Mayfaire-by-the-Lake Festival**

(941/688-7743), complete with a Saturday night Street Dance, held on Mother's Day weekend. There's a **Fourth of July** celebration at historic Munn Park featuring music and fireworks. The country's second largest **Experimental Aircraft Association Fly-In** takes place each spring at the Sun 'n' Fun Air Museum.

Florida Southern College

The largest single collection of buildings designed by architect Frank Lloyd Wright is not located in Illinois, nor in New York, nor in Wisconsin. It's in central Florida, on the bright, sunny campus of Florida Southern College, a small, private liberal arts college associated with the United Methodist Church. Frank Lloyd Wright and the church—an odd pairing, indeed. Equally remarkable is that the construction took place despite the Depression and World War II.

Visitors are welcome to view the exteriors and interiors of Wright's buildings, which range from chapels to a planetarium. They also may stroll the 1.5 miles of his covered walkways—called Esplanades—that link them. A Visitor Center has interesting exhibits dedicated to Wright's work here and elsewhere, as well as a small gift shop. Students and staff—some of whom can remember Wright walking around the campus in his wide-brim hat, flowing coat, and menacing cane—seem eager to answer questions and offer opinions about the man and, in the words of the architect, the "only true American campus."

In 1938, then college president Dr Ludd Spivey approached 70-year-old Wright about designing a "great education temple in Florida." Spivey admitted that he had no money, but said that if Wright designed the buildings, he would use every means to raise the funds. Wright visited the site, a hillside of orange groves overlooking a lake, and envisioned the buildings in harmony, rising "out of the ground, into the light and into the sun."

Designed during his organic period, his 18 buildings use "steel for strength; sand because it was native to Florida; and glass to bring God's outdoors into man's indoors." The first three buildings in his Child of the Sun collection were completed by 1945 using student labor in exchange for tuition. Nine more buildings were erected through 1958. The final six were never built.

Time and use have aged the buildings, but major restoration efforts are underway. This is a rare opportunity to explore Wright's work slowly and closely.

Information
Florida Southern College, 111 Lake Hollingsworth Dr, Lakeland, FL 33801, 941/680-4110 or 941/680-4597. Lakeland Area Chamber of Commerce, 35 Lake Morton Dr, PO Box 3607, Lakeland, FL 33802; 941/688-8551; chamber@lakeland.net; www.lakeland.net/chamber.

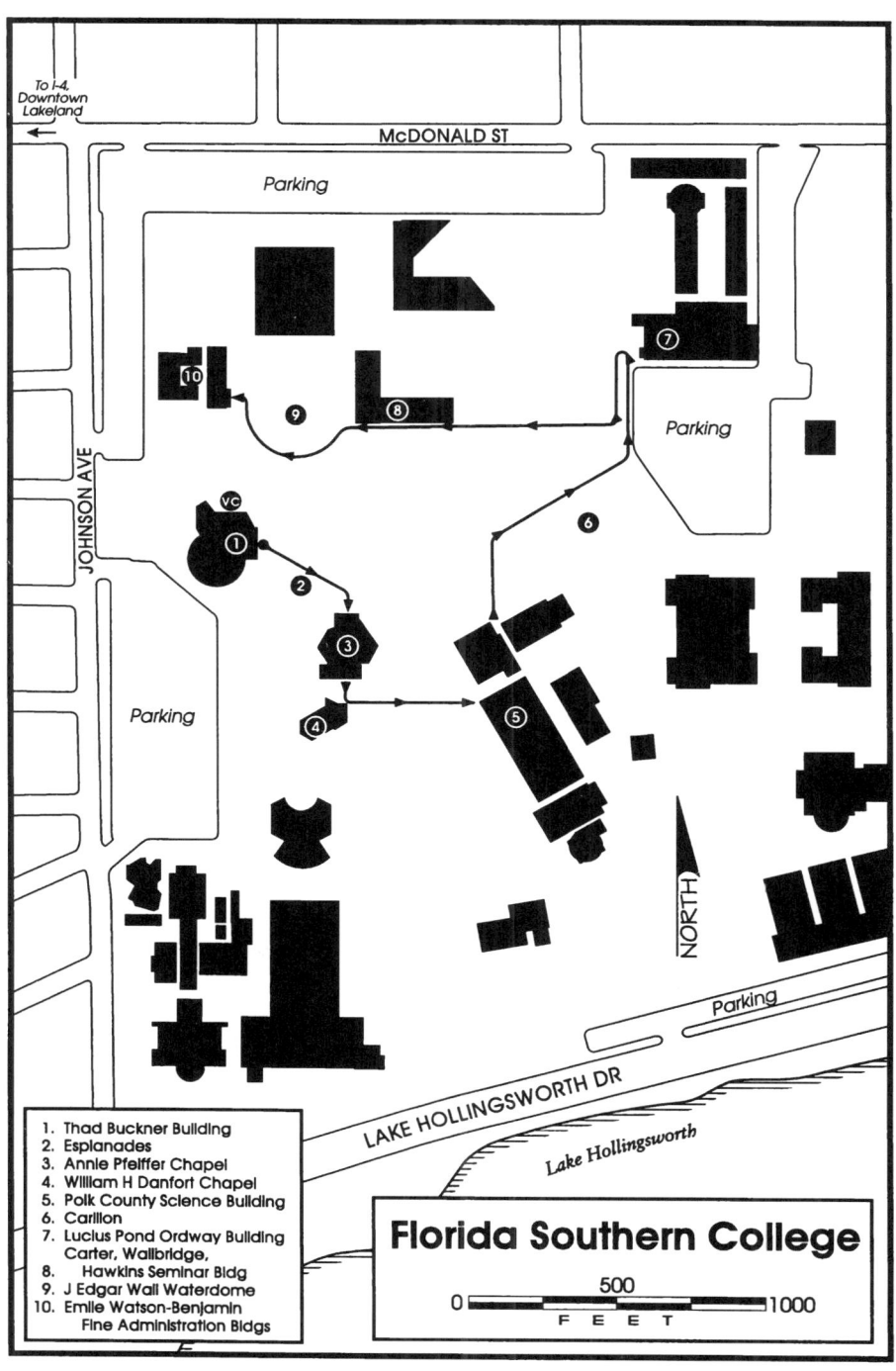

To I-4,
Downtown
Lakeland

McDONALD ST

Parking

JOHNSON AVE

VC

Parking

Parking

NORTH

Parking

LAKE HOLLINGSWORTH DR

Lake Hollingsworth

1. Thad Buckner Building
2. Esplanades
3. Annie Pfeiffer Chapel
4. William H Danfort Chapel
5. Polk County Science Building
6. Carillon
7. Lucius Pond Ordway Building
   Carter, Wallbridge,
8.   Hawkins Seminar Bldg
9. J Edgar Wall Waterdome
10. Emile Watson-Benjamin
     Fine Administration Bldgs

Florida Southern College

0   500   1000

F E E T

Getting there

Take I-4 to exit 18 (Florida Ave/Hwy 98) south, then left onto Memorial Blvd (Hwy 98/92). Turn right onto Ingraham Ave, then right onto McDonald. Turn left into the parking lot on the southeast corner of McDonald and Johnson. Park in Visitor Parking at the southwest corner of the lot. The closest airports are in Tampa and Orlando, approximately one hour away. Amtrak's (800/USA RAIL, 941 /683-6368) station is at 600 Lake Mirror Dr, downtown. Greyhound (800 /231-2222, 941/682-3107) has a station downtown at 303 N Massachusetts Ave.

First steps

For tour maps and background information on Frank Lloyd Wright's architecture, contact **Florida Southern College's Frank Lloyd Wright Visitor Center**, which is open Tuesday to Friday 11 am to 4 pm, Saturday 10 am to 2 pm, Sunday 2 pm to 4 pm. It's closed some holidays and special academic occasions. The campus is open year round, although some buildings are locked when school is not in session and on weekends. For area maps and information, contact the **Lakeland Area Chamber of Commerce**. It's open Monday to Friday 9 am to 5 pm. For an in-depth look at Frank Lloyd Wright and his architecture, read *Wright Sites: A Guide to Frank Lloyd Wright Public Places* by Arlene Sanderson ($13) and *The Life and Works of Frank Lloyd Wright* by Maria Costantino ($20).

Tours

Docents lead guided tours of the Wright buildings Thursdays at 11 am. Tours are free, but donations benefit the Visitor Center.

Historic Florida Southern College. *This 1.5-mile walk covers seven buildings and the Waterdome, Wright's outdoor water garden. Allow one hour, longer if you have a serious interest in architecture.*

Start at the Visitor Center. When it was built in 1945, the circular **Thad Buckner Building** was called the E.T. Roux Library. Today, it houses a museum of Wright's work, including original architectural drawings, blueprints, prototype construction blocks, and donated furniture. An exhibit of dinnerware and fabrics explains that Wright designed textiles, ceramics, and silverware. The room's continuous band of glass (curtained in Wright-designed fabric) makes the space feel undefined. *Walk along the Esplanades straight ahead to the Annie Pfeiffer Chapel.*

From 1941 to 1958 students constructed frames for the **Esplanades,** the covered concrete walkways that link Wright's buildings. The first thing you'll notice is how low they are. Some say it's because Wright was short and he built the Esplanades low to feel taller. Others say he believed they were cooler. The names at the base of the columns designate benefactors who donated $500. Note the copper trim that is richly verdigris-aged along the outer edge.

Students spent two years constructing the **Annie Pfeiffer Chapel,** Wright's first campus building. When it opened in 1941, onlookers commented that it reflected the architect's sense of rising from the ground into light. Go upstairs and look up. Light filters in from the translucent skylights in the tower above and colored light streams in from the small glass squares embedded in the wall's concrete blocks. The only way to see outside is from the balcony. *Walk out the south door down the red steps to the Danforth Chapel.*

Wright used Florida's native tidewater red cypress to frame the smaller **William H. Danforth Chapel,** which has red, gold, and clear geometric-patterned stained-glass windows. Notice the matching pattern on the lectern in front of the large window. The simple, straight-back wooden pews and their cushions are original, designed by Wright and built by students. *Return to the Esplanades that run parallel to the building. Walk east to the Polk County Science Building.*

The way students learn science has changed since the **Polk County Science Building** was constructed in 1958 at a cost of one million dollars, so the building is being renovated. It still features the same kind of labs that you see in vintage movies. The building's planetarium is the only one Wright designed that was ever constructed. *Leave the Science building at the opposite end of the planetarium. Walk north past the Carillon, a tall, three-part concrete structure with a cross on top, then turn right at the first intersection and continue to the Lucius Pond Ordway Building.*

Wright liked the simplicity of the **Lucius Pond Ordway Building.** It is futuristic architecture, a lesson in geometry. The roofline is a series of triangles lying on their hypotenuses. So timeless is its appeal, that it was used as a futuristic setting in a *SeaQuest* television show episode. Today, it houses a student lounge, theater-in-the-round, and fine arts department. Walk through the building and out the far right door, which opens onto a courtyard with a small pond and fountain at the end. If the theater is open, look inside. Continue left around the theater and you'll find yourself parallel to the Esplanades. *Follow the Esplanades to the first right, which lead to the Seminar Building.*

Now the Financial Aid building, the **Carter, Wallbridge, Hawkins Seminar Building** uses the same colored glass pieces embedded in blocks as found in the Annie Pfeiffer Chapel. The building was originally designed with three buildings separated by courtyards. *Walk west along the Esplanades in front of the building to the J Edgar Wall Waterdome.*

Wright designed the **J. Edgar Wall Waterdome** as a single pool with multiple fountains, keeping close to his organic concept of earth, water, and sun. It was redesigned in the 1960s. *Continue west to the Emile Watson-Benjamin Fine Administration Buildings.*

Wright personally supervised the construction of the **Emile E. Watson-Benjamin Fine Administration Buildings**, the first to be constructed by an outside company. That he was influenced by Native American architecture, particularly the Mayans, is evident in the Watson building. The best view is from the parking lot. In keeping with his organic theme, there's another pool with a fountain in the courtyard between the two buildings. Go inside the first building and look at the ceiling. This building also houses the public relations offices, where you can learn more about Wright and his relationship with the college. *While the tour ends here, the area north and west of the college is the South Lake Morton Historic District. More than half of the structures are well preserved Craftsman Bungalows. The remaining are Frame Vernacular, with a few good examples of Wright's Prairie School style (see Lodging). You can see many of these by walking or driving north along Johnson St as you leave the area.*

Lodging
See Munn Park Historic District Walking Tour

Arts & culture
Along with local events (see Munn Historic District, Lakeland), the college sponsors numerous cultural events such as Mark Russell, Alvin Ailey Repertory Ensemble, the Child of the Sun Jazz Festival, and London City Opera through its **Festival of Fine Arts** program from October through April. For information, call 941/680-4296 or 941/680-3089.

The on-campus **Melvin Gallery** features half a dozen faculty and student traveling art exhibits with Meet-the-Artist receptions at each opening September through April. Call 941/680-4111.

Food & drink, Nightlife
See Munn Park Historic District, Lakeland Walking Tour.

Cypress Gardens

Long before Walt Disney set his sights on California or Florida, barefoot skiers and ski jumpers were making headlines against a backdrop of tropical gardens at Cypress Gardens, Florida's first theme park. More than 60 years later, the show goes on and the gardens are even more spectacular with 8,000 varieties of plants and flowers from more than 90 countries.

Founders Dick and Julie Pope carved the park's original 16 acres of subtropical and tropical flora out of a cypress swamp, hence its name. It opened in 1936 to much fanfare with gardens and traditionally costumed Southern Belles featured in newsreels and on the covers of magazines and newspapers. Cypress Gardens quickly gained fame as the "water ski capital of the world" with shows during World War II. Since then, the park has expanded to 203 acres, its gardens blanket 23 acres, its performers have introduced more than 50 waterskiing "firsts," and it has added a butterfly conservatory, radio and history museums, animals, restaurants, and gift shops.

While most of Central Florida's theme parks are hectic and crowded with long lines and neck-wrenching rides, Cypress Gardens still presents a calm, relaxed atmosphere, where the only thing fast-paced is the music that accompanies the waterski shows.

Information

Cypress Gardens, PO Box 1, Cypress Gardens, FL 33884; 800/282-2123 or 941/324-2111; fax 941/324-7946; www.cypressgardens.com. **Central Florida Visitors and Convention Bureau**, 1339 Helena Rd, Winter Haven, FL 33884; 800/828-7655, 941/298-7565; www.cfdc.org/tourism. **Winter Haven Area Chamber of Commerce** 401 Ave B NW, PO Box 1420, Winter Haven, FL 33882; 941/293-2138.

Getting there

Cypress Gardens is located near Winter Haven, off US-27, about 22 miles south of I-4 between Orlando and Tampa, which have the closest airports with service by major carriers. Greyhound (800/231-2222, 941/293-5935) offers service to Winter Haven at 900 6th St NW. Amtrak (800/USA RAIL) services Winter Haven at 1800 7th St SW.

First steps

For information about the gardens, contact **Cypress Gardens**. For area maps and information, contact the **Central Florida Visitors and Convention Bureau**.

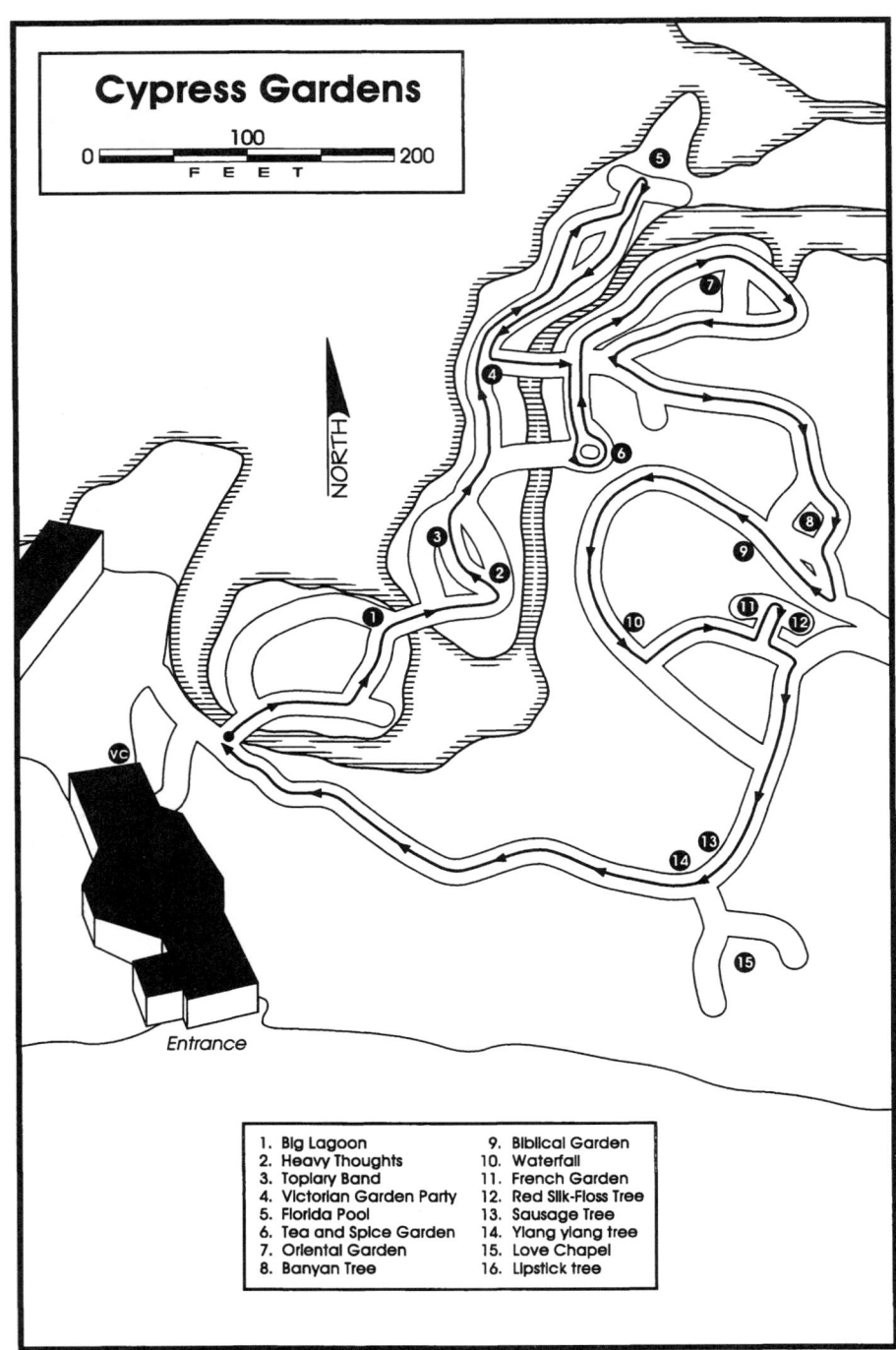

Cypress Gardens

0 ▮▮▮ 100 ▮▮▮ 200
F E E T

NORTH

VC

Entrance

1. Big Lagoon
2. Heavy Thoughts
3. Toplary Band
4. Victorian Garden Party
5. Florida Pool
6. Tea and Spice Garden
7. Oriental Garden
8. Banyan Tree
9. Biblical Garden
10. Waterfall
11. French Garden
12. Red Silk-Floss Tree
13. Sausage Tree
14. Ylang ylang tree
15. Love Chapel
16. Lipstick tree

Admission is $31.95 for adults, $27.15 for seniors, and $14.95 for children ages 6–17.

Seasonal highlights
The most plants are in bloom during the spring and summer months. See Events for specific flower festivals.

Historic Cypress Gardens. *This half-mile route covers the original 16-acre garden devoted to plants, trees, landscaping, and ornamental garden sculpture. Allot one hour for a leisurely walk.*

Begin at the entrance to the Botanical Gardens. The original gardens stretch along the east side of scenic Lake Eloise, north of the Ski Stadium. Towering bald cypress trees (*Taxodium distichum*) and their stubby "skinned" knees line the lake's shore. The path crosses a bridge onto a small island in the middle of **Big Lagoon**, an area that has been used as the backdrop for hundreds of commercials and photographed for thousands of newspapers and magazines. There has been a costumed Southern Belle posing here for almost 60 years. After a frost killed off plants near the front entrance in December 1940, visitors would drive up—the entrance was close to here at that time—see the dead plants, and drive away. So Julie Pope, originally from Alabama, and young ladies on the staff dressed up and sat on a bench in front of the dead plants to hide them. Visitors, distracted from the dead plants by the lovely women, drove up, waved, parked, and came into the gardens. The small island is planted with tropical plants like calathea (*calathea spp.*), philodendron (*Monstera obliua*), monstera (*Monstera deliciosa*), and numerous ferns. There's an overlook and a pool with a fountain and water lilies (*Nymphea hybrids*) backed by a hedge of hibiscus. *Take the right fork after the path crosses over the next bridge.*

Just after crossing is a bronze statue of a frog in Rodin's classic *The Thinker* pose. This fanciful rendition by John Skurja is called *Heavy Thoughts* and is one of more than a score of sculptures throughout the garden. Some are on permanent exhibit, others are for sale. At the intersection, take the Lakeside Trail to pass the **Topiary Band**, a whimsical group of uniform-clad musicians playing their instruments while standing on a bandstand. Two topiary couples dance to their imaginary music. There are 90 such creeping fig (*ficus pumila*)-covered, life-size topiary sculptures in the garden. *At the next set of signs, follow the Florida Pool Loop.*

The path passes more topiary figures, including a **Victorian Garden Party.** At the end of the loop is the **Florida Pool** in the shape of the state. It cost $30,000 and was built in 1951 for the film *Easy to Love* starring Esther Williams and Van Johnson. Esther Williams also came here to film *On an Island with You.* Betty Grable and Robert Cummings starred in *Moon over Miami*, which was shot in the gardens in 1940. The park's Cypress Roots history museum has film clips and exhibits about the filmings. *The path loops back. Cross the first bridge on the left and bear right for a short detour to the Tea and Spice Garden before returning to the intersection and bearing left to the Oriental Garden.*

The **Tea and Spice Garden** offers a respite with shade and a cool water fountain. The most striking feature in the **Oriental Garden** is a large Buddha. *The path loops back. At the intersection make a left hairpin turn.*

The path curves, then opens onto a clearing and big surprise. An enormous **banyan tree** (*ficus benghalensis*) straddles the path. It was purchased 50 years ago in a five-gallon pot for 25 cents. Today it is 38 feet tall and has giant aerial roots bigger than a man. They grow down from the branches to support its weight. This is probably the first place where you will notice heaters planted around the garden to keep the plants from freezing when cold fronts sweep down from the north. *Take the left path as you pass the banyan tree. Pass the Rose Garden, then make a hairpin turn at the railroad, passing the banyan again on your right. Take a left to the Biblical Garden. Don't follow the path to the right, which leads to the French Garden.*

The **Biblical Garden** features Mediterranean accents and fruits, vegetables, spices, grains, trees, shrubs, and flowers inspired by botanical and herbal references in the Bible. Among the plants are aloe (*Aloe Barbadensis vera*), hibiscus (*Hibiscus rosa sinensis*), figs, cedar, crown of thorns (*Euphorbia splndens Bojer*), bitter herbs, and nettle. The path curves to the left and passes a **waterfall,** pond, and sculpture surrounded by hidden ginger (*Curcuma ionodora*), a ponytail palm (*Beaucarnea recurvata*), bromeliads, and various ferns. There's a water fountain and a shaded rest area opposite the waterfall. *The path curves, then detours left to the French Garden Loop. Then it returns to the main trail.*

The two-level **French Garden** earns its name for its design, not for its plants, which include tropical specimens such as border grass (*Liriope spp.*), a red silk-floss tree (*Chorisia speciosa*) and a princess tree (*Tibouchina spp.*), which blooms beautifully several times a year. Take a close look at the **red silk-floss tree.** Thousands of sharp, protective thorns cover its greenish-colored trunk. It blooms in fall with bright pink flowers, then drops seeds encased in silky fibers in spring. The fibers are collected and used in packing in Latin America, where the tree is native. It's obvious how the next two trees earned their names. Pendulous brown fruits that look like sausages on the outside and potatoes on the inside hang from the **sausage tree** (*Kigelia pinnata*). Some African tribes mix the fruit with honey and water to make a beer-like beverage. Its flowers have a strong, unpleasant odor. That's not the case of the nearby **ylang ylang** or perfume tree (*Cananga odorata*), which earns it name for the intense fragrance of its flowers, which are used to make Chanel #5 perfume.

The gazebo on the right is the **Love Chapel**, a popular site for outdoor weddings and one of the most photographed spots in the park. If there is no wedding in progress, walk up and take a closer look. Its dome is an old radar dish from WWII and its original pillars came from an old cigar factory in Ybor City. The latter have since been replaced by fiberglass pillars. On the left, near a bench past the gazebo is a beautiful **lipstick tree** (*bixa orellana*). A red dye is extracted from its seed pods and used to color clothing, paint, and lipstick. *Follow the trail back to the entrance.*

Lodging

Lodging options near Cypress Gardens are limited, but if you're willing to drive 10 to 20 minutes, you can choose from a bed-and-breakfast and several chain hotels and motels.

JD's Southern Oaks ($$–$$$$, 941/293-2335), a restored three-story Colonial with wrap-around porches on two levels, is a picture of Southern gentility at 3800 Country Club Rd S, Winter Haven. The mansion, moved to this 37-acre site on the edge of the woods, once belonged to a citrus magnate. There are seven antique-filled guestrooms in the main house and adjacent "barn."

The **Best Western Admiral's Inn** ($$–$$$, 941/324-5950) is across the parking lot from Cypress Gardens. There's nothing fancy about the 157-room hostelry, but it is comfortable, convenient, and has a large pool, discount tickets to Cypress Gardens, friendly service, two guest laundries, an average restaurant, and a lounge at 5665 Cypress Gardens Blvd. Another option is the 225-room **Holiday Inn Cypress Gardens** ($$, 941/294-4451), located in Winter Haven, about five miles from the park at 1150 Third St SW. Rooms are clean and comfortable. There's a pool and restaurant that's open until 10 pm.

Food & drink

Unless you dine within Cypress Gardens, which has theme-park priced food, your choices are the hotel restaurant across the parking lot or a 5- to 10-minute drive into Winter Haven. If it's rush hour, make that 15 to 20 minutes.

The seafood at **Harry's** ($$–$$$, 941/324-0301), a popular long-established family-owned waterfront restaurant, is fresh and the service is friendly at 3751 Cypress Gardens Rd. For breakfast, lunch, and dinner, the price is right and the soups, meatloaf, pot roast, and desserts are filling at **Ray and Fran's** ($–$$, 941/293-0069), a family-owned, family-style restaurant at 842 Sixth St NW. **Christy's Sundown Restaurant** ($$–$$$, 941/293-0069) at 700 Third St SW is known for its prime rib. It also serves seafood, pasta, and chicken. For authentic Japanese fare prepared with flair and served from the grill, as well as sushi, and rolls, try **Mikasa Japanese Steak House** ($$–$$$, 941/294-3667) at 1124 Havendale Blvd, Spring Lake Square.

Events

The annual **Spring Flower Festival** features the world's largest topiary show from mid-March to mid-May. In early November more than 3 million mums bloom during the annual **Mum Festival**. From Thanksgiving through the New Year the **Poinsettia Festival** showcases about 8,000 poinsettias.

Highlands Hammock State Park

In 1931, local citizens purchased a large tract of land with a virgin hardwood hammock near Sebring, Florida, when it was slated to be turned into farmland. Four years later, when Florida started its state park system, the land became Highlands Hammock State Park, one of the four original parks. It was built by the Civilian Conservation Corps (CCC), one of President Franklin D. Roosevelt's most popular New Deal agencies. Between 1935 and 1942, the men developed eight Florida parks, planted 18,924,000 trees, built 3,620 miles of trails and roads, constructed 2,736 bridges and spent 97,993 worker-days fighting fires. The CCC was disbanded in 1942 because of World War II, but the corps is honored here in Florida's CCC Museum, which is open 3–4 hours a day whenever there are volunteers to staff it.

Today, the 4,896-acre park terrain looks much as it did when European explorers saw it in the early 1500s. It has diverse plant communities of cypress swamp, pine flatwoods, sand pine scrub, scrubby flatwoods, bayheads, and marsh and is home to more than 175 bird species and other wildlife, including white-tailed deer, wild turkey, wild pigs, alligators, river otters, bobcats, Florida panthers, pileated woodpeckers, wading birds, bald eagles, swallow-tailed kites, barred owls, anhingas, Florida scrub jays, red-shouldered hawks, and many butterflies.

A one-way 3.1-mile paved loop road with a fitness parcourse along the grassy verge connects the eight trail heads, restrooms, campgrounds, museum, amphitheater, and picnic and concession areas.

The most popular trails are the Cypress Swamp Trail and the Fern Garden Trail. Both have boardwalks and are wheelchair accessible. Because of alligators, pets are allowed on the paved loop road, but not on the trails.

Information
Highlands Hammock State Park, 5931 Hammock Rd, Sebring, FL 33872; 941/386-6094. Department of Environmental Protection, Division of Recreation and Parks, Mail Station #535, 3900 Commonwealth Blvd, Tallahassee, FL 32399-3000; 800/488-9872; www.dep.state.fl.us/parks. Greater Sebring Chamber of Commerce, 309 S Circle Dr, Sebring, FL 33870; 941/385-8448; www.sebring.com.

Getting there
Take US 27 to Sebring, then drive west 2.4 miles on County Road 634 (Hammock Road) to the entrance. The closest airports are about an hour away in Orlando,

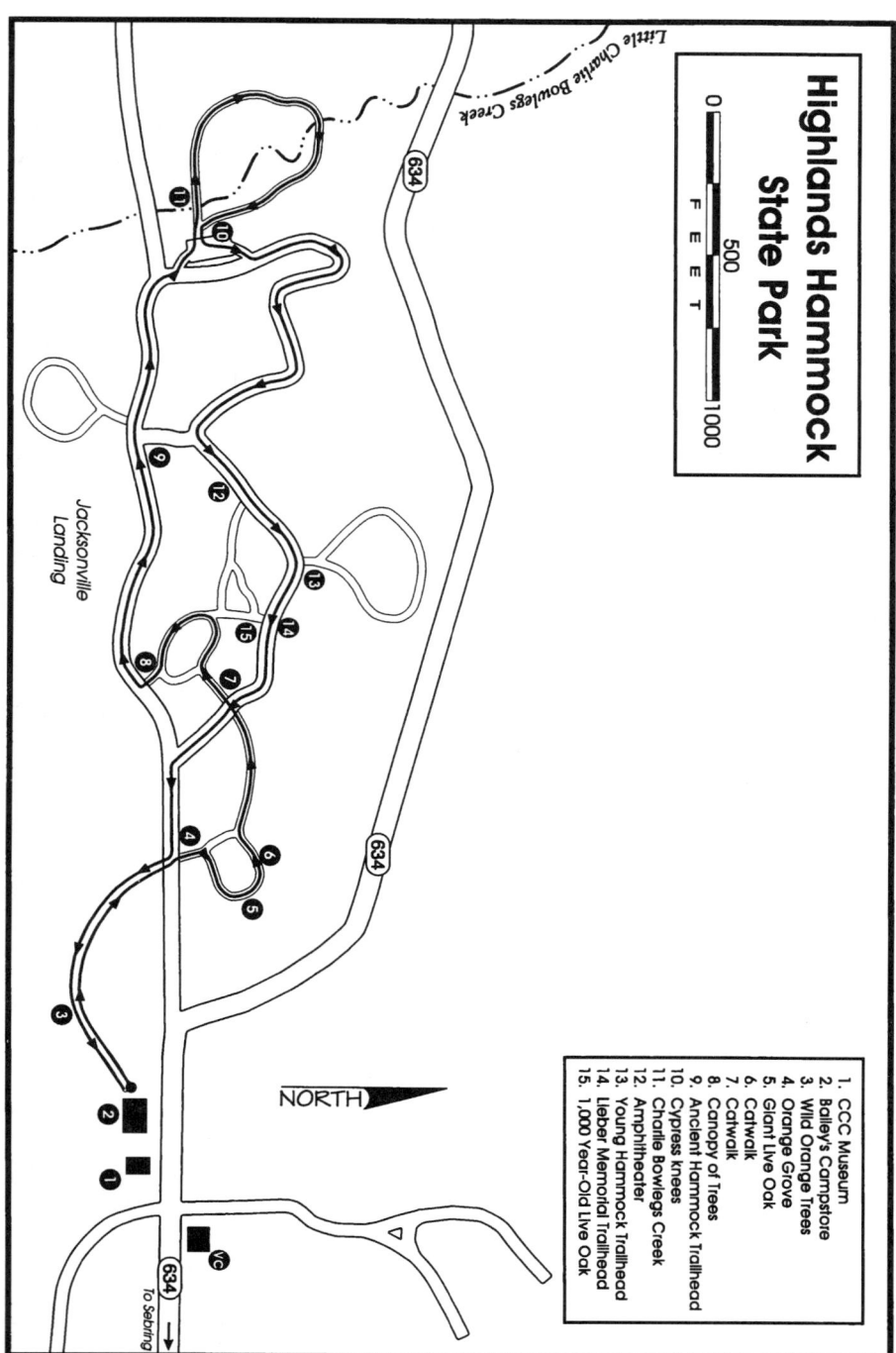

Highlands Hammock
State Park

Little Charlie Bowlegs Creek

Jacksonville
Landing

NORTH ▶

To Sebring

1. CCC Museum
2. Bailey's Campstore
3. Wild Orange Trees
4. Orange Grove
5. Giant Live Oak
6. Catwalk
7. Catwalk
8. Canopy of Trees
9. Ancient Hammock Trailhead
10. Cypress Knees
11. Charlie Bowlegs Creek
12. Amphitheater
13. Young Hammock Trailhead
14. Lieber Memorial Trailhead
15. 1,000 Year-Old Live Oak

Tampa, and Sarasota. Amtrak (800/USA RAIL) and Greyhound Bus Lines (800/231-2222, 941/385-7741) serve Sebring.

First steps
For information, contact the Highlands Hammock State Park ranger station, which is open daily 8 am to sunset; or the Department of Environmental Protection, Division of Recreation and Parks, whose hours are weekdays 9 am to 5 pm.

Walking tours
Rangers lead interpretive nature walks November 1 through April 30 at 10 am each Monday.

Seasonal highlights
October to April is the most pleasant time to visit. It's cooler and there are fewer insects. The annual Civilian Conservation Corps Festival with entertainment, tours, and a chance to meet former CCC workers is held the first Saturday in November. The busiest and most expensive time is March, during Sebring's annual Grand Prix Auto Race.

Natural Highlands Hammock. *At 4.5 miles, this route covers the paved loop road and five trails: Wild Orange Grove Trail (2,929 feet), Big Oak Trail (975 feet), Hickory Trail (2,196 feet), Fern Garden Trail (1,641 feet), and Cypress Swamp Trail (2,355 feet). Allot four hours for a leisurely trip. If the museum is open, allot another 20 minutes. Bring a lunch and use the picnic facilities located near the CCC Museum.*

Start at the CCC Museum. The trailhead for the **Wild Orange Grove Trail** is behind Bailey's Campstore, opposite the museum. The trail's best features are the wild orange trees, whose blossoms give off a heavenly scent in early spring. *Follow the trail through pine flatwoods and young hammock communities* with slash pines (*Pinus elliotti var. densa*), laurel oaks (*Quercus laurifolia*), wax myrtles (*Myrica cerifera*) and gallberries (*Ilex glabra*) before crossing the main paved road at a meadow with an orange grove planted in 1909. Keep quiet. It's a popular grazing spot for white-tail deer.

*Pick up the trail as it merges with the **Alexander Blair Big Oak Trail**,* aptly named for one of the largest trees in the park, a giant live oak that measures 36 feet around the trunk. The trail merges with **Hickory Trail** as it crosses a catwalk. Look for pignut hickory trees (*Carya glabra*). *The trail continues across the north fork of the paved road,* then connects with the **Fern Garden Trail.** *Take a right onto the catwalk* that carries you over marshy ground dense with ferns, cattails, lilies, grasses and bay trees. Heed the "Slippery When Wet" sign. Quietly approach pools of water, where flocks of ibis feed. Check the muddy areas alongside the boardwalk for animal tracks and be on the lookout for Fern, a resident female alligator. Don't connect with the Lieber Memorial Trail, instead, *continue south (counterclockwise) and leave the trail at the south fork of the paved road.* As you head west, the paved road is quickly swallowed up in a canopy of towering trees. The understory is dotted with saw palmetto (*Serenoa repens*), wild coffee (*Psychotria nervosa*) and American beautyberry (*Callicarpa americana L.*). In late summer and fall, the latter displays conspicuous clusters of small, magenta-colored berries. Birds love it for its fruit; butterflies for its pink flowers.

You'll pass the Ancient Hammock trailhead and eventually reach the looped **Cypress Swamp Trail**, locally called The Catwalk. Cypress knees and ancient cypress trees (*Taxodium ascendens* and *Taxodium distichum*) draped with moss, delicate ferns, butterflies, alligators, birds, and reflecting water make this one of the most beautiful places in the park. The trail crosses Charlie Bowlegs Creek twice before returning to the trailhead.

Continue around the paved loop road past the amphitheater, Young Hammock trailhead, and Lieber Memorial trailhead. Just inside the latter is the oldest living thing in the hammock, a 1,000 year-old live oak. Head back to the road and return to the CCC Museum.

Lodging
Make reservations well in advance during the March racing season. Rates are slightly higher in winter season.

The recently renovated **Kenilworth Lodge** ($$–$$$/$–$$, 800/423-5939, 941/385-0111) downtown at 836 SE Lakeview Dr is a 130-room historic hotel built by Sebring's founder, George Sebring, in 1916, to attract wealthy Northerners. The grounds and large Spanish-style building with rooms, apartments, poolside villas, and efficiencies spread out over 6 acres overlooking Lake Jackson.

Jan and Don Bowden operate the 25-room **Santa Rosa Inn & 1924 Cafe** ($$–$$$/$–$$, 941/385-0641) at 509 N Ridgewood Dr. Large oak trees surround the renovated three-story brick building that was built in 1924. It has first-floor suites, second-floor rooms, and a sun porch. It's cozy and warm.

The closest hotel to the park is the **Inn on the Lakes** ($$, 800/531-5253, 941/471-9400), a modern 161-room resort overlooking Little Lake Jackson. It has a pool, restaurant, and comfortable rooms.

Food & drink

Call ahead for reservations during the March racing season.

The **1924 Cafe** ($$, 941/385-0641) in the Santa Rosa Inn at 509 N Ridgewood Dr serves tasty continental cuisine for lunch and dinner in a very pleasant setting. **A.J.'s Fine Dining at Magnolia Village** ($–$$, 941-385-5044) at 143 SE Lakeview Drive prepares seafood, steaks, as well as light fare in a picturesque setting on Lake Jackson. Despite its name, **Buon Appetito's** ($–$$, 941/385-6713) menu isn't strictly Italian. Rather, it offers a diverse menu with European accents. It's at 2310 US Hwy 27 N.

Southwest Florida

"If we painted her (Florida), we should not represent her as a neat, trim damsel, with starched linen cuffs and collar: she would be a brunette, dark but comely, with gorgeous tissues, a general disarray and dazzle, and with a sort of jolly untidiness, free, easy, and joyous."—Harriet Beecher Stowe in *Palmetto Leaves*

Introduction

While Henry Flagler was pushing his railroad south along the east coast, Henry Bradley Plant, a Connecticut businessman, forged his line and luxury hotels down the west coast during the late 1880s and 1890s. He also brought shipping lines. Wealthy northern tourists followed to spend their winters in booming tourist towns like Tampa and Sarasota.

Tampa had grown up out of Fort Brooke, established in 1824 as a pioneer outpost, then played a strategic role during the Second Seminole War and port of embarkation for Native Americans being removed from Florida.

Cigar manufacturers Don Vincente Martinez Ybor and Ignacio Haya took an interest in Plant's new transportation system with an eye towards using it to ship tobacco from Cuba to Tampa and send the finished cigars by train to New York. In 1885 Ybor purchased 40 acres near the harbor and rail lines on the northeast edge of Tampa and began hiring workers and constructing a factory town. Thus, Ybor City was founded and became America's cigar-making capital until the Castro Revolution in 1959. After 30 years of neglect Ybor City was revived and is now an historic district and Tampa's primary tourist destination.

Sarasota's population remained sparse until the 1880s, when affluent Scottish families arrived by steamer. Circus magnate John Ringling moved his winter home and circus to Sarasota in 1910 and built a museum to house his European art collection. Artisans, the arts, wealthy visitors, and like-minded investors followed and Sarasota quickly became a major cultural winter resort.

Farther south along the coast, Fort Myers got its start as Fort Harvie in 1841 during the Second Seminole War. It was abandoned, then reoccupied during the Civil War. After the military left again, settlers disassembled the buildings and used the lumber to build the town. Today, it's a winter resort with many natural attractions.

A string of barrier islands extends down Florida's Gulf Coast from Tampa to Fort Myers. The islands, some developed, others pristine with refuges and parks like Caladesi Island State Park and Ding Darling National Wildlife Refuge, offer superb opportunities for outdoor recreation and wildlife watching on beaches and tidal lagoons. On the mainland, the natural landscape varies from mangroves and cypress and hardwood swamps to sawgrass marshes and scrub and flatwoods. It can all be enjoyed in dozens of national, state, and county parks.

Caladesi Island State Park

Caladesi Island, located about a mile offshore of Dunedin, in the Tampa/St Petersburg area, is one of the few remaining undeveloped barrier islands in the state. For most of its 4,000 years it has been uninhabited. The exceptions were Native Americans, who left burial mounds dating from the 1500s, and pioneer Henry Scharrer, who homesteaded and lived on the island with his daughter for about 50 years from the late 1800s.

Up until 1921 Caladesi was part of Hog Island, now Honeymoon Island. That year, a hurricane split the land and formed two separate islands. Honeymoon Island derives its name from an early 1940s advertising campaign for newlyweds who entered a contest to win a two-week Florida vacation in a resort of 50 palm-thatched bungalows on the island. The island managed to remain uninhabited until 1964, when a causeway connected it to the mainland and threatened its charm. Spurred by locals to protect the islands from development, the state purchased Caladesi Island in 1968 and Honeymoon Island six years later.

Today's visitors drive the causeway to Honeymoon Island State Recreation Area, which has nature trails, beaches (including a pet beach), and a ferry landing for trips to Caladesi Island State Park.

The beach at Caladesi Island is consistently rated among the best in the country. That's because along with it being long, wide, shallow, and pretty, it's never crowded and the facilities are well maintained, even on the busiest holidays. How does it manage to remain unspoiled? The island is accessible only by public ferry or private or rented boats, kayaks, and canoes. With a handful of other top-ranked beaches in the area, many people choose not to pay the park entrance and ferry fees. However, it's worth the trip, especially if you want the best of two worlds—an interesting nature trail and a beautiful beach. One disadvantage is that to limit the number of people on the island, ferry tickets allow you to stay no longer than four hours.

Shore birds, ospreys, wading birds, gopher tortoises, otters, and rattlesnakes are the primary wildlife. During summer, stingrays settle into the sandy surf along all the Gulf Coast beaches, and Caladesi is no exception. Signs advise swimmers to shuffle their feet as they enter the water.

The plant communities on the island range from beach scrub, coastal hammock, and pine flatwoods to mangrove swamps, seagrass beds, salt marshes, tidal flats, and sand dunes. The sandy bottom trail is well maintained and well marked, with 23 points of interest, a few of which need to be updated. Numerous benches—most provided by local Boy Scout troops—are located along the trail. Most of the trail has limited shade. Island facilities include a visitor center, marina, food concession, lockers, restrooms, and showers.

Information

Caladesi Island State Park and Honeymoon Island State Recreation Area, GEOpark, One Causeway Blvd, Dunedin, FL 34698; 727/469-5918 and 727/469-5942, respectively. Dunedin Chamber of Commerce, 301 Main St, Dunedin, FL 34698; 727/733-3197.

Getting there

Take I-75 to I-275, where you'll exit west onto Ulmerton Rd (Hwy 688) from Tampa (exit 18) or St Petersburg (exit 17). Turn north onto Hwy 19, then west onto Curlew Rd (Hwy 586) into Honeymoon Island State Recreation Area. Follow the signs to the Ferry. The Caladesi Connection ferry service runs daily from 10 am to sunset. Round-trip tickets for the 12-minute crossing cost $6 per adult, $3.50 per child. St Petersburg-Clearwater Airport is about 20 minutes southeast. Tampa International Airport is about 30 minutes southeast. Amtrak's (800/USA RAIL, 813/221-7600) closest station is at 601 Nebraska Ave N, Tampa. Greyhound (800/231-2222, 727/796-7315) has a station at 2811 Gulf-to-Bay Blvd, Clearwater.

First steps

Stop at the ranger station at Honeymoon Island State Recreation Area for brochures and trail maps for both islands. For area maps and information, visit the Dunedin Chamber of Commerce. It's open 8:30 am to 4:30 pm Monday to Friday. You can also stop at the Clearwater/Pinellas County Suncoast Welcome Center, 3350 Courtney Campbell Causeway Blvd (Hwy 60); 727/726-1547. It's hours are 9 am to 5 pm daily.

Tours

Linda Taylor offers two-hour nature/history tours of the island through It's Our Nature, Inc (888/535-7448, 727/441-2599) for $10 per adult, $6 per child.

Seasonal highlights

Honeymoon Island State Recreation Area has night Sea Turtle Beach Walks once a month July through September. The same months, but different nights, the park also has History of Honeymoon Island evening walks, and an Astronomer's Star Gazing program.

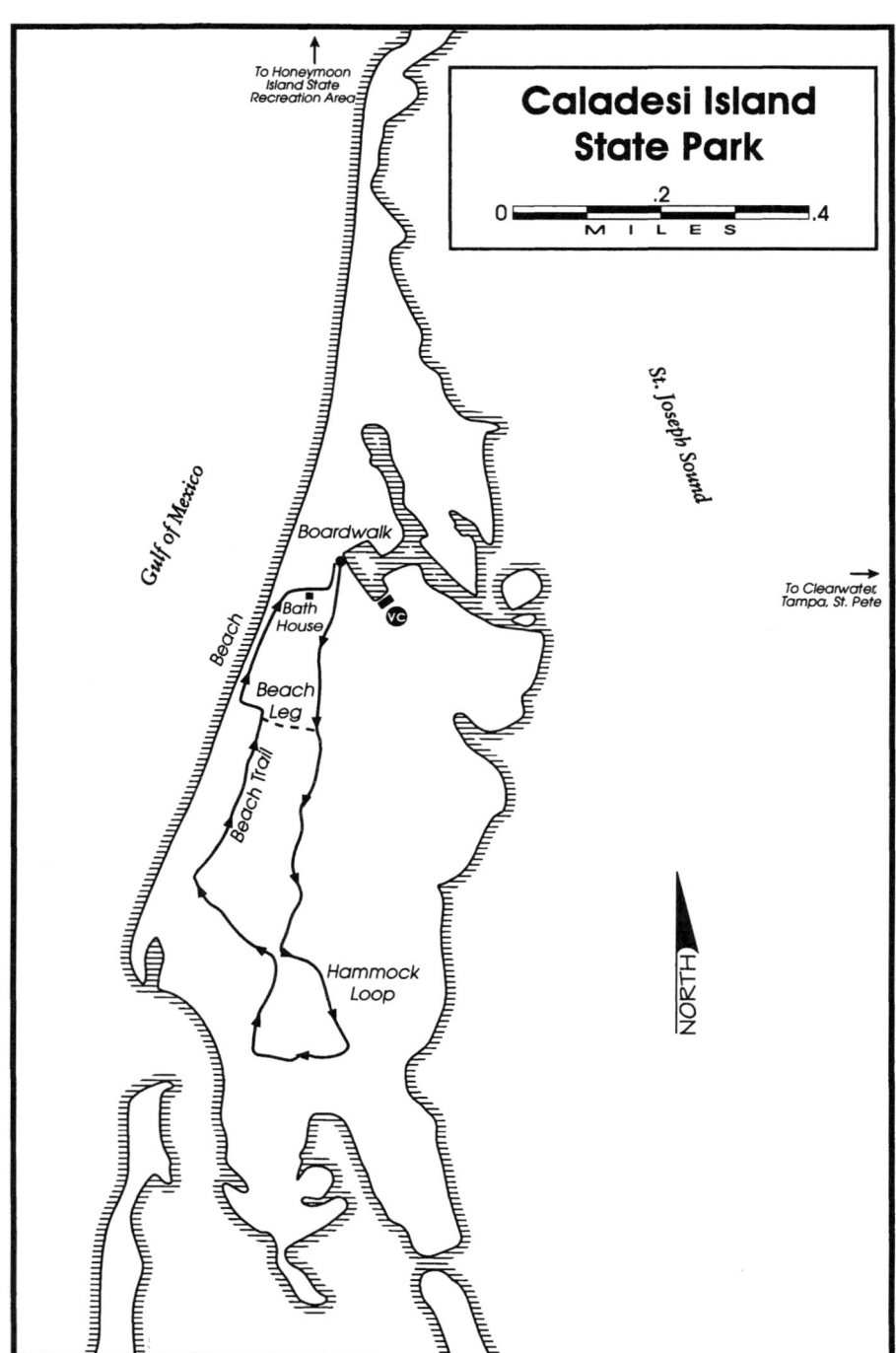

To Honeymoon
Island State
Recreation Area

Caladesi Island
State Park

.2

0 |_____| .4

M I L E S

St. Joseph Sound

Gulf of Mexico

Boardwalk

Bath
House

VC

Beach

Beach
Leg

Beach Trail

Hammock
Loop

To Clearwater,
Tampa, St. Pete

NORTH

Natural Caladesi Island State Park. *This three-mile route covers a short boardwalk and four natural habitats: beach scrub, pine flatwood, coastal hammock, and beach.*

Start at the boardwalk behind the Visitor Center. Follow the boardwalk to the trailhead sign next to the old building foundation. The trail turns left off the boardwalk, just before the boardwalk dead-ends into a T that continues to the beach. At 0.2 miles the trail crosses a road, continue straight about 15 feet to the interpretive sign and trail guide box. Not surprisingly, the trail begins in a beach scrub community of tall cabbage palms (*Sabal palmetto*) with a moderately dense understory of low-growing saw palmettos (*Serenoa repens*), wax myrtle (*Myrica cerifiera*) with leaves that are narrow at their base and toothed near their tips, broom sedge (*Andropogon virginicus*), hair grass (*Muhlenbergia capillaris*), prickly pear cactus (*Opuntia stricta*), and the very showy beautyberry (*Callicarpa americana*) with its tiny, bright purple (and sometimes white) clustered fruits. You're also likely to spot gopher tortoises or their burrows alongside the trail.

At 0.5 miles, there's an interpretive sign for sabal palm and a resting bench on the left. However, most noticeable next to the bench is a saw palmetto with a trunk that's growing 90 degrees. At 0.62 miles, there's an interpretive sign for a saw palmetto and a spur trail to the beach. On the left a few feet ahead is a conspicuously large sand pine (*Pinus clausa*). Thirty feet beyond it is a pair of live oaks on either side of the trail.

Before you reach Marker 7 at mile 0.75, the landscape changes and the elevation rises slightly as the beach scrub community gives way to a pine flatwood habitat that cannot withstand prolonged flooding. The understory thins noticeably. Just ahead at mile 0.82, there's a patch of ferns on the left. Beyond it, as the trail curves, is a cabbage palm on the left surrounded by wildflowers, including saltmarsh fleabane (*Pluchea odorata*) with pinkish flowers that bloom June to November and seashore mallow (*Kosteletzkya virginica*).

The toothed, heart-shaped to round southern fox grape, also called scuppernong and bullace grape (*Vitis rotundifolia*), is abundant on either side of the trail once it crosses a small wooden bridge and climbs slightly at one mile. Avoid touching or rubbing against the tread softly (*Cnidoscolus stimulosus*), the pretty, five-lobed trumpet-shaped white flowers with hairs on the leaves and stems. It gives a severe sting, much like stinging nettle. *At 1.08 miles the trail divides, with one leg going to the beach, the other to the hammock loop. Take the latter.*

This part of the trail is shaded with tall, strong, yet graceful live oaks

(*Quercus virginiana*) and towering slash pines (*Pinus elliottii densa*) as it traverses pine flatwoods and coastal hammock communities. Several features make it worth the trip. This is one of the few remaining virgin stands of South Florida slash pine in the region. Its biggest threat today is lightning strikes. Tampa Bay is one of the most active thunderstorm areas in the world. Look for charred scars on the bottom section of the trees as well as dead trees, which amount to three or four a year.

At mile 1.44, the two large live oaks signal that the trail has left the pine flatwoods and entered the coastal hammock. The number of live oaks increases significantly, as does the three-leaflet poison ivy (*Toxicodendron radicans*), seen on both sides of the trail throughout the hammock loop. Just beyond it on the right is the island's only natural source of freshwater. On a day without a lot of visitors, wading birds and even otters frequent the pond.

Marker 14 describes vines like the thick, woody grapevine growing up the nearby tree. About 30 feet farther on the left is an interpretive sign for aerial gardens, describing the epiphytes—resurrection ferns (*Polypodium polypodioides*), shoestring ferns (*Vittaria lineata*), and bromeliads that grow on the spectacular oaks to the left of the trail. Looking at these multi-branched beauties, it's easy to see where the oaks get their name, *Quercus*, from the Celtic words *quer* meaning beautiful, and *cuez* meaning tree.

About 30 feet ahead are several pines that were struck by lightning. Another 20 feet beyond them is a clearing with benches and Marker 15, which describes a most unusual double-trunk pine. Visitors to the area have been photographing the tree—usually with someone standing in front of it—since the late 1800s. *At mile 1.8 the trail crosses a service road. Continue straight ahead. At 1.93 miles the loop returns to the intersection for the beach and hammock. Follow the left leg to the beach.*

Marker 17 at mile 2 marks a hercules club (*Zanthoxylum clava-herculis*), a small tree with spines on its trunk. To relieve toothaches, Native Americans chewed the leaves, which have a numbing effect. The one here has died, but there is another one—unmarked but unmistakable—on the north side of the boardwalk about 100 feet from the Visitor Center.

The beach trail is bordered by grasses that give way to mangroves on the left, cabbage palms on the right. At mile 2.2 on the left is a thicket of inkberry or Florida privet (*Forestiera segregata*), a straggly shrub or small tree with 2-inch leaves, smooth gray bark and half-inch blue-black fruits that are slightly smaller and more olive shaped than blueberries. Thirty feet beyond it is Marker 20, indicating a 30-foot-long stand of necklace pod (*Sophora tomentosa*), which derives its name from its strand-like beaded seed pods. It's a favorite food for ruby throated hummingbirds. *Just beyond here the trail turns left to the beach, right to the shortcut back to the trailhead. Take the beach route.*

The last section before the trail reaches the beach passes through mangroves and traverses two short wooden bridges that cross dune tidal ponds. These are good spots to watch wading birds year round and migrating mergansers and blue-winged teals in winter. After you've crossed the second bridge, the back dune area is dominated by hairgrass, Florida privet, cabbage palm, and palmettos before giving way to the tall endangered sea oats (*Uniola paniculata*), panic grass (*Panicum amarum*), sea purslane (*Sesuvium portulacastrum*), and beach croton (*Croton punctatus*), among others.

The beach is wide, gently sloping, and hard packed near the water's edge, where small shells wash ashore. A display on the beach side of the Visitor Center shows the types of shells found here. *It's a half mile back to the Visitor Center. Take the first boardwalk, which passes restrooms and showers.*

Lodging

Places to rest one's head at night are as varied as the heads that rest on them. The range is from small 1940s-era mom-and-pop establishments with more character than amenities to turn-of-the-century resorts with more activities than hours in the day. High (most expensive) season is February through April. The lowest season is the summer.

The 1897 **Belleview Biltmore** ($$$$, 800/237-8947, 727/442-6171) recalls the glamour era of turn-of-the-century beachfront Victorian inns with many of its original charms, albeit updated, including a golf-course built in 1925, clay tennis courts, a spa and fitness center, pool, and beach at 25 Belleview Blvd, Clearwater. More modern, but chock-full of amenities is the **Sheraton Sand Key** ($$$$, 727/595-1611) with a beach, lighted tennis courts, pool, playground, massage, and charter fishing at 1160 Gulf Blvd, Clearwater Beach.

Bring a book to read while swinging on the front porch or sitting by the pool of the historic 1878 **J O Douglas House B&B** ($$–$$$, 877/64BandB, 727 /735-9006), a Victorian beauty listed on the National Register of Historic Places at 209 Scotland St, Dunedin. Rooms are decorated in antiques—some family heirlooms— and Victorian frills. Whether you watch the sunset on the private dock or watch the sky darken from a rocker on one of the two porches, you'll be relaxed at the spacious 1910 **Lanning's Green Gables B&B** ($$ 813/443-3675) at 1040 Sunset Point Rd, Clearwater. There are three themed rooms, boat slips and dock, a nearby sandy beach, bathrobes, and antiques at the **Harbour Lights** on the Beach ($$, 800/953-8134, 727/441-1393) at 205 Brightwater Dr, Clearwater. The **Bay Queen Motel** ($$, 727/441-3295) has beautifully landscaped grounds, spotless rooms and efficiencies, and a great view of Clearwater Harbor at an attractive price. Besides having the oldest beach concession in Florida, the 30-room beachfront Art Deco style **Palm Pavilion Inn** ($$–$$$, 800/433-PALM, 727 /446-6777) has a pool, deck, restaurant, and entertainment at 18 Bay Esplanade, Clearwater Beach.

Food & drink
At resort towns like Dunedin, Clearwater, and Clearwater Beach, restaurants vie for the attention and admiration of both locals and international visitors. As a result, there's a seemingly endless choice of good, diverse restaurants. Prices range from anyone-can-afford-it to better-have-an-expensive-account.

Freshly made pasta, homemade desserts, and properly cooked seafood make **Pastels** ($$$, 727/733-5449) a good choice for an Italian restaurant, at 461 Main St, Dunedin. After almost 30 years, locals still consider **Bon Appetit** ($$$, 727 /733-2151) one of their favorite restaurants for consistently good bistro-style food overlooking the Intracoastal Waterway at 148 Marina Plaza, Dunedin. It's hard to decide which is a better reason to go to **Tio Pepe Restaurante** ($$, 727/799-3082) at 2930 Gulf-to-Bay Blvd in Clearwater, its extensive wine list or the consistently good Spanish/Mediterranean cuisine. Either way, it's a winner. The atmosphere is laid-back, but the cooking is seriously creative at **Cafe Alfresco** ($–$$, 727 /736-4299) in Dunedin, overlooking the Pinellas Trail at 344 Main St.

Two favorite haunts for inexpensive seafood in very casual settings are **Frenchy's Rockaway Grill** ($$, 727/446-4844) with a lively beachfront atmosphere at 7 Rockaway St, Clearwater, and **Crabby Bill's** ($$, 727/789-9383), a local chain, at 2901 Alt Hwy 19 N, Clearwater.

When you just want soup, a salad, or sandwich, try **Deli News Cafe** ($, 727/735-0505) in an artsy setting at 680 Main St, Dunedin, or **Palm Harbor Natural Foods** ($, 727/786-1231), which serves tasty, healthy dishes at Hwy19 at Curlew Rd, in the Seabreeze Shopping Center, Dunedin.

Events
Honeymoon Island State Recreation Area has an all-day **Fourth of July C elebration,** starting with the annual Kiwanis Mease Independence Day Midnight Run and ending with a Dunedin-sponsored fireworks show.

Safety Harbor

It's easy to feel overwhelmed by the size, distances, crowds, and traffic of the Tampa-St Petersburg-Clearwater megalopolis. So it's a comfort be able to turn off the fast-paced highways, follow a meandering two-lane bayside road past century-old oak trees shading big houses and find yourself in the middle of a quiet, picturesque five-acre waterfront village of 15,000 residents.

Safety Harbor has many of the attractions of its big neighbors, just done to a much smaller, more personal scale. There's a nationally recognized spa, a first-class history museum, fine restaurants, a marina, fishing opportunities, and two bayfront parks.

Native Americans made seasonal visits to the Safety Harbor area as early as 3,000 BC. By AD 1400 a thriving population of a more advanced culture, the Tocobago Indians, had established villages and was practicing limited agriculture and building mounds. They remained until shortly after the arrival of the Spanish explorers. In time, they were replaced by the Seminole Indians.

The first non-Native American settlers, Odet Philippe and his family, arrived in the late 1830s and established a citrus plantation on the north end of what would become Safety Harbor. His homestead is the town's 88-acre bayfront park, the largest in the county. Other settlers followed in the mid-1850s, including Colonel William J Bailey, who purchased the land on which the famous natural springs are located and on which the Safety Harbor Resort and Spa was developed. As more tourists came to bathe in the legendary curative waters, hotels sprang up and the town became a well-known tourist and health resort. Celebrities such as Harry Houdini, the Seagrams of Canada, Russ Kresge, and the Ebbets family made the pilgrimage to the springs.

Over the years, Safety Harbor took on the moniker "Health Giving City" and several different names, including Espiritu Santo Springs (Springs of Holy Water)—after Hernando de Soto drank from the waters—and Green Springs, after Jesse Green who was cured after drinking the spring waters that bubble up from the earth. The water was bottled and shipped around the world.

Shortly after its incorporation with a population of 200 in 1917, Safety Harbor grew rapidly during the 1920s Florida real estate boom. Historic buildings such as the Safety Harbor Spa and the St James Hotel remain from that era.

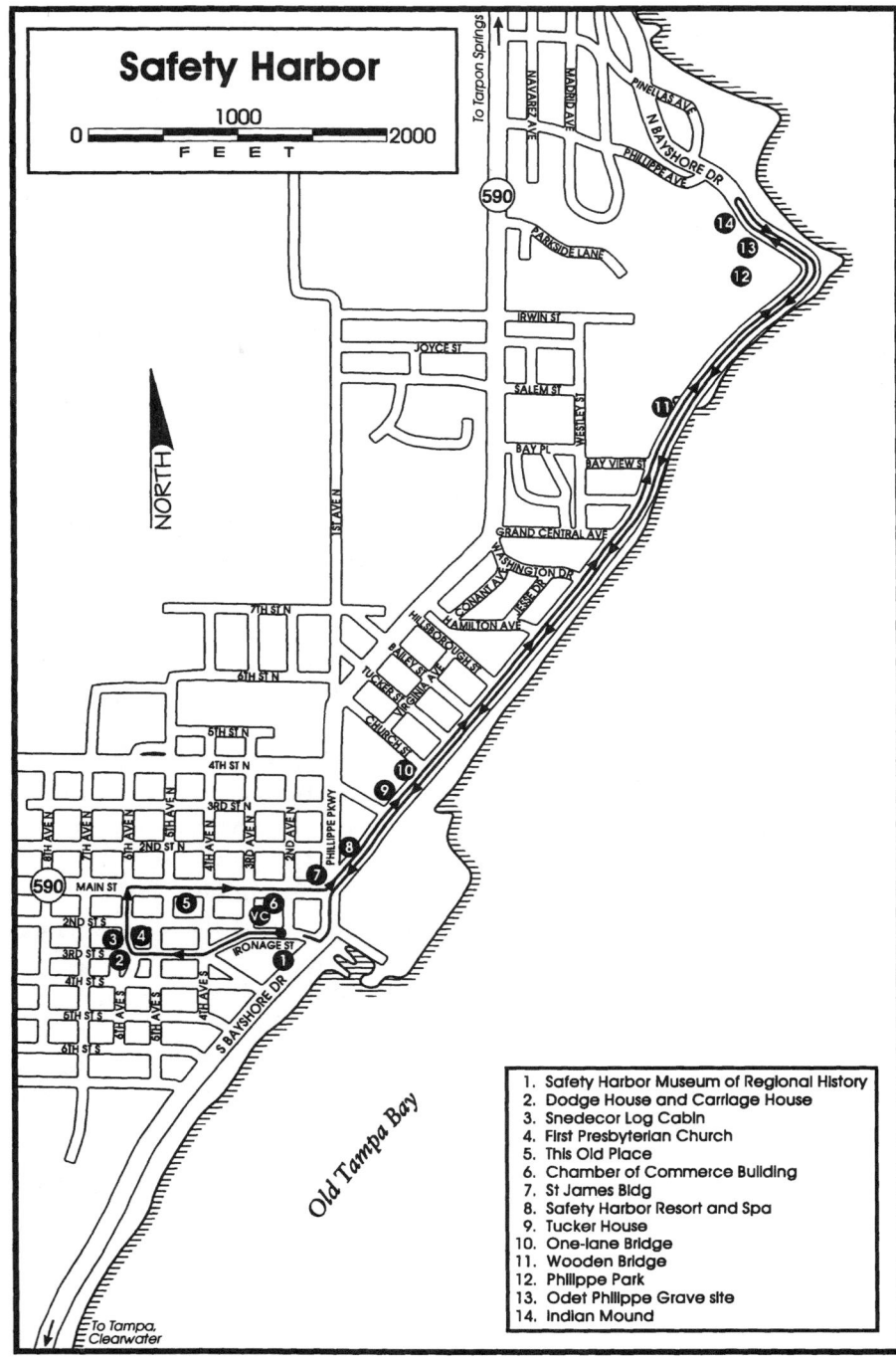

Safety Harbor

0 ▬▬▬▬▬▬▬▬▬▬ 2000
1000
F E E T

NORTH

To Tarpon Springs

590

To Tampa,
Clearwater

Old Tampa Bay

1. Safety Harbor Museum of Regional History
2. Dodge House and Carriage House
3. Snedecor Log Cabin
4. First Presbyterian Church
5. This Old Place
6. Chamber of Commerce Building
7. St James Bldg
8. Safety Harbor Resort and Spa
9. Tucker House
10. One-lane Bridge
11. Wooden Bridge
12. Phillippe Park
13. Odet Phillippe Grave site
14. Indian Mound

Information
Safety Harbor Chamber of Commerce, 200 Main St, Safety Harbor, FL 34695; 727/726-2890; fax 727/726-2733; imagesm@aol.com. Pinellas County Park Department, Philippe Park, 2525 Philippe Pkwy, (mailing 2455 Rajael Ave), Safety Harbor, FL 34695; **727/669-1947**.

Getting there
Take I-75, then I-275 to exit 20 (Tampa International Airport). Drive west on Hwy 60 (Courtney Campbell Causeway), then turn right onto Bayshore Blvd, the first light back on the mainland, and follow it into the village. Tampa International Airport is about 15 minutes east at 5507 Spruce St, at I-275 exit 20. Amtrak's (800/USA RAIL, 813/221-7600) closest station is at 601 Nebraska Ave N, Tampa. Greyhound (800/231-2222, 813/229-2112) has a station in downtown Tampa at 610 Polk St.

First steps
For maps and information, contact the Safety Harbor Chamber of Commerce. For information about Philippe Park, contact the Pinellas County Park Department, Philippe Park. If you're going in summer, plan your walk in the early morning or late afternoon, when there's shade along N Bayshore Blvd.

Odet Philippe: Peninsular Pioneer by J Allison DeFoor, II, relates the history of the namesake pioneer.

Historic and Natural Safety Harbor. *This 4-mile walk covers downtown Safety Harbor, the waterfront, and historic Philippe Park. Allot two hours. However, a more leisurely trip of four hours can include a visit to the history museum, a stop for lunch or refreshments at the Safety Harbor Resort and Spa, and a rest on a bench on an Indian mound overlooking Tampa Bay.*

Begin at the Safety Harbor Museum of Regional History. The Safety Harbor Museum of Regional History's excellent collection of local artifacts and exhibits provides an extensive look at Safety Harbor's development from a Native American village through the mid 1900s. The staff is knowledgeable and helpful.

On the north side of the museum's parking lot are two turn-of-the-century buildings: the Dodge House, brought over from Tampa by barge and altered over the years, and the Carriage House, once a carriage house that possibly belonged to the spa. In front of the latter is a tabby well shaped as an arrow pointing north built by Native Americans. *Turn right out of the parking lot behind the Carriage House, then left onto Iron Age St, and left onto Short St, which becomes 3rd St S.*

At mile 0.2 the road dead-ends in front of the circa 1880 **Snedecor Log Cabin** (3rd St S and 6th Ave S), built for pioneer James George Snedecor. It's believed that the house was moved to this site around 1920. The house features dovetail notching, an indoor and outdoor fireplace, outside pillars made of palm trunks, the original shake roof, and chinking of scrap sticks with mortar. It's being beautifully restored by its owner, Betty Quibell, who will gladly answer questions about the house when you're at the history museum, where she works. *Turn right onto 6th Ave S.*

The Spanish Revival **First Presbyterian Church** (corner 6th Ave S and 2nd St S) was built in 1932. *Turn right onto Main St.*

On the right, **This Old Place** (454 Main) has housed businesses, a hotel, and a restaurant since it was built in 1914 as the Hotel Francis by the McElveen family, whose descendants still live in town. Across the street is John Wilson Park with a gazebo. Two blocks down, on the corner of Second Ave, the pink **Chamber of Commerce Building** (200 Main) was constructed around the same time of brick with stucco. It also served as a town hall and bank. Diagonally across the street is a stunning live oak tree.

Across the street on the corner of Main St and Philippe Pkwy is the restored 1920s **St James Bldg**, formerly the Espiritu Santo Springs Hotel and now offices and shops. It was named after James Tucker, a Civil War veteran and 1920s developer. *Cross the street and turn left onto N Bayshore Blvd, between the parking lot and the resort.*

James Tucker formed the Espiritu Santo Springs Corporation and developed the springs and constructed The Safety Harbor Sanitorium on the site of today's **Safety Harbor Resort and Spa** (105 N Bayshore) in the mid-1920s. Guests overnighted in their hotel across the street. Advertisements claimed "to visit the Sanatorium is to bestow upon yourself the gift of health brewed by the Great Chemist." The sanatorium and springs were sold in 1936 for back taxes. The new owner restored the resort and built a large spring-fed swimming pool. Their promotional pieces referred to the sanatorium and springs as "a Florida haven for those in search of health, recreation and rest." During the 1940s and 1950s two subsequent owners turned it into the modern resort, spa, and health center it is today. *Continue north on N Bayshore Blvd.*

On the left the **Tucker House** (311 N Bayshore) is a grand mansion built by James Tucker and his wife Virginia. Most of the exterior remains unchanged. However, the interior, which has 12-foot ceilings, has been totally altered. Attractive modern houses line the left side of N Bayshore Blvd. The right side's sidewalk and bayfront verge are covered by native plants and turf.

The walk crosses an idyllic old one-lane bridge at mile 0.75. Native vegetation around it includes mangroves (*Rhizophora mangle and Avicennia germinans*), pine (*pinus spp*), oak (*Quercus spp*), and cabbage palms (*Sabal palmetto*). It's a great spot for bird watching. Look for herons, egrets, and ducks. The mangrove eco-system farther along on the right also has non-native cattails, pines, and bananas. Wild rabbits scamper in and out of the brush and woodpeckers and purple martins zoom in and out of the trees and bushes.

At mile 1.15 on the right, there's a garden of bromeliads, bamboos, and a large Hong Kong orchid tree (*Bauhinia blakeana*) with fragrant orchid-shaped lavender flowers. On the right, opposite Grand Central St, elephant ears (*Alocasia spp*) and Queen Anne's lace (*Daucus carota*) wave in the wind. The red flowers across from Washington Avenue are hibiscus (*hibiscus rosa-sinensis*). *North Bayshore Blvd is closed at this end to all but park traffic north of Marshall St. Cross the footpath and continue north into Philippe Park.*

The small wooden bridge at mile 1.50 is a popular spot among bird watchers, especially early morning and early evening. Look for ibis, herons, ducks, and other wading birds. Enjoy the nice breezes off Tampa Bay. The walk continues into **Philippe Park**. At mile 2 on the right an historical marker interprets the history of the eponymous Odet Philippe. Across the street a short stairway leads to his grave site. Much controversy surrounds where he came from and his background. Not debatable is that Philippe was the first person to cultivate grapefruit as a crop in Florida. Philippe also imported tobacco seed from Cuba and became the region's first cigar maker. *Return to the street, cross over to the historical marker. Walk north about 100 feet and climb the embankment on the right, passing between a small stand of pines.*

The ancient live oak (*Quercus virginiana*) ahead of you has graceful sprawling limbs hung with Spanish moss. From the oak you can see a concrete path leading to a marker and a large mound at about 90 degrees. The National Historic Landmark sign marks a mound built by the Tocobago Indians for ceremonial purposes. Park excavations began in 1880. In 1930 subsequent diggings revealed a large, flat-topped temple mound measuring five meters high, several burial mounds, and a large village. It's believed that the site was the Tocobago village visited by Pedro Menéndez de Avilés in 1567. Odet Philippe's house is believed to have been southwest of here, between the mound and the water. *Walk to the top of the mound for a commanding view of the harbor, where Odet*

Philippe kept his boat. Return to the street and retrace your steps back to the museum. Instead of turning onto Main St, continue south on Bayshore after passing the resort.

Lodging

Safety Harbor is primarily a residential community with a main street and one hotel. Other accommodations are available in nearby Clearwater (see Caladesi Island State Park Walking Tour) and Tampa (see Ybor City Walking Tour).

A national historical and Florida landmark, the 193-room **Safety Harbor Resort and Spa** ($$$, 888/237-8772, 727/726-1161) is a comprehensive spa and fitness center with three spring-fed pools, tennis courts, a golf academy, weight-training room, and two restaurants overlooking Tampa Bay at 105 N Bayshore Blvd.

Arts & culture

Major arts and cultural activities are available in neighboring Clearwater and Tampa.

You would expect a small-town museum in a small town. That's not the case at the **Safety Harbor Museum of Regional History** (727/726-1668, 329 S Bayshore Blvd) whose collection has great depth in pre-historic and historic artifacts that trace the history of Safety Harbor and the surrounding Tampa Bay area. Rotating exhibits and lectures complement the permanent collection. Admission is $2 adults/$1 children.

For nearly 20 years **Syd Entel Galleries** (727/725-1808, 247 Main St) has exhibited contemporary paintings, sculpture, hand-blown glass, and prints by international artists.

Food & drink

Safety Harbor has one or two very good restaurants and several good neighborhood hangouts. Neighboring Clearwater (see Caladesi Island State Park Walking Tour) and Tampa (see Ybor City Walking Tour) have scores of restaurants.

The light, attractive atmosphere sets the tone for the healthy indulgences artfully prepared at **The Cafe at Safety Harbor Resort and Spa** ($$–$$$, 727/726-1161, ext 7825) at 105 N Bayshore Blvd. There's yucca and sweet potato encrusted grouper served on a bed of greens; mahi mahi and shrimp meuniere served over a spicy gumbo; Thai vegetarian stir-fry, and several meat dishes like seared filet mignon with crisp onions and a rich porcini-merlot sauce. **Blue Gardenia** ($$–$$$, 727/712-0645) at 231 Main St bills itself as "an eclectic trattoria" and serves creative New World cuisine with a taste of the Mediterranean. Live music adds to the magic on Thursday and Friday evenings. **K Cello's Charhouse Restaurant** ($$, 727/723-0909) features steaks and pasta in a 1940s retro setting at 143 Seventh Ave N.

Two inexpensive options include the nearly 20-year-old **Captain's Italian Restaurant and Pizzeria** ($–$$, 727/725-2846), which offers pizzas, lasagna, manicotti, and lots of daily specials at 324 Main St, and **Paul's Athens Restaurant** ($–$$, 727/726-3471), which serves Greek specialties for breakfast, lunch, and dinner at 226 Main St.

Nightlife

You'll have to travel to nearby Clearwater or Tampa to take in the night lights. Safety Harbor rolls up the carpet after dinner.

Events

May is a busy month in Safety Harbor, with three annual events part of the Heritage Celebration Weekend: **Concert by the Water** (727/726-2890) kicks off the weekend with concerts, activities for kids, storytelling, a run, and other activities. The Safety Harbor Museum of Regional History has revived the annual **Green Springs Fish Fry** (727/726-1668), an historic tradition that dates back to the early 1900s when the city was known as Green Springs. It features a fish fry, storytelling, live folk music, and games. The **Heritage Days Arts & Crafts Show** (727/725-1562) brings vendors and food stretching for six blocks through the streets of Safety Harbor.

Hyde Park Historic District, Tampa

In an article dated August 31, 1893, the *Tampa Morning Tribune* wrote that Hyde Park was the most "aristocratic" section of Tampa. The same could be said today about the 600-acre historic district that lies adjacent to downtown Tampa. Large shade trees still line nearly every pedestrian-oriented street and broad lawns front numerous houses, many of which are in their original condition. Likewise, many streets retain the original bricks, asphalt paving blocks, and granite curbstones.

An 1886 to 1933 construction boom spawned houses, schools, churches, commercial structures, and a fire station in a cross-section of architectural styles. With a common thread of spacious front porches and uniform height, the neighborhood offers a remarkable impression of continuity and cohesiveness. The majority of the more spectacular houses in the 600-acre district lie south of Swann Avenue and east of Rome Avenue and along Bayshore Boulevard.

When Tampa grew up on the east side of the Hillsborough River after Fort Brooke was established on Hillsborough Bay in 1824, the town grew north because there was no bridge across the river. The west bank "frontier" remained undeveloped until the 1870s, when citrus farming began in what is now the heart of Hyde Park. Around 1880 growers James Watrous and William A. Morrison purchased 80 acres of land overlooking Hillsborough Bay and erected mansions that remain today.

Aware of plans for the Lafayette Street Bridge to span the river in 1888, O.H. Platt bought 20 acres of land immediately adjacent to downtown Tampa and created the Hyde Park subdivision west of the Hillsborough River near its confluence with Hillsborough Bay.

Two years later Henry Bradley Plant, a Connecticut businessman, laid the cornerstone for his luxurious Tampa Bay Hotel, now the University of Tampa, and extended his railroad across the river along the western edge of Hyde Park. With the railroad's arrival, Hyde Park became a favored site for upscale dwellings. Other residential districts spread across the river as affluent residents began buying land and building houses in the new "territory." Many of the district's streets are named after these men.

The main thoroughfare, Bayshore Boulevard, ran along Hillsborough Bay. In 1914 it was paved and a sea wall was constructed. Later, the road was widened to six lanes and a sidewalk and elaborate balustrade were added along the waterfront.

Today, Bayshore Boulevard is known as the "world's longest sidewalk." It runs along the picturesque bay for 4.5 miles without a break.

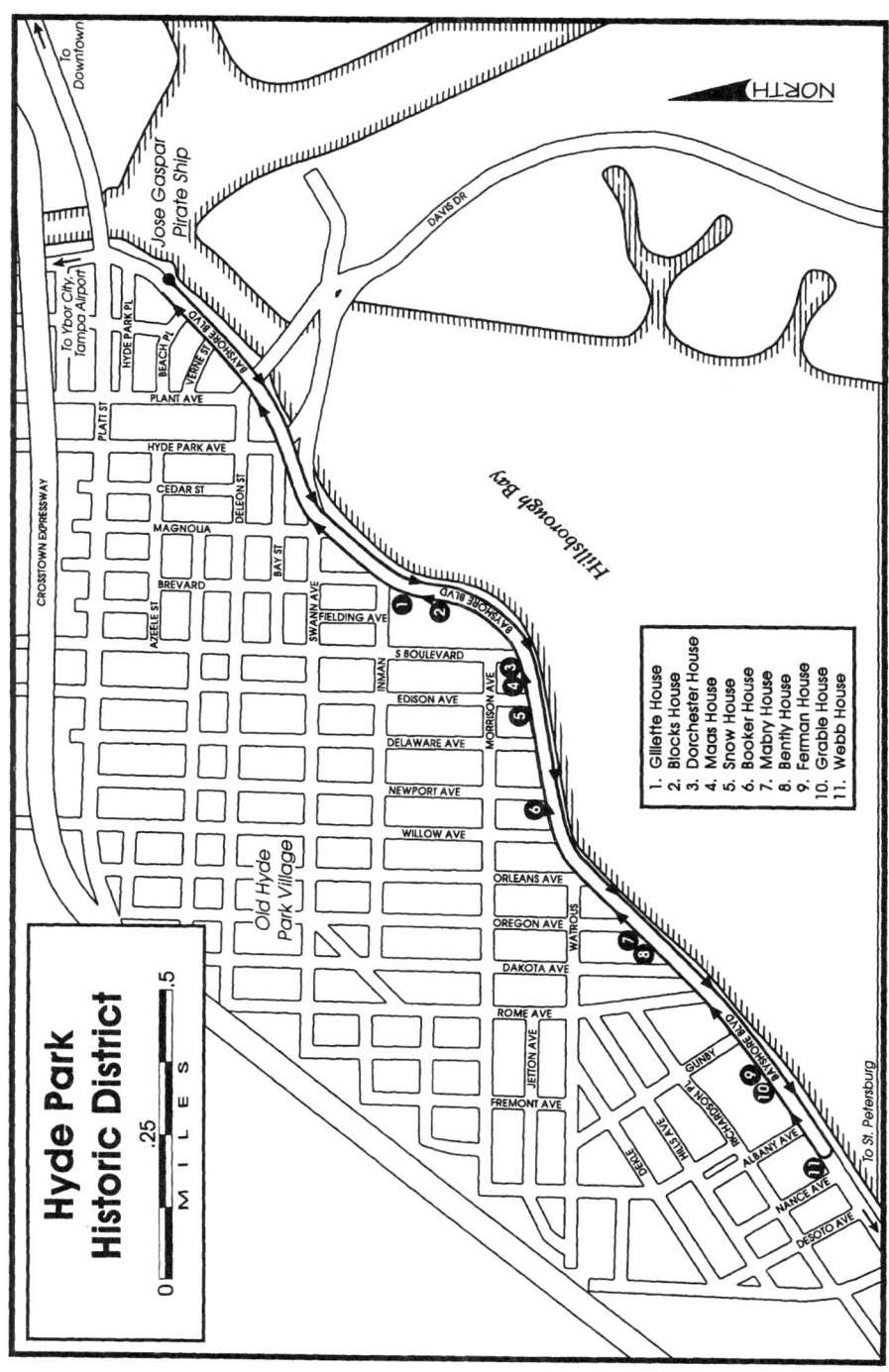

Hyde Park Historic District

MILES

0   .25   .5

1. Gillette House
2. Blocks House
3. Dorchester House
4. Maas House
5. Snow House
6. Booker House
7. Mabry House
8. Bently House
9. Ferman House
10. Grable House
11. Webb House

Walkers, joggers, skaters, and bikers frequent it day and evening. The scenic—and sometimes busy—venue is quite a meeting place for the athletically inclined. Beautiful Bayshore Boulevard was named one of AAA's "Top Roads" for its panoramic view, park-like setting, and architectural features to accommodate motorists, bicyclists, and pedestrians with equal facility.

Information

Tampa-Hillsborough Convention and Visitors Association, 400 N Tampa St, Tampa, FL 33602; 800/44-TAMPA, 813/223-2752; fax 813/229-6616; www.gotampa.com. Tampa Historical Society, 245 S. Hyde Park Ave; 813 /259-1111.

Getting there

Take I-275 or I-4 to I-275 to exit 25 (Tampa St/Ashley Dr), bear left onto Tampa St, then right onto Brorein St over the Hillsborough River, then left onto Bayshore Blvd. Tampa International Airport is about 15 minutes northwest at 5507 Spruce St, at I-275 exit 20. Amtrak's (800/USA RAIL, 813/221-7600) station is at 601 Nebraska Ave N. Greyhound (800/231-2222, 813/229-2112) has a bus station downtown at 610 Polk St.

First steps

For area maps and information, contact the Tampa/Hillsborough Convention & Visitors Association. For historical information, contact the Henry B Plant Museum (813/254-1891, www.plantmuseum.com) at 401 W Kennedy Blvd. It provides wonderful insight into the development of Tampa and its early neighborhoods. Or the Tampa Historical Society, which makes its home in Hyde Park, near Bayshore Boulevard.

Historic Hyde Park and Bayshore Blvd. *This four-mile route covers two miles of Bayshore Boulevard and a return on the same route. Stay on the waterside of the street. You'll get a better view of the bay and of the houses and neighborhood. Be careful—traffic moves very quickly along Bayshore Boulevard.*

There's no parking along Bayshore Boulevard, so do as the local joggers and walkers do and leave your car at the parking lot for the Jose Gaspar pirate ship barge on Bayshore Blvd opposite Hyde Park Place and Beach Place. Begin walking southwest along Bayshore Boulevard. The Gillette House (#819) has had several notable owners. It was constructed in 1916 for D. Collins Gillette, who with his father, developed Temple Terrace, a large community north of downtown. He was president of the Tampa Southern RR, Florida Citrus E-Z Change Exchange Supply Co, and Secretary of the Lucerne Park Fruit Assoc. Dr Louis A. Bize bought it in 1922, gave up his practice and became president of the Citizens-American Bank & Trust Co and the Bank of Ybor City. Later, he headed a syndicate that bought the *Tampa Tribune*.

Hyde Park tongues wagged furiously in 1937 over the **Blocks House** (#829). Residents in the exclusive neighborhood considered the multi-colored house gaudy. A totem pole, "exciting" statues, and variously colored lamps in the garden added to its "charm." Neighbors probably had similar thoughts about its owner, W.L. Blocks, described as "colorful," who ran the steamship terminal bearing his name at the foot of Franklin St.

Dr Watson E. Dorchester, a realtor, was quite the socialite. He was one of the organizers of the Tampa Yacht and Country Club, was a member of the Palma Ceia Golf Club, the Rotary, Board of Trade, Episcopal Church, Masons, Shriners, Odd Fellows, and Knights of Pythias. His namesake home, the **Dorchester House** (#901), was built in 1912. Its odd shape, according to Tampa Preservation, Inc, was caused by the City Council making the good doctor "shave off a portion of the house and porch to conform to setback requirements."

In designing the "Italian style" **Maas House** (#907) in 1924, Tampa architect Franklin O. Adams incorporated a *sgraffitto* frieze and Cretan stone fireplace for Isaac Maas, German immigrant who became General Manager of Maas Brothers Clothiers and Haberdashers. He later served as vice counsel to Belgium.

The Colonial Revival brick and stucco **Snow House** (#1001) was constructed in 1919 for Massachusetts-born Henry E. Snow, president of the Snow & Bryan Co, a wholesale grocer. Snow and his wife Bessie lived there until 1926, when Antonio Santaello, of the A. Santaello & Co cigar manufacturing firm, and his wife Winifred moved in.

The three-story Georgian **Booker House** (#1201) is red bricks painted white and has a two-story porch across the front and a balcony with an iron railing over the front door. It was constructed in 1924 for George V. Booker, president of Booker and Co. An industrious young man, Booker began working as a lineman for the Peninsular Telephone Company at age 14. In 1904 he moved to Jacksonville, where he worked as an electrician, then moved to Lake City and opened an electrical and plumbing supply house. He returned to Tampa in 1907 and opened a lumber business, but there was little new construction. He closed the business and worked with the county tax collector's office until 1913, when he joined a bank. After WWI he returned to Tampa and the bank. A year later he purchased a building supply firm, then established Booker and Co, Inc, which become one of the largest building materials companies in South Florida.

Giddings E. Mabry, president of the law firm of Mabry, Reaves, and Carlton commissioned the Colonial Revival **Mabry House** (#1503) in 1925. He served as city attorney from 1910 to 1913 and county attorney from 1917 to 1923.

The wood frame Mediterranean Revival **Bently House** (#1507) features a stucco exterior and hip roof. It was built in 1924 for Frank Bently. After arriving from Iowa in 1891, he joined the Gulf National Bank. A year later he went into the wholesale grocery business with I.S. Giddens. In 1899 he sold his interest and co-partnered the Bentley-Gray Wholesale Dry Goods Company, the first in South Florida.

William Frederick Ferman arrived in Tampa as a youngster in 1883 and founded Tampa's oldest automobile dealership. A serious bicycle racer, at the age of 21 he opened his first business, the Tampa Cycle and Sporting Good Company in 1895. Four years later he and Victor James constructed the first gasoline-motored automobile ever seen in Tampa. It was made mostly from bicycle parts. Instead of producing cars, he decided to sell them. He opened the first dealership in Tampa in 1902, starting with Oldsmobiles, then later selling Cadillacs, Dodges, and Chevrolets. His brick 1923 Mediterranean Revival **Ferman House** (#1815) served as residence for the presidents of the University of Tampa during the late 1950s.

The Colonial Revival style **Grable House** (#1821) belonged to J.A.M. Grable, who came to Tampa from St Louis with his parents when he was 21 years old. He lived here for 65 years. In 1900 he founded the Tampa Book and News Company.

Cigars were big business in Tampa in the late 19th and early 20th centuries (see Ybor City Walking Tour). Many families became quite prosperous and built houses in Hyde Park. Among them was William I Webb, president of J.M. Martinez and Co, who owned the 1923 Neo-Classical Revival style **Webb House** (#1925). *Return to the start. The interior streets of Hyde Park are lined with more architecturally rich houses.*

Lodging

Accommodations in Tampa are pretty much limited to large chain hotels and motels. There's one exception, a lovely bed-and-breakfast. Prices go up in high season, January to May.

To really appreciate the beauty of the five-room **Behind The Fence Bed and Breakfast Inn** ($$, 813/685-8201), you have to stand behind the fence. Hence, its name. Ever since it was featured in a January 1999 *Country Living* magazine article, travelers have been flocking to the inn, which looks like an old country farmhouse, but actually was built by the owners in the late 1970s out of wood and materials salvaged from 19th-century houses. With the exception of a few 20th-century conveniences—TV, phone, appliances—the decor and atmosphere take you back to the 1800s. It's a delightful place with delightful owners at 1400 Viola Drive at Countryside.

The **Courtyard by Marriott Downtown** ($$–$$$, 800/321-2211, 813/229-1100) is conveniently located across the river from Hyde Park with a restaurant, laundry facilities, health club, and 141 spacious rooms and suites at 902 N Tampa St. One of the best buys in town, especially if you have a family and especially for weekends and holidays (it caters to the business crowd), is the **Sheraton Suites Tampa Airport** ($$$, 813/873-8675) at 4400 W Cypress St. The spacious suites sleep four in two rooms with a mini-kitchen, bar, two televisions and telephones, upholstered furnishings, and French doors looking out over a center courtyard. There's a pool, restaurant, and rooms have hair dryers and irons. One of the closest hotels to Hyde Park is the **Wyndham Harbour Island Hotel** ($$$, 813/229-5000) with 300 rooms near the convention center. There's a pool, boat dock, free breakfast, and oodles of amenities at 725 S Harbour Island Blvd. Budget-conscious travelers can stay 15 minutes away at the **Holiday Inn Express Hotel & Suites Stadium/Airport** ($$, 813/877-6061), which has comfortable, standard rooms, suites, and efficiencies with a gym, in-room coffee, and a pool.

Arts & culture

Tampa's cultural scene earns high marks for its range and quality. There is truly something for everybody.

You can enjoy opera, alternative theater, a Broadway Series, and other performances at the **Tampa Bay Performing Arts Center** (813/229-7827) downtown at 1010 N MacInnes Pl. The Center is also home to the **Spanish Lyric Theater** (813/936-0217), a 40-year-old theatrical group that grew out of the Spanish Club at the University of Tampa in 1959 and now performs both traditional Spanish theater as well as American musicals. **The Florida Orchestra** (813/286-2403) performs classical and pops concerts.

Hyde Park Fine Arts (813/258-8883) specializes in paintings, sculptures, and decorative furnishings by regional artists as well as traveling shows featuring works by international artists at 937 S Howard Ave. **Old Hyde Park Art Center** (813/254-1046) presents monthly exhibits of works in various media created by member artists at 705 Swann Ave. **New Heights Gallery** (813/234-9758) presents works ranging from furniture to paintings to art glass as well as changing exhibitions at 6310 N Nebraska, downtown. North of Hyde Park, the highly regarded **Centre Gallery** (813/974-5464) has changing shows by leading regional artists at the Phyllis P Marshall Center, 4202 E Fowler Ave.

The elegantly restored 1926 **Tampa Theatre** (813/274-8286) presents films, concerts, and special events at 711 Franklin StMall. **Shakespeare In The Park** (813/229-STAR) is a delightful annual outdoor theatrical production at the Curtis Hixon Park downtown on Ashley Street near the Tampa Bay Performing Arts Center.

For Ybor City museums, see the Ybor City Walking Tour. Kids can touch and kids can learn in the **Childrens Museum of Tampa** (813/935-8441) at 7550 North Blvd. Especially interesting is a kid's life-size village, where they can pretend to go to the store and do other everyday things. Admission costs $4 for ages 2 and up.

You can pick and choose your art of interest in the seven galleries plus permanent collection of classical and contemporary art at the **Tampa Museum of Art** (813/274-8130) at 600 N Ashley Dr. Admission for adults is $5, seniors $4, children $3, plus parking.

Take time to see the Tampa history exhibits at the **Henry B Plant Museum** (813/254-1891), a National Historic Landmark at 401 W Kennedy Blvd, University of Tampa, downtown. It's housed in the former Tampa Bay Hotel, a Victorian structure with Moorish-influenced minarets that are visible for miles. Its namesake, transportation magnate Henry Bradley Plant, was instrumental in the development of Tampa and the west coast of Florida.

Even if you grew up hating history, you'll like the way the **Tampa Bay History Center** (813/228-0097) tells the story of the Tampa Bay region through timeline displays, maps, and artifacts as well as rotating exhibits at 225 S Franklin St. Admission is free, but donations are accepted.

There are hundreds of exhibits at the **Museum of Science and Industry** (813/987-6300) at 4801 E Fowler Ave, making it the largest science center in the southeastern United States, and that doesn't even take into account its IMAX Dome Theatre. Admission for adults is $12, seniors $10, children ages 2 to 13 $8.

Borders Books (813/874-5722) has books, speakers, signings, magazines and newspapers at 909 N Dale Mabry.

Food & drink

There's no shortage of fine eateries in Hyde Park and neighboring areas, including downtown. And there's always Ybor City (See Ybor City Walking Tour), about 15 minutes away.

You will think you've died and gone to Paris while dining at **Mise en Place** ($$$, 813/254-5373) at 442 W Kennedy Blvd, Suite 250, an "American Bistro" whose creative French cuisine is oh so good and whose wines-by-the-glass list tops 35 choices. Even with more than 300 seats, there's usually a waiting list at **Bern's Steak House** ($$$, 813/251-2421), a Tampa landmark for more than 40 years at 1208 S Howard Ave. Its reputation was built on well-aged US Prime beef, the largest wine list in the world, one of the best caviar lists in the world, home-grown fresh vegetables and greens, and a 65-page dessert menu. **Armani's** ($$$, 813/281-9165) at 6200 Courtney Campbell Pkwy, in the Hyatt Regency Westshore is right up there with the two aforementioned Tampa culinary stars. Not only do you have the perfect romantic view, but the antipasto, North Italian pasta dishes, desserts, and wine list are also exceptional .

Not only is the Tuscan style cuisine fabulous at **Caffee Firenze** ($$$, 813/228-9200), but the service and Italian atmosphere are remarkable and worth a second trip at 719 N Franklin St, downtown. There's more excellent Italian cuisine at **Donatello** (813/875-6660) at 232 N Dale Mabry, where the elegant setting complements the traditional dishes prepared with a modern, creative touch: linguini with fresh crab and agnolotti with cream and Parmesan, for examples.

Le Bordeaux (813/254-4387) is a French Provençale style bistro with style, flavor, and after dinner music in the lounge at 1502 S Howard Ave.

Take a trip to a European cafe without leaving the city at **Cafe Winberie** ($$, 813/253-6500) in Old Hyde Park Village at 1610 West Swann Ave. While the setting is very, very European, the food is more international, ranging from European to Asian.

Locals might argue that **The Cactus Club** ($$–$$$, 813/251-4089) at 1601 Snow Ave, Old Hyde Park Village serves the best Southwestern food in Florida. It just might. If not the best, then possibly the best in a fun atmosphere. If your partner prefers something north of the border, don't hesitate to order a burger. They're a house specialty.

Nightlife

While you can dance, drink, and listen to music just about anywhere in Tampa, the area's best nightlife is in Ybor City (see Ybor City Walking Tour). Hyde Park Village presents outdoor music, from jazz to reggae, the last Wednesday of every month from June to October.

Downtown Tampa's business crowd meets after hours at **Nickalouie's** at 604 1/2 N Franklin St. There's good Italian food, too, but many folks just go for the bar.

Club 442 at Mise en Place is one of the city's most popular jazz clubs at 442 W Kennedy. **Crawdaddy's** is another jazz club at 2500 Rocky Point Dr.

Sides are splitting with the laughs at **Side Splitters**, a comedy club with national entertainment at 12938 N Dale Mabry.

Events

Approximately 400,000 people attend February's annual two-day **Gasparilla Pirate Festival** (813/353-8108), which has been taking place since 1910 in honor of the mythical legendary pirate Jose Gaspar. There are parades, arts and crafts, entertainment, pirate shows, games, rides, and food. For the past 30 years, the March **Gasparilla Festival of the Arts** (813/876-1747) has showcased the arts, crafts, and fine arts of hundreds of painters, artisans, photographers, sculptors, and jewelers from around the world. At October's **Taste of Florida** (813/259-7376) nearly 50 restaurants and food vendors from the Tampa Bay area prepare and serve delicious food and participate in a chili cook-off. Plus, there's a fireworks show and entertainment.

Ybor City, Tampa

By day, Ybor City is a lively National Historic Landmark District, one of only three in the state of Florida. Tour guides and tour groups shuffle along the streets admiring the collection of 19th-century former cigar factories and other unique buildings that now house eclectic shops, restaurants, and a micro-brewery. By night, visitors change from walking shoes to dancing shoes as Ybor City metamorphoses into the "Nightlife Capital of Florida's West Coast," with about 40,000 people converging on a typical weekend night.

Ybor City is one of several neighborhoods that grew up in Tampa once Henry Bradley Plant, a Connecticut businessman, brought railroad and shipping lines into the town in 1884 and opened his elegant Tampa Bay Hotel, now the University of Tampa.

Don Vincente Martinez Ybor and Ignacio Haya were among those who took an interest in Plant's new transportation system. They were looking for a new location for their Key West and New York cigar factories, respectively, which were experiencing serious labor strikes. Tampa would be ideal. There was plenty of fresh water, the humid climate was conducive to cigar making, the tobacco could be shipped from Cuba to Tampa, and the finished cigars could be sent by train to New York.

In 1885 Ybor purchased 40 acres near the harbor and rail lines on the northeast edge of Tampa and began hiring workers and constructing a factory town. Thus, Ybor City was founded. At its peak, there were 200 cigar factories with 12,000 cigar makers producing an estimated 700 million cigars a year. Women and even children worked in cigar factories.

The city was a melting pot of cultures that worked in harmony. Spaniards from Asturias and Galicia ran the factories. White and black Cubans rolled the cigars. Germans designed the stylish lithographic labels for the cigar boxes. Italian immigrants from Sicily opened grocery stores. And Jews from Romania set up stores and banks.

Each of these groups formed mutual aid societies and built clubhouses—some of which still exist—to help new immigrants adjust, provide medical assistance and affordable burial services, and serve as a place to socialize. The Spanish developed El Centro Español and El Centro Asturiano. White Cubans joined El Circulo Cubano. Cubans of African ancestry started Sociedad La Union Marti-Maceo. The Italians established L'Unione Italiana and the Germans formed the German-American Club.

In the century's last decade, Cuban patriots, particularly José Martí, often visited Tampa to raise money and morale for Cuba's independence from Spain. It is believed that he ordered the invasion of Cuba by smuggling a message in a cigar.

Ybor City's cigar industry began to decline in the 1930s with the advent of machine-made cigars, the Depression, and Prohibition. The district began to decay, too. Urban renewal and Interstate 4 threw the final punches, leveling eight blocks and destroying 600 houses and businesses in the 1960s. That's when preservationists intent on retaining the unique multicultural heritage stepped in to preserve this important neighborhood. The results have been spectacular. Since 1990, a few small cigar shops are again rolling cigars for profit and almost 200 new restaurants, shops, galleries, nightclubs, and other businesses have opened, making Ybor City once again the showcase of Tampa.

Information

Ybor City Chamber of Commerce, 1800 E Ninth Ave, Tampa, FL 33605; 813/248-3712; fax 813/247-1764; info@ybor.org; www.ybor.org. Tampa-Hillsborough Convention and Visitors Association, 400 N Tampa St, Tampa, FL 33602; 800/44-TAMPA or 813/223-2752; fax 813/229-6616; www.thcvacom.

Getting there

Take I-275 to I-4 to Ybor City exit 2, go south on 21st St to Seventh Ave, which is the main street through the historic district. Tampa International Airport is about 15 minutes west at 5507 Spruce St, at I-275 exit 20. Amtrak's (800/USA RAIL, 813/221-7600) station is at 601 Nebraska Ave N. Greyhound (800/231-2222, 813/229-2112) has a station downtown at 610 Polk St.

First steps

Stop at the **Ybor City Chamber of Commerce**, located in a renovated "cigar maker's" house, for maps and information. Or visit the **Tampa-Hillsborough Convention and Visitors Association**. Just as in the old days, a trolley (free) connects Ybor City to downtown Tampa and a few major attractions such as the Henry B Plant Museum. Refurbished electric street cars that once plied the historic districts streets are scheduled to return by 2000.

The 128-page *Images of America: Ybor City* by AM de Quesada captures Ybor City's rich heritage through photographs and captions. For the latest happenings around town, pick up a free copy of the *Weekly Planet*. The *Tampa Tribune* is the local daily.

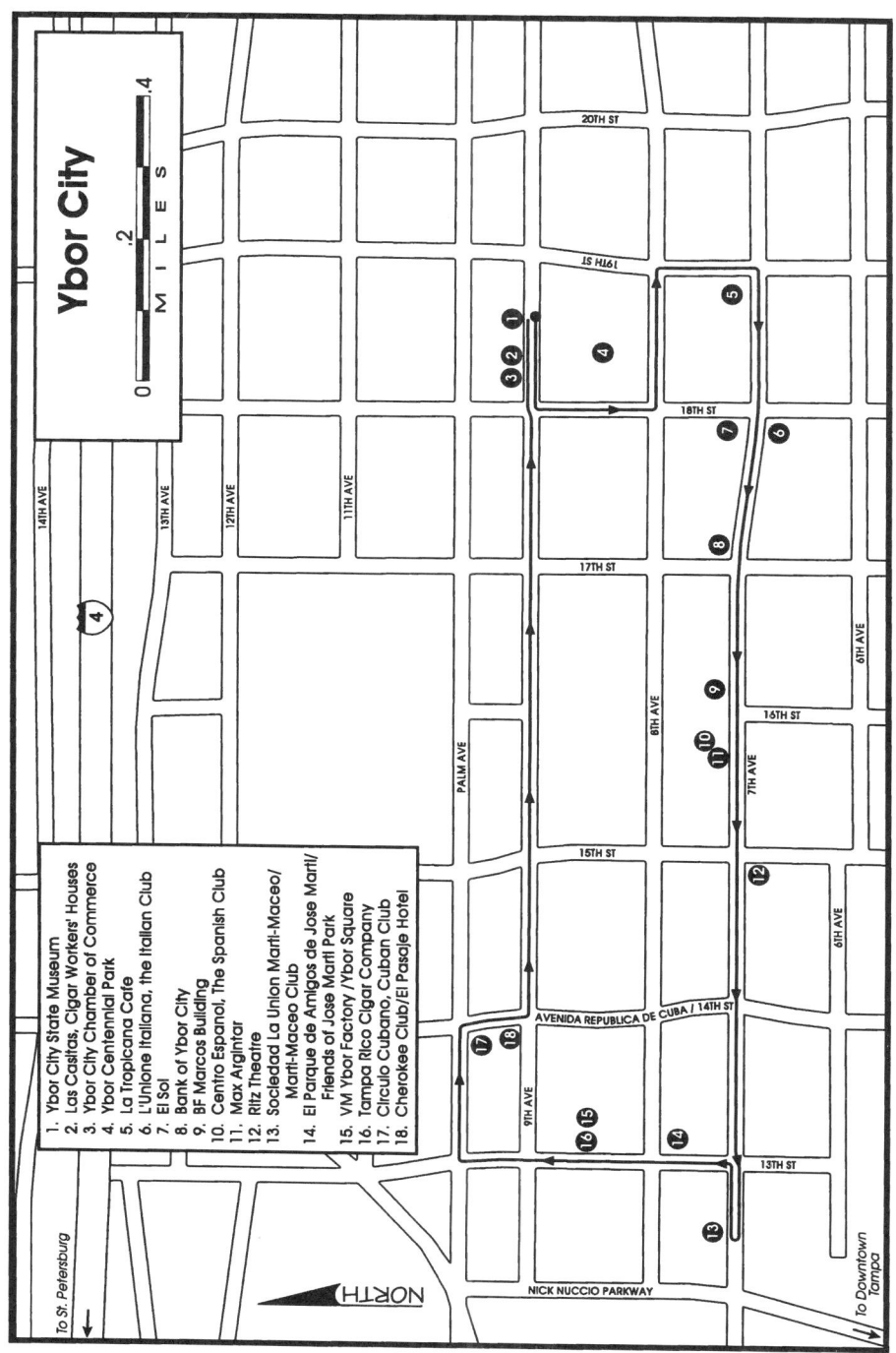

Ybor City

MILES

0   .2   .4

NORTH

Legend:
1. Ybor City State Museum
2. Las Casitas, Cigar Workers' Houses
3. Ybor City Chamber of Commerce
4. Ybor Centennial Park
5. La Tropicana Cafe
6. L'Unione Italiana, the Italian Club
7. El Sol
8. Bank of Ybor City
9. BF Marcos Building
10. Centro Espanol, The Spanish Club
11. Max Argintar
12. Ritz Theatre
13. Socledad La Union Marti-Maceo/
    Marti-Maceo Club
14. El Parque de Amigos de Jose Marti/
    Friends of Jose Marti Park
15. VM Ybor Factory /Ybor Square
16. Tampa Rico Cigar Company
17. Circulo Cubano, Cuban Club
18. Cherokee Club/El Pasaje Hotel

To St. Petersburg
To Downtown Tampa

20TH ST
19TH ST
18TH ST
17TH ST
16TH ST
15TH ST
13TH ST

14TH AVE
13TH AVE
12TH AVE
11TH AVE
8TH AVE
7TH AVE
6TH AVE
9TH AVE

PALM AVE

AVENIDA REPUBLICA DE CUBA / 14TH ST

NICK NUCCIO PARKWAY

Walking tours

Stretch your legs and learn about the city's spicy history and architecture on the actor-led 90-minute **Ybor City Ghost Walk** (813/242-9255). It departs at 6 pm from Joffrey's Coffee Company (1616 E 7th Ave) Thursday to Sunday ($12.50, $10 in advance).

For a more serious take on the city's history, the 60-minute **Ybor City Walking Tour** (813/247-1434) begins at the Ybor City State Museum (1818 E Ninth Ave) at 10:30 am Thursday and Saturday, except May to September only on Saturday ($4).

Tours of the **Ybor City Brewing Company** (813/242-9222), home of Ybor Gold, are given Tuesday to Saturday between 11 am and 3 pm at 2205 N 20th St ($2).

Historic Ybor City. *This 1.5-mile route covers the major landmarks in Ybor City. Allow one hour. However, a more leisurely trip of two or three hours will allow you to shop, visit the museum, and explore one or two of the social clubs.*

Begin at the Ybor City State Museum. The **Ybor City State Museum** (1818 E 9th Ave) gives a fascinating look at the history of Ybor City, tobacco, the cigar-making process, and the people who worked there. It is housed in the Ferlita Bakery building, which baked bread for the town from 1896 until 1973. Every morning boys delivered the long, slender loaves of bread throughout the town, hanging the loaves on a nail next to each front door. Outside in the courtyard is a bust of Don Vincente Martinez Ybor. There are also restrooms, a fountain and garden, and places to rest. Admission costs $2 just for the museum, $4 for a 90-minute walking tour and the museum. *Leave the museum and walk to the first house on the right.*

Las Casitas, Cigar Workers' Houses, (1800 E 9th Ave) are six relocated and renovated late 19th-century shotgun-style houses where cigar workers lived. The one-story wood-frame houses are built on brick pilings and have a porch and balustrade. One of the *casitas* (Spanish for little house) has been furnished to recreate a typical worker's home in 1895. *Turn left onto 18th St, left onto 8th Ave, right onto 19th St, then right onto 7th Ave, also known as La Septima (Spanish for the seventh).*

Seventh Avenue always has been Ybor City's main street. Major businesses were here and streetcars plied the wide street. The green space you've walked around is **Ybor Centennial Park** (between 9th and 8th Ave, 18th and 19th St), dedicated in 1986 for the district's 100th anniversary. Among the memorials in the park are the Immigrant Statue, honoring the immigrant families of Ybor City, and a statue of Anthony "Tony" Pizzo, an historian and businessman, who was born in this block, founded the

Tampa Historical Society, Ybor City Rotary Club and other civic organizations, and wrote a book about everyday living in Ybor City.

La Tropicana Cafe (1822 E 7th Ave) is hardly a distinguished building inside or outside, but it was here that Roland Manteigo, the publisher of the weekly *La Gaceta*, the only tri-lingual—English, Spanish, and Italian—newspaper in the United States, came to eat and hold court at a private corner table with a telephone. The newspaper is still published by his son. *Continue across 18th St.*

L'Unione Italiana, The Italian Club, (1731 E 7th Ave) was the heart and soul of immigrant Italian life in Ybor City during the cigar-making heyday. Formed in 1894 as a mutual aid society, in 1914 members constructed a clubhouse, which burned and was reconstructed in 1918 in an elaborate Neo-Classical style with a 500-seat theater, medical clinic, ballroom, bar, and lavish marble staircase. Still active today, it serves as a gathering place for about 500 members and offers language classes, Italian films, and cultural events. Visitors are welcome to come in to see the beautiful building.

Across the street is El Sol (1728 E 7th Ave), Ybor City's oldest cigar store. They still roll cigars by hand. At the end of the block on the right is the two-story brick Bank of Ybor City building (1702–1706 E 7th Ave), constructed in 1905 and used as a bank for 50 years. In the next block, part of the BF Marcos Building (1610–1612 E 7th Ave) is still in use for retail stores as it when it was built in 1908. Back then, the second floor had residences.

When Centro Español, The Spanish Club, (1526–1536 E 7th Ave) received its charter in September 1891, it became the first immigrant mutual aid society. In return for their $1.50 a month dues, members, who had to be born in Spain or be loyal to Spain, received social and recreational benefits and medical coverage. Their building was erected in 1912. It had a cantina, bar, and theater for stage productions, operas, and movies. The club also maintained its own hospital, which closed in the 1960s. A radical faction split in 1902 and formed the Centro Asturiano (1913 Nebraska Ave). The state purchased Centro Español and is restoring it. Next door the Max Argintar (1522 E 7th Ave) men's store was established in 1908.

The Ritz Theatre (southwest corner of 7th Ave and 15th St) opened in 1917 as one of Florida's early movie houses with elaborate decoration inside and out. Today it houses a nightclub. *Cross 13th St and walk half way up the block.*

Halfway up the next block on the right is the **Sociedad La Union Marti-Maceo, Marti-Maceo Club**, (1226 E 7th Ave). The club's original building met the wrecking ball in 1965, so members moved to this former union hall, where 10 years earlier, in December 1955, Fidel Castro had given a speech to a large crowd, exclaiming, "My movement will end only when tyranny is dead or we are dead." *Return to 13th St and turn right.*

Created in the 1950s with funds from Cuban President Fulgencio Batista and others, **El Parque de Amigos de José Martí, Friends of José Martí Park**, (southeast corner of 13th St and 8th Ave) was established on the site of the former home of Paulina and Ruperto Pedroso, friends and hosts of Cuban patriot José Martí. The property was deeded to the government of Cuba and remains free Cuban soil. *Continue to the next block.*

VM Ybor Factory/Ybor Square (1912 Avenida Republica de Cuba, aka 14th St) was laid out in an east to west orientation, so that the selector could sit by a north-facing window where the lighting was best for selecting the cigars' outer wrappers. *El lector*, the reader, entertained and educated the workers by reading material selected by cigar workers who paid for the service. Eventually, they were eliminated because factory owners felt that their readings of philosophical, social, and political books and articles incited workers to labor unrest. In 1893 José Martí spoke to members and supporters of the Cuban Revolutionary Party on the factory steps. An historical plaque marks the spot. Today, the factory contains shops, restaurants, and offices. Among the businesses in Ybor Square is the **Tampa Rico Cigar Company** (1901 N 13th St), which has been hand rolling cigars for more than 50 years. *Turn right onto Palm Ave, then right onto Avenida Republica de Cuba, aka 14th St.*

Circulo Cubano, Cuban Club, (2010 Avenida Republica de Cuba, aka 14th St) formed in 1902 with the charter, "to bind all Cuban residents of Tampa into a fraternal group, to offer assistance and help the sick." Its original building burned in 1916 and was rebuilt as this four-story yellow-brick Beaux-Arts beauty with a stained-glass seal above the main entrance, a theater, pharmacy, library, outdoor patio, cantina, gym, and ballroom with a lavishly decorated ceiling. The architects, Bonfoey and Elliot, designed most of the city's club buildings.

Ybor City's prominent businessmen and cigar factory owners formed a gentlemen's club called the **Cherokee Club** (1318 E 9th Ave) in 1888. They met there to play cards and socialize, among other activities. Later, they built the luxurious **El Pasaje Hotel** to house their club and accommodations for important visitors. Today, it contains offices and the popular

Cafe Creole Restaurant. *Turn left onto 9th Ave and return to the Ybor City State Museum.*

Lodging

Ybor City welcomed its first hotel in May of 1999. It's the only accommodation in the historic district, but there are many within an easy two- to five-mile drive. Tampa's hotels cater to the business crowd; motels to families planning visits to nearby Busch Gardens, the zoo, and other attractions. The closest bed and breakfasts or small inns are across the bay in St Petersburg. Prices are higher in winter.

Occupying the catbird seat in Ybor City is the new 95-room **Hilton Garden Inn** ($$, 813/769-9267) with a pool, exercise room, self laundry, complimentary business services and parking, a breakfast cafe, and lots of in-room amenities at 1700 E 9th Ave.

Located an easy two miles from Ybor City, **Days Inn Eastgate** ($–$$, 800/523-7513, 813/247-3300) at 2520 N 50th St features a lush tropical courtyard and pool, simply furnished rooms, and a lounge. On a much grander scale and also two miles away is the **Hyatt Regency Tampa** ($$$$, 800/233-1234, 813-225-1234) at 2 Tampa City Center with 521 plushly decorated rooms on 17 floors, a heated pool, two restaurants, and a lounge. Newly refurbished rooms with good lighting, recliners, and dataports on oversized desks, as well as free breakfast and phone calls make **La Quinta Inn East/State Fair** ($$, 800/687-6667, 813/623-3591) an attractive choice at 2904 Melbourne Blvd, about two miles away. Another moderately priced alternative about the same distance from Ybor City is the **Milner Hotel** ($$, 800/237-1510, 813/621-2081) with standard rooms, a heated pool and whirlpool, restaurant overlooking the pool courtyard, and a laundry room at 2708 N 50th St. Guests wanting a bit more room can choose **Sumner Suites** ($$, 800/747-8483, 813/622-8557), whose rooms have a small refrigerator and microwave, and coffee maker at 10007 Princess Palm Ave.

The historic waterfront Queen Anne **Bayboro House Bed & Breakfast** ($$–$$$, 813/823-4955) at 1719 Beach Dr SE, St Petersburg features a wrap-around verandah, pool and spa, expanded continental breakfast, complimentary wine and soft drinks, morning paper delivered to your door, plus antique-furnished rooms with a private bath, color TV, VCR & movies. Not to be confused with the former is the very comfortable **Bayboro Inn and Hunt Room** ($$–$$$, 727/823-0498) at 357 3rd St S, St Petersburg. Built in 1914 and an inn since the 1940s, this historic house has six well-appointed rooms with private baths. Breakfast is an event here, as can be socializing in one of the common areas in front of the fireplace. The **Mansion House**'s ($$–$$$, 800/274-7520 or 813/821-9391) six rooms are divided between two mirror image houses built in 1904 for a noted physician and his wife at 105 5th Ave NE, St Petersburg. Rooms are decorated in eclectic furniture collected from around the world. Hand-made bedding, guest robes, a pool, wine and cheese in the fridge, rich wood, and pastel colors make it a very pleasant place to stay.

Arts & culture

Visitors looking for art galleries, performing arts, museums, and bookstores will find more options in downtown Tampa.

Ybor City has two significant cultural attractions. **Historical Hand Painted Tile** (813/247-6817), a custom tile studio, produces hand-painted tiles reflecting the Mediterranean heritage of the district, at 2104 E 7th Ave. The **Oscar Trevino Spanish Dance Company** performs two to three 45-minute shows nightly except Sunday at the **Columbia Restaurant** (813/248-3000) at 2025 E 7th Ave.

Food & drink

There are many good dining choices in Ybor City. You can dig into a steamy paella, linger over a spicy jambalaya, or savor creative American cuisine. Even the most conservative budgets can enjoy good food in Ybor City.

Choose from a menu of Italian, Spanish, and American selections at **Carmine's** ($–$$, 813/248-3834) at 1802 7th Ave E. **Little Sicily** ($, 813/248-2940) is a good bet for a quick calzone or other Italian specialty at 1724 8th Ave E. **La Tropicana Cafe** ($, 813/247-4040), a large, plain, noisy room, is a gathering place at 1822 E. 7th Ave. It serves typical Cuban fare like toast, pastries, and high-octane Cuban coffee for breakfast, as well as black beans and rice, Spanish bean soup, Cuban sandwiches, and sweet, flavorful guava pastries.

Since 1905 the **Columbia Restaurant** ($$$, 813/248-3000) at 2117 E 7th Ave has been a favorite landmark restaurant specializing in savory Spanish cuisine. Adding to the fine, though pricey dining, is an opulent setting of antiques, wrought iron gates, and hundreds of hand-painted tiles depicting Don Quixote's world. Go for the superb Louisiana oysters, gumbo, crawfish, and andouille at **Cafe Creole** ($$–$$$, 813/247-6283)at 1330 9th Ave E, then if it's the weekend, stay for the live jazz entertainment. While the sushi and sashimi at **Sushi on Seventh** ($$–$$$, 813/247-8744) at 1919 E 7th Ave is some of the finest in the county, those who are less adventurous can enjoy well-prepared Asian-influenced seafood and steaks. At **Atomic Age Cafe & Lounge** ($$, 813/247-6547) at 1518 E Seventh Ave vegetarians, carnivores, and those in between will be satisfied with the eclectic menu of everything from big, juicy hamburgers to pad Thai noodles. The cocktail bar is worth a stop if you aren't hungry. The artistic setting and live acoustical music at **Ovo Cafe** ($$–$$$, 813/248-6979) at 1901 East 7th Ave, located next to an art gallery make this bistro-style restaurant popular with the artsy crowd.

Nightlife

Ybor City exudes a high-level of nocturnal energy. Its nightlife—the best in Tampa—starts early and ends late at jazz, blues, dance, alternative, new wave, and country clubs, as well as coffeehouses. Seventh Avenue is the hot spot, with a few exceptions on side streets.

Blues Ship Cafe on Top takes its name from its blues shows and second-floor location at 1910 E 7th Ave. There's a gospel Sunday supper featuring live gospel music and delicious food. Similarly, the **Jazz Cellar** is in a basement and has live jazz nightly at 1916 N 14th St. **Empire** blasts the latest in house, techno, hip-hop, and booty music under a dazzling color laser and three moving light systems at 1902 E 7th Ave. The motto at the popular **Green Iguana** is "It's not jungle music, it's music in the jungle," referring to its live entertainment and tropical ambiance at 1708 E 7th Ave. **The Masquerade**, with Ybor City's largest dance floor, pumps out the hottest dance sounds, and has touring acts at 1503 E 7th Ave. At the **Rare Olive** at 1601 E. 7th Ave a trendy clientele sips martinis with exotic names, puffs on expensive cigars, and listens to live entertainment. Ybor City has its share of java joints too, such as **El Molino Coffee Shop**, which serves Cuban and international coffees at 2012 E 7th Ave, and **Joffrey's Coffee Co**, which along with Joe has desserts, a smoothie, and very, very late night hours Wednesday to Saturday.

Events

Ybor City has a toll-free events hotline, 877/9FIESTA.

Ybor City's biggest event is February's **Fiesta Day**, which celebrates the historic district's multicultural heritage with live entertainment, children's activities, guava treats, and a guava cooking contest, and an International Parade of Flags. At the end of October, the district revels with Guavaween (813/621-7121), a zany tropical Halloween street festival. November's **Ybor Art Walk** (813/248-3712) brings thousands of people to the district to view and purchase arts and crafts from regional and national vendors.

Sarasota

When it comes to culture in Florida, this elegant town is in a class by itself. You need two hands to count the theaters and more than all of your fingers and toes to count the galleries. Yet the city has only 60,000 year-round residents. The arts and, to a lesser degree, the white sand beaches, double Sarasota's population each winter with well-heeled Snow Birds and visitors.

Like other Florida cities, Sarasota boomed in the 1920s. Many of that era's buildings have been renovated and now are personal homes and home to theaters, restaurants, galleries, and museums. The city, a little less than halfway from Tampa to Fort Myers on Florida's west coast, forms a crescent around Sarasota Bay. A short causeway away from the mainland is a chain of barrier islands developed with more upscale shops, resorts, and restaurants.

Native Americans fished and hunted in the forests, bays, and rivers of Sarasota, then disappeared after the arrival of European explorers and settlers. Seminoles, Native Americans from Georgia and the Carolinas, moved south into the abandoned areas. Fish camps run by American and Cuban Americans to export fish and turtles began appearing along Sarasota Bay around 1825. A few years later, the US Army established Fort Armistead at one of the camps. Settlers with enslaved African workers started arriving to set up cattle ranches in the 1840s. Soon after, the Seminoles were forced to move west to Oklahoma.

Sarasota's population remained sparse until the 1880s, when the town was surveyed and affluent Scottish families arrived by steamer. These aristocratic pioneers defined Sarasota's style.

Enter John Ringling, the show biz tycoon who invested in the town and upped the level of sophistication in the 1910s by erecting palaces, bringing in artisans, art, and like-minded investors, and building the causeway. By the time the 1920s land boom came around, the city was already a major cultural winter resort. Roads, railroads, and in the 1940s, the war, brought thousands more. The WPA gave the city a major boost with the construction of the Lido Casino, post office, and airport.

Historic preservation got underway in the mid-1970s and continues enthusiastically. Unfortunately, several important buildings were destroyed, including some of the most prominent hotels and casinos.

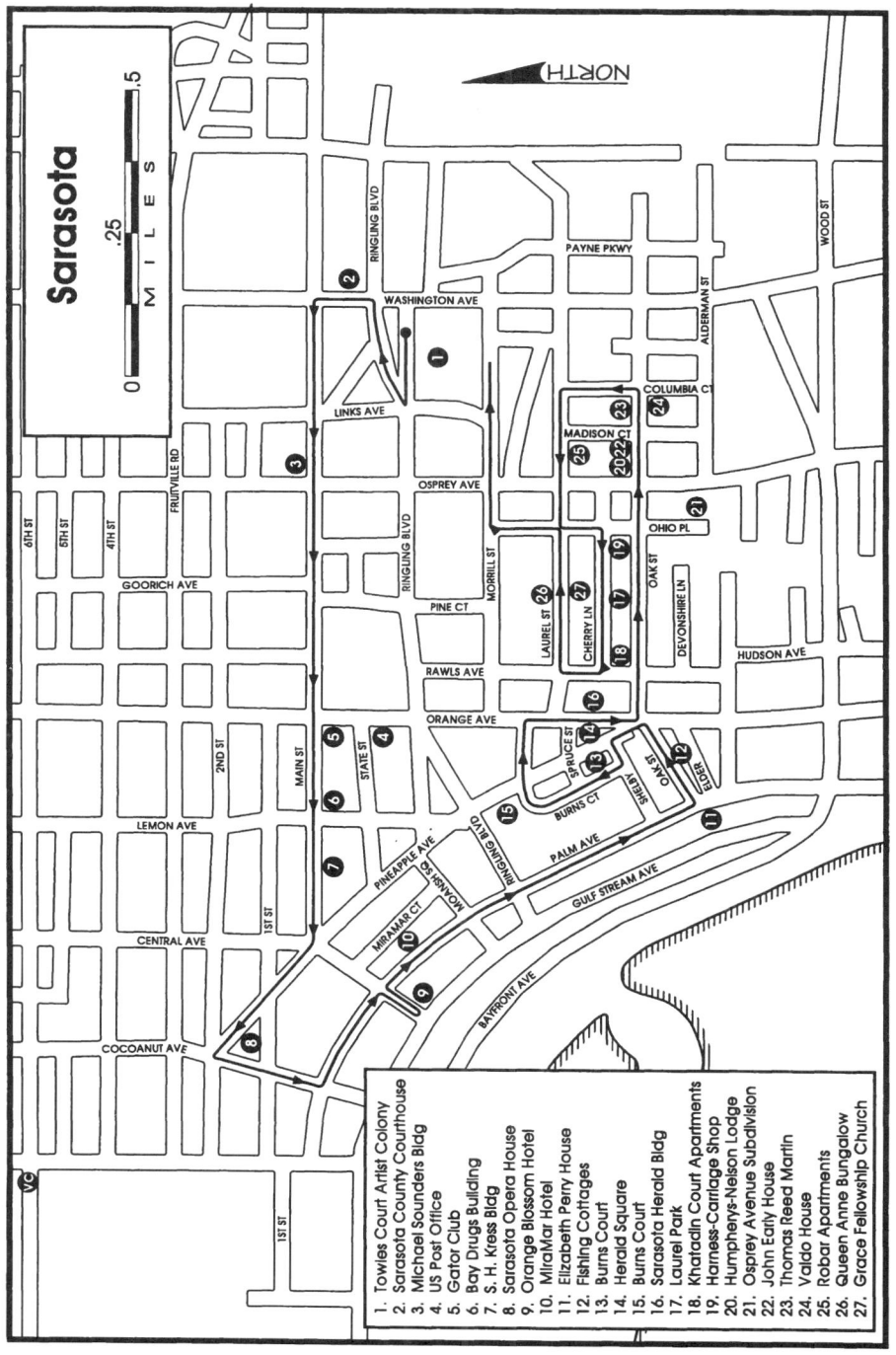

Sarasota

MILES

0   .25   .5

NORTH

1. Towles Court Artist Colony
2. Sarasota County Courthouse
3. Michael Saunders Bldg
4. US Post Office
5. Gator Club
6. Bay Drugs Building
7. S. H. Kress Bldg
8. Sarasota Opera House
9. Orange Blossom Hotel
10. MiraMar Hotel
11. Elizabeth Perry House
12. Fishing Cottages
13. Burns Court
14. Herald Square
15. Burns Court
16. Sarasota Herald Bldg
17. Laurel Park
18. Khatadin Court Apartments
19. Harness-Carriage Shop
20. Humpherys-Nelson Lodge
21. Osprey Avenue Subdivision
22. John Early House
23. Thomas Reed Martin
24. Valdo House
25. Robar Apartments
26. Queen Anne Bungalow
27. Grace Fellowship Church

Information
Sarasota Convention & Visitors Bureau, 655 N Tamiami Trail, Sarasota, FL 34236; 941/957-1877; www.sarasotafl.org. The Sarasota County Department of Historical Resources, 701 Plaza de Santo Domingo, Sarasota, FL 34235; 941/316-1115, provides information on history and preservation of Sarasota. Sarasota Alliance for Historic Preservation, 941/953-8727.

Getting there
Sarasota Bradenton International Airport (941/359-5200, www.srq-airport.com) offers jet and commuter service at 6000 Airport Circle on the north end of Sarasota.

Greyhound (800/231-2222, 941/955-5735) operates from 575 N Washington Blvd. Amtrak (800/USA RAIL) offers connecting bus service departing from 1995 Main St to Orlando for trains north and south.

Sarasota is a few miles west of exit 39 on I-75 for travelers coming from the north, south, and Miami/Fort Lauderdale. Visitors coming from the east can take Hwy 70 from Fort Pierce or any cross-state highway that connects to I-75.

First steps
For maps and information, contact the Sarasota Convention & Visitors Bureau. It's open Monday to Saturday 9 am to 5 pm, Sunday 11 am to 3 pm. Contact the Sarasota Alliance for Historic Preservation for information about other historic districts. Author Jeff LaHurd has three books that provide insight into Sarasota through words and pictures: Sarasota Then and Now, Quintessential Sarasota: Stories and Pictures From the 1920s–1950s, and Sarasota...A Sentimental Journey. To learn more about the local architecture, read Sarasota School of Architecture by John Howey.

Walking tours
Sarasota Alliance for Historic Preservation (941/953-8727) offers an annual tour ($10) of five historic houses in February. The 2000 tour will focus on Five Decades of Building in the 1900s.At press time, Towles Court Artist Colony (941/362-0960, 941/955-0050) was organizing a two-hour walking tour that would include lunch ($20-$25) one Saturday a month.

Historic Sarasota. *This 4.25-mile route covers historic downtown, commercial, and residential communities. Allot 3–4 hours for a leisurely trip with a stop for lunch at a cafe.*

Begin at Towles Court Artist Colony. If you want to see what Florida artists are doing, look at Towles Court Artist Colony (1945 Morrill St), made up of almost 30 galleries, studios, and a restaurant in a charming restored

1920s subdivision of bungalow-style cottages for winter visitors, built by Chicago busniessman William B. Towles. *Go west on Adams Lane, right onto Links Ave, then right onto Ringling Blvd and left onto Hwy 301.*

The **Sarasota County Courthouse** (2000 Main St) was designed by architect Dwight Baum and in its day was described as "the most beautiful building south of Washington DC." *Turn left onto Main St.*

The **Michael Saunders Bldg** (1801 Main St) was formerly the Saprito Bros Fruit Company. *Cross Orange Avenue and look south toward the* former **US Post Office** (111 S Orange) built in a Classic Revival style in 1934 by nationally known architect George Albee Freeman and now housing Federal offices.

Originally built in 1912 as a grocery store for William Worth, the **Gator Club** (1490 Main St) was also a brothel and other businesses before becoming a popular nightclub. The landmark **Bay Drugs Building** (SE corner Lemon Ave and Main St) opened in 1940 with fluorescent lighting. Now it's a Burger King. In the next block, the Art Deco **S.H. Kress Bldg** (1442 Main) remains as beautiful as it was when it was constructed in 1932. *Turn right onto Pineapple Ave.*

The **Sarasota Opera House** (61 N Pineapple Ave) was once the Edwards Theater, which opened in 1926 showing the film *Skinner's Dress Suit.* The $350,000 theater had seats for 1,500, an organ, and two large fans. It later became the Florida Theater, a movie house. Fittingly, in 1952 it served as the set for the movie *The Greatest Show on Earth*, which upon completion made its world premier in the theater. *Turn left onto Coconut Ave.*

Along with theaters, this district has many art galleries. *Turn left onto Palm Ave. At Main St detour right.*

The **Orange Blossom Hotel** (Main St between Gulfstream Ave and Palm Ave) started as the DeSoto Hotel for "people of wealth and influence" in 1887. During the 1920s land boom, it was demolished and replaced by the American National Bank, which went bankrupt, and has served as a hotel and apartment since then. *Return to Palm Ave and turn right.*

Scottish-born, Chicago-raised developer Andrew McAnsh completed the lovely Mediterranean Revival **MiraMar Hotel** (Palm Ave between Main St and McAnsh) in 1924 to fulfill Sarasota's need for a "modern" hotel. It contained hotel rooms and apartments, a 1,200-seat auditorium that was completed in just 60 days, formal gardens, and an upstairs casino that was off limits to locals. Today, it has been considerably altered and now houses upscale shops, galleries, and restaurants. The **Elizabeth Perry**

House (624 Palm) was built in 1924. Next door is the back entrance to The Cypress, an historic bed and breakfast. *Turn left onto Oak St.*

Judge J.D. Chapline, an early mayor and judge in Sarasota, built the Fishing Cottages (1500 block) for winter tourists and sportsmen. *Turn left onto Orange Ave, which immediately divides at what's called Little Five Points. Take the left fork, which becomes Pineapple Ave.*

This is the heart of historic Burns Court, on the left, an early subdivision, and Herald Square, on the right, both built by Owen Burns during the 1920s. Many of the 15 identical, original Mediterranean Revival single-family houses with garages remain well-preserved and contain unique shops, galleries, and restaurants. *Turn left onto Selby Lane, then right onto Burns Court.*

Burns Court curves right at the USG Building (330 S Pineapple), formerly the US Garage built by Calvin Payne and W.L. Pearsall in 1924 to provide automobile storage for seasonal visitors. Today, it's an architectural firm. *Turn right onto Pineapple Ave. Turn left onto Orange Ave for a short detour.*

On the right is the Sarasota Herald Building (539 S Orange), the original home of the *Sarasota Herald* newspaper. The first paper rolled off the presses on October 4, 1925. *Return to Oak St and turn left.*

The neighborhood east of Burns Court and Herald Square is called Laurel Park. The large number of restored Mission, Mediterranean Revival, and Craftsman Bungalow cottages and apartments from the 1920s and 1930s makes it a pleasant neighborhood to stroll.

On the left is the Khatadin Court Apartments (637 Oak), built in 1925 by Logan & Currin Contractors. A few doors down is the old Harness-Carriage Shop (1739) built in 1914 to supply and service buggies, carriages, and early automobiles. On the corner of Osprey is the Humphreys-Nelson Lodge (555 S Osprey), moved to this location in 1935 by Irving Nelson, a circus strongman. To the right, the Osprey Avenue Subdivision (659 Ohio) was developed by the Land & Broker Baxter Company in 1914 with the slogan "Closer, Cheaper, Dryer, Better." The John Early House (1841 Oak) was built in 1925, then moved here 10 years later by John Early, a mayor, judge, and state representative.

In 1925 architect Thomas Reed Martin designed and Owen Burns built the namesake house (1855 Oak). Martin, who designed more than 500 buildings in the United States from 1910 to 1949, is known as the "father of Sarasota architecture." Pat Valdo, general manager of the Ringling Brothers Barnum & Bailey Circus, lived across the street in the Valdo House (1922 Oak), built in 1925 and moved here 10 years later.

Turn left onto Columbia Ct, then left onto Laurel St.
Mr Roades and Mr Bar, real estate speculators during the 1920s, lent their names to the **Robar Apartments** (1836 Laurel). *Turn left onto Ohio Pl, right onto Cherry Lane, right onto Rawls Ave, then right onto Laurel St.*
The 1600-block of Laurel Street has wonderful architecture, including a **Queen Anne bungalow** (1677 Laurel) that was built in 1890 on Gulfstream Ave and moved here during the 1920s, and the Mission style **Grace Fellowship Church** (1702 Laurel) with polychromatic tiles above the windows. It was built by Sarasota's first Seventh Day Adventist congregation in 1926. *Turn left onto Ohio Pl, right onto Morrill St. Cross Links Ave to return to Towles Court.*

Lodging

For such a sophisticated city, the variety of accommodations is surprisingly limited. Most of the offerings are chain hotels, motels, and resorts and mom-and-pop motels either along the bay or on the barrier islands.

The Cypress Bed & Breakfast Inn's ($$$–$$$$, 941/955-4683) three intriguing owners, a former New York photographer and two teachers, totally pamper their guests with a five-course breakfast, concierge and services, evening cocktails with hors d'oeuvres, turn-down service with fresh-baked cookies, fresh flowers, and chilled beverages in the fridge. It's a wonderfully elegant, yet comfortable, five guestroom B&B in a 1940s-era house made of pond cypress at 621 S Gulfstream Ave, downtown.

The **Crescent House Bed & Breakfast** ($$–$$$$, 941/346-0857), a restored 1914 weathered beachhouse on quiet Siesta Key, is across the street from the beach. Pastel-colored walls with white trim, polished hardwood floors, bright upholstered furniture, ceiling fans, and antiques give the room a bright, light, airy feel. It has a deck, spa, and lots of personality at 459 Beach Rd. Breakfast is expanded continental.

Other downtown properties include the **Hyatt Sarasota** ($$$$, 941/953-1234) with restaurants, a pool, health club, recreation, and lots of amenities in more than 300 rooms and suites, many of which have a balcony overlooking Sarasota Bay at 1000 Blvd of the Arts. The **Holiday Inn Downtown By The Bay** ($$–$$$, 941/365-1900) has 100 spacious rooms—some with waterfront balconies—an outdoor pool, and a central location at 1 N Tamiami Trail.

There are several places to stay on St Armands Key, just across the Ringling Causeway that links downtown. The 34 rooms decorated in a contemporary Florida style at the waterfront **Coquina on the Beach Resort** ($$–$$$$, 941/388-2141) are spacious and have a balcony or patio at 1008 Ben Franklin Dr. Lots of recreation options make it suitable for families. Nearby is the **Half Moon Beach Club**

($$–$$$, 941/388-3694), a slightly less expensive waterfront option with a restaurant, similar facilities, and 85 rooms at 2050 Ben Franklin Dr.

Arts & culture

Sarasota has six professional theater companies and three dinner theaters, two large performing arts centers, a symphony orchestra, opera and ballet companies, choral and jazz ensembles, nearly 50 commercial galleries, six community arts organizations, and a world-class collection of Baroque and circus art. *Sarasota Arts & Entertainment* is a free monthly newspaper covering the arts and cultural scene.

Sarasota Film Society's Burns Court Cinema (941/955-FILM) shows foreign and independent films and hosts the annual Cine-World Film Festival at 506 Burns Lane.
The **Golden Apple Dinner Theatre** (941/366-5454) presents musicals and Broadway shows year round at 25 N Pineapple Ave. **Florida Studio Theatre** (941/366-9017) stages contemporary plays December to August at 1241 N Palm Ave. **Theatre Works** (941/952-9170) bills itself as an "actor-driven theater" presenting a five-play series from November to May, plus summer productions in the historic Palm Tree Playhouse at 1247 First St. At almost 70 years old, **The Players of Sarasota** (941/365-2494) is the city's oldest community theater. It presents musicals, live music, and other programs at 838 N Tamiami Trail. Professional artists and graduate acting students at the Florida State University comprise the **Asolo Conservatory Theatre Company** (941/351-9010), which performs five plays at the FSU Center. The **Asolo Theatre Company** (941/351-8000) is a professional company that stages five plays November to June and the Asolo Theatre Festival.
The **Sarasota Opera Association** (941/366-8450, ext 405), now in its 41st season, produces four operas in repertory in February and March in the historic Sarasota Opera House at 61 N Pineapple Ave. **Jazz Club of Sarasota** (941/366-1552) stages more than 100 live performances. **Sarasota Friends of Florida Folk** (941/377-9256) presents national and international artists and companies. **Sarasota Ballet of Florida's** (941/359-0771) season begins in September. **Florida West Coast Symphony** (941/953-3434) produces symphonic and chamber music concerts September through June.
Galleries on Palm Avenue stay open late, often with hors d'oeuvres and entertainment, on the first Friday of the month for **First Friday Palm Walk** (941/365-8700). **La Maison Dubrocq** (941/917-0231, 1515 Main St) features contemporary works by Latin American artists, including paintings by Javier Dubrocq. At **Towles Court** (941/362-0960, 941/955-0050, 1945 Morrill St) almost 30 artists with galleries and studios create everything from trompe l'oeil paintings and faux finishes at Trompe Art Studio (#203) to watercolors and acrylics at Rosalie Silver Gallery (#102) to custom tiles at Paddy Dugan Tile (#201) and abstract art at Claudia Porter Abstract Expressionism (#205). **Selby Gallery** at the Ringling School of Art and Design (941/359-7563, 2700 N Tamiami Trail) presents

revolving exhibits of American and international artists. See the sea through the eyes of one-name environmental marine life artist, Wyland, at **Wyland Gallery** (941/388-5331, St Armands Circle). He uses art, an educational foundation, and 82 "Whaling Walls" murals around the world to save the ocean. **Chasen Galleries** (941/366-4278, 16 S Palm Ave) specializes in original oils, glass, and sculpture from around the world. **William Hartman Gallery** (941/955-4785, 48 S Palm Ave) features 19th-century Japanese wood block prints, Florida landscape paintings, and antique natural history prints.

The **Main Bookshop** (941/366-7653, 1962 Main St) boasts that it is the country's largest publisher's overstock book shop outside of New York. **Sarasota News & Books** (941/351-9681, 1341 Main St) holds frequent book discussions and signings. **Barnes & Noble** (941/923-9907, 4010 S Tamiami Trail) offers books, concerts, wine discussions, art talks, author talks, and other interesting events.

Sarasota's journey toward becoming an international center for arts and culture started at the **John and Mable Ringling Museum of Art** (941/359-5700, 5401 Bay Shore Rd), a combination indoor and outdoor art museum, historic 1920s mansion, circus showcase, and cafe. The **Marie Selby Botanical Gardens** (941/366-5731, 811 S Palm Ave) features a botanical garden, museum, and art gallery.

Food & drink

Pockets of dining establishments offer superb choices in the historic districts along the tour.

Burns Lane Cafe ($–$$$, 941/955-1653) is a casually chic indoor/outdoor bistro serving contemporary New World cuisine in a tropical Old Florida setting at 516 Burns Lane. Critics consider **Yoshino** ($$–$$$, 941/366-8544) the best Japanese restaurant in town at 417 Burns Ct. **Picasso's** ($–$$, 941/362-9006) at 443 Burns Ct is extremely popular for its coffees and desserts, as well as hummus and pita, brie and crackers, and veggie platters.

It is good fortune indeed to dine indoors or outdoors at **Kismet** ($$, 941/355-2168), which prepares creative healthy fare for lunch and dinner at Towles Court, 1938 Adams Lane.

Healthy and delicious describe the food at two eateries: After church, one of the most popular spots in town is **Mim's Healthy Gourmet** ($–$$, 941/364-8561) serving natural, organic, and healthy food at 301 S Pineapple Ave. For breakfast, lunch, and dinner **Wild Eats** ($–$$, 941/954-1330) at 3800 S Tamiami Trail prepares healthy innovative salads, sandwiches, salmon cakes, pasta and fish dishes, burgers (veggie and salmon), and desserts that would make you cry if you were on a diet.

Alley Cat Cafe ($$$–$$$$, 941/954-1228) is an unconventional restaurant serving a delicious, eclectic, and sophisticated menu in a ramshackle garden setting with candlelight, flowers in the food, and live music for lunch and dinner at 1558

Fourth St.

The menu at **Sage** ($$$–$$$$, 941/954-2226) features divine dishes like lobster and tobiko ravioli with a light fresh lime and ginger cream sauce at 1371 Main St. One of Sarasota's most popular meeting places for breakfast and lunch is **First Watch** ($–$$, 941/957-3579) at 1395 Main St and 8383 S Tamiami Trail.

At the authentic **Thai Garden Restaurant** ($$–$$$, 941/922-0032) tender squid salad, curries, and garlic chicken are prepared just right at 4804 The Landings Shopping Center.

Nightlife

Nightlife varies from comedy clubs to dance clubs, offering everything from belly dancing shows to line and reel dancing.

McCurdy's Comedy Club tickles your funny bone with live local and national acts at 3900 Clark Rd. **Spats** has swing dancing, ballroom dancing, and live band music at 501 N Beneva Rd. The **US Amateur Ballroom Dancers Association** holds monthly dances at the Ballroom of Sarasota at 5660 Swift Rd. **Alley Cat Cafe** presents live contemporary music and jazz Wednesday to Saturday and steel drum tunes for weekday lunch in the Hot Tin Roof Bar at 1558 Fourth St. At the **Blue Parrot** Tuesday night is open microphone, Thursday is a funky rock and roll band with an island feeling, and Friday and Saturday nights feature solo blues acts at 1377 Main St. **The Five O'clock Club**, which has nightly blues acts, bills itself as "the neighborhood club with a national sound" at 1930 Hillview St. Befitting its historic location, **Gator Club** has an Old Florida atmosphere. Downstairs the tunes blast dance music nightly. Upstairs patrons play pool and chess and sip cocktails at 1490 Main St.

Events

In March there's a five-day **Jazz Festival** (941/366-1552) and the **Sarasota Africana Film Festival** (941/953-6424) shows foreign, independent, classic, and contemporary films. April brings **La Musica International Chamber Music Festival** (941/364-8802), featuring musicians from Europe and the Americas in a traditional and contemporary program. The **Sarasota Concert Band Summer Season** (941/316-1172) features free outdoor concerts around Sarasota County from May through September. **Florida Studio Theatre** (941/366-9000) presents the National Playwright's Festival in May. The Florida West Coast Symphony hosts the **Sarasota Music Festival** (941/953-9634), a visual and performing arts celebration, in June.

Fort Myers

Electricity literally brought the world new light. It also brought to light Fort Myers, where in 1886 Thomas Alva Edison built his winter home, now the city's biggest tourist attraction.

Edison chose to spend winters in Fort Myers—situated on Southwest Florida's Gulf Coast between Naples and Sarasota—because of its warm climate. He became one of the first "snowbirds" when he constructed his luxurious winter home facing McGregor Boulevard and backing the Caloosahatchee River. Just after the turn of the century, he replaced the street's citrus groves with a mile of stately palm trees. Other residents added more trees, and now about 1,800 palms line the 12-mile street, thus giving the city its diminutive, the City of Palms.

The Edison Winter Home is less than a mile from the Fort Myers Downtown Historic District, which retains many buildings dating from 1888 to 1939 that housed the hotels, homes, businesses, eateries, and stores that Edison probably frequented. Today, the vibrant district's historic structures actively serve as offices, trendy restaurants and cafes, theaters, and fashionable shops.

The district, listed on the National Register of Historic Places in 1990, began humbly in 1841 as a Seminole Indian War post called Fort Harvie. It was abandoned a year later, then reestablished as Fort Myers in 1850 for the Civil War. After the occupying Union forces withdrew, new settlers salvaged the fort's lumber to build houses and businesses.

Over the next 100 years a mix of Commercial Vernacular, Neo-Classical Revival, Mediterranean Revival, Moderne, and Art Deco buildings were erected downtown. When documenting the district's historical significance, researchers cited "the rich textures found on many of the buildings ranging from polychrome terra cotta inlay...bas relief carved in granite or oolitic limestone...applied sculptural details...textured brick surfaces...rough cast stucco finishes...polychrome designs in low relief." These textural features distinguish the district from surrounding modern buildings and from other Florida downtowns. The district is considered one of the best examples of intact early 20th-century commercial architecture in South Florida.

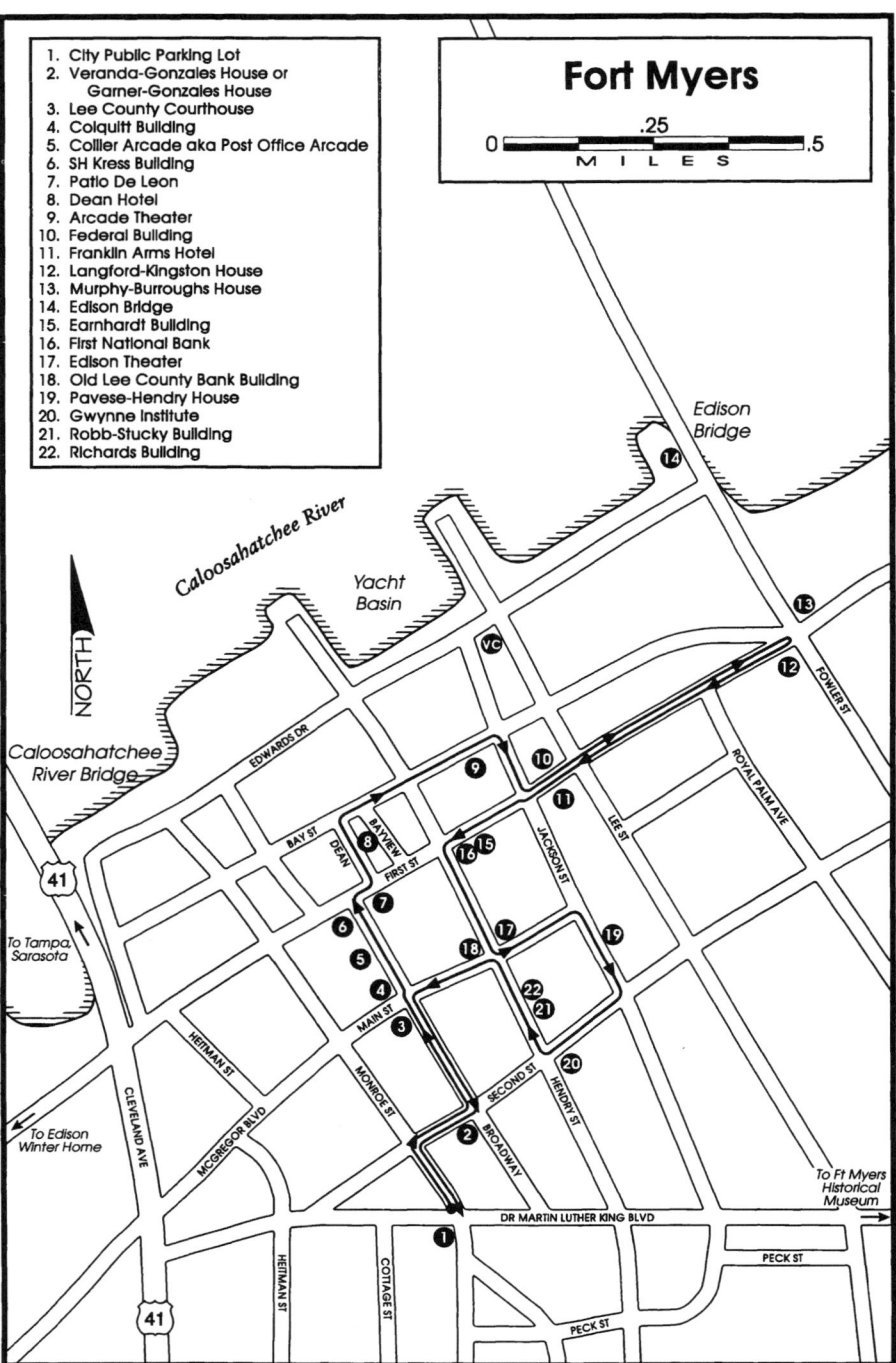

Fort Myers

1. City Public Parking Lot
2. Veranda-Gonzales House or Garner-Gonzales House
3. Lee County Courthouse
4. Colquitt Building
5. Collier Arcade aka Post Office Arcade
6. SH Kress Building
7. Patio De Leon
8. Dean Hotel
9. Arcade Theater
10. Federal Building
11. Franklin Arms Hotel
12. Langford-Kingston House
13. Murphy-Burroughs House
14. Edison Bridge
15. Earnhardt Building
16. First National Bank
17. Edison Theater
18. Old Lee County Bank Building
19. Pavese-Hendry House
20. Gwynne Institute
21. Robb-Stucky Building
22. Richards Building

Information

Lee Island Coast Visitor & Convention Bureau, Suite 100, 2180 W First St, Fort Myers, FL 33901; 800/237-6444, 941/338-3500; fax 941/334-1106; LIC @Cyberstreet.com; www.LeeIslandCoast.com. There's also a branch at the Southwest Florida International Airport near the baggage claim area.

Getting there

Major carriers serve the Southwest Florida International Airport (941/768-1000), located on the city's southeast border at 16000 Chamberlin Pkwy. Greyhound (800/231-2222, 941/334-1011) has service into Fort Myers at 2275 Cleveland Ave. Amtrak (800/USA RAIL) offers connecting bus service via Orlando to Fort Myers at 6050 Plaza Dr. Buquebus (941/461-0999) runs a high-speed ferry between downtown Fort Myers and Key West. By car from the north or east, take I-75 to exit 23 (Immokalee Rd/Dr Martin Luther King Jr Blvd). From the south or east take Alligator Alley west to Hwy 951 north, then I-75 north to exit 23.

First steps

For area maps and information, contact the **Lee Island Coast Visitor & Convention Bureau.**

Historic downtown Fort Myers. *This 1.5-mile route covers the downtown historic district and a few historically significant houses on the fringe.*

Park at the City Public Parking lot on the corner of Dr Martin Luther King Jr Blvd and Monroe St. Walk up to the corner of Broadway and Second streets to start the walk. The **Veranda-Gonzales House** or **Garner-Gonzales House** (2112 Second St) is actually two houses built by Manuel Gonzales, whose father was one of the city's first settlers. The two-story J. Franklin Garner House was built in 1902 at this site. The Gonzales House, also two-story, was built on Broadway in 1912 and moved here in 1973 by Peter Pulitzer, the grandson of the famous publisher. Both may contain wood salvaged from the fort. Together, they form the highly acclaimed Veranda Restaurant. *Walk north along Broadway to the corner of Main St.*

On the southwest corner, the two trees in front of the second **Lee County Courthouse** (2120 Main) are as historic as the judicial building. The live oak is believed to be at least 100 years old, the banyan tree about 50 years old. In 1915, many residents objected to spending the $85,000 to replace the frame courthouse with this new two-story buff-colored Neo-Classical Revival building. Henry Colquitt, a developer from Detroit, built the **Colquitt Building** (northwest corner of Broadway and Main) across Main Street in a Mediterranean Revival style in 1925. It features a second-story bell tower on the corner, barrel tiles, and ornamental stucco work. *Continue north on Broadway.*

On the left, the one-story, L-shaped stucco-over-brick **Collier Arcade** aka **Post Office Arcade** (1520 Broadway and 2118 First St) was built in 1925 by a Michigan developer who made his fortune in New York advertising. If buildings could talk, this one could tell some stories. Its first tenant was the US Post Office, which moved out in 1933. Among its other tenants were the Poinsettia Pharmacy, a jewelry store, Hendry Brothers & Bowden Real Estate, the Pollack Lumber Company offices, the Gift and Kodak Shop, and a barber shop. In 1934 South Florida developer Barron Collier purchased it and built an addition (now removed) for his Tamiami Trail Tours bus company here. Two later occupants were the *Fort Myers News-Press* and the famous Snack House Restaurant.

When Florida boomed in the 1920s, the stately three-story **SH Kress Building** (2132–2138 First St) was one of the first to go up at a cost of $136,000. Its brick exterior belies the fact that it was built over a steel skeleton. Look for its name molded on the outside. *Turn right onto First St.*

Patio De Leon (First St to Hendry St to Main St) began as the Stone Block, the first business block, on the southwest corner of First and Hendry streets. Retired Michigan businessman and banker Peter Tonnelier purchased the Stone Block in 1912 for $150,000, considered an astronomical amount at the time. Eventually, he purchased and/or developed the entire block with hotels, restaurants, and businesses between First and Main streets into what became known as Tonnelier Court, then later Patio de Leon. It formed a courtyard that had flowers, benches, and later an aquarium (now removed) with alligators. Tonnelier became the county's second largest property owner. *Turn left onto Dean St.*

During the Florida Boom, John Morgan Dean built the 22-room Mediterranean Revival style **Morgan Hotel** (northeast corner of First and Dean streets) and named it after his mother. Later the same year, he enlarged it to 70 rooms and added a telephone booth, lobby fireplace, new carpets and furnishings, and, according to Sanborn Fire Insurance documents, a rare safety feature, an automatic fire sprinkler system. On its reopening, the *Fort Myers News-Press* commented that it was "one of the most attractive (hotels) in the city." An astute businessman, Dean created his namesake street so that the hotel would have exposure on First and Dean streets. In 1938 the property was renamed the **Dean Hotel**. It recently underwent major restoration as an apartment/office complex.

Turn right onto Bay St.
Originally, Bay Street bordered the river, but land infilling during the early 20th century added two blocks. On the right, the two-story 1915 **Arcade Theater** (Bay St) featured shops and a theater. It was built by Harvie and Gilmer Heitman. Harvie Heitman opened one of the first marine supply stores for recreational fishermen in 1894. Two years later he r n one of the first tourist transportation services between Fort Myers and Naples and in 1904 he built a popular hotel. *Turn right onto Jackson St, then left onto First St.*
Walk up to the **Federal Building** (2301 First St) and take a close look at the fossilized sealife in the Florida Keys limestone that was used for its exterior walls. It was constructed in 1933 during the New Deal Era as the Fort Myers Post Office, but since the 1960s has been used to house Federal offices. From humble beginnings in 1889 as a small boarding house, ⠄ Mediterranean Revival influenced **Edison Regency Building** (2320 First St), became the **Franklin Arms Hotel** (2320 First St), one of the most fashionable hotels in Fort Myers in the first half of the century. It was renovated in the 1970s and given its current name. Today, it is a luxury apartment complex. *Continue on First St.*
There are several historically significant houses in the two to three blocks west of the historic downtown district. Businessman Walter G. Langford built the two-and-a-half-story Bungalow **Langford-Kingston House** (2460 First St) in 1919. Note the contrasting white masonry on red brick. It was purchased by inventor George Kingston in 1925 and is now owned by a church. It may be moved from this site to preserve it. On the opposite side of the street on the corner of Fowler St is the Georgian Revival style **Murphy-Burroughs House** (2505 First St), Fort Myers' first year-round luxury home. Built in 1901 for rancher John Murphy, it features an ornate verandah on three sides, a second-floor balcony, balustraded widow's walk, 10 dormers, and two fireplaces. Nelson Burroughs purchased it in 1918. The Murphy-Burroughs House is open for historic tours ($3). Look up Fowler Street to the **Edison Bridge**, which spans the Caloosahatchee River. It was named for Thomas Edison, who attended the dedication ceremony on his 84th birthday. *Before retracing your steps back along First St, look at the other houses in the 2500 block of First St.*
In historic designation documents, researchers noted "a striking image of two to three story historic building façades continuous in a solid pattern for blocks fronting both sides of First Street. The impact...is one of the most distinguishing features of the district." Among those façades are

Harvie Heitman's elaborately decorated 1915 **Earnhardt Building** (2258 First St), which features spiral scrolls between green borders and polychrome terra cotta inlay on the brick façade, and the elegant granite 1914 **First National Bank** (2248 First St), built in a Neoclassic-Revival style with two-story columns and Palladian windows. *Turn left onto Hendry St.*

At the end of the block on the left is the **Edison Theater** (1533 Hendry St), one of the best examples of Moderne architecture with Art Deco influence in Fort Myers. It has retained such style elements as streamlined details, applied ornamentation, fluted roofline, and a tall marquee. On the right, the two-story **Old Lee County Bank Building** (1534 Hendry St) was constructed in 1911 by James Hendry for a general store. It also served as the post office and the namesake bank before being converted into offices. *Turn left onto Main St, then right onto Jackson St.*

Pioneer builder Manuel S Gonzales used heart-pine to construct the two-story, nine-bedroom **Pavese-Hendry House** (1619 Jackson St) in 1909 for the Pavese family. In 1940 May Hendry converted it into a rooming house. Almost 40 years later, two attorneys purchased, restored, and converted it into offices. *Turn right onto Second St.*

Nearly 90 years after the **Gwynne Institute** (2253 Second St) was constructed as a school, it is still used for educational purposes. The two-story red brick building was named for Colonel Andrew D. Gwynne, a cotton magnate whose family donated funds for its construction. *Turn right onto Hendry St.*

Restoration has made the Florida Boom-era **Robb-Stucky Building** (1625 Hendry St) one of downtown's most notable 1920s commercial Neo-Classical buildings. It cost more than $50,000 to build this showroom and warehouse for the Robb and Stucky Furniture Company in 1925. The four-story brick **Richards Building** (1615 Hendry St) is another expensive Florida Boom-period construction. Developer Albertus A. Gardner sunk $150,000 into the building, which was to serve as the headquarters of the Knights of Pythias. *Turn left onto Main St, then left onto Broadway and retrace your steps back to the start.*

Lodging

Fort Myers is a beautiful, relaxing, engaging place to take a vacation. So why are its accommodation choices so limited? There's only one bed and breakfast establishment and no high-quality non-chain hotels.

Craig and Claire Poe of the **Li-Inn Sleeps Bed & Breakfast** ($$, 941/332-2651) were destined to become innkeepers. Not because they have the business wisdom of a JW Marriott—although they are pretty business savvy—but because they are two of the most welcoming individuals on earth. Their restored 1912 house has four large pleasantly decorated guestrooms with private baths and queen-size beds, as well as one disabled-accessible room with a private bath, daybed, and single bed at 2135 McGregor Blvd. Each night's stay is complemented by a full family-style breakfast and a memorable visit with the Poes. Li-Inn Sleeps is within walking distance of downtown, the Edison and Ford estates, and Boston Red Sox spring training fields.

Ta Ki-Ki Motel ($–$$, 941/334-2135) at 2631 First St is a relaxing 23-room family-oriented resort offering a heated pool, poolside dining, a BBQ grill, and great view of the Caloosahatchee River. Service is friendly. It's located on the edge of the downtown historic district. If you fancy a modern, 25-story, amenities-chocked resort with a great view of a river and yacht basin, you can't beat the **Amtel Marina Hotel & Suites** ($$–$$$, 800/833-1620 in US, 800/325-3535 in Canada, 941/337-0300) in the heart of the downtown historic district at 2500 Edwards Dr. It has two outdoor pools, lighted tennis courts, privileges at nearby golf courses, a gourmet restaurant, poolside lounge, and nightclub with entertainment. The 146-room **Holiday Inn SunSpree Resort** ($$, 941/334-3434) is situated downtown on the banks of the Caloosahatchee River at 2220 W First St. Vacationers can take advantage of the pools, boat dock, marina, restaurant, and charter fishing services. It's also popular with groups using the nearby Harborside Convention Center.

Arts & culture
The **Lee County Alliance of the Arts** sponsors a 24-hour Arts Hot Line (941 /433-INFO or 941/939-ARTS). The Friday entertainment section of the *Fort Myers News-Press* lists upcoming events.

The **Symphony of Southwest Florida** (941/433-3040), the county's only professional symphony, performs classical, pops, and chamber music. The **William R Frizzell Cultural Center**, which includes an exhibition gallery, the 200-seat Claiborne & Ned Foulds Theatre, an outdoor amphitheater, and art education classrooms is home to the **Company Inc**, a professional equity theater group, which performs from fall through late spring, as well as **The Film Society of Southwest Florida**, the **Southwest Florida Historical Society**, and the **Lee County Art in Public Places**. The **Barbara B Mann Performing Arts Hall** (941/481-4849) showcases national Broadway productions, prominent entertainers, dance performances, and popular and classical music concerts year-round at 8099 College Pkwy SW.

Restored historic buildings serve as homes for three galleries. The **De Leon Gallery**

(941/461-5522) features functional and decorative pottery and paintings in various media in Patio de Leon, between First and Main streets, off Hendry St. **Up The Creek Too** (941/332-4350) is a snazzy little gallery selling folk art, wall hangings, sculptures, and ceramics at 2273 First St. **WyldeStyle** (941/461-9292) brings the arts and crafts of the world to Fort Myers in a gallery that adheres to the principles of the Fair Trade Federation, ie not exploiting artisans in Third World countries, at 2149 First St.

You'll find works by local artists and craftsmen as well as traveling exhibitions at the **Alliance of the Arts Gallery** (941/939-2787) at 10091 McGregor Blvd. The **Edison Community College Gallery of Fine Art** (941/489-9313) exhibits works by well-known national and international artists at 8099 College Pkwy, Fort Myers, FL 33906.

Restoration efforts at the turn-of-the-century **Arcade Theatre** (941/332-4488) at 2267 First St have turned the 393-seat Victorian playhouse into a delightful place to enjoy live theater by local and touring companies, dance, and musical productions, downtown in the historic district.

The 100-seat **Broadway Palm Dinner Theatre** (941/278-4422) at 1380 Colonial Blvd serves up buffet meals along with professional, Broadway-style, live theatrical matinee and evening performances.

See how the rich and famous lived in Victorian-era Fort Myers at the **Murphy-Burroughs Home** (941/332-6125) at 2505 First St, a turn-of-the-century home on the National Register of Historic Places. Admission is $3 per adult.

Learn about the region's natural history and the stars at the **Calusa Nature Center and Planetarium** (941/275-3435) at 3450 Ortiz Ave. Admission to the nature center is $4 for adults, $2.50 for children under 12 years. Planetarium shows cost $3 for adults and $2 for children under 12 years.

Take a guided walking tour of the **Edison-Ford Winter Homes and Gardens** (941/334-3614), then explore the Edison Museum's inventions and memorabilia at 2350 McGregor Blvd. Admission is $11.

The **Fort Myers Historical Museum** (941/332-5955) at 2300 Peck St explores the region's history from the Calusa Indians and Spanish explorers to the turn-of-the-century pioneers and 20th-century power brokers. Entrance costs $4.

Children are encouraged to touch everything at the **Imaginarium Hands-on Museum** (941/337-3332), a science and nature center with interactive exhibits at 2000 Cranford Ave. Admission is $6 for adults, $5.50 for seniors, $3 for children ages 3 to 12.

This is sort of cheating, but the best bookstore for Florida books in Fort Myers—actually the company is in Fort Myers Beach—is on the Internet, **paradise-books.com**, which specializes in books set in, written by authors living in, or concerning the Sunshine State. They also keep a list of their personal favorite non-Florida books.

Among the chains there is **Barnes & Noble** (941/437-0654) at 13751 S Tamiami Trl and **Books-A-Million** (941/936-8871) at 4329 Cleveland Ave.

Food & drink

While some of the downtown restaurants cater to the business community and are only open on weekdays for breakfast and lunch, many attract the theater crowd and are open for lunch and dinner.

Fort Myers has two restaurants in the stellar category, both in the downtown historic district. **Peter's La Cuisine** ($$$, 941/332-2228) serves masterfully prepared and artfully presented foods fit for the gods like caviar, lobster bisque, and venison in a restored building at 2224 Bay St . The other heavenly option, which is also in a landmark building, is **The Veranda** ($$$, 941/332-2065), serving creative seafood, lamb, beef, and vegetable dishes with a touch of the South in a romantic indoor and al fresco setting at 2122 Second St.

There are two options that are not downtown, but are worth the drive. You don't have to love seafood to enjoy the wonderful food and service at the **Prawnbroker Restaurant and Seafood Market** ($$–$$$, 941/489-2226), but you'll have many more options if you do. Along with traditionally and creatively prepared fish and shellfish, the restaurant serves steak and poultry dishes at 13451 McGregor Blvd. It's a few steps back in time—and price—to **Mel's Diner** ($, 941/275-7850), where the mashed potatoes, soups, steaks with gravy, and fruit pies are better than mom's and grandma's at 4820 Cleveland Ave.

Nightlife

After dinner at Peter's La Cuisine, head upstairs to the **Brick Bar** for blues at 2224 Bay St. A younger crowd meets at **Liquid Cafe** for live popular music and open-mike nights at 2236 First St.

Life's a big joke at the **Laugh-In Comedy Cafe** (941/338-6127), where nationally recognized comedians and local talent yuck it up weekends at American Pie on the corner of College Pkwy and Winkler Rd.

For music you can snap your fingers to, try **Churchill's Pub** (941/936-1776) at 3732 Cleveland Ave, and the **Orbit Night Club** 941/461-0550, where there's a DJ or live music at 3057 Cleveland Ave.

Events

The year begins with the **Edison Festival of Light** (941/334-2999), one of the area's biggest and most celebrated annual events, commemorating Thomas Edison's birthday with three weeks of activities. Blues fans can enjoy music down by the river and feast on food at the **River and Blues Festival** (941/939-1300) in April. In

November, the Junior League of Fort Myers kicks off its annual **Taste of the Town** with a country music concert, then follows up with more than a dozen area restaurants serving their most popular recipes while bands entertain the audience. In December the fancy historic houses brighten the night with more than a million lights at the Edison and Ford estates during the annual **Edison/Ford Homes Holiday Houses Festival** (941/461-2687).

J.N. Ding Darling National Wildlife Refuge

The J.N. "Ding" Darling National Wildlife Refuge stretches along 6,000 acres of mangroves, shallow bays, and white sand beaches of Sanibel, a 12-mile subtropical barrier island on Florida's west coast, between Naples and Sarasota.

Evidence suggests that Native Americans inhabited the island for more then 2,000 years. They were followed by European settlers, who fished and farmed until a hurricane devasted the area in1926. Today, the island is home to an affluent community and a major eco-tourist destination with the wildlife refuge, a conservation center, wildlife rehabilitation center, and shell museum.

Native wading birds, migratory waterfowl, and shorebirds flock to the refuge by the thousands. On foot, by car, and by kayak or canoe, visitors can observe nearly 300 species of birds, 50 types of reptiles and amphibians, and at least 32 different mammals within the refuge's boundaries. An observation tower and mangrove overlook facilitate viewing.

By car, visitors can drive the five-mile, one-way Wildlife Drive at 15 mph on an impacted earthen dike built in 1965 as part of a mosquito control program. Birds feed in the impounded waters on both sides of the dike, one freshwater/brackish, the other saltwater. On foot, visitors can walk the Wildlife Drive or any of three trails, Shell Mound at one-third mile, Indigo Trail at two miles, and a number of small trails totaling almost two miles at the Bailey Tract.

Originally called Sanibel National Wildlife Refuge when it was established in 1945, the refuge's name was changed in 1967 to honor J.N. "Ding" Darling, a pioneer in the conservation movement. He played a major role in establishing the National Wildlife Refuge System, designed the first "Duck Stamp," whose funds are used to purchase wetlands, and designed the system's logo, a blue goose with a flat back and extended wings.

Information

J.N. "Ding" Darling National Wildlife Refuge, 1 Wildlife Dr, Sanibel Island, FL 33957; 941/472-1100. Sanibel & Captiva Islands Chamber of Commerce, 1159 Causeway Rd, Sanibel Island, FL 33957; 941/472-1080; fax 941/472-1070; Island@sanibel-captiva.org; www.sanibel-captiva.org.

Getting there

The closest airport is Southwest Florida International Airport (941/768-1000), about 30 miles north in Fort Myers. Greyhound (800/231-2222, 941/334-1011) has bus service into Fort Myers at 2275 Cleveland Ave. Amtrak (800/USA RAIL) offers connecting bus service via Orlando to Fort Myers at 6050 Plaza Dr. By car, connect with I-75 from all points to Exit 21 west (Daniels Pkwy) to Summerlin Rd. Follow Summerlin Rd to the Sanibel Causeway ($3 toll). At the four-way stop sign turn right onto Periwinkle Way, then right onto Tarpon Bay Rd and left onto Sanibel-Captiva Rd. Follow signs to the park entrance on the right.

First steps

Write or call in advance for refuge information and maps from the J.N. "Ding" Darling National Wildlife Refuge. For Sanibel maps and information, contact the Sanibel & Captiva Islands Chamber of Commerce.

Exhibits at the Refuge Visitor Center explain the ecosystem. You can purchase the "Wild Drive Guide," a 28-page illustrated guide to some of the flora and fauna in the refuge for $1. Admission to the visitor center is free. Walkers and bicyclists pay $1, drivers $5 to access the Wildlife Drive. Trails are open daily from sunrise to sunset.

There is little shade on the route, so drink water ahead of time and bring a bottle with you. There are no water fountains along the route.

Walking tours

During winter months (the high season) Jack Rushworth, a refuge volunteer and roving interpreter, gives one-hour tours of the Indigo Trail on Tuesday and Wednesday mornings for $1.

Seasonal highlights

Migrating songbirds are abundant March through May and again September through November. Look for migrating ducks December through February. The best time to see alligators is in winter during midday when they sun themselves on the banks and dikes. On any given day, the best time to see wildlife is during low tide, which is one to two hours after the times stated on island charts, and around sunrise and sunset. Roseate spoonbills congregate around watering holes at sunset.

Natural Ding Darling National Wildlife Refuge. *This nearly 4-mile route covers the Indigo Trail, a hard-packed dirt trail that joins the shell and hard-packed sand Wildlife Drive. Allot two hours. Plan on another hour if you want to spend more time observing the birds and touring the visitor center.*

Begin at the Refuge Visitor Center, then pick up the trail behind the center. A boardwalk runs for 0.15 miles through a mangrove wetlands community.

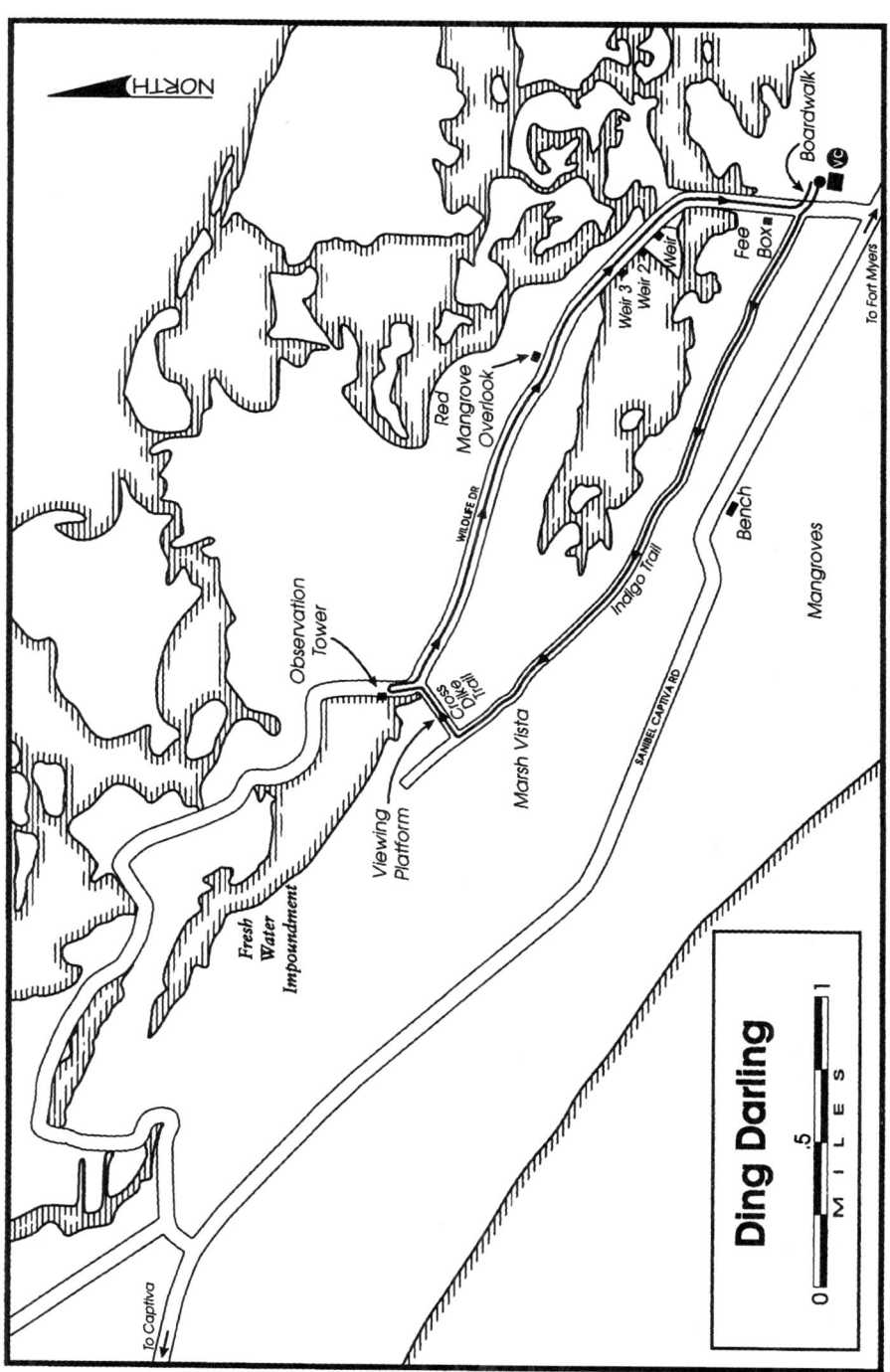

Markers along the boardwalk identify some plants, which include black mangroves (*Avicennia germinans*), buttonwoods (*Conocarpus erectus*), and white stoppers (*Eugenia axillaris*). In fall and winter, migratory songbirds flitter among the tree branches. The trail crosses over the Wildlife Drive, then continues as a sand dike running between two ditches for two miles. Beyond the mangroves on the left, you can see many birds feeding in the water. Look for egrets, different types of herons, and anhingas perched with outspread wings. The vegetation nearest the waters is primarily mangroves. A little higher up the sides of the dike, it changes to a mix of cabbage palms (*Sabal palmetto*), sea grapes (*Coccoloba uvifera*), gumbo limbo (*Bursera simaruba*), poison ivy (*Toxicodendron radicans*), wild coffee (*Psychotria nervosa*), wild olive (*Forestiera segregata*), and goldfoot ferns (*Phlebodium aureum*), among others.

If you're ready for a short rest or need to load film, use the bench at about 1 mile. When you reach 1.5 miles, note the gumbo limbo on the left. Locals nicknamed it the "tourist tree" after its red peeling bark.

As the trees clear on the right at 1.75 miles, the vista opens to marsh, where hundreds of roseate spoonbills, egrets, and shorebirds feed in the low waters. It's a beautiful scene of pink and white against brown earth, green vegetation, and blue sky.

At just under 2 miles, the trail turns right and becomes the **Crossdike Trail**. The view is unobscured. Scan the environs from the covered **Viewing Platform** and you can see myriad birds, including reddish, snowy, and great egrets; tricolored herons; and roseate spoonbills, as well as numerous ducks and shore birds. Alligators may be seen basking in the sun on the left. *Continue along the Crossdike Trail, then at the Wildlife Drive take a short detour left to the Observation Tower.*

Through manipulation of the water level in the freshwater impound pool on the left, the Water Management Program inhibits mosquito production and provides brackish and freshwater habitats for wildlife. It's a popular area for ducks, including mergansers, grebes, and teals. On the right, the view is of a mangrove-dotted tidal zone, where the tide rises and drops up to two feet. When the tide is low and small fish and crustaceans are left behind, there's a feeding frenzy of shorebirds, roseate spoonbills, and ibis. At high tide, look for birds roosting in the trees.

Climb the **Observation Tower** for a panoramic view of the impound, tidal flats, and Pine Island Sound. *Retrace your steps back to the Crossdike Trail, cross it and continue against the slow moving traffic on the Wildlife Drive. There's plenty of room on the road and wide shoulder for cars, bicyclists, and pedestrians to move about safely.*

A series of weirs along the Wildlife Drive controls the level of water—and its salinity—in the impoundments. Refuge managers open the weirs to let off excess rain water or introduce tidal waters. The sandbars near the weirs are good spots to find birds. Watch for small crabs skitting across the road.

The road is intermittently lined with red mangroves, conspicuous for their bow-shaped prop roots. Among them, on higher ground are black mangroves and buttonwoods. Look for propagules, the red mangroves fully developed, pendulous, 10-inch torpedo-shaped seedlings that fall into the water and float to a mud flat, shoal, or sandbar, and take root. Within a year, the seedlings grow three feet and produce arching aerial prop roots. The roots trap and stabilize waterborne sediments and create a complex microhabitat.

From 2.75 miles to 2.95 miles, starting at about 30 feet after the Wrong Way sign, look into the heart of the dense mangrove swamp. Look and listen. The mangrove swamp is active with mangrove tree crabs and other crustaceans. Birds flit about. Raccoons crawl about the tangled prop roots. Observe the lichen on the trees and the oysters on the roots.

At around 3 miles, you'll reach the **Red Mangrove Overlook**, a short boardwalk that looks out beyond the mangrove swamp to a tidal pond and the islands in Sanibel Bayou and San Carlos Bay. Time it right—low tide and just as the tides are rising and lowering—and you'll be treated to a striking view of thousands of wading birds feeding on the flats. When the flats are visible, thousands of such shorebirds as willets, sandpipers, and plovers race about the mud feeding. At high water, look across at the trees, where birds roost and wait. *Continue along the Wildlife Drive.*

The sandbars on the left and right near Weir 3, Weir 2, and Weir 1 are excellent spots to see birds throughout the day. They attract anhingas, pelicans, herons, egrets, gulls, ducks, and shorebirds. The larger birds are usually farther away, but can be seen easily from the road. Look for anhingas and cormorants. They swim with their bodies submerged and only their heads and necks above the water. This has given them the moniker "snakebird".

As you pass Weir 1, note the wildflowers and other vegetation growing along the bank. There are firecrackers, ferns, sea grapes, and poison ivy. *Continue along the Wildlife Drive. Remember to put $1 into the fee envelope and drop it into the box. At the gate, turn left and retrace your steps along the boardwalk back to the visitor center.*

Lodging
There are numerous lodging options, mostly mid- to high-priced, including small, personable inns, condos, bed-and-breakfasts, and large resorts on Sanibel Island and adjacent Captiva Island. Sanibel and Captiva Central provides free reservations to all types of accommodations. Call 800/325-2352 or 941/472-0457. Rates are considerably higher in peak season, December through April.

Captiva Island Inn Bed & Breakfast ($$–$$$$, 941/395-0882) at 11509 Andy Ross Lane, Captiva has cottages and apartments with all the usual facilities, plus child care and picnic and barbecue facilities. **Sanibel's Song of the Sea** ($$$$, 941/472-2200, 800/231-1045) at 836 E Gulf Dr, Sanibel is a 30-room European-style inn on the Gulf of Mexico. Pampering service and amenities include flowers, complimentary wine, daily continental breakfast on the terrace, bikes, a pool and whirlpool, plus a sandy beach.

Among the less pricey accommodations are the friendly **Kona Kai Motel** ($$, 941/472-1001) at 1539 Periwinkle and the **Anchorage Inn** ($$, 941/395-9688) at 1245 Periwinkle Way.

Food & drink
On Sanibel and Captiva islands, there is no shortage of restaurants. Most are pricey, especially in winter.

LaVigna Restaurant ($$$, 941/472-5453) at 1625 Periwinkle Way is a fine Italian eatery with an open kitchen and a chef who knows how to please customer by offering a varied menu or you can request your own entree. For a quick coffee, dessert, or bagels, try **The Bean** ($–$$, 941/395-1919) at 2240 Periwinkle. The black and red beans and rice are superb and inexpensive at the **East End Deli** ($–$$, 941/472-9622) at 359 Periwinkle. And the made-to-order pizza is worth coming back a second day at **The Canoe and the Kayak Waterfront Deli** ($$, 941/472-5161) at 15951 Captiva Drive, at the 'Tween Waters Marina. The moderatly priced **Bubble Room** ($$–$$$, 941/472-5558) at 15001 Captiva Dr is not for the calorie conscious. It serves steaks, seafoods, pastas and the most incredible homemade desserts you can imagine.

Corkscrew Swamp Sanctuary, Naples

Within its 11,000 acres the National Audubon Society's Corkscrew Swamp Sanctuary encompasses the largest known old-growth, bald cypress forest on earth. Some of the cypress trees here are more than 500 years old. They share this magnificent sanctuary with other habitats such as pine flatwoods, prairies, marshes and lakes, where birds, alligators, turtles, otters, deer, and diverse vegetation flourish.

During the 1940s and 1950s, Florida's cypress forests were being cut for their timber at an alarming rate. The Audubon Society, which had protected wood storks and great egrets in the area since 1912, teamed up with other conservation organizations and individuals and purchased the first 2,240 acres in 1954. Over the next 20 years, more land was acquired north and south of the park. In 1955, the first boardwalk was constructed to give visitors access to the sanctuary. Today, the two-mile boardwalk has been redesigned to take visitors through major habitats abundant with wildlife on a short (1.04 miles) and long (2.25 miles) walk.

Information

Corkscrew Swamp Sanctuary, 375 Sanctuary Rd West, Naples, Florida 34120; 941/348-9151; amackie@audubon.org; www.audubon.org/local/sanctuary/corkscrew. Naples Visitor Center, 895 Fifth Ave S, Naples, FL 34102; 941/262-6141.

Getting there

Take I-75 to Naples, exit 17 (Hwy 846). Go east on Hwy 846 about 15 miles to Sanctuary Rd. Turn left and continue to the end of the road. The closest airport is Southwest Florida Regional Airport, about 30 miles north in Fort Myers. Amtrak (800/USA RAIL) and Greyhound (800/231-2222, 941/385-7741) serve Naples.

First steps

For sanctuary information, contact Corkscrew Swamp Sanctuary, which is open daily 7 am to 5 pm. Adult admission is $7.00; college students $5.50; children 6-18 years $3.50; children under 6 years free; Audubon members $5.00. For maps and accommodation information, contact the Naples Visitor Center, which is open weekdays 9 am to 5 pm, to 7 pm December to March.

Seasonal highlights

October to April is the most pleasant time to visit. It's cooler and there are fewer insects, but more visitors in the park and surrounding communities. It's also the most expensive time for accommodations.

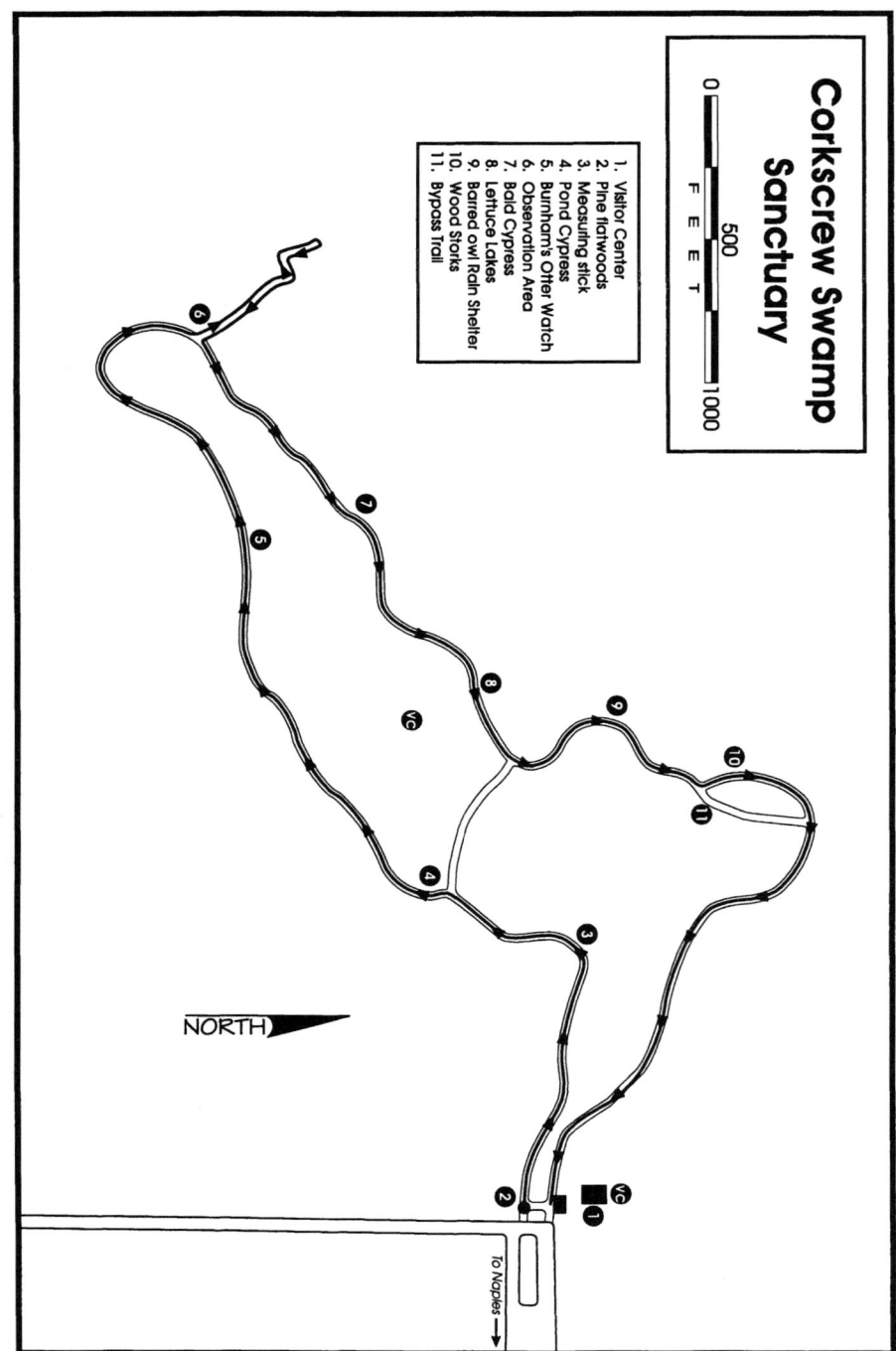

**Corkscrew Swamp
Sanctuary**

1. Visitor Center
2. Pine flatwoods
3. Measuring stick
4. Pond Cypress
5. Burnham's Otter Watch
6. Observation Area
7. Bald Cypress
8. Lettuce Lakes
9. Barred owl Rain Shelter
10. Wood Storks
11. Bypass Trail

NORTH

To Naples →

Natural Corkscrew Swamp Sanctuary. *The 2.25-mile route covers a short paved path and two miles of elevated wood boardwalk. Allow two to three hours. There are picnic facilities near the sanctuary entrance.*

Start at the Interpretive Displays behind the Visitor Center.
The trail begins crossing **Pine Flatwoods**, dense with slash pines (*Pinus elliottii*), sabal palms (*Sabal palmetto*), and saw palmettos (*Serenoa repens*) on both sides. The charred trunks are from recent fires. The first of more than a dozen interpretive signs on the trail (mile .06) explains how plants benefit from fires.

The pine flatwoods gradually give way to a **Wet Prairie**, a broad expanse of sand cordgrass (*Spartina bakerii*), St John's wort (*Hypericum reductum*) and blue flag iris (*Iris hexagona*) among other plants. Check the depth of water at the measuring stick on the right at mile 0.2. In severe drought periods, the ground beneath can be dry in late winter and early spring. The resurrection ferns (*Polypodium polypodioides*) that grow on the tree branches shrivel and wildlife congregates in the remaining watering areas. By late spring and summer, rains raise the water level and wildflowers abound.

As the swamps take over the landscape around mile 0.37, a dense forest of pond cypress (*Taxodium distichum var. nutans*)appears along with red maples (*Acer rubrum*), strangler figs (*Ficus aurea*), and pond apples (*Annona glabra*). The latter is a favorite food for raccoons. Look for splotches of red lichen on the trunks of cypress, as well as 12 species of air plants (*Tillandsia spp*), Spanish moss (*Tillandsia usneoides*) and what looks like moss, but is actually the small filamentous old man's beard lichen (*Usnea strigosa*). At their feet grow broad-leafed aquatic plants like alligator flag (*Thalia geniculata*), swamp lily (*Crinum americanum*), and numerous ferns, especially when you reach mile 0.4. *Continue on the long trail or turn right to take the short trail.*

At **Burnham's Otter Watch**, there are benches under a rain shelter that overlooks a slough, where otters often play. Mosquito fish and sailfin molly are two of the fish found in the waters below. Continue to mile 0.62, where there's an impressive red maple just before the road divides. The left walk leads to an observation area over a broad, open marsh before you must turn around and rejoin the main trail, which continues right to a rain shelter.

The trees, primarily bald cypress (*Taxodium distichum*) and red maples, grow taller (up to 120 ft) here, where the lower bedrock and increased organic matter provide ideal growing conditions. Their massive trunks reach a circumference of several feet. Wildlife live in the holes in the trunks. Swamp ferns (*Blechnum serrulatum*) and tall, clumping, gray-green narrow-leafed sawgrass (*Mariscus jamaicensis*) grow at their wide base. Unusual looking strap ferns (*Campyloneuron phyllitidis*) have sword-like leaves and grow in clumps in the trees, on logs or mounds of earth.

Audubon volunteers can be identified by their khaki uniforms. They walk the trail answering questions, pointing out wildlife, and setting up telescopes with placards identifying the bird, reptile, or mammal that can be seen if you stop to take a peek. There are always two or three around Lettuce Lakes.

Lettuce Lakes derives its name from the abundance of water lettuce (*Pistia stratiotes*), a floating aquatic plant that resembles a head of Boston lettuce and provides cover for small fish and crayfish. It's one of the most popular areas within the sanctuary. There are always American alligators, as well as Florida redbelly turtles, gallinules, great egrets, little blue and black- and yellow-crowned night herons, and such songbirds as white-eyed vireos and northern Parula warblers.

The **Barred Owl Rain Shelter** at mile 1 derives its name from the large (up to 24 in) owls that often rest in the trees in this area. The boardwalk splits, then rejoins a little farther along the trail. The left trail is often closed in late winter and early spring so that the endangered wood storks in North America can nest high in the bald cypress trees. On the right Bypass Trail is an aquarium showing life under Lettuce Lake.

The trail swings right, heading back to the Visitor Center. As it recrosses the pine flatwood, note the numerous tiny holes in the patchwork bark of the slash pines. They're made by the large (up to 18 in) pileated woodpecker and the red-bellied woodpecker. Both can be heard and seen pecking the trees throughout the sanctuary. *Return to the Visitor Center.*

Lodging

Accommodations are numerous in affluent Naples, the closest town. The selection is mostly upscale resort or moderately priced chains. There are a few pleasant exceptions.

The restored **Inn by the Sea** ($$$/$$$, 941/649-4124) bed-and-breakfast, built in 1937 at 287 11th Ave, has the feel of a posh estate's beach house with polished pine floors, light-filled rooms, wicker furnishings, private baths, and a fireplace. Though the 318-room **Naples Beach Hotel & Golf Club** ($$$$/$$$, 941/261-2222) at 851 Gulf Shore Blvd N has been around since the 1940s, it has colorful contemporary

Florida decor, right down to the local art on the walls. The most elegant hotel on the coast is the **Ritz-Carlton Naples** ($$$$/$$$$, 941/598-3300), a five-star resort at 280 Vanderbilt Beach Road.

Nicely appointed and attractively priced options are the 107-room **Baymont Inn** ($$/$, 941/352-8400)at 185 Bedzel Circle, which includes continental breakfast; the 44-room **Fairways Resort** ($$$/$$, 941/597-8181) with beautiful tropical landscaping at 103 Palm River Blvd; and the 35-room **Lemon Tree Inn** ($$$/$, 941/262-1414) with a tranquil courtyard in Old Naples at 250 9th St S.

Food & Drink

There are lots of good choices in Naples, where the selection includes sophisticated dining, fast food, ethnic and all-American.

The **Key Wester Fish & Pasta House** ($$$, 941/649-7770) serves moderately priced seafood in a laid-back setting with water views. It's all Italian fare at family-owned **Farino's/Gilda's Casa Italiana** ($–$$$, 941/262-2883) at 4000 N Tamiami Trail. Eat in or out at the open-air waterfront **Riverwalk Fish & Ale House** ($–$$, 941/263-2734) at 1200 5th Ave S. The theme is Old World nautical at **St George & The Dragon** ($$–$$$, 941/262-6546), where the food is surf and turf at 936 5th Ave S.

There's no shortage of sophisticated dining. Favorites include **Sign of the Vine** ($$$, 941/261-6745) at 980 Solana Rd, where guests dine in a renovated house on creative specialties. The fine wine list compliments the contemporary Italian dishes at **Villa Pescatore** ($$–$$$, 941/597-8119) at 8920 N Tamiami Trail. Fine French cuisine is featured on **Chardonnay**'s menu ($$$, 941/261-1744) in the Best Western at 2331 Tamiami Trail N. At the Ritz-Carlton at 280 Vanderbilt Beach Rd, **The Grill Room** ($$$, 941-598-6644) serves up old money ambiance with a menu of seafoods, beef, and pasta, and **The Dining Room** ($$$/941-598-6644) offers an innovative, eclectic, upscale-menu and indoor/outdoor dining.

Index

About the Author

Diane Marshall lives in the Florida Keys, where she walks 3–5 miles every day with her two dogs, the Pointer Sisters. She will donate 5 percent of her earnings from the book to the Florida Trust for Historic Preservation and 5 percent to the Friends of Florida State Parks.